CW00322033

Keep this book. You will
need it and use it throughout
your career.

STRATEGIC
HOTEL/MOTEL
MARKETING

MIRELLA (MA1)

Educational Institute Courses

Introductory

INTRODUCTION TO THE HOSPITALITY INDUSTRY
Third Edition
Gerald W. Lattin

AN INTRODUCTION TO HOSPITALITY TODAY
Second Edition
Rocco M. Angelo, Andrew N. Vladimir

TOURISM AND THE HOSPITALITY INDUSTRY
Joseph D. Fridgen

Rooms Division

FRONT OFFICE PROCEDURES
Fourth Edition
Michael L. Kasavana, Richard M. Brooks

HOUSEKEEPING MANAGEMENT
Margaret M. Kappa, Aleta Nitschke, Patricia B. Schappert

Human Resources

HOSPITALITY SUPERVISION
Second Edition
Raphael R. Kavanaugh, Jack D. Ninemeier

HOSPITALITY INDUSTRY TRAINING
Second Edition
Lewis C. Forrest, Jr.

HUMAN RESOURCES MANAGEMENT
Robert H. Woods

Marketing and Sales

MARKETING OF HOSPITALITY SERVICES
Revised Edition
Christopher W. L. Hart, David A. Troy

HOSPITALITY SALES AND MARKETING
Second Edition
James R. Abbey

CONVENTION MANAGEMENT AND SERVICE
Leonard H. Hoyle, David C. Dorf, Thomas J. A. Jones

MARKETING IN THE HOSPITALITY INDUSTRY
Third Edition
Ronald A. Nykiel

Accounting

UNDERSTANDING HOSPITALITY ACCOUNTING I
Third Edition
Raymond Cote

BASIC FINANCIAL ACCOUNTING FOR THE HOSPITALITY INDUSTRY
Raymond S. Schmidgall, James W. Damitio

FINANCIAL ACCOUNTING FOR THE HOSPITALITY INDUSTRY II
Second Edition
Raymond Cote

MANAGERIAL ACCOUNTING FOR THE HOSPITALITY INDUSTRY
Third Edition
Raymond S. Schmidgall

Food and Beverage

FOOD AND BEVERAGE MANAGEMENT
Second Edition
Jack D. Ninemeier

QUALITY SANITATION MANAGEMENT
Ronald F. Cichy

FOOD PRODUCTION PRINCIPLES
Jerald W. Chesser

FOOD AND BEVERAGE SERVICE
Anthony M. Rey, Ferdinand Wieland

HOSPITALITY PURCHASING MANAGEMENT
William P. Virts

BAR AND BEVERAGE MANAGEMENT
Lendal H. Kotschevar, Mary L. Tanke

FOOD AND BEVERAGE CONTROLS
Third Edition
Jack D. Ninemeier

General Hospitality Management

HOTEL/MOTEL SECURITY MANAGEMENT
Raymond C. Ellis, Jr., Security Committee of AH&MA

HOSPITALITY LAW
Third Edition
Jack P. Jefferies

RESORT MANAGEMENT
Second Edition
Chuck Y. Gee

INTERNATIONAL HOTEL MANAGEMENT
Chuck Y. Gee

HOSPITALITY INDUSTRY COMPUTER SYSTEMS
Second Edition
Michael L. Kasavana, John J. Cahill

MANAGING FOR QUALITY IN THE HOSPITALITY INDUSTRY
Robert H. Woods, Judy Z. King

Engineering and Facilities Management

FACILITIES MANAGEMENT
David M. Stipanuk, Harold Roffman

HOSPITALITY INDUSTRY ENGINEERING SYSTEMS
Michael H. Redlin, David M. Stipanuk

HOSPITALITY ENERGY AND WATER MANAGEMENT
Robert E. Aulbach

STRATEGIC HOTEL/MOTEL MARKETING

Revised Edition

Christopher W.L. Hart
and
David A. Troy

EDUCATIONAL INSTITUTE
of the American Hotel & Motel Association

Disclaimer

This publication is designed to provide accurate and authoritative information in regard to the subject matter covered. It is sold with the understanding that the publisher is not engaged in rendering legal, accounting, or other professional service. If legal advice or other expert assistance is required, the services of a competent professional person should be sought.

  —*From the Declaration of Principles jointly adopted by the American Bar Association and a Committee of Publishers and Associations*

The authors, Christopher W.L. Hart and David A. Troy, are solely responsible for the contents of this publication. All views expressed herein are solely those of the authors and do not necessarily reflect the views of the Educational Institute of the American Hotel & Motel Association (the Institute) or the American Hotel & Motel Association (AH&MA).

Nothing contained in this publication shall constitute a standard, an endorsement, or a recommendation of the Institute or AH&MA. The Institute and AH&MA disclaim any liability with respect to the use of any information, procedure, or product, or reliance thereon by any member of the hospitality industry.

©Copyright 1985, 1986, 1996
By the EDUCATIONAL INSTITUTE of the
AMERICAN HOTEL & MOTEL ASSOCIATION
1407 South Harrison Road
P.O. Box 1240
East Lansing, Michigan 48826

The Educational Institute of the American
Hotel & Motel Association is a nonprofit
educational foundation.

Printed in the United States of America
  2 3 4 5 6 7 8 9 10 00 99 98 97 96

Library of Congress Cataloging-in-Publication Data
Troy, David A.
  Strategic hotel/motel marketing

Includes bibliographies and index.
  1. Hotels, taverns, etc. 2. Marketing. I. Hart, Christopher. II. Title
TX911.3.M3T76 1986 647'.94'0688 86-19926
ISBN 0-86612-031-9
ISBN 0-86612-111-0 (pbk.)

Editors: George A. Glazer
            Ann M. Halm

Contents

Congratulations. . .

You have a running start on a fast-track career!

Developed through the input of industry and academic experts, this course gives you the know-how hospitality employers demand. Upon course completion, you will earn the respected American Hotel & Motel Association certificate that ensures instant recognition worldwide. It is your link with the global hospitality industry.

You can use your AH&MA certificate to show that your learning experiences have bridged the gap between industry and academia. You will have proof that you have met industry-driven learning objectives and that you know how to apply your knowledge to actual hospitality work situations.

By earning your course certificate, you also take a step toward completing the highly respected learning programs—Certificates of Specialization, the Hospitality Operations Certificate, and the Hospitality Management Diploma—that raise your professional development to a higher level. Certificates from these programs greatly enhance your credentials, and a permanent record of your course and program completion is maintained by the Educational Institute.

We commend you for taking this important step. Turn to the Educational Institute for additional resources that will help you stay ahead of your competition.

Preface

In writing this textbook, the purpose has been to gather into one manageable volume the best of contemporary hospitality marketing ideas and practices. We, the authors, have been aided in this task by many friends, colleagues, and competitors, who agreed to put in writing their thoughts about our discipline so they could be shared with you, the reader. Taken as a whole, their comments in this book reflect the state of the art of marketing in the hospitality industry.

To supplement these ideas, we have researched other educational materials produced by the Educational Institute of the American Hotel & Motel Association (AH&MA), as well as periodicals and trade magazines, for successful approaches and techniques that could be included in this text. Also, we have not hesitated to draw on other sources containing information about the marketing programs of various hotel organizations—the giant chains that have traditionally dominated the field; the newer, more specialized companies which have emerged in recent years; and even individual properties.

Every hotel—whether it is part of a vast organization or a small, independently owned property—must engage in marketing planning and execution. Therefore, regardless of what marketing resources are at your disposal, the principles of sound marketing planning and careful follow-up presented in this book will help your hotel achieve significantly better financial results.

This text is divided into five parts. The first part, which includes Chapters 1 and 2, defines the marketing concept and other important terms in order to put the subject of hospitality marketing in perspective. Part I also identifies distinctive aspects of service marketing and discusses the various circumstances which have shaped the evolution of marketing thought.

Part II introduces the concept of strategic marketing planning. Comprising Chapters 3 through 6, Part II examines the types of planning and analyses which form the base for successful hospitality marketing programs.

In Part III, the focus turns to individual properties in contrast to previous discussions which center on marketing approaches of major hotel chains. Chapters 7 through 10 discuss the typical structure of a marketing and sales division in addition to exploring some of the techniques and tools of marketing.

Part IV, which embraces Chapters 11 through 14, illustrates marketing tools in action. Readers are walked through the strategic planning process to see how these seemingly separate tools can be correlated in a successful hotel marketing program. Because examples are given at the property level, this section should be particularly useful to small hotels, whether they fall at the budget end of the market, at the world-class end, or somewhere in between.

Part V discusses strategic planning as a growth philosophy and some of the current trends in the hospitality industry. Growth strategies, market conditions, product lines, new hotel types, and management considerations are among the topics presented in Chapters 15 and 16 in terms of their potential impact on hospitality marketing in the future.

Some chapters in the text are followed by supplemental readings. These materials are intended to help facilitate your understanding and further study of hospitality marketing.

We have undertaken the preparation of this book with humility and consider its contents a beginning, not a conclusion. Twenty-five years ago, the discipline of hospitality marketing was virtually nonexistent, but it has grown rapidly in the intervening years. Nevertheless, from the standpoint of marketing practices, the hospitality industry has yet to mature to the level of sophistication enjoyed by some industries. If this book contributes to that maturing process, it will have accomplished its task.

The authors would like to acknowledge Gary Spizizen, independent consultant in the hospitality industry, for his contributions and invaluable assistance in developing this text.

The Educational Institute of AH&MA, the publisher of this textbook, is committed to the improvement of marketing education in the hospitality industry. So, too, is its peer organization, the Educational Foundation of the Hotel Sales and Marketing Association, International (HSMAI). Thanks to these two outstanding organizations, the quality of marketing education in our industry has been and continues to be greatly enhanced.

Christopher W. L. Hart, Ph.D.
Professor of Economics and Marketing
School of Hotel Administration
Cornell University

David A. Troy, CHSE, President
Inn America, Braintree, Massachusetts
Past President, TIMA Corporation
Past President, HSMAI

Study Tips for Users of
Educational Institute Courses

Learning is a skill, like many other activities. Although you may be familiar with many of the following study tips, we want to reinforce their usefulness.

Your Attitude Makes a Difference

If you want to learn, you will: it's as simple as that. Your attitude will go a long way in determining whether or not you do well in this course. We want to help you succeed.

Plan and Organize to Learn

- Set up a regular time and place for study. Make sure you won't be disturbed or distracted.

- Decide ahead of time how much you want to accomplish during each study session. Remember to keep your study sessions brief; don't try to do too much at one time.

Read the Course Text to Learn

- *Before* you read each chapter, read the chapter outline and the learning objectives. If there is a summary at the end of the chapter, you should read it to get a feel for what the chapter is about.

- Then, go back to the beginning of the chapter and *carefully* read, focusing on the material included in the learning objectives and asking yourself such questions as:

  —Do I understand the material?

  —How can I use this information now or in the future?

- Make notes in margins and highlight or underline important sections to help you as you study. Read a section first, then go back over it to mark important points.

- Keep a dictionary handy. If you come across an unfamiliar word that is not included in the textbook glossary, look it up in the dictionary.

- Read as much as you can. The more you read, the better you read.

Testing Your Knowledge

- Test questions developed by the Educational Institute for this course are designed to measure your knowledge of the material.

- End-of-the-chapter Review Quizzes help you find out how well you have studied the material. They indicate where additional study may be needed. Review Quizzes are also helpful in studying for other tests.

- Prepare for tests by reviewing:

  —learning objectives

  —notes

  —outlines

  —questions at the end of each assignment

- As you begin to take any test, read the test instructions *carefully* and look over the questions.

We hope your experiences in this course will prompt you to undertake other training and educational activities in a planned, career-long program of professional growth and development.

Part I

Introduction

This section defines the marketing concept and identifies distinctive aspects of service marketing that apply to the hospitality industry. Chapter 1 addresses the marketing concept as a means by which companies achieve their business goals by first determining the needs and wants of target markets and then delivering products and services to satisfy those markets more effectively and efficiently than the competition. The chapter also discusses the circumstances which influence companies to fully adopt the marketing concept and closes with a brief account of the evolution of hospitality marketing thought. The marketing concept is further defined in Chapter 2 where the focus shifts to the differences between the marketing of services in the hospitality industry and the marketing of products in manufacturing industries. Supplemental readings which follow each chapter elaborate on the material presented in the text.

Chapter Outline

Trends in the U.S. Lodging Industry
    Consolidation
    Market Saturation
    Brand Proliferation
Well-Marketed Hotels of the Future
The Managers of the Future
Evolving Hospitality Technology

Learning Objectives

1. List what lodging marketers must do to gain and sustain a competitive advantage in the market.

2. Identify current trends affecting the lodging industry.

1

The Marketing Concept

THE MARKETING FUNCTION IS ESSENTIAL to the success of a hospitality operation. This function encompasses a broad range of activities. While many of these activities are the direct responsibility of the marketing staff, every employee in the hospitality operation has a marketing responsibility.

> 66 Everyone is involved in marketing at a Sheraton property, from the general manager on through to the doorman. Selling hotel services is not done by salespeople alone. While it requires the cooperative effort of sales, advertising, and public relations people to seek out good business prospects and develop them into good customers, they are not really 'sold' on a hotel unless they enjoy the real product that a Sheraton sells—a quality guest experience.
>
> Assuring our customers of that quality experience means providing a warm welcome; clean, comfortable, and convenient facilities; fine cuisine and courteous service. It involves the cooperation of a unified staff, working at every position in the hotel. This is a hotel's true marketing strength, and it has been very successful for Sheraton. 99

> —Howard P. James
> Former Chairman of the Board
> The Sheraton Corporation

This statement by Bud James, who has been such a dominant figure in the hotel industry, indicates the new depth of commitment to marketing called for at all levels of today's lodging industry, and it sets the stage for your study of hospitality marketing.[1]

Hospitality is already a big industry, and it's still growing. As the industry expands, competition becomes keener. Because today's guests expect more services, amenities, and value, the industry is responding by becoming more specialized and sophisticated. As more and more companies equip themselves to surpass the competition and to meet these new customer demands, marketing will play an increasingly important role in the hospitality industry.

Marketing is often mistakenly equated with selling, or advertising, or public relations. While it does include these activities, it is much more. Marketing integrates such basic business functions as sales, advertising, public relations, promotions, merchandising, and pricing in order to produce the maximum obtainable profit.

> 66 My personal philosophy about selling and marketing in the hospitality industry is to constantly involve yourself in the basics—the basic knowledge of your industry and the service involved, basic selling and marketing skills with

complete knowledge of your customer's needs—and finally to develop those creative skills that separate you as an individual and your hotel from that of your competition. I have always felt the people are buying you, your ideas, your sincere desire to follow through and make it happen. The final ingredient in my personal philosophy is to **do it at a profit.** It doesn't take a genius to give it away. It takes hard work, perseverance, and a love for what we are doing to truly succeed. I have never thought I was better than anybody else, but I've always worked overtime to try to be better. **"**

—Sig Front
Senior Vice President of Marketing
The Sheraton Corporation

The most basic task of marketing is to bring buyers and sellers together. Strategic marketing planning is the process of accomplishing this task by first learning who the buyers are. Markets must be identified by grouping current or potential customers on the basis of such categories as geographic location, industry sector, economic status, or behavioral and lifestyle characteristics. Next, the markets must be narrowed into the particular segments toward which the operation will direct its marketing efforts. Once these target markets have been selected, strategic marketing planning must develop the appropriate marketing mix—the particular combination of marketing objectives, strategies, and tactics by which to attract the targeted mix of market segments.

Above all, marketing attempts to see the business of the hospitality operation through the eyes of the customer. From this perspective, it is obvious that activities other than selling, advertising, and public relations become important. For example, discovering what your guests want and need, how your property can deliver the appropriate services, and planning strategies for competing against other properties catering to the same customers are among marketing activities which are critical to the success of today's hospitality operation.

The Marketing Orientation

The marketing concept proposes that the best way to achieve organizational goals consists of determining the needs and wants of target markets and delivering products and services to satisfy those needs and wants more effectively and efficiently than competitors. Today's marketers begin by asking what personal needs and wants customers desire to satisfy. The company then creates products and services to satisfy those wants. Profits come about through customer satisfaction and repeat purchasing.

The marketing concept has a long history behind it. Peter Drucker suggests that the marketing concept first appeared in Japan around 1650 when a member of the Mitsui family settled in Tokyo as a merchant and opened what might be called the first department store.[2] He became the buyer for his customers, designed the right products for them, and developed sources for their production. He implemented a money-back, no-questions-asked policy, and adopted the strategy of offering a large assortment of products to his customers rather than focusing on any single craft or product category.

Despite occasional manifestations of these kinds of marketing techniques throughout history, the actual tenets of the marketing concept did not crystalize, at least in the United States, until the late 1950s. From our position today, we can view the emergence of the marketing concept as one step in the progressive evolution of a business philosophy. This business philosophy addresses the following concern: in the manufacture and creation of products and services, what weights should be given to the interests of the company, the customers, and society?

The specific weights, or emphases, that a company places on its own interests, the interests of its customers, and the interests of the society within which it conducts business will define that particular company's business orientation. There are essentially four competing concepts, or orientations, under which businesses conduct their economic activities: (1) product orientation, (2) selling orientation, (3) marketing orientation, and (4) the societal marketing orientation.

Product Orientation

Companies that are product-oriented aim to provide products or services that are low in cost, capable of a wide distribution, and which offer the best quality, performance, and features. Product-oriented companies assume that consumers are primarily interested in product availability and low prices.

This assumption appears to be valid in a business situation in which the demand for a product exceeds supply. For the most part, this situation prevailed in the United States from the latter part of the nineteenth century to about 1920. At that time, there was little demand for products not associated with satisfying basic family needs. Businesses placed their emphasis on meeting the general demand for basic commodities and satisfying the relatively homogeneous needs of a population having relatively limited discretionary income. Companies concentrated their efforts on ways to streamline their production processes while, at the same time, holding down costs. Ford Motor Company, with its standardized Model-T, is a classic example of this product-oriented approach to the marketplace.

The problem with the product orientation is that it leads to what Theodore Levitt terms "marketing myopia"—an undue concentration on the product rather than on the needs of consumers. Product-oriented managers seem to focus all their attention on their products and channel all their energies to improving them. They fail to notice significant changes in the marketplace which may affect their businesses, such as changing consumer needs, new competitors entering the market with better products, or substitute products which more accurately satisfy consumer needs. Ford Motor Company learned this lesson when other car manufacturers began turning out automobiles in hundreds of different styles and colors.

A classic example which illustrates an extreme product orientation to the marketplace is the story about a manufacturer of office files who complained that his files should be selling better because they are the best in the world. "They can be dropped from a four-story building and not be damaged." "Yes," agreed the sales manager, "but our customers aren't planning to push them out of four-story buildings."[3]

Selling Orientation

Selling-oriented companies generally operate under the assumption that buyers are naturally reluctant to part with their money and, therefore, they need to be persuaded to purchase products and services. The selling orientation reached its zenith in the United States during the period from 1920 to 1950. During this time, many companies turned out increasing quantities of goods through improved mass-production processes. Many businesses found a situation in which supplies of their products or services exceeded demand. Given this economic condition, the success, or failure, of many businesses hinged on the ability of the sales force to move inventories. Many companies developed sophisticated sales techniques by which to locate prospects and convince them through persuasive personal selling techniques to purchase their companies' products or services.

Today, the selling orientation to the marketplace is still a crucial and effective perspective for many businesses, especially for those businesses that provide products or services which consumers do not normally think of buying. At times, these businesses are accused of using "high-pressure" sales techniques. However, it is only reasonable to expect sales representatives of these kinds of businesses to be as persuasive as possible, because they often have only one opportunity to convince their sales prospects to purchase the products or services offered.

Although the selling orientation has connotations of "hard driving," "high-pressure," and "pushy" salespeople, some kind of sales push is necessary in almost every business. However, for a selling orientation to be most effective, it must be integrated within a more general marketing effort—one which identifies the necessity and the limitations of the sales effort in relation to a customer needs assessment, market research, product development, pricing, and distribution. If the customer needs are accurately identified, and if the appropriate distributing, promoting, and pricing tactics have been implemented, then the personal selling task should not be terribly difficult or "high-pressured."

Marketing Orientation

During the 1950s, competition for markets grew. As consumer discretionary income rose, so too did the demand for an increasingly wide variety of products and services. In this more competitive environment, selling skills alone were insufficient. Sophisticated companies developed new skills to enable them to produce products and services more attuned to a discriminating market. These conditions ushered in the marketing-oriented era.

A marketing orientation begins by asking what personal needs the consumer wants to satisfy. Needs may be defined very broadly to include not only the basic services such as a room and a meal, but ancillary services as well, such as a reservations system, valet parking, express check-in and check-out, and many others.

The personal needs of consumers can also be viewed as a bundle of intangible benefits which they expect to receive by purchasing a company's products or services. These bundles of benefits may range from the sensual (for example, the sight and sound of the facility and of other guests), to the psychological (for example, the comfort, status, or just plain well-being associated with staying at a particular property).

Identifying the bundle of benefits which consumers seek to receive from purchasing a specific product or service is a critical task for marketing efforts within service industries. Once the consumer needs have been identified, a property then begins to develop the products or services which will satisfy those needs better than the competition.

The difference between the marketing concept and the product concept is really the difference between an internal and an external focus. Peter F. Drucker notes that it is often necessary to step outside a business in order to get inside the heart of the operation:

> **❝**I do not believe that one can manage a business by reports. One must spend a great deal of time outside, where the results are. Inside a business one only has costs. One looks at markets, at customers, at society, and at knowledge, all of which are outside the business, to see what is really happening. This, reports will never tell you.**❞**4

It is easy for managers to lose a marketing-oriented focus. Just as a fish doesn't know that it's wet because it has been in the water all of its life, so managers often lose track of the environment in which their businesses exist. The demand of day-to-day operations frequently locks managers' attention onto short-term concerns and hinders their perceptions of long-term considerations which may be critical to the success of their companies. Indeed, one of the most difficult tasks that managers face today is setting aside time to take off the hat of the operating manager and put on the hat of the strategist.

Marketers need to be strategists because marketing activities begin not after products or services are offered, but long before they are produced. Long before construction ever begins with a new hotel project, efforts must be made to determine whether a market actually exists for the hotel's services, and, if a market does exist, its location, size, segments, perceptions, preferences, and buying habits must also be identified.

This is critically important for the lodging industry for at least two reasons. First, with the enormous variety of lodging properties on the market, a new hotel must be sure that its product meets a specific need. Consumers want to purchase *exactly* what satisfies their needs. Second, opening a hotel requires a long lead time—up to two years from conception, through design and construction, to the actual opening ceremonies. The ability to identify and anticipate trends through sophisticated market research reduces the probability that by the time the hotel opens it will be obsolete.

Once this market research has been done, the best possible products and services for the target market must be developed. Marketing must also design the pricing, distribution, and promotional plan for launching the hotel into the marketplace. Then comes implementation of the plan, monitoring of results, and, where necessary, corrective action(s) when goals are not being met.

As you can see, marketing activities begin long before the products or services exist, and they continue long after the products or services are purchased by customers. All along the way, marketing must interpret what is happening in the marketplace and seek new ways to constantly improve customer satisfaction.

Societal Marketing Orientation

Contemporary marketing scholars have identified yet another stage in the evolution of business philosophy which has been termed a societal marketing orientation. This perspective focuses a company's attention on the broader, social implications of satisfying consumer needs.

One example of a societal marketing orientation is the introduction of returnable cans and bottles. Supporters of this policy argue that despite initial consumer resistance and the immediate increase in prices which would arise from processing bottle and can returns, the one-way, disposable bottles and cans wasted resources and contributed to littering. Another example is the introduction of bio-degradable detergents to prevent the pollution of lakes, rivers, and streams. Managerial decisions in the lodging industry are sometimes affected by societal concerns. For example, the Delta Landing Project, a mixed-use development in Antioch, California, near San Francisco, has included a nature preserve in its development plans.[5]

When Companies Adopt the Marketing Concept

Most companies don't really grasp the marketing concept until driven to it by circumstances. Philip Kotler has identified the following five possible developments which could influence companies to adopt the marketing concept.[6]

Sales Decline. When companies which have been product-focused experience falling sales, they become desperate and start looking for answers in the marketplace. Many lodging firms have encountered sales declines and have had to take a hard look at their products and how well they meet the needs of consumers.

Slow Growth. Slow growth gives companies the impetus to look for new markets. They recognize a need for marketing know-how if they are to successfully identify, evaluate, and select new opportunities. Many lodging companies, faced with slow growth in their traditional markets, are diversifying or developing new products for different market segments.

Changing Buying Patterns. Many industries are marked by rapidly changing consumer wants and needs. In the restaurant industry, for example, concepts come and go. In fact, the variety seems to stimulate fickleness on the part of consumers—knowing that more is available, they seem to constantly demand even more.

Increasing Competition. Complacent companies may suddenly be attacked by powerful marketing strategies launched by their competitors. When this happens, they are forced to learn sophisticated marketing techniques in order to meet the challenge. The classic example of an industry in which the level of competition suddenly escalated from a state of relative calm to a ferocious marketing pitch is the beer business.

Before Philip Morris acquired Miller Brewing in 1970, the majority of beer producers were regional firms, which typically concentrated their competitive efforts on such mundane practices as hiring professional football players to push their products in local taverns and bars during the off-season. Philip Morris, possessing considerable marketing acumen honed through years of competition in the hotly competitive tobacco industry, changed the face of competition by executing a sophisticated and aggressive national marketing strategy. By segmenting the market and completely repositioning the Miller product line, market share rose from 4% in 1970 to over 22% in 1981. Anheuser-Busch, the market leader, responded in force by successfully copying Miller's strategy, but most other brewing firms were caught short by the radical shift in the competitive environment.

Increasing Marketing Expenditures. Companies may find their expenditures for advertising, sales promotion, marketing research, and consumer service getting out of control. In these kinds of situations, management may decide that it is time to adopt a strategic marketing planning process.

The Evolution of Hospitality Marketing Thought

The rest of this chapter concerns how thinking about marketing in the hospitality industry has evolved over the last few decades. We asked a number of industry leaders who took an active part in those decades of development to give us their points of view. Among the most thorough and thought-provoking responses we received was the following.

❝It isn't so much *who* as *what* has had the largest influence on our evolution from a sales-oriented industry to a marketing-oriented industry. I think of it in terms of multiple, interrelated factors, the most important of which is mass transportation. The airline industry has had a profound effect on our business. As airlines learned to do mass-marketing well, we in the hotel business scooped up ideas and ways of doing things that made sense to our industry. We have borrowed shamelessly from the airlines over the years to the ultimate good of all concerned, I think. We have also learned, more and more, how to do joint marketing with them....

The economy is another factor, obviously. After World War II, increasing affluence and levels of discretionary income led to an even broader and more complex marketplace of travelers, each segment of which had to be understood and courted. Group business, convention business, pleasure travel, business travel—they all had their special needs and peculiarities which had to be addressed. [Today] the basic need of people to get together and communicate involves traveling greater and greater distances as more and more companies decentralize or add regional offices. Conglomerates grow, multi-national corporations spring up, and we get closer and closer to becoming the 'global village' McLuhan envisioned. I don't think teleconferencing, which is high-tech, will ever replace the 'high-touch' of face-to-face meetings, however.

I should also give credit to the Hilton organization. I think they were the first to express a marketing philosophy that caught the imagination of the industry. The building of the Shamrock Hilton was a harbinger of what was to come … the first big hotel after the war. You didn't necessarily agree with them, but you sure knew they were there. Competition has always depended on people sticking their heads above the crowd, and you either follow the leader or you learn to do what they're doing 'differently' or 'better.' So, when Hilton started describing how they did business, it gave rise to all sorts of competitive reactions: 'We can do it better'; 'we'll do it differently'; 'we can ride on their coattails'; 'we'd never stoop to that sort of thing'; and so on.

Prior to World War II, all you had to do was open a hotel on the corner and sit on your hands, and people came in and rented a room. You were an innkeeper in the grand tradition. You met the people as they left in the morning and greeted them as they returned in the evening. After the war, things got a little more competitive and then a lot more competitive. First there was one hotel across the street, then another. Somebody had to manage the hotel, and somebody had to go out and market the hotel or people [would go] to the competition. Some companies didn't make the transition very well. Competition forces people to ask themselves, what do I have to do to compete? The better the answer, the more effective the marketing becomes. When a whole bunch of people who are very good at what they do ask themselves, 'What do I have to do to compete?' then a whole industry benefits, and the ultimate benefit goes to the consumer.

We went from being innkeepers to being managers in a very short period of time as hotels got bigger and more complex.... The innkeeper functions of meeting and greeting guests and making them feel welcome were passed ... along to the directors of marketing, who found ways to convey that sense of being welcome, even if [they didn't do it] in person. **"**

—**Bill Newman**
Senior Vice President, Marketing
Westin Hotels

As you can see from Bill Newman's capsule, hospitality marketing is a relatively new discipline. People who have been in the business for the last 35 years have witnessed during the course of their careers virtually the entire development of marketing as a concept and an activity within the hospitality industry. This does not mean that certain marketing functions were not very well developed earlier than that. For example, good hotel advertising was produced during the nineteenth century, and hotel selling became a fairly professional activity during the post-World War II era of declining hotel occupancies. Also, during the forties and early fifties, great promotions were launched for hotels. In one classic case, Glen McCarthy created a tremendous fanfare nationwide as he opened the Shamrock Hotel in what was then the outskirts of Houston.

Although the elements of marketing had not been brought together into a collective body of thought 35 years ago, they certainly have been integrated in recent years out of necessity. Hospitality marketing became a recognizable discipline during the years after World War II. It was about that time that a gentleman by the name of Kemmons Wilson conceived of building roadside motor inns with consistent quality standards at a reasonable price. His idea eventually became the vast Holiday Inn empire.

Another gentleman was responsible for developing a great deal of the hospitality marketing theory of the post-World War II era. C. DeWitt Coffman, affectionately known as "Witt," was a pioneer in the field. When most of today's senior practitioners were just beginning to seek resources that would give them a working knowledge of the hospitality marketing discipline, the only writings on the subject were by Witt. His textbooks *The Full House* and *Marketing for a Full House,* both published by the Cornell Press, broke new ground. In 1980, Witt's last book, *Hospitality for Sale*, was published by the Educational Institute of the American Hotel & Motel Association, and this fine marketing text is still in circulation today.

Buck Hoyle, the Executive Vice President of the Hotel Sales and Marketing Association, International, said of Witt, a past president of HSMAI:

> 66 As an individual, the late Witt Coffman has had a tremendous influence on hospitality marketing. A prolific writer and speaker, he had, in addition, a presence and charisma which personified professionalism as well as structured academic knowledge. He did a great deal to influence hospitality marketers to think of themselves as professionals and [to think] of their skill as a discipline. More than any single individual, he popularized the technique of customer, client, and facilities analysis; [the] developing of long-range marketing strategies; and the integration of sales, advertising, and promotion in the total marketing approach. 99

There were many others, however, who profoundly changed the way the hospitality industry did business. In the late fifties, Jack Neumann took charge of a group of eager, young hotel salespeople working for the Hotel Corporation of America (now Sonesta). With the strong support of the Sonnabend family (and using professional educators from the Harvard Business School, the University of New Hampshire's Whittemore School of Business, and other schools), Neumann began to teach the academic subjects of sales, advertising, and public relations. These teachers forced the young salespeople to learn marketing but, more important, they taught them how to teach marketing. It is significant that so many of today's industry leaders came through that tough HCA marketing school of the late fifties and the early sixties.

At the same time, Bud Grice, Tom McCarthy, and Al LeFaivre were building the hotel side of the Marriott Corporation as a marketing force to be reckoned with. In the fifties all three of these marketing giants recognized an opportunity which had, oddly enough, never been seized. That is, a tremendous amount of hotel usage was attributable to the corporate market, and yet very little attention was paid to the business traveler as a market segment. Grice, McCarthy, and LeFaivre wisely concentrated the early efforts of the Marriott Corporation on the business traveler and worked closely with their operating group to formulate a product most acceptable to this market segment. The result was that, in a very short period of time, Marriott became THE hotel company for the business traveler in the early sixties. Of course, since that time Marriott has radically altered its product line to include the entire spectrum of convention hotels, destination resorts, and so on, but the company still remains a favorite among corporate business travelers.

Other changes were occurring during the early sixties. Hotels in Las Vegas, which had originally catered exclusively to the pleasure-seeking, gambling-oriented traveler, now faced enormous gaps in their occupancy. As more and more legitimate companies, such as Del Webb, began taking over Las Vegas properties and easing out some of the previously unsavory elements, the business of running hotels (and not merely casinos) became important. At this time, convention sales leaders, such as Charlie Monahan and Sig Front, began to approach large corporations and organizations with the crazy notion that they ought to go into the desert for a meeting or convention. The meeting planners responded, and the risk paid off. Enormous amounts of investment capital and space were committed to the construction of more Las Vegas hotels "on the come." Come it did, and for the next 25 years conventions and Las Vegas became synonymous. Conventions in the desert—the fledgling idea of a few courageous people—mushroomed beyond anyone's wildest dreams.

Moving into the seventies, a new school of hospitality marketing thought came to the forefront. It held that the general manager of a hotel should be its number one salesperson. Until that time, most general managers had treated their marketing and sales departments with "benign neglect" at best. This sprang from the fact that many GMs had felt that sales was a necessary evil. In those days, salespeople were considered an unusual breed. What they did to bring in business was not the affair of the general manager. In fact, it was not necessarily even the concern of the property's operations management. This attitude was taken to the extreme by some companies whose marketing departments at the properties were told to report not to the general managers of those hotels but to the central headquarters or regional headquarters of the chains. Besides allowing the managers to be uninvolved, this arrangement in effect relieved them of bottom-line responsibility for the hotel's overall financial performance. After all, if the general manager didn't control revenues, how could they control costs?

Fortunately, these practices were changed under the strong direction of industry leaders such as Bud James (see related quotation at the beginning of this chapter); Jon Canas, Chief Operating Officer of Dunfey Air Lingus Corporation; and others. The new school of thought insisted on interactive marketing planning and implementation programs, led by general managers with a deep respect for and involvement in their marketing programs at every level. This interactive process has worked to produce stronger and better results in hotels. Marketing-minded management is an important characteristic of virtually every successful hotel company today. It is also the reason for the growth of the emerging hotel organizations, the future leaders of the industry.

No discussion of hospitality marketing in the seventies would be complete without some mention of the phenomenon of Atlantic City's rebirth. In the mid-seventies a group of community leaders, in what was then a stagnant and economically depressed Atlantic City, determined that the only way to revitalize their local economy was to legalize casino gambling. This proposal was followed by an enormous public outcry to the effect that casino gambling would attract more crime and that Atlantic City would become a haven for criminals. Many citizens feared that Atlantic City would be doomed to go through the same evolutionary process as Nevada's cities allegedly had in their infancy.

Because of this outcry, highly restrictive legislation was passed so that casino gambling would be accepted by the public. Extensive controls were imposed on the casino hotels through a state bureaucracy, which significantly increased their costs of construction. For a time, these administrative constraints held back the growth of the casino hotel industry in Atlantic City. Nevertheless, the appeal of the early casinos to day trippers—people who come by bus to spend part of the day at a casino and then return to one of the major metropolitan centers—made these

Exhibit 1   Ads for Atlantic City Casino Hotels

Courtesy of The Claridge, Atlantic City, New Jersey

operations extremely profitable, despite the constraints under which they were obliged to do business.

Soon sales and marketing came into play. These new hotels, built with outstanding meeting facilities, became increasingly popular as sites for meetings and conferences. Overnight motor coach tours also were attracted to Atlantic City. The enormous weight of advertising in the major metropolitan markets (see Exhibit 1) contributed mightily to the growth of Atlantic City's casino business with the curious result that, in some respects, the casino gambling industry became much healthier in Atlantic City than in Nevada.

Endnotes

1. For our purposes, hotel is a broad generic term for all types of lodging operations including luxury hotels, motels, motor inns, and inns.
2. Peter F. Drucker, *Management: Tasks, Responsibilities, Practices* (New York: Harper & Row, 1973), p. 62.
3. Philip Kotler, *Marketing Management: Analysis, Planning, and Control* (Englewood Cliffs, N.J.: Prentice-Hall, Inc., 1984), p. 18.
4. Peter F. Drucker, *Technology, Management, and Society* (New York: Harper Colophon, 1977), pp. 95–96.
5. "3 Props Planned in Shore Project," *Hotel & Motel Management*, March 1985, p. 11.
6. Philip Kotler, *Marketing Management: Analysis, Planning, and Control* (Englewood Cliffs, N.J.: Prentice-Hall, 1984), pp. 23–24.

Exhibit 1 *(continued)*

Supplemental Reading

What is a Business?

by Peter F. Drucker

> *Peter Drucker was one of the earliest management writers to define the purpose of a business as that of satisfying consumer needs. His statements on this purpose as well as those on the entrepreneurial functions have been widely quoted.*
>
> *The following material is included because of its significance to all those interested in management.*

If we want to know what a business is we have to start with its *purpose.* And its purpose must lie outside of the business itself. In fact, it must lie in society since a business enterprise is an organ of society. There is only one valid definition of business purpose: *to create a customer.*

Markets are not created by God, nature or economic forces, but by businessmen. The want they satisfy may have been felt by the customer before he was offered the means of satisfying it. It may indeed, like the want for food in a famine, have dominated the customer's life and filled all his waking moments. But it was a theoretical want before; only when the action of businessmen makes it effective demand is there a customer, a market. It may have been an unfelt want. There may have been no want at all until business action created it—by advertising, by salesmanship, or by inventing something new. In every case it is business action that creates the customer.

It is the customer who determines what a business is. For it is the customer, and he alone, who through being willing to pay for a good or for a service, converts economic resources into wealth, things into goods. What the business thinks it produces is not of first importance—especially not to the future of the business and to its success. What the customer thinks he is buying, what he considers "value," is decisive—it determines what a business is, what it produces and whether it will prosper.

The customer is the foundation of a business and keeps it in existence. He alone gives employment. And it is to supply the consumer that society entrusts wealth-producing resources to the business enterprise.

The Two Entrepreneurial Functions

Because it is its purpose to create a customer, any business enterprise has two—and only these two—basic functions: marketing and innovation. They are the entrepreneurial functions.

Marketing is the distinguishing, the unique function of the business. A business is set apart from all other human organizations by the fact that it markets a product or a service. Neither Church, nor Army, nor School, nor State does that. Any organization that fulfills itself through marketing a product or a service is a business. Any organization in which marketing is either absent or incidental is not a business and should never be run as if it were one.

The first man to see marketing clearly as the unique and central function of the business enterprise, and the creation of a customer as the specific job of management, was Cyrus McCormick. The history books mention only that he invented a mechanical harvester. But he also invented the basic tools of modern marketing: market research and market analysis, the concept of marketing standing, modern pricing policies, the modern service-salesman, parts and service supply to the customer and installment credit. He is truly the father of business management. And he had done all this by 1850. It was not until fifty years later, however, that he was widely imitated even in his own country.

The economic revolution of the American economy since 1900 has in large part been a marketing revolution caused by the assumption of responsibility for creative, aggressive, pioneering marketing by American management. Fifty years ago the typical attitude of the American businessman toward marketing was still: "The sales department will sell whatever the plant produces." Today it is increasingly: "It is our job to produce what the market needs." But our economists and government officials are just beginning to understand this: only now, for instance, is the U.S. Department of Commerce setting up an Office of Distribution.

In Europe there is still almost no understanding that marketing is the specific business function—a major reason for the stagnation of the European economies of today. For to reach full realization of the importance of marketing requires overcoming a deep-rooted social prejudice against "selling" as ignoble and parasitical, and in favor of "production" as gentlemanly, with its resultant theoretical fallacy of considering production as the main and determining function of a business.

A good example of this historical attitude toward marketing are those big Italian companies which have no domestic sales managers even though the home market accounts for 70% of their business.

Actually marketing is so basic that it is not just enough to have a strong sales department and to entrust marketing to it. Marketing is not only much broader than selling, it is not a specialized activity at all. It encompasses the entire business. It is the whole business seen from the point of view of its final result, that is, from the customer's point of view. Concern and responsibility for marketing must therefore permeate all areas of the enterprise.

One illustration of this concept of marketing is the policy worked out by General Electric Company over the last ten years, which attempts to build customer and market appeal into the product from the design stage on. It considers the actual act of selling but the last step in a sales effort that began before the first engineer put pencil to drawing paper. This, according to a statement in the company's 1952 annual report, "introduces the marketing man at the beginning rather than the end of the production cycle and would integrate marketing into each phase of the business. Thus marketing, through its studies and research, will establish for the engineer, the designer and the manufacturing man what the customer wants in a given product, what price he is willing to pay, and where and when it will be wanted. Marketing would have authority in product planning, production scheduling and inventory control, as well as in the sales distribution and servicing of the product."

The Enterprise as the Organ of Economic Growth

But marketing alone does not make a business enterprise. In a static economy there are no "business enterprises." There are not even "businessmen." For the "middleman" of a static society is simply a "broker" who receives his compensation in the form of a fee.

A business enterprise can exist only in an expanding economy, or at least in one which considers change both natural and desirable. And business is the specific organ of growth, expansion and change.

The second function of a business is therefore *innovation*, that is, the provision of better and more economic goods and services. It is not enough for the business to provide just any economic goods and services; it must provide better and more economic ones. It is not necessary for a business to grow bigger; but it is necessary that it constantly grow better.

Innovation may take the form of lower price—the form with which the economist has been most concerned, for the simple reason that it is the only one that can be handled by his quantitative tools. But it may also be a new and better product (even at a higher price), a new convenience or the creation of a new want. It may be finding new uses for old products. A salesman who succeeded in selling refrigerators to the Eskimos to prevent food from freezing would be an "innovator" quite as much as if he had developed brand-new processes or invented a new product. To sell the Eskimos a refrigerator to keep food cold is finding a new market; to sell a refrigerator to keep food from getting too cold is actually creating a new product. Technologically there is, of course, only the same old product; but economically there is innovation.

Innovation goes right through all phases of business. It may be innovation in design, in product, in marketing techniques. It may be innovation in price or in service to the customer. It may be innovation in management organization or in management methods. Or it may be a new insurance policy that makes it possible for a businessman to assume new risks. The most effective innovations in American industry in the last few years were probably not the much publicized new electronic or chemical products and processes but innovations in materials handling and in manager development.

Innovation extends through all forms of business. It is as important to a bank, an insurance company or a retail store as it is to a manufacturing or engineering business.

In the organization of business enterprise innovation can therefore no more be considered a separate function than marketing. It is not confined to engineering or research but extends across all parts of the business, all functions, all activities. It is not, to repeat, confined to manufacturing business alone. Innovation in distribution has been as important as innovation in manufacturing; and so has been innovation in an insurance company or in a bank.

The leadership in innovation with respect to product and service can normally be focused in one functional activity which is responsible for nothing else. This is always true in a business with a strong engineering or chemical flavor. In an insurance company, too, a special department charged with leadership responsibility for the development of new kinds of coverage is in order; and there might well be another such department charged with innovation in the organization of sales, the administration of policies and the settling of claims. For both together are the insurance company's business.

A large railroad company has organized two centers of innovation, both under a vice-president. One is concerned with systematic work on all physical aspects of transportation: locomotives and cars, tracks, signals, communications. The other is concerned with innovation in freight and passenger service, the development of new sources of traffic, new tariff policies, the opening of new markets, the development of new service, etc.

But every other managerial unit of the business should also have clear responsibility and definite goals for innovation. It should be responsible for its contribution to innovation in the company's product or service; and it should in addition strive consciously and with direction toward advancement of the art in the particular area in which it is engaged: selling or accounting, quality control or personnel management.

Marketing Myopia

by Theodore Levitt

Shortsighted managements often fail to recognize that in fact there is no such thing as a growth industry.

How can a company ensure its continued growth? In 1960 "Marketing Myopia" answered that question in a new and challenging way by urging organizations to define their industries broadly to take advantage of growth opportunities. Using the archetype of the railroads, Mr. Levitt showed how they declined inevitably as technology advanced because they defined themselves too narrowly. To continue growing, companies must ascertain and act on their customers' needs and desires, not bank on the presumptive longevity of their products. The success of the article testifies to the validity of its message. It has been widely quoted and anthologized, and HBR has sold more than 265,000 reprints of it. The author of 14 subsequent articles in HBR, Mr. Levitt is one of the magazine's most prolific contributors. In a retrospective commentary, he considers the use and

---

*misuse that have been made of "Marketing Myopia," describing its many inter-
pretations and hypothesizing about its success.*

*At the time of the article's publication, Theodore Levitt was lecturer in busi-
ness administration at the Harvard Business School. Now a full professor there,
he is the author of six books, including* The Third Sector: New Tactics for a
Responsive Society *(1973) and* Marketing for Business Growth *(1974).*

Every major industry was once a growth industry. But some that are now riding a
wave of growth enthusiasm are very much in the shadow of decline. Others which
are thought of as seasoned growth industries have actually stopped growing. In
every case the reason growth is threatened, slowed, or stopped is *not* because the
market is saturated. It is because there has been a failure of management.

Fateful purposes: The failure is at the top. The executives responsible for it, in
the last analysis, are those who deal with broad aims and policies. Thus:

The railroads did not stop growing because the need for passenger and freight
transportation declined. That grew. The railroads are in trouble today not because
the need was filled by others (cars, trucks, airplanes, even telephones), but because
it was *not* filled by the railroads themselves. They let others take customers away
from them because they assumed themselves to be in the railroad business rather
than in the transportation business. The reason they defined their industry wrong
was because they were railroad-oriented instead of transportation-oriented; they
were product-oriented instead of customer-oriented.

Hollywood barely escaped being totally ravished by television. Actually, all
the established film companies went through drastic reorganizations. Some simply
disappeared. All of them got into trouble not because of TV's in-roads but because
of their own myopia. As with the railroads, Hollywood defined its business incor-
rectly. It thought it was in the movie business when it was actually in the entertainment business. "Movies" implied a specific, limited product. This produced a
fatuous contentment which from the beginning led producers to view TV as a
threat. Hollywood scorned and rejected TV when it should have welcomed it as an
opportunity—an opportunity to expand the entertainment business.

Today, TV is a bigger business than the old narrowly defined movie business
ever was. Had Hollywood been customer-oriented (providing entertainment),
rather than product-oriented (making movies), would it have gone through the fiscal purgatory that it did? I doubt it. What ultimately saved Hollywood and ac-
counted for its recent resurgence was the wave of new young writers, producers,
and directors whose previous successes in television had decimated the old movie
companies and toppled the big movie moguls.

There are other less obvious examples of industries that have been and are
now endangering their futures by improperly defining their purposes. I shall discuss some in detail later and analyze the kind of policies that lead to trouble. Right
now it may help to show what a thoroughly customer-oriented management *can*
do to keep a growth industry growing, even after the obvious opportunities have
been exhausted; and here there are two examples that have been around for a long
time. They are nylon and glass—specifically, E.I. du Pont de Nemours & Company
and Corning Glass Works.

Both companies have great technical competence. Their product orientation is unquestioned. But this alone does not explain their success. After all, who was more pridefully product-oriented and product-conscious than the erstwhile New England textile companies that have been so thoroughly massacred? The Du Ponts and the Cornings have succeeded not primarily because of their product or research orientation but because they have been thoroughly customer-oriented also. It is constant watchfulness for opportunities to apply their technical know-how to the creation of customer-satisfying uses which accounts for their prodigious output of successful new products. Without a very sophisticated eye on the customer, most of their new products might have been wrong, their sales methods useless.

Aluminum has also continued to be a growth industry, thanks to the efforts of two wartime-created companies which deliberately set about creating new customer-satisfying uses. Without Kaiser Aluminum & Chemical Corporation and Reynolds Metals Company, the total demand for aluminum today would be vastly less.

Error of analysis: Some may argue that it is foolish to set the railroads off against aluminum or the movies off against glass. Are not aluminum and glass naturally so versatile that the industries are bound to have more growth opportunities than the railroads and movies? This view commits precisely the error I have been talking about. It defines an industry, or a product, or a cluster of know-how so narrowly as to guarantee its premature senescence. When we mention "railroads," we should make sure we mean "transportation." As transporters, the railroads still have a good chance for very considerable growth. They are not limited to the railroad business as such (though in my opinion rail transportation is potentially a much stronger transportation medium than is generally believed).

What the railroads lack is not opportunity, but some of the same managerial imaginativeness and audacity that made them great. Even an amateur like Jacques Barzun can see what is lacking when he says:

"I grieve to see the most advanced physical and social organization of the last century go down in shabby disgrace for lack of the same comprehensive imagination that built it up. [What is lacking is] the will of the companies to survive and to satisfy the public by inventiveness and skill."[1]

Shadow of Obsolescence

It is impossible to mention a single major industry that did not at one time qualify for the magic appellation of "growth industry." In each case its assumed strength lay in the apparently unchallenged superiority of its product. There appeared to be no effective substitute for it. It was itself a runaway substitute for the product it so triumphantly replaced. Yet one after another of these celebrated industries has come under a shadow. Let us look briefly at a few more of them, this time taking examples that have so far received a little less attention:

Dry cleaning—This was once a growth industry with lavish prospects. In an age of wool garments, imagine being finally able to get them safely and easily clean. The boom was on.

Yet here we are 30 years after the boom started and the industry is in trouble. Where has the competition come from? From a better way of cleaning? No. It has come from synthetic fibers and chemical additives that have cut the need for dry cleaning. But this is only the beginning. Lurking in the wings and ready to make chemical dry cleaning totally obsolescent is that powerful magician, ultrasonics.

Electric utilities—This is another one of those supposedly "no-substitute" products that has been enthroned on a pedestal of invincible growth. When the incandescent lamp came along, kerosene lights were finished. Later the water wheel and the steam engine were cut to ribbons by the flexibility, reliability, simplicity, and just plain easy availability of electric motors. The prosperity of electric utilities continues to wax extravagant as the home is converted into a museum of electric gadgetry. How can anybody miss by investing in utilities, with no competition, nothing but growth ahead?

But a second look is not quite so comforting. A score of nonutility companies are well advanced toward developing a powerful chemical fuel cell which could sit in some hidden closet of every home silently ticking off electric power. The electric lines that vulgarize so many neighborhoods will be eliminated. So will the endless demolition of streets and service interruptions during storms. Also on the horizon is solar energy, again pioneered by nonutility companies.

Who says the utilities have no competition? They may be natural monopolies now, but tomorrow they may be natural deaths. To avoid this prospect, they too will have to develop fuel cells, solar energy, and other power sources. To survive, they themselves will have to plot the obsolescence of what now produces their livelihood.

Grocery stores—Many people find it hard to realize that there ever was a thriving establishment known as the "corner grocery store." The supermarket has taken over with a powerful effectiveness. Yet the big food chains of the 1930s narrowly escaped being completely wiped out by the aggressive expansion of independent supermarkets. The first genuine supermarket was opened in 1930, in Jamaica, Long Island. By 1933 supermarkets were thriving in California, Ohio, Pennsylvania, and elsewhere. Yet the established chains pompously ignored them. When they chose to notice them, it was with such derisive descriptions as "cheapy," "horse-and-buggy," "cracker-barrel storekeeping," and "unethical opportunists."

The executive of one big chain announced at the time that he found it "hard to believe that people will drive for miles to shop for foods and sacrifice the personal service chains have perfected and to which Mrs. Consumer is accustomed."[2] As late as 1936, the National Wholesale Grocers convention and the New Jersey Retail Grocers Association said there was nothing to fear. They said that the supers' narrow appeal to the price buyer limited the size of their market. They had to draw from miles around. When imitators came, there would be wholesale liquidations as volume fell. The current high sales of the supers was said to be partly due to their novelty. Basically people wanted convenient neighborhood grocers. If the neighborhood stores "cooperate with their suppliers, pay attention to their costs, and improve their service," they would be able to weather the competition until it blew over.[3]

It never blew over. The chains discovered that survival required going into the supermarket business. This meant the wholesale destruction of their huge investments in corner store sites and in established distribution and merchandising methods. The companies with "the courage of their convictions" resolutely stuck to the corner store philosophy. They kept their pride but lost their shirts.

Self-deceiving cycle: But memories are short. For example, it is hard for people who today confidently hail the twin messiahs of electronics and chemicals to see how things could possibly go wrong with their galloping industries. They probably also cannot see how a reasonably sensible businessman could have been as myopic as the famous Boston millionaire who 50 years ago unintentionally sentenced his heirs to poverty by stipulating that his entire estate be forever invested exclusively in electric streetcar securities. His posthumous declaration, "There will always be a big demand for efficient urban transportation," is no consolation to his heirs who sustain life by pumping gasoline at automobile filling stations.

Yet, in a casual survey I recently took among a group of intelligent business executives, nearly half agreed that it would be hard to hurt their heirs by tying their estates forever to the electronics industry. When I then confronted them with the Boston streetcar example, they chorused unanimously, "That's different!" But is it? Is not the basic situation identical?

In truth, *there is no such thing* as a growth industry, I believe. There are only companies organized and operated to create and capitalize on growth opportunities. Industries that assume themselves to be riding some automatic growth escalator invariably descend into stagnation. The history of every dead and dying "growth" industry shows a self-deceiving cycle of bountiful expansion and undetected decay. There are four conditions which usually guarantee this cycle:

1. The belief that growth is assured by an expanding and more affluent population.

2. The belief that there is no competitive substitute for the industry's major product.

3. Too much faith in mass production and in the advantages of rapidly declining unit costs as output rises.

4. Preoccupation with a product that lends itself to carefully controlled scientific experimentation, improvement, and manufacturing cost reduction.

I should like now to begin examining each of these conditions in some detail. To build my case as boldly as possible, I shall illustrate the points with reference to three industries—petroleum, automobiles, and electronics—particularly petroleum, because it spans more years and more vicissitudes. Not only do these three have excellent reputations with the general public and also enjoy the confidence of sophisticated investors, but their managements have become known for progressive thinking in areas like financial control, product research, and management training. If obsolescence can cripple even these industries, it can happen anywhere.

Population Myth

The belief that profits are assured by an expanding and more affluent population is dear to the heart of every industry. It takes the edge off the apprehensions everybody understandably feels about the future. If consumers are multiplying and also buying more of your product or service, you can face the future with considerably more comfort than if the market is shrinking. An expanding market keeps the manufacturer from having to think very hard or imaginatively. If thinking is an intellectual response to a problem, then the absence of a problem leads to the absence of thinking. If your product has an automatically expanding market, then you will not give much thought to how to expand it.

One of the most interesting examples of this is provided by the petroleum industry. Probably our oldest growth industry, it has an enviable record. While there are some current apprehensions about its growth rate, the industry itself tends to be optimistic.

But I believe it can be demonstrated that it is undergoing a fundamental yet typical change. It is not only ceasing to be a growth industry, but may actually be a declining one, relative to other business. Although there is widespread unawareness of it, I believe that within 25 years the oil industry may find itself in much the same position of retrospective glory that the railroads are now in. Despite its pioneering work in developing and applying the present-value method of investment evaluation, in employee relations, and in working with backward countries, the petroleum business is a distressing example of how complacency and wrongheadedness can stubbornly convert opportunity into near disaster.

One of the characteristics of this and other industries that have believed very strongly in the beneficial consequences of an expanding population, while at the same time being industries with a generic product for which there has appeared to be no competitive substitute, is that the individual companies have sought to outdo their competitors by improving on what they are already doing. This makes sense, of course, if one assumes that sales are tied to the country's population strings, because the customer can compare products only on a feature-by-feature basis. I believe it is significant, for example, that not since John D. Rockefeller sent free kerosene lamps to China has the oil industry done anything really outstanding to create a demand for its product. Not even in product improvement has it showered itself with eminence. The greatest single improvement—namely, the development of tetraethyl lead—came from outside the industry, specifically from General Motors and Du Pont. The big contributions made by the industry itself are confined to the technology of oil exploration, production, and refining.

Asking for trouble: In other words, the industry's efforts have focused on improving the *efficiency* of getting and making its product, not really on improving the generic product or its marketing. Moreover, its chief product has continuously been defined in the narrowest possible terms, namely, gasoline, not energy, fuel, or transportation. This attitude has helped assure that:

Major improvements in gasoline quality tend not to originate in the oil industry. Also, the development of superior alternative fuels comes from outside the oil industry, as will be shown later.

Major innovations in automobile fuel marketing are originated by small new oil companies that are not primarily preoccupied with production or refining. These are the companies that have been responsible for the rapidly expanding multipump gasoline stations, with their successful emphasis on large and clean layouts, rapid and efficient driveway service, and quality gasoline at low prices.

Thus, the oil industry is asking for trouble from outsiders. Sooner or later, in this land of hungry inventors and entrepreneurs, a threat is sure to come. The possibilities of this will become more apparent when we turn to the next dangerous belief of many managements. For the sake of continuity, because this second belief is tied closely to the first, I shall continue with the same example.

Idea of indispensability: The petroleum industry is pretty much persuaded that there is no competitive substitute for its major product, gasoline—or, if there is, that it will continue to be a derivative of crude oil, such as diesel fuel or kerosene jet fuel.

There is a lot of automatic wishful thinking in this assumption. The trouble is that most refining companies own huge amounts of crude oil reserves. These have value only if there is a market for products into which oil can be converted—hence the tenacious belief in the continuing competitive superiority of automobile fuels made from crude oil.

This idea persists despite all historic evidence against it. The evidence not only shows that oil has never been a superior product for any purpose for very long, but it also shows that the oil industry has never really been a growth industry. It has been a succession of different businesses that have gone through the usual historic cycles of growth, maturity, and decay. Its overall survival is owed to a series of miraculous escapes from total obsolescence, of last-minute and unexpected reprieves from total disaster reminiscent of the Perils of Pauline.

Perils of petroleum: I shall sketch in only the main episodes.

First, crude oil was largely a patent medicine. But even before that fad ran out, demand was greatly expanded by the use of oil in kerosene lamps. The prospect of lighting the world's lamps gave rise to an extravagant promise of growth. The prospects were similar to those the industry now holds for gasoline in other parts of the world. It can hardly wait for the underdeveloped nations to get a car in every garage.

In the days of the kerosene lamp, the oil companies competed with each other and against gaslight by trying to improve the illuminating characteristics of kerosene. Then suddenly the impossible happened. Edison invented a light which was totally nondependent on crude oil. Had it not been for the growing use of kerosene in space heaters, the incandescent lamp would have completely finished oil as a growth industry at that time. Oil would have been good for little else than axle grease.

Then disaster and reprieve struck again. Two great innovations occurred, neither originating in the oil industry. The successful development of coal-burning domestic central-heating systems made the space heater obsolescent. While the industry reeled, along came its most magnificent boost yet—the internal combustion engine, also invented by outsiders. Then when the prodigious expansion for gasoline finally began to level off in the 1920s, along came the miraculous escape of a central oil heater. Once again, the escape was provided by an outsider's invention and development. And when that market weakened, wartime demand for aviation fuel came to the rescue. After the war the expansion of civilian aviation, the dieselization of railroads, and the explosive demand for cars and trucks kept the industry's growth in high gear.

Meanwhile, centralized oil heating—whose boom potential had only recently been proclaimed—ran into severe competition from natural gas. While the oil companies themselves owned the gas that now competed with their oil, the industry did not originate the natural gas revolution, nor has it to this day greatly profited from its gas ownership. The gas revolution was made by newly formed transmission companies that marketed the product with an aggressive ardor. They started a magnificent new industry, first against the advice and then against the resistance of the oil companies.

By all the logic of the situation, the oil companies themselves should have made the gas revolution. They not only owned the gas, they also were the only people experienced in handling, scrubbing, and using it, the only people experienced in pipeline technology and transmission, and they understood heating problems. But, partly because they knew that natural gas would compete with their own sale of heating oil, the oil companies pooh-poohed the potentials of gas.

The revolution was finally started by oil pipeline executives who, unable to persuade their own companies to go into gas, quit and organized the spectacularly successful gas transmission companies. Even after their success became painfully evident to the oil companies, the latter did not go into gas transmission. The multibillion dollar business which should have been theirs went to others. As in the past, the industry was blinded by its narrow preoccupation with a specific product and the value of its reserves. It paid little or no attention to its customers' basic needs and preferences.

The postwar years have not witnessed any change. Immediately after World War II the oil industry was greatly encouraged about its future by the rapid expansion of demand for its traditional line of products. In 1950 most companies projected annual rates of domestic expansion of around 6% through at least 1975. Though the ratio of crude oil reserves to demand in the Free World was about 20 to 1, with 10 to 1 being usually considered a reasonable working ratio in the United States, booming demand sent oil men searching for more without sufficient regard to what the future really promised. In 1952, they "hit" in the Middle East; the ratio skyrocketed to 42 to 1. If gross additions to reserves continue at the average rate of the past five years (37 billion barrels annually), then by 1980 the reserve ratio will be up to 45 to 1. This abundance of oil has weakened crude and product prices all over the world.

Uncertain future: Management cannot find much consolation today in the rapidly expanding petrochemical industry, another oil-using idea that did not originate in the leading firms. The total United States production of petrochemicals is equivalent to about 2% (by volume) of the demand for all petroleum products. Although the petrochemical industry is now expected to grow by about 10% per year, this will not offset other drains on the growth of crude oil consumption. Furthermore, while petrochemical products are many and growing, it is well to remember that there are nonpetroleum sources of the basic raw material, such as coal. Besides, a lot of plastics can be produced with relatively little oil. A 50,000-barrel-per-day oil refinery is now considered the absolute minimum size for efficiency. But a 5,000-barrel-per-day chemical plant is a giant operation.

Oil has never been a continuously strong growth industry. It has grown by fits and starts, always miraculously saved by innovations and developments not of its own making. The reason it has not grown in a smooth progression is that each time it thought it had a superior product safe from the possibility of competitive substitutes, the product turned out to be inferior and notoriously subject to obsolescence. Until now, gasoline (for motor fuel, anyhow) has escaped this fate. But, as we shall see later, it too may be on its last legs.

The point of all this is that there is no guarantee against product obsolescence. If a company's own research does not make it obsolete, another's will. Unless an industry is especially lucky, as oil has been until now, it can easily go down in a sea of red figures—just as the railroads have, as the buggy whip manufacturers have, as the corner grocery chains have, as most of the big movie companies have, and indeed as many other industries have.

The best way for a firm to be lucky is to make its own luck. That requires knowing what makes a business successful. One of the greatest enemies of this knowledge is mass production.

Production Pressures

Mass-production industries are impelled by a great drive to produce all they can. The prospect of steeply declining unit costs as output rises is more than most companies can usually resist. The profit possibilities look spectacular. All effort focuses on production. The result is that marketing gets neglected.

John Kenneth Galbraith contends that just the opposite occurs.[4] Output is so prodigious that all effort concentrates on trying to get rid of it. He says this accounts for singing commercials, desecration of the countryside with advertising signs, and other wasteful and vulgar practices. Galbraith has a finger on something real, but he misses the strategic point. Mass production does indeed generate great pressure to "move" the product. But what usually gets emphasized is selling, not marketing. Marketing, being a more sophisticated and complex process, gets ignored.

The difference between marketing and selling is more than semantic. Selling focuses on the needs of the seller, marketing on the needs of the buyer. Selling is preoccupied with the seller's need to convert his product into cash, marketing with the idea of satisfying the needs of the customer by means of the product and the whole cluster of things associated with creating, delivering, and finally consuming it.

In some industries the enticements of full mass production have been so powerful that for many years top management in effect has told the sales departments, "You get rid of it; we'll worry about profits." By contrast, a truly marketing-minded firm tries to create value-satisfying goods and services that consumers will want to buy. What it offers for sale includes not only the generic product or service, but also how it is made available to the customer, in what form, when, under what conditions, and at what terms of trade. Most important, what it offers for sale is determined not by the seller but by the buyer. The seller takes his cues from the buyer in such a way that the product becomes a consequence of the marketing effort, not vice versa.

Lag in Detroit: This may sound like an elementary rule of business, but that does not keep it from being violated wholesale. It is certainly more violated than honored. Take the automobile industry.

Here mass production is most famous, most honored, and has the greatest impact on the entire society. The industry has hitched its fortune to the relentless requirements of the annual model change, a policy that makes customer orientation an especially urgent necessity. Consequently the auto companies annually spend millions of dollars on consumer research. But the fact that the new compact cars are selling so well in their first year indicates that Detroit's vast researches have for a long time failed to reveal what the customer really wanted. Detroit was not persuaded that he wanted anything different from what he had been getting until it lost millions of customers to other small car manufacturers.

How could this unbelievable lag behind consumer wants have been perpetuated so long? Why did not research reveal consumer preferences before consumers' buying decisions themselves revealed the facts? Is that not what consumer research is for—to find out before the fact what is going to happen? The answer is that Detroit never really researched the customer's wants. It only researched his preferences between the kinds of things which it had already decided to offer him. For Detroit is mainly product-oriented, not customer-oriented. To the extent that the customer is recognized as having needs that the manufacturer should try to satisfy, Detroit usually acts as if the job can be done entirely by product changes. Occasionally attention gets paid to financing, too, but that is done more in order to sell than to enable the consumer to buy.

As for taking care of other customer needs, there is not enough being done to write about. The areas of the greatest unsatisfied needs are ignored, or at best get stepchild attention. These are at the point of sale and on the matter of automotive repair and maintenance. Detroit views these problem areas as being of secondary importance. That is underscored by the fact that the retailing and servicing ends of this industry are neither owned and operated nor controlled by the manufacturers. Once the car is produced, things are pretty much in the dealer's inadequate hands. Illustrative of Detroit's arm's-length attitude is the fact that, while servicing holds enormous sales-stimulating, profit-building opportunities, only 57 of Chevrolet's 7,000 dealers provide night maintenance service.

Motorists repeatedly express their dissatisfaction with servicing and their apprehensions about buying cars under the present selling setup. The anxieties and problems they encounter during the auto buying and maintenance processes are probably more intense and widespread today than 30 years ago. Yet the automobile companies do not *seem* to listen to or take their cues from the anguished consumer. If they do listen, it must be through the filter of their own preoccupation with production. The marketing effort is still viewed as a necessary consequence of the product, not vice versa, as it should be. That is the legacy of mass production, with its parochial view that profit resides essentially in low-cost full production.

What Ford put first: The profit lure of mass production obviously has a place in the plans and strategy of business management, but it must always *follow* hard thinking about the customer. This is one of the most important lessons that we can learn from the contradictory behavior of Henry Ford. In a sense Ford was both the most brilliant and the most senseless marketer in American history. He was senseless because he refused to give the customer anything but a black car. He was brilliant because he fashioned a production system designed to fit market needs. We habitually celebrate him for the wrong reason, his production genius. His real genius was marketing. We think he was able to cut his selling price and therefore sell millions of $500 cars because his invention of the assembly line had reduced the costs. Actually he invented the assembly line because he had concluded that at $500 he could sell millions of cars. Mass production was the *result* not the cause of his low prices.

Ford repeatedly emphasized this point, but a nation of production-oriented business managers refuses to hear the great lesson he taught. Here is his operating philosophy as he expressed it succinctly:

"Our policy is to reduce the price, extend the operations, and improve the article. You will notice that the reduction of price comes first. We have never considered any costs as fixed. Therefore we first reduce the price to the point where we believe more sales will result. Then we go ahead and try to make the prices. We do not bother about the costs. The new price forces the costs down. The more usual way is to take the costs and then determine the price; and although that method may be scientific in the narrow sense, it is not scientific in the broad sense, because what earthly use is it to know the cost if it tells you that you cannot manufacture at a price at which the article can be sold? But more to the point is the fact that, although one may calculate what a cost is, and of course all of our costs are carefully calculated, no one knows what a cost ought to be. One of the ways of discovering ... is to name a price so low as to force everybody in the place to the highest point of efficiency. The low price makes everybody dig for profits. We make more discoveries concerning manufacturing and selling under this forced method than by any method of leisurely investigation."[5]

Product provincialism: The tantalizing profit possibilities of low unit production costs may be the most seriously self-deceiving attitude that can afflict a company, particularly a "growth" company where an apparently assured expansion of demand already tends to undermine a proper concern for the importance of marketing and the customer.

The usual result of this narrow preoccupation with so-called concrete matters is that instead of growing, the industry declines. It usually means that the product fails to adapt to the constantly changing patterns of consumer needs and tastes, to new and modified marketing institutions and practices, or to product developments in competing and complementary industries. The industry has its eyes so firmly on its own specific product that it does not see how it is being made obsolete.

The classical example of this is the buggy whip industry. No amount of product improvement could stave off its death sentence. But had the industry defined itself as being in the transportation business rather than the buggy whip business, it might have survived. It would have done what survival always entails, that is, changing. Even if it had only defined its business as providing a stimulant or catalyst to an energy source, it might have survived by becoming a manufacturer of, say, fanbelts or air cleaners.

What may some day be a still more classical example is, again, the oil industry. Having let others steal marvelous opportunities from it (e.g., natural gas, as already mentioned, missile fuels, and jet engine lubricants), one would expect it to have taken steps never to let that happen again. But this is not the case. We are getting extraordinary new developments in fuel systems specifically designed to power automobiles. Not only are these developments concentrated in firms outside the petroleum industry, but petroleum is almost systematically ignoring them, securely content in its wedded bliss to oil. It is the story of the kerosene lamp versus the incandescent lamp all over again. Oil is trying to improve hydrocarbon fuels rather than develop *any* fuels best suited to the needs of their users, whether or not made in different ways and with different raw materials from oil.

Here are some things which nonpetroleum companies are working on:

Over a dozen such firms now have advanced working models of energy systems which, when perfected, will replace the internal combustion engine and eliminate the demand for gasoline. The superior merit of each of these systems is their elimination of frequent, time-consuming, and irritating refueling stops. Most of these systems are fuel cells designed to create electrical energy directly from chemicals without combustion. Most of them use chemicals that are not derived from oil, generally hydrogen and oxygen.

Several other companies have advanced models of electric storage batteries designed to power automobiles. One of these is an aircraft producer that is working jointly with several electric utility companies. The latter hope to use off-peak generating capacity to supply overnight plug-in battery regeneration. Another company, also using the battery approach, is a medium-size electronics firm with extensive small-battery experience that it developed in connection with its work on hearing aids. It is collaborating with an automobile manufacturer. Recent improvements arising from the need for high-powered miniature power storage plants in rockets have put us within reach of a relatively small battery capable of withstanding great overloads or surges of power. Germanium diode applications and batteries using sintered-plate and nickel-cadmium techniques promise to make a revolution in our energy sources.

Solar energy conversion systems are also getting increasing attention....

As for oil companies, they are more or less "watching developments," as one research director put it to me. A few are doing a bit of research on fuel cells, but almost always confined to developing cells powered by hydrocarbon chemicals. None of them are enthusiastically researching fuel cells, batteries, or solar power plants. None of them are spending a fraction as much on research in these profoundly important areas as they are on the usual run-of-the-mill things like reducing combustion chamber deposit in gasoline engines. One major integrated petroleum company recently took a tentative look at the fuel cell and concluded that although "the companies actively working on it indicate a belief in ultimate success ... the timing and magnitude of its impact are too remote to warrant recognition in our forecasts."

One might, of course, ask: Why should the oil companies do anything different? Would not chemical fuel cells, batteries, or solar energy kill the present product lines? The answer is that they would indeed, and that is precisely the reason for the oil firms having to develop these power units before their competitors, so they will not be companies without an industry.

Management might be more likely to do what is needed for its own preservation if it thought of itself as being in the energy business. But even that would not be enough if it persists in imprisoning itself in the narrow grip of its tight product orientation. It has to think of itself as taking care of customer needs, not finding, refining, or even selling oil. Once it genuinely thinks of its business as taking care of people's transportation needs, nothing can stop it from creating its own extravagantly profitable growth.

'*Creative destruction*': Since words are cheap and deeds are dear, it may be appropriate to indicate what this kind of thinking involves and leads to. Let us start at the beginning—the customer. It can be shown that motorists strongly dislike the bother, delay, and experience of buying gasoline. People actually do not buy gasoline. They cannot see it, taste it, feel it, appreciate it, or really test it. What they buy is the right to continue driving their cars. The gas station is like a tax collector to whom people are compelled to pay a periodic toll as the price of using their cars. This makes the gas station a basically unpopular institution. It can never be made popular or pleasant, only less unpopular, less unpleasant.

To reduce its unpopularity completely means eliminating it. Nobody likes a tax collector, not even a pleasantly cheerful one. Nobody likes to interrupt a trip to buy a phantom product, not even from a handsome Adonis or a seductive Venus. Hence, companies that are working on exotic fuel substitutes which will eliminate the need for frequent refueling are heading directly into the outstretched arms of the irritated motorist. They are riding a wave of inevitability, not because they are creating something which is technologically superior or more sophisticated, but because they are satisfying a powerful customer need. They are also eliminating noxious odors and air pollution.

Once the petroleum companies recognize the customer-satisfying logic of what another power system can do, they will see that they have no more choice about working on an efficient, long-lasting fuel (or some way of delivering present fuels without bothering the motorist) than the big food chains had a choice about going into the supermarket business, or the vacuum tube companies had a choice about making semiconductors. For their own good the oil firms will have to destroy their own highly profitable assets. No amount of wishful thinking can save them from the necessity of engaging in this form of "creative destruction."

I phrase the need as strongly as this because I think management must make quite an effort to break itself loose from conventional ways. It is all too easy in this day and age for a company or industry to let its sense of purpose become dominated by the economies of full production and to develop a dangerously lopsided product orientation. In short, if management lets itself drift, it invariably drifts in the direction of thinking of itself as producing goods and services, not customer satisfactions. While it probably will not descend to the depths of telling its salesmen, "You get rid of it; we'll worry about profits," it can, without knowing it, be practicing precisely that formula for withering decay. The historic fate of one growth industry after another has been its suicidal product provincialism.

Dangers of R & D

Another big danger to a firm's continued growth arises when top management is wholly transfixed by the profit possibilities of technical research and development. To illustrate I shall turn first to a new industry—electronics—and then return once more to the oil companies. By comparing a fresh example with a familiar one, I hope to emphasize the prevalence and insidiousness of a hazardous way of thinking.

Marketing shortchanged: In the case of electronics, the greatest danger which faces the glamorous new companies in this field is not that they do not pay enough attention to research and development, but that they pay *too much* attention to it. And the fact that the fastest growing electronics firms owe their eminence to their heavy emphasis on technical research is completely beside the point. They have vaulted to affluence on a sudden crest of unusually strong general receptiveness to new technical ideas. Also, their success has been shaped in the virtually guaranteed market of military subsidies and by military orders that in many cases actually preceded the existence of facilities to make the products. Their expansion has, in other words, been almost totally devoid of marketing effort.

Thus, they are growing up under conditions that come dangerously close to creating the illusion that a superior product will sell itself. Having created a successful company by making a superior product, it is not surprising that management continues to be oriented toward the product rather than the people who consume it. It develops the philosophy that continued growth is a matter of continued product innovation and improvement.

A number of other factors tend to strengthen and sustain this belief:

1. Because electronic products are highly complex and sophisticated, managements become top-heavy with engineers and scientists. This creates a selective bias in favor of research and production at the expense of marketing. The organization tends to view itself as making things rather than satisfying customer needs. Marketing gets treated as a residual activity, "something else" that must be done once the vital job of product creation and production is completed.

2. To this bias in favor of product research, development, and production is added the bias in favor of dealing with controllable variables. Engineers and scientists are at home in the world of concrete things like machines, test tubes, production lines, and even balance sheets. The abstractions to which they feel kindly are those which are testable or manipulatable in the laboratory, or, if not testable, then functional, such as Euclid's axioms. In short, the managements of the new glamour-growth companies tend to favor those business activities which lend themselves to careful study, experimentation, and control—the hard, practical, realities of the lab, the shop, the books.

What gets shortchanged are the realities of the *market*. Consumers are unpredictable, varied, fickle, stupid, shortsighted, stubborn, and generally bothersome. This is not what the engineer-managers say, but deep down in their consciousness it is what they believe. And this accounts for their concentrating on what they know and what they can control, namely, product research, engineering, and production. The emphasis on production becomes particularly attractive when the product can be made at declining unit costs. There is no more inviting way of making money than by running the plant full blast.

Today the top-heavy science-engineering-production orientation of so many electronics companies works reasonably well because they are pushing into new frontiers in which the armed services have pioneered virtually assured markets. The companies are in the felicitous position of having to fill, not find markets; of not having to discover what the customer needs and wants, but of having the customer voluntarily come forward with specific new product demands. If a team of consultants had been assigned specifically to design a business situation calculated to prevent the emergence and development of a customer-oriented marketing viewpoint, it could not have produced anything better than the conditions just described.

Stepchild treatment: The oil industry is a stunning example of how science, technology, and mass production can divert an entire group of companies from their main task. To the extent the consumer is studied at all (which is not much), the focus is forever on getting information which is designed to help the oil companies improve what they are now doing. They try to discover more convincing advertising themes, more effective sales promotional drives, what the market shares of the various companies are, what people like or dislike about service station dealers and oil companies, and so forth. Nobody seems as interested in probing deeply into the basic human needs that the industry might be trying to satisfy as in probing into the basic properties of the raw material that the companies work within trying to deliver customer satisfactions.

Basic questions about customers and markets seldom get asked. The latter occupy a stepchild status. They are recognized as existing, as having to be taken care of, but not worth very much real thought or dedicated attention. Nobody gets as excited about the customers in his own backyard as about the oil in the Sahara Desert. Nothing illustrates better the neglect of marketing than its treatment in the industry press.

The centennial issue of the *American Petroleum Institute Quarterly*, published in 1959 to celebrate the discovery of oil in Titusville, Pennsylvania, contained 21 feature articles proclaiming the industry's greatness. Only one of these talked about its achievements in marketing and that was only a pictorial record of how service stations' architecture has changed. The issue also contained a special section on "New Horizons," which was devoted to showing the magnificent role oil would play in America's future. Every reference was ebulliently optimistic, never implying once that oil might have some hard competition. Even the reference to atomic energy was a cheerful catalogue of how oil would help make atomic energy a success. There was not a single apprehension that the oil industry's affluence might be threatened or a suggestion that one "new horizon" might include new and better ways of serving oil's present customers.

But the most revealing example of the stepchild treatment that marketing gets was still another special series of short articles on "The Revolutionary Potential of Electronics." Under that heading this list of articles appeared in the table of contents:
"In the Search for Oil"
"In Production Operations"
"In Refinery Processes"

"In Pipeline Operations"

Significantly, every one of the industry's major functional areas is listed, *except* marketing. Why? Either it is believed that electronics holds no revolutionary potential for petroleum marketing (which is palpably wrong), or the editors forgot to discuss marketing (which is more likely, and illustrates its stepchild status).

The order in which the four functional areas are listed also betrays the alienation of the oil industry from the consumer. The industry is implicitly defined as beginning with the search for oil and ending with its distribution from the refinery. But the truth is, it seems to me, that the industry begins with the needs of the customer for its products. From the primal position its definition moves steadily backstream to areas of progressively lesser importance, until it finally comes to rest at the "search for oil."

Beginning & end: The view that an industry is a customer-satisfying process, not a goods-producing process, is vital for all businessmen to understand. An industry begins with the customer and his needs, not with a patent, a raw material, or a selling skill. Given the customer's needs, the industry develops backwards, first concerning itself with the physical *delivery* of customer satisfactions. Then it moves back further to *creating* the things by which these satisfactions are in part achieved. How these materials are created is a matter of indifference to the customer, hence the particular form of manufacturing, processing, or what-have-you cannot be considered as a vital aspect of the industry. Finally, the industry moves back still further to *finding* the raw materials necessary for making its products.

The irony of some industries oriented toward technical research and development is that the scientists who occupy the high executive positions are totally unscientific when it comes to defining their companies' overall needs and purposes. They violate the first two rules of the scientific method—being aware of and defining their companies' problems, and then developing testable hypotheses about solving them. They are scientific only about the convenient things, such as laboratory and product experiments.

The reason that the customer (and the satisfaction of his deepest needs) is not considered as being "the problem" is not because there is any certain belief that no such problem exists, but because an organizational lifetime has conditioned management to look in the opposite direction. Marketing is a stepchild.

I do not mean that selling is ignored. Far from it. But selling, again, is not marketing. As already pointed out, selling concerns itself with the tricks and techniques of getting people to exchange their cash for your product. It is not concerned with the values that the exchange is all about. And it does not, as marketing invariably does, view the entire business process as consisting of a tightly integrated effort to discover, create, arouse, and satisfy customer needs. The customer is somebody "out there" who, with proper cunning, can be separated from his loose change.

Actually, not even selling gets much attention in some technologically-minded firms. Because there is a virtually guaranteed market for the abundant flow of their new products, they do not actually know what a real market is. It is as if they lived in a planned economy, moving their products routinely from factory to retail outlet. Their successful concentration on products tends to convince them of the soundness of what they have been doing, and they fail to see the gathering clouds over the market.

Conclusion

Less than 75 years ago American railroads enjoyed a fierce loyalty among astute Wall Streeters. European monarchs invested in them heavily. Eternal wealth was thought to be the benediction for anybody who could scrape a few thousand dollars together to put into rail stocks. No other form of transportation could compete with the railroads in speed, flexibility, durability, economy, and growth potentials.

As Jacques Barzun put it, "By the turn of the century it was an institution, an image of man, a tradition, a code of honor, a source of poetry, a nursery of boyhood desires, a sublimist of toys, and the most solemn machine—next to the funeral hearse—that marks the epochs in man's life."[6]

Even after the advent of automobiles, trucks, and airplanes, the railroad tycoons remained imperturbably self-confident. If you had told them 60 years ago that in 30 years they would be flat on their backs, broke, and pleading for government subsidies, they would have thought you totally demented. Such a future was simply not considered possible. It was not even a discussable subject, or an askable question, or a matter which any sane person would consider worth speculating about. The very thought was insane. Yet a lot of insane notions now have matter-of-fact acceptance—for example, the idea of 100-ton tubes of metal moving smoothly through the air 20,000 feet above the earth, loaded with 100 sane and solid citizens casually drinking martinis—and they have dealt cruel blows to the railroads.

What specifically must other companies do to avoid this fate? What does customer orientation involve? These questions have in part been answered by the preceding examples and analysis. It would take another article to show in detail what is required for specific industries. In any case, it should be obvious that building an effective customer-oriented company involves far more than good intentions or promotional tricks; it involves profound matters of human organization and leadership. For the present, let me merely suggest what appear to be some general requirements.

Visceral feel of greatness: Obviously the company has to do what survival demands. It has to adapt to the requirements of the market, and it has to do it sooner rather than later. But mere survival is a so-so aspiration. Anybody can survive in some way or other, even the skid-row bum. The trick is to survive gallantly, to feel the surging impulse of commercial mastery; not just to experience the sweet smell of success, but to have the visceral feel of entrepreneurial greatness.

No organization can achieve greatness without a vigorous leader who is driven onward by his own pulsating *will to succeed*. He has to have a vision of grandeur, a vision that can produce eager followers in vast numbers. In business, the followers are the customers.

In order to produce these customers, the entire corporation must be viewed as a customer-oriented and customer-satisfying organism. Management must think of itself not as producing products but as providing customer-creating value satisfactions. It must push this idea (and everything it means and requires) into every nook and cranny of the organization. It has to do this continuously and with the kind of flair that excites and stimulates the people in it. Otherwise, the company will be merely a series of pigeonholed parts, with no consolidating sense of purpose or direction.

In short, the organization must learn to think of itself not as producing goods or services but as *buying customers*, as doing the things that will make people *want* to do business with it. And the chief executive himself has the inescapable responsibility for creating this environment, this viewpoint, this attitude, this aspiration. He himself must set the company's style, its direction, and its goals. This means he has to know precisely where he himself wants to go, and to make sure the whole organization is enthusiastically aware of where that is. This is a first requisite of leadership, for *unless he knows where he is going, any road will take him there*.

If any road is okay, the chief executive might as well pack his attaché case and go fishing. If an organization does not know or care where it is going, it does not need to advertise that fact with a ceremonial figurehead. Everybody will notice it soon enough.

Retrospective Commentary

Amazed, finally, by his literary success, Isaac Bashevis Singer reconciled an attendant problem: "I think the moment you have published a book, it's not any more your private property.... If it has value, everybody can find in it what he finds, and I cannot tell the man I did not intend it to be so." Over the past 15 years, "Marketing Myopia" has become a case in point. Remarkably, the article spawned a legion of loyal partisans—not to mention a host of unlikely bedfellows.

Its most common and, I believe, most influential consequence is the way certain companies for the first time gave serious thought to the question of what business they are really in.

The strategic consequences of this have in many cases been dramatic. The best-known case, of course, is the shift in thinking of oneself as being in the "oil business" to being in the "energy business." In some instances the payoff has been spectacular (getting into coal, for example) and in others dreadful (in terms of the time and money spent so far on fuel cell research). Another successful example is a company with a large chain of retail shoe stores that redefined itself as a retailer of moderately priced, frequently purchased, widely assorted consumer specialty products. The result was a dramatic growth in volume, earnings, and return on assets.

Some companies, again for the first time, asked themselves whether they wished to be masters of certain technologies for which they would seek markets, or be masters of markets for which they would seek customer-satisfying products and services.

Choosing the former, one company has declared, in effect, "We are experts in glass technology. We intend to improve and expand that expertise with the object of creating products that will attract customers." This decision has forced the company into a much more systematic and customer-sensitive look at possible markets and users, even though its stated strategic object has been to capitalize on glass technology.

Deciding to concentrate on markets, another company has determined that "we want to help people (primarily women) enhance their beauty and sense of youthfulness." This company has expanded its line of cosmetic products, but has also entered the fields of proprietary drugs and vitamin supplements.

All these examples illustrate the "policy" results of "Marketing Myopia." On the operating level, there has been, I think, an extraordinary heightening of sensitivity to customers and consumers. R&D departments have cultivated a greater "external" orientation toward uses, users, and markets—balancing thereby the previously one-sided "internal" focus on materials and methods; upper management has realized that marketing and sales departments should be somewhat more willingly accommodated than before; finance departments have become more receptive to the legitimacy of budgets for market research and experimentation in marketing; and salesmen have been better trained to listen to and understand customer needs and problems, rather than merely to "push" the product.

A Mirror, Not a Window

My impression is that the article has had more impact in industrial-products companies than in consumer-products companies—perhaps because the former had lagged most in customer orientation. There are at least two reasons for this lag: (1) industrial-products companies tend to be more capital intensive, and (2) in the past, at least, they have had to rely heavily on communicating face-to-face the technical character of what they made and sold. These points are worth explaining.

Capital-intensive businesses are understandably preoccupied with magnitudes, especially where the capital, once invested, cannot be easily moved, manipulated, or modified for the production of a variety of products—e.g., chemical plants, steel mills, airlines, and railroads. Understandably, they seek big volumes and operating efficiencies to pay off the equipment and meet the carrying costs.

At least one problem results: corporate power becomes disproportionately lodged with operating or financial executives. If you read the charter of one of the nation's largest companies, you will see that the chairman of the finance committee, not the chief executive officer, is the "chief." Executives with such backgrounds have an almost trained incapacity to see that getting "volume" may require understanding and serving many discrete and sometimes small market segments, rather than going after a perhaps mythical batch of big or homogeneous customers.

These executives also often fail to appreciate the competitive changes going on around them. They observe the changes, all right, but devalue their significance or underestimate their ability to nibble away at the company's markets.

Once dramatically alerted to the concept of segments, sectors, and customers, though, managers of capital-intensive businesses have become more responsive to the necessity of balancing their inescapable preoccupation with "paying the bills" or breaking even with the fact that the best way to accomplish this may be to pay more attention to segments, sectors, and customers.

The second reason industrial products companies have probably been more influenced by the article is that, in the case of the more technical industrial products or services, the necessity of clearly communicating product and service characteristics to prospects results in a lot of face-to-face "selling" effort. But precisely because the product is so complex, the situation produces salesmen who know the product more than they know the customer, who are more adept at explaining what they have and what it can do than learning what the customer's needs and problems are. The result has been a narrow product orientation rather than a liberating customer orientation, and "service" often suffered. To be sure, sellers said, "We have to provide service," but they tended to define service by looking into the mirror rather than out the window. They *thought* they were looking out the window at the customer, but it was actually a mirror—a reflection of their own product-oriented biases rather than a reflection of their customers' situations.

A Manifesto, Not a Prescription

Not everything has been rosy. A lot of bizarre things have happened as a result of the article:

Some companies have developed what I call "marketing mania"—they've become obsessively responsive to every fleeting whim of the customer. Mass production operations have been converted to approximations of job shops, with cost and price consequences far exceeding the willingness of customers to buy the product.

Management has expanded product lines and added new lines of business without first establishing adequate control systems to run more complex operations.

Marketing staffs have suddenly and rapidly expanded themselves and their research budgets without either getting sufficient prior organizational support or, thereafter, producing sufficient results.

Companies that are functionally organized have converted to product, brand, or market-based organizations with the expectation of instant and miraculous results. The outcome has been ambiguity, frustration, confusion, corporate infighting, losses, and finally a reversion to functional arrangements that only worsened the situation.

Companies have attempted to "serve" customers by creating complex and beautifully efficient products or services that buyers are either too risk-averse to adopt or incapable of learning how to employ—in effect, there are now steam shovels for people who haven't yet learned to use spades. This problem has happened repeatedly in the so-called service industries (financial services, insurance, computer-based services) and with American companies selling in less-developed economies.

"Marketing Myopia" was not intended as analysis or even prescription; it was intended as manifesto. It did not pretend to take a balanced position. Nor was it a new idea—Peter F. Drucker, J. B. McKitterick, Wroe Alderson, John Howard, and Neil Borden had each done more original and balanced work on "the marketing concept." My scheme, however, tied marketing more closely to the inner orbit of business policy. Drucker—especially in *The Concept of the Corporation* and *The Practice of Management*—originally provided me with a great deal of insight.

My contribution, therefore, appears merely to have been a simple, brief, and useful way of communicating an existing way of thinking. I tried to do it in a very direct, but responsible, fashion, knowing that few readers (customers), especially managers and leaders, could stand much equivocation or hesitation. I also knew that the colorful and lightly documented affirmation works better than the tortuously reasoned explanation.

But why the enormous popularity of what was actually such a simple preexisting idea? Why its appeal throughout the world to resolutely restrained scholars, implacably temperate managers, and high government officials, all accustomed to balanced and thoughtful calculation? Is it that concrete examples, joined to illustrate a simple idea and presented with some attention to literacy, communicate better than massive analytical reasoning that reads as though it were translated from the German? Is it that provocative assertions are more memorable and persuasive than restrained and balanced explanations, no matter who the audience? Is it that the character of the message is as much the message as its content? Or was mine not simply a different tune, but a new symphony? I don't know.

Of course, I'd do it again and in the same way, given my purposes, even with what more I now know—the good and bad, the power of facts and limits of rhetoric. If your mission is the moon, you don't use a car. Don Marquis's cockroach, Archy, provides some final consolation: "an idea is not responsible for who believes in it."

Supplemental Reading Notes

1. Jacques Barzun, "Trains and the Mind of Man," *Holiday,* February 1960, p. 21.
2. For more details see M. M. Zimmerman, *The Super Market: A Revolution in Distribution* (New York: McGraw-Hill Book Company, Inc., 1955), p. 48.
3. Ibid, pp. 45–47.
4. *The Affluent Society* (Boston: Houghton-Mifflin Company, 1958), pp. 152–160.
5. Henry Ford, *My Life and Work* (New York: Doubleday, Page & Company, 1923), pp. 146–147.
6. Barzun, p. 20.

REVIEW QUIZ

When you feel you have covered all of the material in this chapter, answer these questions. Choose the *best* answer. Check your answers with the correct ones found on the Review Quiz Answer Key at the end of this book.

True (T) or False (F)

T F 1. The most basic task of marketing is to bring buyers and sellers together.

T F 2. Marketing attempts to see the business of the hospitality operation through the eyes of the customer.

T **F** 3. Marketing-oriented companies assume that customers are primarily interested in product availability and low prices.

T F 4. A product-oriented business philosophy may be appropriate for a company if the demand for its products exceeds supply.

T F 5. Marketing activities begin after products and services are produced.

T F 6. From the latter part of the nineteenth century to about 1920, businesses in the United States were primarily selling-oriented.

T F 7. Strategic marketing planning develops objectives, strategies, and tactics by which to attract a targeted mix of market segments.

T F 8. The early development of the Ford Motor Company, with its standardized Model-T, is a classic example of a marketing-oriented approach to the marketplace.

T F 9. The product-oriented business philosophy reached its zenith in the United States during the period from 1920 to 1950.

T F 10. Pre-opening hotel marketing activities include designing the pricing, distribution, and promotional plan for launching the hotel into the marketplace.

T F 11. Stable consumer buying patterns are typical in the restaurant industry.

T F 12. The hotel industry learned basic marketing techniques from marketers in the airline industry.

T F 13. Hospitality marketing is a relatively new discipline.

T F 14. General managers should not be involved in the marketing efforts of their operations.

T F 15. In the early 1960s, the Marriott Corporation concentrated its marketing efforts on attracting the vacationing pleasure traveler.

Multiple Choice

16.   Today's marketers begin by:

a. determining the needs and wants of consumers.
b. creating products and services to satisfy consumer needs.
c. developing an appropriate marketing mix.
d. coordinating objectives, strategies, and tactics by which to attract a mix of market segments.

17.   Which of the following basic business functions does marketing include?

a. sales
b. advertising
c. pricing
d. all of the above

18.   Which of the following circumstances may lead companies to adopt the marketing concept?

a. rising sales
b. stable buying patterns
c. increasing competition
d. none of the above

19.   Which of the following business philosophies may be most appropriate for a situation in which supply exceeds demand?

a. product orientation
b. selling orientation
c. marketing orientation
d. societal marketing orientation

20.   Which of the following business philosophies focuses a company's attention on the broader, social implications of satisfying consumer needs?

a. product orientation
b. selling orientation
c. marketing orientation
d. societal marketing orientation

Chapter Outline

Service Intangibility
Consumer Perceptions of Risk
Quality Control and Quality Assurance
Seasonality of Business
Balancing Supply and Demand
    Adjusting Demand to Supply
    Adjusting Supply to Demand

Learning Objectives

1. Explain what is meant by the intangibility of services.

2. Define positioning.

3. Explain why consumer perceptions of risk may be greater when purchasing services than when purchasing manufactured products.

4. Define what is meant by quality control and quality assurance in the context of service industries.

5. Explain how the seasonality of business affects the hospitality industry.

6. Describe four basic demand situations experienced by hospitality businesses.

7. Explain how differential pricing can be used to adjust demand to supply.

8. Explain how developing supplemental services can be used to adjust demand to supply.

9. Explain how cultivating non-peak demand can be used to adjust demand to supply.

2

Distinctive Aspects of Service Marketing

MANUFACTURING INDUSTRIES have successfully developed many sophisticated product marketing techniques. However, some of these techniques are not easily transferred into the realm of service marketing because there are fundamental differences between product industries and service industries.

There are distinctive aspects of service marketing because service industries face unique situations in relation to the intangibility of services, consumer perceptions of risk, seasonality of business, and balances of supply and demand.

Service Intangibility

Modern approaches to hospitality marketing recognize that hoteliers are not simply in the business of selling tangible products such as clean beds and good food. Marketing-minded hoteliers recognize that they are mainly in the business of providing relatively intangible services that produce an experience of hospitality.

Manufacturing industries produce objects, devices, things that can be touched and that persist beyond a consumer's purchase. Service industries, on the other hand, are mainly in the business of providing intangible services. These services are not so much things as they are actions, deeds, performances, or efforts. After a service has been delivered, the purchaser generally has nothing tangible to show for it. Money has been spent, but there is no "thing" that persists beyond the purchase. Customers do not leave with objects to place in their living rooms or to hang in their closets. In most cases, customers leave only with memories of their experiences.

While tangibility seems to be an obvious difference between a product and a service, in reality, there are very few pure products or pure services. Most products and services are actually combinations of tangible and intangible elements. Even the purchase of a highly tangible product, such as a new automobile, usually involves on the part of the consumer the perception of such intangible elements as the feel of the steering wheel, the excitement of the design, and the unique new-car smell of the interior. Months after the purchase, these intangible elements become less and less "real" until they eventually become distant memories. However, while the consumer's new car experience becomes more and more intangible, the automobile still sits in the driveway and represents a tangible clue capable of reminding the consumer of all that was experienced when the car was new.

The services provided by the hospitality industry are not completely intangible. For example, food served in the dining room is certainly a tangible element of a

The Greenbrier, White Sulphur Springs, West Virginia.

guest's experience. However, the dining room is not just in the food business, it is in the hospitality business. This involves providing more than just a good meal, it means surrounding the meal with a particular ambience of hospitality which includes not only the decor and atmosphere but also the geniality of hosts/hostesses, servers, and even cashiers. These intangible elements are just as important as the tangible elements that the guest experiences while enjoying a satisfying meal.

The difficulty facing hospitality marketers is that, for the most part, guests leave a hotel with only the memories of their experiences. There are no tangible clues (like the automobile sitting in the driveway) to bring back the liveliness and hospitality experienced during their stay at the hotel. The challenge facing today's hospitality service marketer is to make the intangible tangible by creating an image of the hotel's services that is so powerful, clear, and precise that the image itself appears to the public to take on the solid, tangible characteristics of an actual product. When a property is marketed well, the image of the hotel and its position relative to the competition are so clear and credible that the specifics of its service become an instantly recognizable, permanent signature of the hotel, almost like a product.

For example, what frequenter of resort hotels has not heard of the impeccable service of the Greenbrier? Similarly, who can think of the Waldorf-Astoria Hotel and not think of the highest standards of service and the highest quality of food and drink? And among convention-goers, what hotels conjure up a more positive image as convention headquarters than the Sheraton Waikiki or the Opryland Hotel?

Hotel marketers must project an image of what their hotels are all about and the kinds of guests their hotels attempt to serve. The individuals involved in presenting

The Waldorf-Astoria, New York City, New York.

The Sheraton Waikiki, Honolulu, Hawaii.

the hotel to its markets must then make the image a reality by showing that they are totally committed to the appropriate level of service for those markets.

A hotel's level of service is both a difficult idea to market and an extremely difficult program to implement in light of the variety of hotels and the spectrum of services being offered in the hospitality industry today. For instance, what is the proper level of service in an economy hotel versus a hotel that functions without a typical front desk? An example of the latter is the Watertower Hyatt in Chicago, where guests are individually registered and escorted to their rooms by a host or hostess.

Part of the answer lies in recognizing that every service provided by a hotel must meet the expectations of the guests that the property wishes to attract and satisfy. Otherwise, guests will be disappointed or overwhelmed. For example, guests in an economy property probably would be surprised by an attempt to escort them to their rooms. Similarly, an attempt to upgrade the image of a hotel by instituting a nightly turndown service may prompt some guests to complain that their beds have not been properly made. However, given a defined level of service and a specific market that a hotel is trying to attract and satisfy, escorting guests to rooms or a nightly turndown service can become tangible clues to the image that the hotel wishes to project. The more tangible clues that the hotel can provide, the more the image it projects will appear to take on product-like attributes. These tangible clues are marketing tools by which to position the products and services offered by a lodging property.

Positioning is a marketing term that is used to describe how consumers perceive the products and services offered by a particular company in relation to similar products and services offered by competitors. It is one thing for a property to

Opryland Hotel, Nashville, Tennessee.

say, "We're number one" but it is quite another thing for consumers to say "You're number one." Positioning is concerned with image, and positioning strategies attempt to establish in the minds of consumers a particular image of a lodging property's products and services.

Tangible clues not only help a property to position itself in the minds of consumers, they also lead customers to form certain expectations about the hotel's services and reassure them that the performance level will measure up to their expectations. A high ceiling in a hotel lobby furnished in oak with antique fixtures would be appropriate in a property catering to the upscale traveler. The same furnishings in an economy or budget operation appealing to the price-sensitive consumer would convey the wrong set of impressions. Because tangible clues powerfully influence consumers' perceptions of service, the needs of the target market must be kept firmly in mind. Interior design issues should be coordinated by a marketing strategy and should not simply be left to the discretion of interior designers.

Theodore Levitt points out that tangible clues need not be as grandiose as our example of the high-ceiling hotel lobby. They can be simple clues that are no less powerful in conveying the image of a hotel:

      ❝ For instance, hotels wrap their drinking glasses in fresh bags or film, put on the toilet seat a 'sanitized' paper band, and neatly shape the end piece of the toilet tissue into a fresh-looking arrowhead. All these actions say with silent, affirmative clarity that 'the room has been specially cleaned for your use and comfort'—yet no words are spoken to say it. Words, in any case, would be less convincing, nor could employees be reliably depended on to say them each time or to say them convincingly. **99**1

Consumer Perceptions of Risk

An important factor distinguishing service marketing from product marketing is the higher level of risk that consumers perceive when purchasing services as opposed to purchasing manufactured products. One factor contributing to customers' perceptions of risk in purchasing services is the intangibility of services discussed in the previous section.

It seems only natural that customers would perceive a greater risk in purchasing services than in purchasing manufactured products because customers cannot really evaluate many forms of service until they actually purchase and consume them. Services cannot be touched, tasted, or tried on for size. Also, since few service purchases are backed by warranties or guarantees, it is virtually impossible for dissatisfied customers to "return" a service.

Service marketers need to develop strategies by which to overcome these perceptions of risk and increase consumer confidence. Such strategies include forms of advertising and promotion that stress the tangible clues of service discussed in the previous section. Marketers can also emphasize the benefits that consumers receive from the services, rather than merely describing various features of the services themselves. This would mean highlighting guestrooms in terms of comfort, security, and convenience.

A major difference between service marketing and product marketing is that many of the intangible services delivered by people in an atmosphere of hospitality tend to be less standardized, or uniform, than the tangible objects produced by equipment in a manufacturing setting. This service variability may lead customers to perceive more risk to be associated with the purchase of services because they don't know what to expect each time they purchase a particular service. This form of consumer uncertainty may be the direct result of inconsistencies in the product service delivery systems of service industries. One of the most effective strategies which hotels can adopt to increase consumer confidence in this area is to cultivate positive word-of-mouth advertising by satisfying the customers they presently attract. Once a property ensures consistency in the delivery of its products and services, consumer confidence increases and positive word-of-mouth advertising spreads from satisfied guests to potential customers. Ensuring the consistent delivery of products and services leads to the next distinctive feature of service marketing: quality control and quality assurance.

Quality Control and Quality Assurance

Consumers of manufactured products are normally isolated from the production processes. They are rarely present along assembly production lines, except as tourists, and they do not line up outside factory entrances waiting to purchase items directly off the assembly lines. Instead, consumers buy the products at retail outlets, and either consume them there, or take them home and consume them at a later date. This allows manufacturing industries the luxury of being able to inspect and test products before they are sold to consumers.

In the case of hotels, guests are rarely present when room attendants are cleaning guestrooms or when chefs and cooks are preparing meals in the kitchen. In these instances, some of the quality control techniques of manufacturing industries apply: rooms are inspected after they are cleaned, and recipes are tested before new items appear on menus in the dining room.

However, in many instances, guests are not isolated from the production processes of a hotel. For example, the interaction that takes place between front desk employees and guests at the time of check-in, and the interaction between food servers and guests in the dining room represent instances when services are produced, delivered, and consumed simultaneously. In these situations, the way in which the service is delivered is considered just as much a part of the hospitality "product" as a clean guestroom or a satisfying meal in the dining room. This means that traditional quality control techniques of manufacturing industries may not be appropriate for many aspects of service industries. Inspecting service after the service is delivered is too late to ensure satisfied customers.

The intangible nature of services, the presence of consumers at the point of service production and delivery, and the people-intensive nature of service interaction are among the many factors that contribute to service variability. Some service operations, such as fast-food restaurants, have tried to eliminate service variability by isolating a "technological core" of the service and minimizing the interactions between customers and employees. However, in the lodging industry, this strategy of reducing the human element in the service delivery system is seldom possible or even desirable.

One of the greatest challenges facing service marketers in the hospitality industry today is to develop a system by which to control service variability—a system that not only adapts the quality control methods developed by manufacturing industries to the unique problems and situations of service industries, but also one that explores new methods of tracking and controlling the consistent delivery of quality services.

A 1982 survey, directed by the Quality Assurance Committee of the American Hotel & Motel Association, revealed widespread misconceptions about quality. Many hoteliers believed that quality applied only to properties with high room rates, or that quality was a subjective evaluation of the services provided by properties throughout the industry. Few survey respondents thought that the idea of quality could apply to every property in the industry, regardless of size, room rates, or the number of services provided. Even fewer respondents believed that quality could be quantified and measured. Only 9% of the respondents to the survey defined quality in terms of a management system that assures the consistent delivery of products and services according to expected standards.

The key to quality is consistency, and the keys to consistency are the standards that a property develops by coordinating the expectations of guests, employees, and management into agreed-upon levels of performance for every position throughout the organization. However, standards alone do not assure quality; people assure quality. Standards make quality possible for an organization, but only the people within the organization can make quality a reality by working together to develop, communicate, and manage quality standards. This kind of cooperation becomes possible only when everyone within an organization absorbs a common language, a common set of values, and a common set of goals. A quality assurance system can provide a common language of quality (the consistent delivery of products and services according to standards), a common set of values (quality standards as required levels of performance), and a common set of goals (100% conformance to standards).

Quality control and quality assurance are not only methods by which to reduce consumer perceptions of risk, they are also marketing tools for advertising and promotional campaigns.

Seasonality of Business

Although both manufacturing firms and hospitality operations frequently experience fluctuations in demand over long periods of time, hospitality operations must also deal with fluctuations in demand from month to month, from day to day, and from hour to hour.

The seasonality of business throughout a year is a serious factor for many hotels and motels. Some resorts are open for only one season of the year. Other lodging properties, although open year round, experience considerably higher demand during certain months. For example, many south Florida hotels experience higher occupancy during the winter months than during the summer, as vacationers from the north descend to enjoy south Florida's warmth and sunshine.

Occupancy percentage is a prime measure of activity for lodging operations. It expresses what percent of the rooms available for sale are actually sold, and it is calculated by dividing the number of rooms sold by the number of rooms available for sale.

Exhibit 1 shows the monthly occupancy rates in selected U.S. cities and states for 1984. The occupancy percentage nationwide was lowest in December (49%) and highest in both March and June (71%). Boston hotels registered 92% occupancy in October and 48% in December, while Miami hotels registered a high of 74% in February and a low of 51% in September. Thus, Exhibit 1 reveals seasonal fluctuations by month and also considerable differences among selected cities and states.

Seasonality of business throughout a week may often be a consequence of the particular markets which hotels and motels strive to serve. Hotels catering primarily to the business traveler (transient hotels) may experience 100% occupancy Monday through Thursday, but only 30% for Friday through Sunday, thus averaging 70% for the week. Weekly seasonality for many resort hotels is the opposite of that experienced by transient hotels. Busy resort business periods are usually weekends rather than weekdays. In addition, their average number of guests per room, determined by dividing the number of paid guests by the number of rooms sold, is higher than that experienced by transient hotels.

While both manufacturing firms and hospitality operations frequently experience monthly and even weekly fluctuations of demand, only service industries,

Exhibit 1   Monthly Occupancy Rates

	1st Quarter 1985	Average for Year 1984	Dec.	Nov.	Oct.	Sept.	Aug.	July	June	May	April	Mar.	Feb.	Jan.
							1984							
Albuquerque	70%	67%	46%	57%	77%	75%	73%	68%	79%	75%	69%	73%	66%	58%
Atlanta	67	66	47	63	72	65	71	67	71	68	67	73	69	64
Austin	71	73	49	70	76	70	77	77	84	81	77	83	78	69
Baton Rouge	48	57	39	49	62	46	56	58	68	69	64	61	61	66
Boston	N/A	70	48	69	92	81	76	71	80	78	75	62	52	51
Chattanooga	57	66	48	54	72	60	77	75	77	70	69	82	59	49
Chicago	58	66	49	65	81	77	74	63	77	74	61	65	55	50
Colorado Springs	48	67	39	47	62	77	92	91	84	76	62	62	60	44
Corpus Christi	50	57	35	45	50	55	70	70	75	63	50	53	47	43
Dallas/Fort Worth	67	62	46	55	68	63	71	66	67	72	65	72	67	64
Denver	62	59	42	41	56	60	77	66	74	66	64	64	60	51
Fort Lauderdale	N/A	65	60	69	58	50	54	51	54	67	72	90	82	68
Houston	50	53	39	45	52	44	63	55	55	51	51	57	52	52
Knoxville	53	58	44	57	70	62	67	61	65	59	63	56	49	41
Los Angeles	71	68	53	63	67	77	77	55	77	70	66	74	68	62
Memphis	62	69	51	66	73	68	80	76	79	74	69	69	58	52
Miami	79	62	59	64	57	51	62	58	52	57	62	66	74	68
Nashville	59	70	47	61	79	76	80	82	86	74	70	70	59	47
New Orleans	54	67	36	56	84	73	75	69	82	77	62	69	61	52
New York City	65	75	68	81	90	81	82	67	81	80	74	73	67	59
Orlando Area:														
Disney/Kissimmee	69	75	49	60	61	48	86	91	87	82	91	94	79	59
International Drive	75	72	52	59	69	57	74	83	76	76	84	88	79	67
City of Orlando	69	62	46	42	43	41	67	76	64	71	81	92	77	56
Palm Beach	N/A	73	71	73	71	59	71	56	58	72	70	88	88	74
Phoenix	53	62	43	62	76	69	70	61	70	68	63	57	52	47
Philadelphia	82	68	51	71	73	63	44	46	61	70	75	87	91	72
San Antonio	68	74	55	63	71	69	81	78	81	78	82	76	68	54
San Francisco	67	72	50	70	84	82	79	81	79	79	69	68	62	54
Scottsdale	75	60	47	51	59	51	44	43	61	72	65	87	88	69
Tampa Bay	74	73	54	59	68	56	67	70	68	77	79	90	74	57
Tuscon	84	65	60	69	72	53	46	46	53	52	61	77	69	56
Tulsa	46	57	43	44	55	53	59	50	45	49	53	46	48	47
Washington, D.C.	65	70	46	65	82	78	70	67	82	85	83	72	62	50
Alabama	56	66	49	65	71	66	74	72	—	—	—	—	—	—
Arizona	79	66	51	66	69	59	47	46	61	68	70	85	84	69
Colorado	63	61	46	46	61	68	82	72	66	60	71	65	63	58
Hawaii	88	76	72	65	76	70	79	79	78	73	76	88	89	75
Illinois	59	60	41	56	68	66	71	64	68	60	71	62	57	50
Louisiana	52	62	37	53	74	65	70	66	76	72	59	63	59	52
Mississippi	51	61	35	51	63	54	66	72	75	69	68	71	59	52
New Mexico	68	66	49	55	75	72	73	69	73	71	84	70	64	56
New York State	83	74	65	78	88	80	73	67	79	79	72	71	65	58
North Carolina	82	67	46	63	81	70	70	65	70	68	72	66	60	58
Northern California	59	72	52	69	80	78	80	78	80	80	71	70	65	59
Oklahoma	49	57	43	52	61	59	60	59	59	58	59	59	54	53
South Carolina	61	70	48	62	68	68	77	80	77	77	82	73	64	38
Tennessee	57	66	47	60	75	68	77	76	78	69	66	65	56	47
Texas	61	62	45	54	63	58	66	65	67	66	64	67	63	57
Virginia	50	62	43	64	64	66	63	63	62	59	54	67	46	41
Wyoming-Utah-Montana-Nebraska	60	63	44	54	62	71	80	78	74	62	62	65	67	55
Nationwide Averages*	68%	67%	49%	60%	70%	65%	70%	68%	71%	70%	68%	71%	65%	56%

*Estimated occupancies for nation's total hotel-motel industry.

Source: Pannell Kerr Forster & Company, *Trends—USA*, 1985, p. 40. Reprinted with permission.

and the hospitality industry in particular, experience acute fluctuations in demand from hour to hour throughout a day. Check-in time may vary but many hotels are busiest between 3:00 P.M. and 5:00 P.M., while check-out at many hotels is extremely busy between 7:00 A.M. and 9:00 A.M., and between 11:00 A.M. and 1:00 P.M. Similarly, some food service establishments may be operating at full capacity during typical meal periods, but are nearly empty during other hours throughout the day.

Balancing Supply and Demand

Manufacturing industries are often able to balance supply and demand by properly managing inventory levels. Since products can often be stored in inventories, manufacturing industries are relatively unaffected by sharp, unexpected changes in consumer demand. This is not the case with hospitality operations. Services cannot be stored in inventory, and hotel rooms and dining room seats are relatively fixed.

In the lodging industry, supply is relatively fixed because it cannot be increased except by expanding the original facility. This could take months, even years. As we have seen, lodging operations face special problems because demand varies on a seasonal, daily, and even hourly basis. Hospitality operations may also experience conditions of falling demand, no demand, or even negative demand which may occur when past guests form an aversion to the property and simply will not return. In these situations, the primary task of the marketer is to stimulate demand. When demand exceeds available capacity, however, the primary task is to manage demand.

Casino marketers in Great Britain face the unusual situation of managing what is called an unstimulated demand. British gaming facilities must operate as private clubs and cannot advertise, organize groups, or entice customers with floor shows, dancing, or music, nor can they offer complimentary food, drinks, or rooms to clientele. The gaming facilities must depend on what is called unstimulated demand.

There are four basic kinds of demand conditions that face service industries and especially the lodging industry: (1) demand exceeds maximum capacity level, (2) demand exceeds optimum capacity level, (3) demand balances with optimum capacity level, (4) demand falls below optimum capacity level. Each of these demand conditions calls for a separate and distinct marketing strategy.

Demand Exceeds Maximum Capacity Level. When every available room is occupied, the hotel cannot accept any more guests and consumers seek accommodations elsewhere. In this demand condition, potential business is lost. If this condition occurs often enough, the logical business strategy is to increase supply by expanding the property and adding new rooms. An important short-term alternative available to food and beverage marketers which could expand supply in an excess demand situation is to increase operating efficiency and thereby increase turnover time (or service cycle time) during peak-demand periods. This is often the tactic taken by dining room managers for busy business lunch hours and for many special occasion and holiday dinner periods. However, this approach may conflict with the level of service that the property usually provides and which guests have come to expect. A serious deterioration in service quality could result in eventual loss of business for the property and produce problems that usually occur when demand exceeds the optimum capacity level.

Demand Exceeds Optimum Capacity Level. In this demand situation, no customers are turned away, but all guests are likely to perceive a deterioration in the quality of the services delivered. For example, the quality of dining room service will be strained when every seat is occupied and servers cannot spend as much time with guests as they would if the facility were operating at optimum capacity. Long check-in and check-out lines at the front desk of a hotel may be a sign that, when the house is full, a more flexible scheduling of the front desk staff is necessary. In terms of resort properties, crowded ski areas may seem to generate more revenues for owners, but the long lift lines may ultimately create consumer dissatisfaction, reducing repeat business and resulting in an overall loss of business.

Demand Balances with Optimum Capacity Level. Although the potential for handling more business exists in this kind of demand situation, management and customers are usually satisfied with the current operating level of service. The marketing task in this type of situation is to maintain the level of demand in the face of changing consumer preferences and increasing competition. For example, when a hotel balances demand with optimum capacity, management must work to maintain the quality of services the operation provides and continually monitor guest satisfaction.

Demand Falls Below Optimum Capacity Level. In this demand situation, re-sources are underutilized, and, in some cases, customers may find the experience disappointing or begin to have doubts about the viability of the service operation. In the face of falling demand, marketers must analyze the causes of market decline and determine whether demand can be stimulated by appealing to new market segments, changing the service amenities, or developing a more effective advertis-ing and promotional campaign.

Adjusting Demand to Supply

Generally, marketing efforts can do little to smooth out random fluctuations in de-mand or fluctuations that are due to external events such as political turmoil, fluc-tuating currency exchange rates, or changes in the weather. However, if, over time, demand fluctuations follow predictable patterns, then it may be economically worthwhile to develop marketing strategies to adjust demand to supply. Strategies by which to adjust demand to supply include: differential pricing, developing sup-plemental services, and cultivating non-peak demand.

Differential Pricing. Differential, or peak-load, pricing is sometimes used to smooth demand fluctuations by shifting demand from peak to shoulder seasons, or low occupancy periods. Prices will vary according to the lack of demand. For example, a week's vacation at a resort during Christmas week may generally cost more than a week's vacation at the same resort during the time period between Thanksgiving and Christmas. This strategy may work well for price-sensitive mar-kets such as students, senior citizens, families with flexible vacation months, and other groups not constrained by time factors.

Holiday Inns, Inc., Marriott Corporation, and Days Inns of America have of-fered "supersaver" discounts for pleasure travelers who make early reservations. The "Great Rates" promotion of Holiday Inns, Inc. offered discounts off regular room rates available at all 1,500 of its Holiday Inns and Crowne Plaza Hotels in the United States. Reservations had to be made at least seven days in advance and guaranteed by credit card. Days Inns' supersaver rates required reservations 29 days in advance. Marriott's supersaver rates applied mostly to weekends, but were considerably lower than regular weekday rates.

A distinction should be made between differential pricing and price-cutting. Differential pricing can be a useful tactic to shift existing demand from one period to another. Higher rates are maintained during peak periods of demand while lower rates are used to shift some users to periods of lower demand. Price-cutting, on the other hand, is the wholesale lowering of prices in a prolonged attempt to stimulate demand. Price-cutting can occur even during periods of relatively high demand to encourage trial usage and take business away from local competitors.

Many problems may result when price-cutting is used as a competitive strategy. Hotels may encounter consumer resistance when rates are later raised. Also, some evidence suggests that price is often not the major determinant of lodging demand. This means that price cuts might not stimulate much additional demand. For example, widespread price-cutting during the 1981–82 recession did not stop the decline in occupancy percentages. Reducing room rates to bolster occupancy during economic slumps can be a very expensive strategy.

The demand for most commercial hotels may be thought of as a kind of "derived demand." That is, consumers only need hotel rooms because they need to be in an area for some externally driven reason, such as to conduct business. Reducing room rates in this situation may have little effect except to shift demand from one hotel to another. The case is quite different with resort properties. Here rate-cutting can have a major impact on demand.

Extreme and prolonged price-cutting, so-called "price wars," can have serious effects for any service industry. The airline industry is a classic example of price warfare. According to the Air Transport Association, roughly 86% of domestic airline seats sold in the first ten months of 1985 went at a discount, with the average ticket selling for only about 56% of full fare. This industry dilemma stems from at least two factors: (1) major differences in the operating costs of established airlines and newer, low-cost non-union carriers, and (2) the seemingly insatiable desire of practically every airline to expand their base of operations. Industry experts debate whether the airlines will be able to control the spread of fare wars on selected routes or whether the situation will deteriorate into a full-scale price war. A very worrisome trend for airline executives is the growing use of discounted fares for corporations—the last stronghold of full-fare travel—to fill seats on selected routes. It has been estimated that a 10% cut in the $30 billion that corporations annually pay in fares to the 12 major airlines would wipe out those carriers' profits.[2]

Developing Supplemental Services. Another method of managing demand in capacity-strained properties is the creation of service alternatives during peak demand periods. This strategy channels the physical distribution of customers in the service facility. For example, cocktail lounges and other types of facilities are often used by patrons of a hotel dining room to relax and have a drink while waiting for dinner. Liquor service in hotel lobbies is a method of diverting pressure from crowded lounges. Developing supplemental services such as these can also increase the profitability of the overall hotel operation.

Balancing demand and recreation facilities within resort operations may be extremely difficult during peak periods. Developing temporary supplemental services can be an effective strategy by which resort operations manage demand when their facilities are strained to capacity. It may not be economically feasible to respond to peak demand situations by expanding the facilities. Yet, vacationing guests expect access to tennis courts, golf courses, riding facilities, etc., especially if these features are emphasized in the resort advertising and promotional literature. Temporary supplemental services may be able to shift demand to facilities or activities that are not functioning at an overload capacity. For example, an afternoon fashion show by the pool may temporarily relieve an overload demand situation for the tennis courts and serve to spread the use of the tennis facilities more evenly throughout the day.

Cultivating Non-peak Demand. Hotel marketers must often seek to offset the falling demand of one market with the rising demand of another market. Few hotels are fortunate enough to have an equal balance of offsetting markets—markets whose demand peaks and valleys occur during different periods. Tourist traffic at many resorts, for example, normally peaks in summers, on weekends, and at the Christmas holidays. Business travel, on the other hand, is predominantly a Monday through Thursday phenomenon, heaviest in the spring and autumn, and particularly light in December. Convention business also favors the midweek, as well as the January to May, and September to November seasons. Occupancy patterns may vary with location. For example, New York City hotels have significant weekend and tourist business, but may experience lower mid-week occupancy levels. This is a particularly thorny problem for luxury hotels where the incremental revenue from high room rates can have an enormous impact on the bottom line, and where low occupancy percentages can be disastrous due to the high fixed costs involved in operating luxury properties.

In order to cultivate non-peak demand, many marketers take advantage of demand generators such as special events or activities that occur in their areas. Urban hotels, catering to the business traveler, capitalize on cultural and athletic events and also fill rooms on weekends by developing mini-vacation packages for the suburban population in their areas. Resort hotels, jammed with pleasure travelers during school vacations, develop special packages for business groups during off-season periods. For example, the mid-Atlantic oceanfront hotels market beach and sun in the summer, golf and tennis in the spring, conventions in the fall, and seclusion in the winter. Winter ski resorts can become summer golfing centers that also offer hiking, riding, and tennis. In addition, mountain-area hotels can often operate as effective conference centers.

Adopting new concepts to attract new markets can be costly. New concepts often require equipment and skills not found in a hotel's current service delivery system. Attracting and satisfying new types of customers may require a wholly different combination of people, equipment, and facilities. New kinds of training and closer forms of supervision may be necessary. The introduction of a new concept may even reduce operational efficiency and, in some cases, may destroy the delicate balance of supply and demand found in most service delivery systems. Also, when two different markets, such as business travelers and tour groups, patronize a hotel simultaneously, various operational problems may arise.

Adjusting Supply to Demand

Differential pricing, developing supplemental services, and cultivating non-peak demand are useful marketing strategies by which to adjust demand to supply. There are a number of actions that properties can take to adjust supply to demand. These include: hiring part-time employees, maximizing efficiency, and increasing consumer participation.

Automation and, more recently, computerization and robotics have reduced the need for intensive labor in the production processes of many manufacturing firms. However, payroll expense is a major factor in the cost of sales for both the lodging and food service segments of the hospitality industry.

The often acute fluctuations in demand contribute to the labor intensive feature of many hospitality operations. The busy check-in and check-out times during daily hotel operations require considerable amounts of labor in the rooms department in order to provide quality service. Similarly, food service operations have increased labor needs for spurts of activity throughout the day. Another important feature of food and beverage outlets in lodging properties is the need to provide service even when it may not be profitable. For example, food service must usually be provided to guests even on low occupancy days, and room service must always be available in first-class properties.

High school and college students can be hired on a part-time basis for peak demand periods. Also, flexible scheduling techniques can ensure adequate and effective coverage during predictable fluctuations in demand. Employee vacations can be scheduled to coincide with slack business periods and peak-time efficiency routines can be introduced which engage employees only in the most essential tasks. Non-essential tasks can either be eliminated or contracted out.

The disadvantage in contracting out essential services is that managers lose control. Contractors may not adhere to the same standards of service that the facility demands of its employees. Even if contractors perform well, there may still be the risk that guests will perceive inconsistencies between the contractor's methods and the service delivery system of the property.

The more the consumer participates in the production process, the lower the labor requirements of the producer. Lower costs can be passed on to consumers, improving the price/value perceptions of a property's services. Fast-food operations have long understood the value of eliminating table service in favor of having customers place their orders at a central desk, and of eliminating buspersons in favor of customers busing their own tables. Obviously, this approach has limited application to other dining facilities. A different group of customers may resent performing these tasks. However, there are other forms of customer participation that apply to dining room service, such as self-serve salad bars and Sunday brunch buffets. The extent to which properties can increase customer participation will depend on the expectations of the guests they serve.

This discussion of supply and demand has focused on the tactics used by some properties to balance supply and demand situations unique to the hospitality industry. However, modern hospitality marketing is much more than a series of tactical adjustments to emergent problems. Long-range planning and analyses are also becoming increasingly necessary for the successful marketing of hospitality services.

Endnotes

1. Theodore Levitt, "Marketing Intangible Products and Product Intangibles," *Harvard Business Review*, May–June 1981.

2. James E. Ellis, "Fare Wars Are Becoming A Way of Life," *Business Week*, January 13, 1986, p. 102.

Supplemental Reading

Breaking Free from Product Marketing

by G. Lynn Shostack

> *Service marketing, to be effective and successful, requires a mirror-opposite view of conventional "product" practices.*

About the Author:

> *G. Lynn Shostack is Vice President, Citibank, N.A., New York; she is Marketing Director for the Investment Management Group.*

New concepts are necessary if service marketing is to succeed. Service marketing is an uncharted frontier. Despite the increasing dominance of services in the U.S. economy, basic texts still disagree on how services should be treated in a marketing context.[1]

The heart of this dispute is the issue of applicability. The classic marketing "mix," the seminal literature, and the language of marketing all derive from the manufacture of physical goods. Practicing marketers tend to think in terms of products, particularly mass-market consumer goods. Some service companies even call their output "products" and have "product" management functions modeled after those of experts such as Procter & Gamble.

Marketing seems to be overwhelmingly product-oriented. However, many service-based companies are confused about the applicability of product marketing, and more than one attempt to adopt product marketing has failed.

Merely adopting product marketing's labels does not resolve the question of whether product marketing can be overlaid on service businesses. Can corporate banking services really be marketed according to the same basic blueprint that made *Tide* a success? Given marketing's historic tenets, there is simply no alternative.

Could marketing itself be "myopic" in having failed to create relevant paradigms for the service sector? Many marketing professionals who transfer to the services arena find their work fundamentally "different," but have a difficult time articulating how and why their priorities and concepts have changed. Often, they also find to their frustration and bewilderment that "marketing" is treated as a peripheral function or is confused with one of its components, such as research or advertising, and kept within a very narrow scope of influence and authority.[2]

This situation is frequently rationalized as being due to the "ignorance" of senior management in service businesses. "Education" is usually recommended as the solution. However, an equally feasible, though less comforting, explanation is that service industries have been slow to integrate marketing into the mainstream of decision-making and control because marketing offers no guidance, terminology, or practical rules that are clearly *relevant* to services.

Reprinted by permission of the *Journal of Marketing*. "Breaking Free from Product Marketing" by G. Lynn Shostack (April 1977), pp. 73–80. Published by the American Marketing Association.

Making Room for Intangibility

The American Marketing Association cites both goods *and* services as foci for marketing activities. Squeezing services into the Procrustean phrase, "intangible products,"[3] is not only a distortion of the AMA's definition but also a complete contradiction in terms.

It is wrong to imply that services are just like products "except" for intangibility. By such logic, apples are just like oranges, except for their "appleness." Intangibility is not a modifier; it is a state. Intangibles may come with tangible trappings, but no amount of money can buy physical ownership of such intangibles as "experience" (movies), "time" (consultants), or "process" (dry cleaning). A service is rendered. A service is experienced. A service cannot be stored on a shelf, touched, tasted or tried on for size. "Tangible" means "palpable," and "material." "Intangible" is an antonym, meaning "*im*palpable," and "*not* corporeal."[4] This distinction has profound implications. Yet marketing offers no way to treat intangibility as the core element it is, nor does marketing offer usable tools for managing, altering, or controlling this amorphous core.

Even the most thoughtful attempts to broaden the definition of "that which is marketed" away from product synonymity suffer from an underlying assumption of tangibility. Not long ago, Philip Kotler argued that "values" should be considered the end result of "marketing."[5] However, the text went on to imply that "values" were created by "objects," and drifted irredeemably into the classic product axioms.

To truly expand marketing's conceptual boundaries requires a framework which accommodates intangibility instead of denying it. Such a framework must give equal descriptive weight to the components of "service" as it does to the concept of "product."

The Complexity of Marketed Entities

What kind of framework would provide a new conceptual viewpoint? One unorthodox possibility can be drawn from direct observation of the marketplace and the nature of the market "satisfiers" available to it. Taking a fresh look, it seems that there are really very few, if any, "pure" products or services in the marketplace.

Examine, for instance, the automobile. Without question, one might say, it is a physical object, with a full range of tangible features and options. But another, equally important element is marketed in tandem with the steel and chrome—i.e., the service of transportation. Transportation is an *independent* marketing element; in other words, it is not car-dependent, but can be marketed in its own right. A car is only *one* alternative for satisfying the market's transportation needs.

This presents a semantic dilemma. How should the automobile be defined? Is General Motors marketing a *service* a service that happens to include a *by*-product called a car? Levitt's classic "Marketing Myopia" exhorts businessmen to think in exactly this generic way about what they market.[6] Are automobiles "tangible services"? It cannot be denied that both elements—tangible and intangible—exist and are vigorously marketed. Yet they are, by definition, different qualities, and to attempt to compress them into a single word or phrase begs the issue.

Conversely, how shall a service such as airline transportation be described? Although the service itself is intangible, there are certain very real things that belong in any description of the total entity, including such important tangibles as interior decor, food & drink, seat design, and overall graphic continuity from tickets to attendants' uniforms. These items can dramatically affect the "reality" of the service in the consumer's mind. However, there is no accurate way to lump them into a one-word description.

If "either-or" terms (product vs. service) do not adequately describe the true nature of marketed entities, it makes sense to explore the usefulness of a new *structural* definition. This broader concept postulates that market entities are, in reality, *combinations of discrete elements* which are linked together in molecule-like wholes. Elements can be either tangible or intangible. The entity may have either a tangible or intangible nucleus. But the whole can only be described as having a certain dominance.

Molecular Model

A "molecular" model offers opportunities for visualization and management of a total market entity. It reflects the fact that a market entity can be partly tangible *and* partly intangible, without diminishing the importance of either characteristic. Not only can the potential be seen for picturing and dealing with multiple *elements*, rather than a *thing*, but the concept of dominance can lead to enriched considerations of the priorities and approach that may be required of a marketer. Moreover, the model suggests the scientific analogy that if market entities have multiple elements, a deliberate or inadvertent change in a *single* element may completely alter the entity, as the simple switching of Fe_3O_2 to Fe_2O_3 creates a new substance. For this reason, a marketer must carefully manage all the elements, especially those for service-based entities, which may not have been considered previously within his domain.

Diagramming Market Entities

A simplified comparison demonstrates the conceptual usefulness of a molecular modeling system. In Exhibit 1, automobiles and airline travel are broken down into their major elements. As shown, these two entities have different nuclei. They also differ in dominance.

Clearly, airline travel is intangible-dominant; that is, it does not yield physical ownership of a tangible good. Nearly all of the other important elements in the entity are intangible as well. Individual elements and their combinations represent unique satisfiers to different market segments. Thus:

- For some markets—students, for example—pure transport takes precedence over all other considerations. The charter flight business was based on this element. As might be expected during lean economic times, "no frills" flights show renewed emphasis on this nuclear core.

- For business travelers, on the other hand, schedule frequency may be paramount.

Exhibit 1   Diagram of Market Entities

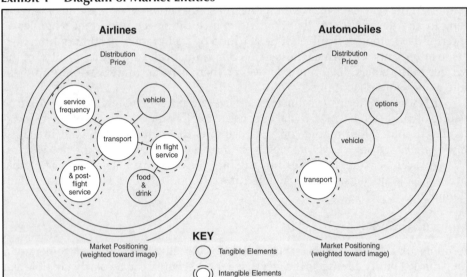

- Tourists, a third segment, may respond most strongly to the combination of in-flight and post-flight services.

As the market entity of airline travel has evolved, it has become more and more complex. Ongoing reweighting of elements can be observed, for example, in the marketing of airline food, which was once a battleground of quasi-gourmet offerings. Today, some airlines have stopped marketing food altogether, while others are repositioning it primarily to the luxury markets.

Airlines vs. Automobiles

In comparing airlines to automobiles, one sees obvious similarities. The element of transportation is common to both, as it is to boats, trains, buses, and bicycles. Tangible decor also plays a role in both entities. Yet in spite of their similarities, the two entities are not the same, either in configuration or in marketing implications.

In some ways, airline travel and automobiles are mirror opposites. A car is a physical possession that renders a service. Airline travel, on the other hand, cannot be physically possessed. It can only be experienced. While the inherent "promise" of a car is service, airline transportation often promises a Lewis Carroll version of "*product*," i.e., *destination*, which is marketed as though it were physically obtainable. If only tropical islands and redwood forests *could* be purchased for the price of an airline ticket!

The model can be completed by adding the remaining major marketing elements in a way that demonstrates their function vis-à-vis the organic core entity. First, the total entity is ringed and defined by a set value or price. Next, the valued entity is circumscribed by its distribution. Finally, the entire entity is encompassed,

Exhibit 2   Scale of Market Entities

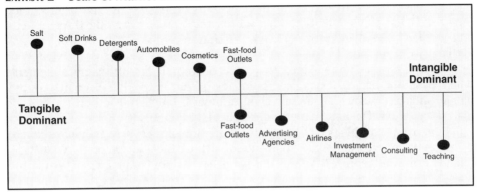

according to its core configuration, by its public "face," i.e., its positioning to the market.

The molecular concept makes it possible to describe and array market entities along a continuum, according to the weight of the "mix" of elements that comprise them. As Exhibit 2 indicates, teaching services might be at one end of such a scale, *intangible or I-dominant*, while salt might represent the other extreme, *tangible or T-dominant*. Such a scale accords intangible-based entities a place and weight commensurate with their true importance. The framework also provides a mechanism for comparison and market positioning.

In one of the handful of books devoted to services, the author holds that "the more intangible the service, the greater will be the difference in the marketing characteristics of the service."[7] Consistent with an entity scale, this axiom might now be amended to read: the greater the weight of intangible elements in a market entity, the greater will be the divergence from product marketing in priorities and approach.

Implications of the Molecular Model

The hypothesis proposed by molecular modeling carries intriguing potential for rethinking and reshaping classic marketing concepts and practices. Recognition that service-dominant entities differ from product-dominant entities allows consideration of other distinctions which have been intuitively understood, but seldom articulated by service marketers.

A most important area of difference is immediately apparent—i.e., that service "knowledge" and product "knowledge" cannot be gained in the same way.

A *product* marketer's first task is to "know" his product. For tangible-dominant entities this is relatively straightforward. A tangible object can be described precisely. It is subject to physical examination or photographic reproduction or quantitative measure. It can not only be exactly replicated, but also modified in precise and duplicate ways.

It is not particularly difficult for the marketer of *Coca-Cola*, for example, to summon all the facts regarding the product, itself. He can and does make reasonable assumptions about the product's behavior, e.g., that it is consistent chemically to the taste, visually to the eye, and physically in its packaging. Any changes he might make in these three areas can be deliberately controlled for uniformity since they will be tangibly evident. In other words, the marketer can take the product's "reality" for granted and move on to considerations of price, distribution, and advertising or promotion.

To gain *service* "knowledge," however, or knowledge of a service element, where does one begin? It has been pointed out that intangible elements are dynamic, subjective, and ephemeral. They cannot be touched, tried on for size, or placed on a shelf. They are exceedingly difficult to quantify.

Reverting to airline travel, precisely what *is* the service of air transportation to the potential purchaser? What "percent" of airline travel is comfort? What "percent" is fear or adventure? What *is* this service's "reality" to its market? And how does that reality vary from segment to segment? Since this service exists only during the time in which it is rendered, the entity's true "reality" must be defined experientially, not in engineering terms.

A New Approach to Service Definition

Experiential definition is a little-explored area of marketing practice. A product-based marketer is in danger of assuming he understands an intangible-dominant entity when, in fact, he may only be projecting his *own* subjective version of "reality." And because there is no documented guidance on acquiring service-knowledge, the chances for error are magnified.

Case Example
One short-lived mistake (with which the author is familiar) occurred recently in the trust department of a large commercial bank. The department head, being close to daily operations, understood "investment management" as the combined work of hundreds of people, backed by the firm's stature, resources, and long history. With this "reality" in mind, he concluded that the service could be better represented by professional salesmen, than through the traditional, but interruptive use of the portfolio manager as main client contact.

Three salesmen were hired, and given a training course in investments. They failed dismally; both in maintaining current client relationships and in producing new business for the firm. In hindsight, it became clear that the department head misunderstood the service's "reality" as it was being experienced by his clients. To the clients, "investment *management*" was found to mean "investment *manager*"—i.e., a single human being upon whom they depended for decisions and advice. No matter how well prepared, the professional salesman was not seen as an acceptable substitute by the majority of the market.

Visions of Reality
Clearly, more than one version of "reality" may be found in a service market. Therefore, the crux of service-knowledge is the description of the major *consensus realities* that define the service entity to various market segments. The determination of consensus realities should be a high priority for service marketers, and marketing should offer more concrete guidance and emphasis on this subject than it does.

To define the market-held "realities" of a service requires a high tolerance for subjective, "soft" data, combined with a rigidly objective attitude toward that data. To understand what a service entity is to a market, the marketer must undertake more initial research than is common in product marketing. More important, it will be research of a different kind than is the case in product marketing. The marketer must rely heavily on the tools and skills of psychology, sociology and other behavioral sciences—tools that in product marketing usually come into play in determining *image*, rather than fundamental "reality."

In developing the blueprint of a service entity's main elements, the marketer might find, for instance, that although tax return preparation is analogous to "accurate mathematical computation" within his firm, it means "freedom from responsibility" to one segment of the consuming public, "opportunity for financial savings" to another segment, and "convenience" to yet a third segment.

Unless these "realities" are documented and ranked by market importance, no sensible plan can be devised to represent a service effectively or deliberately. And in *new* service development, the importance of the service-research function is even more critical, because the successful development of a new service—a molecular collection of intangibles—is so difficult it makes new-product development look like child's play.

Image vs. Evidence—The Key

The definition of consensus realities should not be confused with the determination of "images." Image is a method of *differentiating* and *representing* an entity to its target market. Image is not "product;" nor is it "service." As was suggested in Exhibit 1, there appears to be a critical difference between the way tangible- and intangible-dominant entities are best represented to their markets. Examination of actual cases suggests a common thread among effective representations of services that is another mirror-opposite contrast to product techniques.

In comparing examples, it is clear that consumer product marketing often approaches the market by enhancing a physical object through abstract associations. *Coca-Cola*, for example, is surrounded with visual, verbal and aural associations with authenticity and youth. Although *Dr. Pepper* would also be physically categorized as a beverage, its *image* has been structured to suggest "originality" and "risk-taking;" while *7-up* is "light" and "buoyant." A high priority is placed on linking these abstract images to physical items.

But a service is already abstract. To compound the abstraction dilutes the "reality" that the marketer is trying to enhance. Effective service representations appear to be turned 180° *away* from abstraction. The reason for this is that service images, and even service "realities," appear to be shaped to a large extent by the things that the consumer can comprehend with his five senses—tangible things. But a service itself cannot be tangible, so reliance must be placed on peripheral clues.

Tangible clues are what allow the detective in a mystery novel to surmise events at the scene of a crime without having been present. Similarly, when a consumer attempts to judge a service, particularly before using or buying it, that service is "known" by the tangible clues, the tangible evidence, that surround it.

The management of tangible evidence is not articulated in marketing as a primary priority for service marketers. There has been little in-depth exploration of the *range* of authority that emphasis on tangible evidence would create for the service marketer. In product marketing, tangible evidence is primarily the product itself. But for services, tangible evidence would encompass broader considerations in contrast to product marketing, *different* considerations than are typically considered marketing's domain today.

Focusing on the Evidence

In *product* marketing, many kinds of evidence are beyond the marketer's control and are consequently omitted from priority consideration in the market positioning process. Product marketing tends to give first emphasis to creating *abstract* associations.

Service marketers, on the other hand, should be focused on enhancing and differentiating "realities" through manipulation of *tangible* clues. The management of evidence comes first for service marketers, because service "reality" is arrived at by the consumer mostly through a process of deduction, based on the total impression that the evidence creates. Because of product marketing's biases, service marketers often fail to recognize the unique forms of evidence that they *can* normally control and fail to see that they should be part of marketing's responsibilities.

Management of the Environment

Environment is a good example. Since product distribution normally means shipping to outside agents, the marketer has little voice in structuring the environment in which the product is sold. His major controllable impact on the environment is usually product packaging. Services, on the other hand, are often fully integrated with environment; that is, the setting in which the service is "distributed" *is* controllable. To the extent possible, management of the physical environment should be one of a service marketer's highest priorities.

Setting can play an enormous role in influencing the "reality" of a service in the consumer's mind. Marketing does not emphasize this rule for services, yet there are numerous obvious examples of its importance.

Physicians' offices provide an interesting example of intuitive environmental management. Although the quality of medical service may be identical, an office furnished in teak and leather creates a totally different "reality" in the consumer's mind from one with plastic slipcovers and inexpensive prints. Carrying the example further, a marketer could expect to cause change in the service's image simply by painting a physician's office walls neon pink or silver, instead of white.

Similarly, although the services may be identical, the consumer's differentiation between "Bank A Service" and "Bank B Service" is materially affected by whether the environment is dominated by butcher-block and bright colors or by marble and polished brass.

By understanding the importance of evidence management, the service marketer can make it his business to review and take control of this critical part of his "mix." Creation of environment can be deliberate, rather than accidental or as a result of leaving such decisions in the hands of the interior decorators.

Exhibit 3   Principles of Market Positioning Emphasis

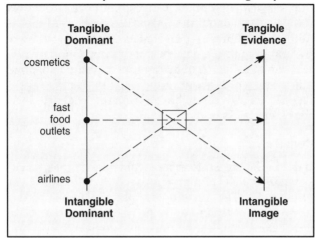

Integrating Evidence

Going beyond environment, evidence can be integrated across a wide range of items. Airlines, for example, manage and coordinate tangible evidence, and do it better than almost any large service industry. Whether by intuition or design, airlines do *not* focus attention on trying to explain or characterize the service itself. One never sees an ad that attempts to convey "the slant of takeoff," "the feel of acceleration," or "the aerodynamics of lift." Airline transport is given shape and form through consistency of a firm's identification, its uniforms, the decor of its planes, its graphics, and its advertising. Differentiation among airlines, though they all provide the same service, is a direct result of differences in "packages" of evidence.

Some businesses in which tangible and intangible elements carry equal weight emphasize abstractions and evidence in about equal proportions. McDonald's is an excellent example. The food *product* is associated with "nutritious" (two all-beef, etc.), "fun" (Ronald McDonald) and "helpful" ("We Do it All for You," "You Deserve a Break Today"). The main *service* element, i.e., fast food preparation, is tangibly distinguished by uniformity of environment, color, and style of graphics and apparel, consistency of delivery (young employee), and the ubiquitous golden arches.

Using the scale developed in Exhibit 2, this concept can be postulated as a principle for service representation. As shown in Exhibit 3, once an entity has been analyzed and positioned on the scale, the degree to which the marketer will focus on either tangible evidence of intangible abstractions for market positioning will be found to be inversely related to the entity's dominance.

The more intangible elements there are, the more the marketer must endeavor to stand in the consumer's shoes, thinking through and gaining control of *all* the inputs to the consumer's mind that can be classified as material evidence.

Some forms of evidence can seem trivial until one recognizes how great their impact can be on service perception. Correspondence is one example. Letters, statements, and the like are sometimes the main conveyers of the "reality" of a service to its market; yet often these are treated as peripheral to any marketing plan. From the grade of paper to the choice of colors, correspondence is visible evidence that conveys a unique message. A mimeographed, non-personalized, cheaply offset letter contradicts any words about service quality that may appear in the text of that letter. Conversely, engraved parchment from the local dry cleaner might make one wonder about their prices.

Profile as Evidence

As was pointed out in the investment management example, services are often inextricably entwined with their human representatives. In many fields, a person is perceived to *be* the service. The consumer cannot distinguish between them. Product marketing is myopic in dealing with the issue of *people as evidence* in terms of market positioning. Consumer marketing often stops at the production of materials and programs for salesmen to use. Some service industries, on the other hand, have long intuitively managed human evidence to larger ends.

Examples of this principle have been the basis for jokes, plays, and literature. "The Man in the Grey Flannel Suit," for example, was a synonym for the advertising business for many years. Physicians are uniformly "packaged" in smocks. Lawyers and bankers are still today known for pin-stripes and vests. IBM representatives were famous for adhering to a "White Shirt" policy. Going beyond apparel, as mentioned earlier, McDonald's even achieves age uniformity—an extra element reinforcing its total market image.

These examples add up to a serious principle when thoughtfully reviewed. They are particularly instructive for service marketers. None of the above examples were the result of deliberate market planning. McDonald's, for instance, backed into age consistency as a result of trying to keep labor costs low. Airlines are the single outstanding example of consciously-planned standards for uniformity in human representation. The power of the human evidence principle is obvious, and the potential power of more deliberately controlling or structuring this element is clear.

Lest this discussion be interpreted as an advocacy of regimentation, it should be pointed out that management of human evidence can be as basic as providing nametags to service representative or as complex as the "packaging" of a political candidate, whose very words are often chosen by committee and whose hair style can become a critical policy issue. Or, depending upon what kind of service "reality" the marketer wishes to create, human representation can be encouraged to display *non*-conformity, as is the case with the "creative" departments of advertising agencies. The point is that service marketers should be charged with tactics and strategy in this area, and must consider it a management responsibility.

Services and the Media

As has been previously discussed, service elements are abstract. Because they are abstract, the marketer must work hard at making them "real," by building a case from tangible evidence. In this context, media advertising presents a particularly difficult problem.

The problem revolves around the fact that media (television, radio, print) are one step removed from tangibility. Media, by its McLuhanesque nature, abstracts the physical.

Even though product tangibility provides an anchor for media representation because a product can be *shown*, media still abstract products. A photograph is only a two-dimensional version of a physical object, and may be visually misleading. Fortunately, the consumer makes the mental connection between seeing a product in the media and recognizing it in reality. This is true even when a product is substantially distorted. Sometimes, only part of a product is shown. Occasionally, as in recent commercials for *7-up*, the product is *not* shown. However, the consumer remembers past experience. He has little difficulty recognizing *7-up* by name or remembered appearance when he sees it or wants to buy it.

Thus, media work *with* the creation of product image and *help* in adding abstract qualities to tangible goods. Cosmetics, for example are often positioned in association with an airbrushed or soft-focus filmed *ideal* of beauty. Were the media truly accurate, the wrinkles and flaws of the flesh, to which even models are heir, might not create such an appealing product association.

Making Services More Concrete

Because of their abstracting capabilities, the media often make service entities more hazy, instead of more concrete, and the service marketer must work *against* this inherent effect. Unfortunately, many marketers are so familiar with product-oriented thinking that they go down precisely the wrong path and attempt to represent services by dealing with them in abstractions.

The pages of the business press are filled with examples of this type of misconception in services advertising. In advertisements for investment management, for instance, the worst examples attempt to describe the already intangible service with *more* abstractions such as "sound analysis," "careful portfolio monitoring," "strong research capability," etc. Such compounded abstractions do *not* help the consumer form a "reality," do *not* differentiate the service and do *not* achieve any credibility, much less any customer "draw."

The best examples are those which attempt to associate the service with some form of tangible evidence, working against the media's abstracting qualities. Merrill Lynch, for instance, has firmly associated itself with a clear visual symbol of bulls and concomitant bullishness. Where Merrill Lynch does not use the visual herd, it uses photographs of tangible physical booklets, and invites the consumer to write for them.

Therefore, the final principle offered for service marketers would hold that effective media representation of intangibles is a function of establishing non-abstract manifestations of them.

Conclusion

This article has presented several market-inspired thoughts toward the development of new marketing concepts, and the evolution of relevant service marketing principles. The hypotheses presented here do not by any means represent an exhaustive analysis of the subject. No exploration was done, for example, on product vs. service pricing or product vs. service distribution. Both areas offer rich potential for creative new approaches and analysis.

It can be argued that there are many grey areas in the molecular entity concept, and that diagramming and managing according to the multiple-elements schema could present considerable difficulties by virtue of its greater complexity. It might also be argued that some distinctions between tangible- and intangible-dominant entities are so subtle as to be unimportant.

The fact remains that service marketers are in urgent need of concepts and priorities that are relevant to their actual experience and needs, and that marketing has failed in evolving to meet that demand. However unorthodox, continuing exploration of this area must be encouraged if marketing is to achieve stature and influence in the new post-Industrial Revolution services economy.

Supplemental Reading Notes

1. See, for example E. Jerome McCarthy, *Basic Marketing: A Managerial Approach*, 4th ed. (Homewood IL: Richard D. Irwin, 1971), p. 303 compared to William J. Stanton, *Fundamentals of Marketing*, 3rd ed. (New York: McGraw-Hill, 1971), p. 567.

2. See William R. George and Hiram C. Barksdale, "Marketing Activities in the Service Industries," *Journal of Marketing*, Vol. 38, No. 4 (October 1974), pp. 65–70.

3. *The Meaning and Sources of Marketing Theory*—Marketing Science Institute Series (New York: McGraw-Hill, 1965), p. 88.

4. *Webster's New Collegiate Dictionary* (Springfield, MA: G. & C. Merriam Company, 1974).

5. Philip Kotler, "A Generic Concept of Marketing," *Journal of Marketing*, Vol. 36, No. 2 (April 1972), pp. 46–54.

6. Theodore H. Levitt, "Marketing Myopia," *Harvard Business Review*, Vol. 38 (July–August 1960), pp. 45–46.

7. Aubrey Wilson, *The Marketing of Professional Services* (New York: McGraw-Hill, 1972), p. 8.

Comparing Marketing Management in Package Goods and Service Organizations

by Gary Knisely

> *After four decades of experience that have firmly established the marketing discipline in the consumer package goods industry, experienced marketers are invading the consumer service industry, bringing with them a new set of skills developed through trial, error, and refinement. How successful will they be? What*

is the likelihood of marketing altering the service sector as fundamentally as it has the consumer products industry?

The answers to these and other questions can perhaps best be given by managers who have served successfully in senior marketing positions in both consumer-package goods and consumer service organizations.

Greater Marketing Emphasis by Holiday Inn Breaks Mold

The interview is with James L. Schorr, then executive vice president-marketing, Holiday Inns Inc. Mr. Schorr previously held positions in account management with Ogilvy & Mather and in brand management with Procter & Gamble. Prior to joining Holiday Inns in 1975, he served in a succession of senior marketing positions with the U.S. Postal Service and as a special consultant to the President of the United States on energy communications. Mr. Schorr's responsibilities at the time of the interview included planning, product development, sales, advertising and promotion activities of the Holiday Inn system of hotels throughout the world.

Knisely: You've marketed soap, postal services, and now hotel rooms. What's the difference between what you were doing five years ago and now, in terms of managing the marketing process?

Schorr: Essentially what I did at Procter & Gamble (or with General Foods when they were my client) and at the Postal Service and here was that in each instance I simply used what we call marketing tools to persuade somebody to do something that I wanted them to do. Whether it's to purchase a service or purchase a product, there really isn't as much difference as a lot of people think—tactically, yes; but not strategically.

Knisely: Convincing me to stay at a Holiday Inn seems more complex than getting me to choose one brand of soap or another. It's a more complex decision from my standpoint, if for nothing more than there are more actions involved in it.

Schorr: Well, I suppose a major difference between product marketing and service marketing is that we can't control the quality of our product as well as a P&G control engineer on a production line can control the quality of his product. When you buy a box of Tide, you can reasonably be 99 and 44/100% sure that this stuff will work to get your clothes clean. When you buy a Holiday Inn room, you're sure at some lesser percentage that it will work to give you a good night's sleep without any hassle, or people banging on the walls and all the bad things that can happen to you in a hotel.

Holiday Inns really brought the brand name into the hotel business. Back in the 50s, the only brand name in the business was Hilton with a lot of downtown aging properties. Today, Holiday Inns is 10 times bigger than the Hilton chain. We brought the brand name concept to the business by providing a uniformity of experience and certain standards which the customer can depend on.

But that's still a far cry below the level of quality control that manufacturers can put on their products.

Knisely: How do you define a "service" business *vis a vis* a "product" business?

Schorr: Simply defined, in our terms, a product is something a consumer purchases and takes with him or consumes, or otherwise uses. If it is not physical, not something that they can take away or consume, then we call it a service.

Knisely: What about a McDonald's, where most people say it's the fast-foods *service* business?

Schorr: I don't agree with that. I think McDonald's sells products. They sell french fries and hamburgers—products. They're also selling the service with which they provide those products, but very few people go to McDonald's for service.

Knisely: Let's talk about the room part of the business. When you think of what somebody is buying, what are those elements you think of?

Selling an Experience

Schorr: What I am really selling, in terms of what people are buying, is a hotel experience. I'm selling the room, the way they treat you at the front desk, the way the bellman treats you, the way the waitress treats you—it's all mixed together in a consumer's mind when he makes a hotel decision. I could go out and convince everybody in the world that I had the world's most superior rooms and it probably wouldn't have much impact on my business, even though that's obviously the most important thing I've got. My sale is much more a service sale and much more a people-on-people sale.

Knisely: How do you sell people-on-people? Are advertising and some of the standard marketing tactics of selling a package goods product as applicable to this business as they are to P&G or General Foods?

Schorr: No. Such tactics are not as directly efficient for us as for somebody who can control the quality of their product or service better than we can. Half of our efforts are in product development, which is part of the marketing organization here. Very unusual. Even in a sophisticated company like P&G, product development is not part of the marketing operation.

I am famous here for what's called the Bucket Theory of Marketing in the service business. I say you've got to think of marketing as a big bucket. It's what the sales programs, the advertising programs, and other programs do that shovels business into the top of that bucket. When the bucket's full, that's 100% occupancy. And we keep building new programs and accelerating existing programs to shovel more and more business into that bucket.

There's only one problem. There's a hole in the bottom of the bucket. When we run our business really well, when we control the quality of our product, then the hole is very small and the business falls out much more slowly than I throw it in at the top.

But when we run weak operations, when our experience, our people contact, our systems, or our rooms degrade or deteriorate, then that hole gets bigger. When I'm in a period of declining occupancy, what's happening is I'm losing them out of the bottom of that bucket faster than I can bring in new ones at the top. Those two functions—product quality and selling—*that* is marketing.

Knisely: Give me some examples of the kinds of things that bucket theory gets you involved in.

Schorr: Take our rules of operation, which every Holiday Inn has to follow if they want to have the sign out front and if they want to have a Holidex machine at the front desk, which fills up half the rooms every night before they do anything. We'll unplug the sign, we'll unplug the Holidex machine, if they don't live by our rules of operation.

It used to be those rules were written by people who would define standards in technical terms. There was almost no consumer orientation in our rules. Our rules now are very consumer oriented. In another six months to nine months, they will be totally consumerized in terms of setting priorities for the inns on what the most important things are and what they must do.

We run test inns here, where we try a number of new programs. The customers at those inns don't know they're in the test inns, but they are guinea pigs for things so we can work out operational glitches and also screen things that people really didn't like before we expand nationally.

Difficult to Test

Knisely: Is market research more difficult in this business than when you're selling a product in a box?

Schorr: Much more difficult. Also much more rewarding. No one else does much of it in the industry but us. You have most competitors flying by the seat of their pants. We are taking the techniques that have been developed in the package goods industry and then putting those techniques to work in this industry.

Knisely: Do you have to fiddle with them to make them work here?

Schorr: Invariably. Things that are applicable to the package goods business are only somewhat applicable here.

The best example would be something we run called "travel audit." That would be this industry's version of a Nielsen, except that only Holiday Inns has it.

Knisely: What about more attitudinal marketing research—qualitative? Are you looking at demographics and psychographics?

Schorr: We don't do much qualitative research. Most of it is quantitative, even the attitudinal research.

We do something annually here that basically splits our market down into whether or not people are traveling to a property as a destination or as an overnight pit stop. Then that splits out by business versus leisure travel. Then we go into the usage of hotel chains by these categories and the attitudinal reasons why. It's very similar to national brand usage studies conducted by a major package goods company.

Knisely: What about the functional linkages? In the classic package goods terms, there are certain relationships between manufacturing, R&D, distribution, etc. What about your linkages?

Schorr: What do you mean by linkages?

Knisely: Who reports to whom—who calls the shots—who has the real power. In the soap business, marketing tells manufacturing, "We want it to be white with blue dots; it should smell a certain way with a certain package"—and it comes out that way. In many of the service businesses, banking particularly, it is operations that calls the shots.

Closely Linked

Schorr: In a service business, marketing and operations are more closely linked than they are in a manufacturing business. My eye is on the same target as the eye of the guy who runs operations. As a result, we tend to walk hand-in-hand.

There's an awareness in the company about marketing. Marketing is not subservient to operations and neither is operations subservient to marketing. If there is a conflict, theoretically the president of the company resolves it.

In the structure of this corporation, there tends not to be the conflicts between operations and marketing. I may go into operations, for example, and say, "Hey, listen, I've got this idea on something we ought to do." His response to me may be, "Sounds nifty, but it would be a nightmare if I did that." My response is, "I know it would be a nightmare, but let's see if we can figure out a way to do it. Put it in our test inns and we'll see if everybody stumbles over themselves and what the customer thinks of it, and what he's going to pay for it."

That's a very easy way to work things out, so you quickly find out first of all if it is a good marketing idea, and secondly if it is an operational infeasibility—it just can't be done.

Knisely: You've worked in two organizations now where you've had to recruit a lot of people from the package goods industry. Did you find that there are certain mind sets that might have come along that make it difficult for them to adapt to this way of thinking? Were there certain surprises that hit a lot of people that they just never thought about?

Schorr: That's the best question you've asked. There definitely are certain kinds of people who should never make the move. There are some that certainly could make it, and should. After all, the service industries are the growth sectors of the U.S. economy.

The biggest difference is that—let's go back to package goods companies. There are essentially two kinds of people. There is the kind who gets his marketing plan from last year, who gets an assignment to ship 8% more cases next year and who develops the marketing plan to do that. And that's a certain mind set that functions very well inside of P&G. That person should probably never leave the package goods industry.

On the other hand, there is a kind of person who is somewhat more pioneering, a person who wants to take those skills that heretofore have not been applied to that industry and to see something dramatic happen, more dramatic than 8%.

They're Pioneers

I think every one of the persons [from package goods] we attracted to Washington when I was there [and now here at Holiday Inns] really comes because his mind set is a little more pioneering, more innovative, more of "I don't want to do that same thing for the next 30 years of my life," and "I want to have a little more fun" and "innovate a little more," to be a builder of things at least as much as a manager.

Knisely: What's the most important skill that ought to be brought from the package goods industry?

Schorr: The most important skill is the creativity and the judgment involved in the ability to recognize when something will be persuasive to people. Successful marketing people, no matter what industry they're in, are people who have a mix of skills that enable them to identify when something will be persuasive to people and who will be able to persuade them to do something.

If you have that skill, then what the package goods industry has done is to identify some 87 media through which you can execute. A guy simply brings a knowledge of "continuity promotions" versus "trial promotions" versus "repurchase promotion" versus "trial incentive" versus "discounts." He's learned all these categories and learned all the different ways to do it and they are all very valuable. I think they apply equally in both industries.

But the successful guys would have the persuasion skills and be able to succeed in either.

Knisely: Are there more surprises here than in package goods?

Schorr: Yes. One of the things I've learned is the difference between our kinds of businesses—tactical, not strategic, but it makes a big difference.

In the process of learning differences about the hotel business, there have been a lot of surprises. I came in believing the classical marketing tactics and I've learned that only about half of the so-called classical beliefs are immutable truths. For example, I was taught by Procter that in marketing you fish where the fish are: In periods of high consumption, that's when you advertise the most.

Well, that's ridiculous in this industry. For example, in periods of high consumption, I'm full. I don't have any rooms to sell. This is not the time that I want to spend all my marketing money. Yet, classical theory would have me spend 40% of my marketing effort in that three-month period to stimulate that activity; I have a capacity problem, so I don't spend any of my marketing funds during that period of time.

There have been, I suppose, a dozen little surprises like that where you just can't operate out of rote. It means a little more open mindedness, a little less moving by rote.

Knisely: Is part of it that you just don't have all the data available that you had at P&G?

Schorr: We have, in the last three years, generated more base data in terms of consumer aspects of the lodging market than P&G possesses in the soap business and the consumer aspects of the soap market. It has to, because as you said earlier, our customer has a more complex purchasing decision.

Can't Transplant P&G

It's not the possession of the data or the rote application of the data. Most of the guys that I've seen come out of P&G who failed someplace else and just really died in the service industry were guys who tried to reinvent P&G wherever they went. The classic way failed. It is not reinventable. P&G has *evolved* to where it is. You cannot walk into any company—I don't care if it's General Foods—and plant your P&G system. It will never work. It took years and years and generations and a lot of personnel and manpower, fine tuning, and training to get where they are.

Lesser Role

So a guy has to be able to go in without the crutches of a P&G media staff department, P&G promotional development staff department, where he was almost unable to fail; he has to be able to throw those crutches away and be willing to operate without that kind of staff support.

There's one other big difference. In service industries, people aren't oriented to the marketing concept; marketing is not as important in the service industry as in the package goods industry. Most organization charts of the service industry show the head of marketing is not the equal of the head of operations; he just doesn't have as much horsepower.

There are several service companies—Holiday Inns is, I think, foremost—which are organized to pay real attention to marketing and to innovate multi-million-dollar annual investments and manpower and staff. They bring in the best marketing people they can find to help them.

I won't say to you that marketing has the acceptance as it has at P&G, but I would say at Holiday Inns that it's maybe 80% of the way there. My image of the service industry, in general, is that it's somewhere around 20% of the way there. But there are service companies that are breaking out of the traditional operations mold and becoming much more marketing oriented.

REVIEW QUIZ

When you feel you have covered all of the material in this chapter, answer these questions. Choose the *best* answer. Check your answers with the correct ones found on the Review Quiz Answer Key at the end of this book.

True (T) or False (F)

T (F) 1. The product marketing techniques developed by manufacturing industries can be easily applied by service industries.

T (F) 2. Marketing-minded hoteliers recognize that they are mainly in the business of selling tangible products such as clean beds and good food.

(T) F 3. Most products and services are actually combinations of tangible and intangible elements.

(T) F 4. The intangible elements of service are just as important as the tangible elements that the guest experiences while staying at a hotel or motel.

(T) F 5. Tangible clues to intangible aspects of service are marketing tools by which to position the products and services offered by a lodging operation.

T (F) 6. Positioning is a marketing term that is used to describe how marketing directors perceive the products and services offered by their hotels.

(T) F 7. Positioning strategies attempt to establish in the minds of consumers a particular image of a lodging property's products and services.

(T) F 8. Customers may perceive greater risks when purchasing services than when purchasing manufactured products.

(T) F 9. One of the most effective strategies which hotels can adopt to reduce consumer perceptions of risk is to satisfy the needs of customers their hotels presently attract.

(T) F 10. The way in which services are delivered may be considered just as much a part of the hospitality "product" as clean guestrooms in the hotel and satisfying meals in the dining room.

T (F) 11. Controlling service variability is a relatively unimportant task for service industries.

(T) F 12. Standards make quality possible for an organization, but only the people within the organization can make quality a reality.

T (F) 13. The occupancy percentage for a lodging operation is calculated by dividing the number of rooms available for sale by the number of rooms sold.

T (F) 14. One of the most effective techniques by which to balance supply and demand in hotels is to effectively manage inventory levels.

T (F) 15. Widespread price-cutting during the 1981–82 recession was an effective strategy by which to stop the decline in occupancy percentages.

Multiple Choice

16.   Which of the following is an example of cultivating non-peak demand?

    a.   a transient hotel lowering room rates during weekdays
    b.   a ski resort offering golfing and hiking facilities during the summer
    c.   a resort organizing fashion shows by the pool to relieve overcrowded facilities
    d.   none of the above

17.   Which of the following is *not* a strategy by which to adjust demand to supply?

    a.   differential pricing
    b.   hiring part-time employees
    c.   developing supplemental services
    d.   cultivating non-peak demand

18.   Which of the following is *not* a strategy by which to adjust supply to demand?

    a.   hiring part-time employees
    b.   maximizing efficiency
    c.   price cutting
    d.   increasing consumer participation

19.   Which of the following best illustrates the difference between service marketing and produce marketing?

    a.   the more sophisticated marketing techniques developed by service industries
    b.   the higher level of risk which consumers perceive when purchasing services as opposed to purchasing products
    c.   the greater variety of services
    d.   the greater variety of products

20.   Reducing room rates may have a major impact on which of the following types of lodging operations?

    a.   commercial hotels
    b.   resorts
    c.   economy motels
    d.   none of the above

Part II
Strategic Marketing

This section explores the kind of planning and analyses necessary for effective strategic marketing. Chapter 3 defines strategic marketing planning and discusses its various stages. The chapter traces the process from the formation of a mission statement, through the development of objectives, strategies, and tactics, to the actual implementation of the plan. Practical concerns in developing marketing strategies are addressed in the supplemental reading at the end of this chapter. From this point, the section turns to an examination of the broad kinds of analyses that form the foundation for strategic marketing planning. Chapter 4 deals with the analysis of threats and opportunities in the business environment which may affect the strategies of marketing plans. Chapter 5 focuses on the analysis of the lodging industry and illustrates how understanding an industry's basic structure forms the logical starting point in determining how an operation should compete in the marketplace. Chapter 6 concentrates on the analysis of markets and the techniques of market segmentation which are most useful to hospitality operations.

Chapter Outline

Strategic Planning
The Mission Statement
Objectives, Strategies, Tactics
Implementation of the Strategic Marketing
    Plan
Analyzing the Environment, the
    Competition, and the Markets
        The Environment
        The Competition
        The Markets

Learning Objectives

1. Define strategic marketing planning.

2. State the purpose of a mission statement.

3. Define objectives, strategies, and tactics.

4. Explain the implementation phase of the strategic marketing planning process.

5. Explain what is meant by the terms market share and market expansion.

6. Describe the purpose of market segmentation.

3

Strategic Marketing Planning

FOR MANY YEARS hotels prepared annual financial forecasts which projected potential revenues, costs, and probable profits. Although hotels have used this general business planning cycle, only in the last 20 years or so have their plans been supported by strategic marketing plans. Therefore, until recently, hotels have been committed to achieving a certain level of revenue without specifying how they were to achieve it. The following comment indicates the importance of the strategic planning process to the industry today:

> ❝Days Inns of America, Incorporated, has been and still is in the developing phases. It began as a real estate company back in the early '70s and has evolved into the seventh largest hospitality company domestically. [At first,] the strategic planning process was basically real estate driven and most of the planning was on a short-term, one- or two-year basis. [However,] the size of the company, numbers of properties, spread of locations, and increasing competition have now made ... long-range planning necessary from ... the operating side, [and] more important, from the marketing side.
>
> [Originally, a typical] 120- to 180-room Days Inn could be built and filled because of its location and price positioning. Now other hotel companies have entered the price-conscious market and are starting to eat away at this market segment. [Therefore,] it is now necessary for [us to do] advanced marketing planning, not only to increase our share but to maintain our share. We are currently in the process of developing a five-year strategic plan.❞

—John Russell
Senior Vice President of Marketing
Days Inns of America, Incorporated

Strategic Planning

Today, all hospitality operations, regardless of size, do some planning. The ongoing nature of business requires that management make estimates about what is likely to happen in the future. Based on these estimates, management decides how the business may adjust to future events.

Definitions of strategic planning abound; some are couched in classical military terminology, others in a vague and obscure academic language. However, a simple definition is possible: strategic planning is the managerial process of developing and maintaining an optimal "fit" between the deployment of an organization's resources and the opportunities in its changing environment. This definition makes it clear that strategic planning is much more than a reactive series of incremental adjustments to changing threats and opportunities in the environment. Strategic planning is a proactive effort of managers to anticipate change by establishing objectives and formulating strategies and tactics by which to organize the marketing effort. Investments can then be made to ensure that the hospitality operation does the volume of business necessary to maximize its revenue and profit potential.

Implicit in the notion of strategy is the idea that the company should not sacrifice long-term considerations for short-term profitability. Management theorists attribute many of the ills afflicting the automobile and steel industries to short-term orientations on the part of management where the immediate focus is on building sales volume rather than on engineering quality into the products. The Japanese, who dominate several world markets, operate strategically with a very long time horizon—100 years or longer.

The distinction between efficiency and effectiveness underscores the need for a longer view. Peter Drucker puts it simply, but elegantly: "Efficiency is concerned with doing things right. Effectiveness is doing the right things."[1] In Drucker's view, an eye to efficiency is an operational perspective which aims to improve what is already being done. Effectiveness, on the other hand, is a more encompassing strategic perspective which focuses on what should be done—such as how a company's resources can capitalize on opportunities that will optimize long-run profitability.

Ultimately, businesses that practice strategic planning are in better competitive positions than businesses that simply drift strategically. Changes in the business environment can seriously affect hospitality operations. Therefore, companies should place themselves in active positions by which to influence the business environment and not merely accept passive positions through which they can only react to change as it occurs, or worse, after it has already occurred.

However, strategic planning can be frustrating. The business environment is often difficult to understand and predict. Also, the kind of communication and decisions that strategic planning requires may create strains and resistance within an organization. Furthermore, strategic planning absorbs a valuable organizational resource—management time. For these reasons, some companies may opt for an opportunistic alternative to strategic planning.

Today, major hospitality firms are aggressively opportunistic in the search for profitable business ventures. Yet, some firms neglect strategic planning in favor of evaluating each emerging opportunity on the merits of its individual profitability. On the surface, this approach does seem to have several advantages. For example, the amount of time, resources, and executive talent is far less than that required by a thorough strategic analysis. Objectives and strategies can also be developed that focus within the limited field of the potential opportunity. In addition, by delaying commitment, a company may be able to act on the basis of the best possible information.

Although the opportunistic alternative to strategic planning may seem tempting to many lodging operations, the disadvantages to the approach outweigh the advantages. In the absence of a long-range strategy, there are few rules to guide a search for new opportunities, either inside or outside of the operation. The company must either wait passively for opportunities to arise in the environment, or search for them in a "shotgun" approach. Internally, the business lacks guidelines by which to develop new products and services. Consequently, new acquisitions, and newly developed products or services may lead to haphazard growth and expansion.

Without a strategic foundation, decisions made throughout an organization may lack coherence and internal consistency. This increases the risk of various divisions and departments acting at cross-purposes. For example, the director of marketing could assume that growth will be attained through adding new products or services, while others in the company could assume that growth will best be accomplished by refining existing products and services. Also, the opportunistic approach may cause managers to act on insufficient information and force extreme forms of behavior: conservatives within the organization may refuse to take risks that, given better information, are actually reasonable ventures; the more entrepreneurial managers may wish to plunge into opportunities with little understanding or appreciation of costs or dangers. Also, without a clear strategic vision, morale in the organization may be low because no definite sense of purpose is communicated to staff members and employees.

Clearly, this opportunistic alternative amounts to little more than drifting strategically. In order for today's managers, especially those in the hospitality industry, to adopt the long-range perspective necessary for effective strategic planning, they must be able to step back from the pressures and demands of day-to-day operations. The tendency of managers to focus on daily operating tasks is often reinforced by the limited nature of the information they usually receive. For example, the data made available to hospitality managers by accounting and management information systems often draws attention to problems or inefficiencies; but, for the most part, the data fails to draw attention to opportunities. To overcome the natural tendency toward a short-term operational focus, many hospitality organizations are formally incorporating the strategic planning process into the structure of their operations and forcing their managers to engage in some semblance of long-range thinking.

However, it is not easy to stand back from the immediacies of everyday business activities and develop a long-range strategic plan that defines marketing objectives along with strategies and tactics for achieving them. In order to set the stage for successful strategic marketing planning, a sense of direction must be established by the preparation of a mission statement.

The Mission Statement

❝Our marketing planning process is very strategic. We always start with our mission statement and follow a planning model, not only to the implementation strategy but also to the measurement of results.❞

—**Michael A. Leven**
Former Executive Vice President
Americana Hotels

The first phase of strategic marketing planning is the preparation of a mission statement that defines what the business is and what it is not. Mission statements are also referred to as "business definitions" or "statements of business purpose."

A mission statement answers the most basic questions regarding a company's business activity: What do we do? How do we do it? For whom do we do it? Preparing a mission statement can be a time-consuming task, yet it is essential to the balance of any strategic marketing plan. When a mission statement includes the company's "distinctive competencies" (its particular business strengths or resources), then it often serves as the basis for determining decision rules, or criteria, that guide not only the allocation of present resources but also the direction for future growth.

Mission statements have a variety of uses. They provide a concise statement of the company's current product-market position as well as clear guidelines on where an organization's resources should be applied. A mission statement may also help a hotel to differentiate its products and services from those of competitors and target specific customer groups. Hilton Hotels, for example, identified its primary thrust as the business and meeting group markets. Accordingly, it made a substantial investment in video-conferencing services and equipment.

Also, the mission statement portion of the strategic planning process may serve as a screening mechanism to keep management's attention focused only on those opportunities that clearly mesh with the company's business purpose. The Registry Hotel Corporation, for example, clearly benefits from a strategic planning orientation. According to Charles W. Lanphere, Chairman and President:

> **"**With Registry, we wanted to go after key markets and build both corporate hotels and resort locations near high-income residential areas where there is a substantial amount of outside catering. We also looked for mixed-use developments with high-end corporate growth and regional office space.**"**2

Mission statements give a clear direction to everyone working in the organization. They foster common basic goals, serve as a basis for communication, assert a philosophy for doing business, and provide a basis for evaluating the organization.

The first of the basic elements of a strategic marketing plan is illustrated by the following mission statement, prepared by the Americana Great Gorge Resort:

> **"**The Americana Great Gorge Resort should be positioned as the only hotel in the New York metropolitan area to offer the corporate meeting planner the perfect combination of meeting facilities and relaxed resort environment.
>
> To be successful the hotel must become the dominant corporate meeting resort hotel in the New York area weekdays and a dominant social/association hotel for weekend business. The marketing philosophy will be that of an EP house.... Our major sales and operations focus must be the discovery, booking and satisfaction of the midweek meeting planner.
>
> The Americana Great Gorge Resort and Conference Center is the closest year-round first class convention/resort facility, 55 miles from New York City. The property is within a one-and-one-half hour drive from our major group area, north central New Jersey (from New Brunswick up), Westchester County and Connecticut up to Stamford. The facilities include 617 sleeping rooms and suites, extensive meeting space for all types of meetings, located on 500 rolling acres. The meeting space is of a magnitude that can comfortably accommodate 2 current conventions of 500, or 25 concurrent corporate meetings of 15 to 50 people. The resort is considered to be in good condition to the corporate market and excellent condition to the association and social market segments.
>
> Summer activities include 27 holes of golf designed by Fazio, 4 lighted outdoor tennis courts, 3 indoor tennis courts, horseback riding, jogging, par course,

paddle boats, indoor pool, and outdoor pool. There's also an excellent family amusement park adjacent to our property. The Vernon Valley ski areas are located within 5 minutes of us. They feature 2 main ski areas with night skiing. Our ski business is totally dependent upon group tour business.

> The hotel will have nightly entertainment to satisfy the corporate entertainment needs, supplemented by additional live entertainment to meet the expectations of the business in-house on any night. **"** [3]

In our quotation of the Americana Great Gorge's mission statement, we have excluded some privileged information regarding pricing strategies. Nevertheless, the portion quoted here indicates just how sophisticated this aspect of Americana's planning really is. They do not set about marketing the property until they know exactly who they are, what markets they intend to serve, and what their policies in regard to pricing and mix of business will be. This sophisticated approach is characteristic of most well-marketed hotels today, and for good reason. In order to evaluate all of the proposed action steps in a marketing program, it is absolutely essential to know these facts exactly. Only then can the hotel launch an effective attack.

Objectives, Strategies, Tactics

Once management has prepared a mission statement, it is necessary to develop objectives for the property. Objectives set the performance levels which a business seeks to achieve. A company always pursues a large number of objectives. Among the most common objectives are profitability, sales growth, market-share improvement, risk diversification, and innovation. Some analysts use the term "goals" to describe objectives that are narrowly focused with respect to magnitude and time. To the extent possible, objectives should be specific and quantified. For example, an objective could be stated as: to increase by 15% the volume of business booked through travel agents.

Objectives might be set for a specific change in occupancy level, or an increase in food and beverage revenue levels, or a shift in position with respect to a given market. As you set these objectives, however, it is extremely important to test them against your mission statement to ensure consistency. Only by making sure there is a one-to-one correspondence between the two will you have a cohesive plan in the end. It is clear, for instance, that increases in occupancy at the Americana Great Gorge Resort are consistent with the mission statement as we have presented it. However, it is not as clear that a plan for increasing food and beverage revenues would naturally evolve from that mission statement.

Objectives for a comparable hotel with a similar mission statement (specifying increased occupancy) might be as follows:

1. To increase by 20% the volume of business booked through corporate meeting planners in and around New York City.

2. To reposition the hotel as a neighbor to the central and northern New Jersey business community from Brunswick up and, therefore, as the logical location for its business meetings.

3. To dramatically increase the appeal of the hotel to motor coach tour operators who are handling winter ski tour movements.

4. To attract more regional association conventions, particularly those booked by unpaid meeting planners who tend to represent drive-in conventions more than fly-in conventions.

Clearly, these objectives all flow logically from the mission statement already quoted. Although they are not the actual objectives developed by Americana, they certainly could be, given its mission statement.

Once major objectives have been selected, a whole series of marketing sub-objectives can be derived. These should be stated in hierarchial fashion from the most important to the least important. Also, major objectives should be well-defined and translated into specific objectives for each employee. For example, each regional sales manager can be assigned a sales quota, and each sales quota can be broken down and assigned to individual sales representatives. Unfortunately, many companies fall into the trap of setting too many objectives and sub-objectives. Consequently, few of them receive enough strategic attention or financial support to be successful.

Strategies are statements about what should be done in order to achieve objectives and reach desired goals. For example, it is one thing to have a goal of increasing weekend occupancy by ten percent. But it is quite another thing to determine what has to be done to achieve that ten percent increase. One manager might cut prices to increase occupancy. Another manager might increase services. Yet another manager might rely more on travel agents to create this increase.

Tactics are plans or methods used to implement strategies. The difference between strategies and tactics is really one of scope. In contrast to a tactical decision, a strategic decision is usually more costly in resources and time to reverse or change. Furthermore, while strategies tend to be ongoing in nature, tactics are relatively short-term and flexible. Additionally, there may be several tactics for each broad strategy.

Thus, objectives, strategies, and tactics point the direction for the business organization. Furthermore, they are stated operationally so that they may guide management decisions and actions. Integrating these elements is not a one-time, mechanical process, rather it is a continuously creative process. Various inputs trigger insight. For example, objectives may be modified by the feasibility of strategic alternatives. Strategies, in turn, may be modified by extraordinary events in the environment.

The strategic plan for a property ought to be only as "global" as it needs to be. Rather than containing one "big bang" idea, most successful strategic plans detail a significant number of individual steps, which taken together will make the hotel successful. Broad-based, grandiose plans that fail to outline the specific tasks that must be accomplished are not implementable and are therefore not successful.

Implementation of the Strategic Marketing Plan

Of course, no matter how sound the mission statement or how specific the objectives and strategies may be, the most important aspect of the strategic marketing process is the implementation of the plan.

A significant problem in the implementation phase of market planning arises when strategies are given up too soon. For instance, a young general manager of a large downtown hotel in one of the slower growth regions of the United States instituted a weekend plan. Two weeks later, he called his advertising agency to cancel the program because the volume of business generated during the first weekend did not pay for the ad, and the second weekend saw only a slight improvement in volume. Worse still, this same general manager (who viewed himself as quite a marketer) was hired years later to open a hotel, and eight months prior to its opening still did not have a mission statement. Needless to say, the hotel had a difficult opening and the general manager learned the value of planning well in advance. Strategies simply cannot be worked out overnight.

Wise marketers in the hotel industry know that if a strategy is broad enough and well developed enough to result in needed large-scale changes, its implementation (or the "tactical" phase of the strategy) will be measured in years rather than in days. Therefore, it is important to have strategies to achieve massive, long-term objectives and, at the same time, tactics for meeting rather limited, short-term objectives. Strategies remain relatively constant over time while tactics are quite flexible. It is important not to confuse the two.

One of the dangers of strategic planning in any industry is the tendency for the manager to hold to his or her own particular plan to the exclusion of all other possibilities. While the successful manager's pride of authorship is understandable, there are times when even a successful strategy must be altered and a property's priorities rearranged. For instance, the strategy may have worked as well as anticipated in the past but now the need may have increased. On the other hand, the strategy may be working but achieving less success than anticipated.

For example, a hotel may be using perfectly adequate tactics to achieve the objective of developing business from the national association market. However, this objective and the tactics which correspond to it constitute only one part of an overall plan. It may turn out that another market segment, which management projected to be strong, is delivering less business than originally anticipated. In this case, the hotel would need to do even more business in the convention market to offset shortfalls elsewhere, and the successful convention component of the strategy would need to be revised.

Finally, a strategy may have outlasted its useful life. Some hotels that do an excellent job of developing a mission statement, projecting a strategic plan, and implementing it, make the mistake of staying with their program long after it can reasonably be expected to succeed. Hotels that are "stuck in a rut" may find that their strategies are working against rather than contributing to their continued success.

Analyzing the Environment, the Competition, and the Markets

Strategic marketing planning is a dynamic and ongoing process of analyzing the ever-changing marketing environment in which hospitality organizations function. Economic conditions within the business environment change, as do competitive conditions within the hospitality industry and the needs and wants of customers. Transitions in these and other forces create new opportunities for alert hospitality managers. Changes can also create threats which, if not countered, could endanger the profitability and perhaps even the survival of hospitality properties.

The Environment

An important consideration in any analysis of the business environment revolves around the concepts of market share and market expansion. Many hoteliers see the market for guestrooms, restaurants, and banquet facilities as finite. According to this view, since there is only a limited amount of business available, a hotel's marketing efforts must be directed toward increasing its share by taking business away from its local competitors. To put it another way, this school of business thought likens the total business available to a pie which can be cut in many different ways. A hotel succeeds only by enlarging its piece of the pie while pieces cut for other properties become correspondingly smaller. Therefore, growth is always at the expense of competitors.

Although a market share philosophy is widespread and popular, there are times when marketing approaches which violate this view are entirely valid. For example, holidays are historically slow periods for hotels, but there are a few organizations that do meet during holidays. For instance, in the northeast United States there are a number of temple youth groups that meet over the Christmas holidays. Either a hotel has one of these rare and valuable holiday meetings or it is empty like the others. If a hotel is fortunate enough to book a convention at Christmastime, it will have virtually *all* the business in town over that period, not just a better share. Therefore, hotel marketers can rest assured that any effort they make to capture a convention during such down times is worthwhile, because if they don't get the business, their hotels will probably be empty.

On the other hand, the concept of market share is not adequate to today's needs when applied to prime business times. Instead of dividing up a limited pie, hoteliers need to expand the pie. The theory of market expansion deals with creating whole new sources of business. Market expansion involves stimulating more travel to a given area. Naturally, the hotel that does the best job of attracting new sources of business will be the primary beneficiary; but if the market expansion is very successful, the entire destination will probably benefit.

The phrase "soft-spot marketing" refers to all types of sales stimulation with the objective of market expansion. Sometimes several hotels can work together to build traffic to their destination. For example, hotels in Vail, Colorado, have done weekend promotions in the summer and fall, which are off-seasons, with excellent results. Most good hotels have market expansion at the root of their marketing plans. However, successful expansion into new markets often depends on a new sensitivity on the part of hotel marketers to such environmental conditions as government legislation, economic trends, and more.

The Competition

Like all other businesses, properties in the hospitality industry operate in a competitive environment. They compete with properties across the street, down the block, or across town. They compete with properties in other cities, and sometimes with properties in other countries. However, in examining their situation in relation to the competition, many hotel managers view the other hotels in the area as the only competition for the consumer dollar. Yet if you look beyond competition within the industry, you may soon realize that many other spending alternatives are available to potential customers. Other businesses offering different diversions are reaching out to the same markets as hospitality operations and probably with some degree of success. Let us consider some of the other attractions competing for the same categories of customers, or market segments, as are lodging properties.

The social/recreational guest who might use a hotel as an escape from the pressures of work has a whole variety of ways to spend disposable income. In this case, hotels are competing for the same dollar that the guest might use for theater tickets, for fine dining at a restaurant outside the hotel, for electronic home entertainment equipment such as videocassette recorders and players, or even for household improvements. In attracting this market, the task is to convince the guest that there will be more "psychic income" or psychological benefit (relaxation, escape from work pressures, enjoyment) from visiting the hotel than from spending the money on these other diversions. Here the marketing approach relies heavily on the imagery you are able to create in the prospect's mind. Of course, the hotel operation will be challenged to deliver what was promised. If the hotel experience does not live up to the image provided, then the guest will not feel that sufficient dollar value has been received for the dollars expended. Of all the market segments hotels attempt to attract, the social/recreational guest is the most fragile and among the most vocal. Therefore, if a lodging operation hopes to improve its performance in the social/recreational segment of the market, it is imperative that the operation be prepared to invest the monies in the operation that will allow the hotel to live up to its claims.

Suppose a hotel wants to increase its convention bookings. In this case, the buyer also has alternatives on which to spend the convention sponsor's dollar. Today, the meeting planner can choose to run a teleconference at a variety of sites instead of hosting a major convention in one location as has been done in the past. But even if the decision is made to hold a traditional annual convention, the audience can choose either to attend or to skip this year's meeting, depending on how attractive the destination and the particular property seem to be. Obviously, today's hotel marketer cannot afford to consider any market segment as a constant.

Similarly, it is very important that, once a property has sold a piece of convention business, the customer is provided with continual reinforcement of the decision. Otherwise, a common phenomenon known as cognitive dissonance may result in cancellation of the purchase agreement. Without reinforcement, the buyer who is responsible for wisely spending a large sum of money can lose faith in the decision he or she has made. After the doubt sets in, the buyer may begin considering alternative decisions and the hotel can end up losing the business it was counting on.

Some hotels have established programs for ongoing, after-decision marketing to the convention-attending public. For example, the Sheraton Washington Hotel, in concert with the Greater Washington Convention and Visitors Bureau, provides a steady stream of materials and information to members of associations that have booked meetings with the property. Exhibit 1 illustrates the newsletters direct-mailed by the Sheraton Washington. Furthermore, whenever an occupancy period

Exhibit 1   The Sheraton Washington's Direct Mail Newsletters

Courtesy of the Sheraton Washington Hotel, Washington, D.C.

appears to be in jeopardy, the hotel helps to underwrite the cost of mailings by associations that are already booked for the occupancy period in danger. This excellent program is being used in many other hotels as well.

Another market segment important to many properties in the lodging industry is the business traveler. Again, there are many distractions to prevent this customer from staying at a lodging facility. When deciding whether or not to make a business trip, the businessperson can opt to conduct a teleconference, send a videotape, or make a phone call instead of traveling. On the other hand, the business traveler may commute to a destination and return on the same day. The task of the hotel marketer is to convince the business traveler that staying at the facility over the dates in question will make the business trip to that area more successful than not staying there. Of course, hotels accomplish this task in a variety of ways.

The economy properties, for example, tell business travelers that their stay will be pleasant, make them feel well rested, cost very little, and add to the value of the trip. Some of the more luxurious properties have accustomed the modern business traveler to in-room amenities, such as special soaps, lotions, and shampoos. Some also invite their frequent guests to special receptions to make business travel more appealing. All these extras have created a buyer who is no longer shy about asking what the hotel is going to do, over and above the ordinary, to attract him or her to the property.

All of these competitive factors must be considered when determining the appropriateness of a hotel's marketing effort. Competition within the hospitality industry is also extremely important.

The Markets

Market analysis is the central focus of strategic marketing planning. Markets consist of people. As hospitality organizations go about the business of serving people, they quickly find that they cannot satisfy the wants and needs of every individual. Therefore, each property should identify what it considers to be the most attractive portion of the market and attempt to provide the products and services that will satisfy the needs and wants of homogeneous groups of people. Each homogeneous group is a distinct market segment and becomes a target market when a property chooses to direct its marketing effort toward that segment.

The purpose of market segmentation is to analyze demand. Consumers with similar needs and wants are grouped together for the purpose of better focusing on and serving that market segment. How a market becomes portioned into segments will depend upon specific characteristics of each particular hospitality operation. For example, the marketing department of a downtown commercial hotel may segment the business travel market into more portions than the marketing department of a rural resort hotel. Similarly, the rural resort hotel may segment the pleasure/personal travel market into more portions than the downtown commercial hotel.

The idea behind market segmentation is that the market for a particular product or service is really made up of groups of consumers with distinctive needs and preferences. These groups are segments of the market. While demographic characteristics such as age, income, gender, and level of education are the most commonly used criteria for segmenting a market, other criteria may prove useful to many hospitality operations. Once the market segments have been identified and profiles have been drawn up, it is necessary to select which segment(s) the hospitality property will seek to attract and serve. The segment(s) selected become the target market for the property's marketing efforts.

Whatever the competitive arena in which hospitality properties function, all hospitality operations have at least three things in common. They all try to develop new sources of business, create a core of repeat business, and make a profit. Strategic marketing planning is an efficient and effective method by which to accomplish these objectives. Effective strategic marketing planning demands that hotel marketers know everything about the environment in which their businesses operate, the competitive structure of the hospitality industry, and the markets which their businesses intend to select as the targets for their properties' marketing efforts.

Endnotes

1. Peter F. Drucker, *Management: Tasks, Responsibilities, Practices* (New York: Harper & Row, 1973), p. 45.

2. Brian McCallen, "The Registry Hotel Corporation: An Expanding Group of Luxury Hotels," *Hotel & Resort Industry,* February 1985, p. 17.

3. We are grateful to Michael Leven and Neil Ostergren, formerly of Americana Hotels, for sharing this information with us.

Supplemental Reading

How to Develop Marketing Strategies

by **Michael Leven**

> *Michael Leven, senior vice president, Americana Hotels, New York, is a recent past president of Hotel Sales Management Association International. Formerly with Dunfey Hotels, Hampton, New Hampshire, he is one of the most respected authorities on marketing in the lodging industry.*

The objective of this article is to increase your awareness and understanding of the term, "Marketing Strategy." By the time you have read what follows, you should be able to (1) see your own marketing universe and (2) see that universe as fragmented to its most important finality: the strategies you need to achieve desired results.

What is "Strategy"?

A strategy is an action you decide to take to initiate activity that will achieve a specific result. A strategy is not an objective; a strategy is a tactic by which you propose to achieve an objective. Here are some examples of the difference:

Objective: Lower percentage of payroll to 32% of dollars of sales.

Strategy: Re-do staffing guides to effect a 10% reduction in fixed payroll.

Objective: To increase penetration of the corporate meeting market, resulting in 10,000 additional room nights a year.

Strategy: Redecorate and rehabilitate present meeting facilities by June 1, 1980.

Do not mix up objectives and strategies. Objectives don't create change. Strategies do create change; they are actions that must be tracked and measured, road maps to results. Objectives are well thought out; they should be inflexible. Strategies are flexible, elastic, malleable. Our problem in the hotel business is that we focus more on objectives and then when things go wrong, assume that our objectives were wrong. We therefore change objectives that were right in the first place. Our failure is not as often in the choice of incorrect objectives as in the choice of incorrect strategies or the failure to change strategies when strategies fail to get us where we want to go.

All strategies generate sub-strategies. In the example above where the strategy calls for "redecoration of meeting rooms," the sub-strategies might be (1) have designs by March 1; (2) select plan by March 30; (3) enter order by April 20—etc. Sub-strategies are planned steps for implementing key strategies.

Why "Marketing Strategy"?

As the lodging industry has matured, it has become a common practice for hotels and motels—chain, franchise or independent properties—to come up with marketing plans. In some cases, as with any planning process—financial, marketing, personnel, etc.—the planning process is personalized by the producer of plans. Most

From *Lodging* (March 1980) pp. 12–16. Reprinted by permission of *Lodging*.

formalized claims standardize planning processes and create shelves of annual and revised documents.

The purpose of a plan is to outline the end results to be achieved; i.e., (A) the annual and 3-year objectives of the unit; (B) the strategic action steps to achieve the objectives; and, (C) ways to measure success or failure or to judge progress.

Frequently, our industry falls into the pattern of simply writing the plan, putting it into the appropriate "in-box" and pulling it out again only when formulating next year's plan.

We must avoid this. A "living plan" should be created with the focus on marketing strategy. Why? Because marketing strategy sets up a frequency for accountability in areas that are trackable. The beautifully typed and bound objectives can be left on the shelf, but the strategies and their measuring apparati can be daily put into the hands of both the executors and the monitors.

Without strategies there are no directions to work with; there is a place to go to (objective) but no road map for getting there. So—how many strategies do we need? How extensive should they be? Is there a general rule?

The number of strategies depends on the diminishing return of each succeeding strategy. Your strategies should start with the *key ones*; e.g., what must be done to achieve the greatest percentage of the objectives? What then can be done to generate the remainder of the desired result, and at what strategy investment, financial and human?

Virtually all hotels fall into the trap of setting down too many strategies. Hence, none get strength in terms of financial and human investment. The successful market strategist simply works more efficiently on fewer strategies and thereby generates the greatest possible progress toward his objective.

How to Develop Strategy

Ideally, marketing strategy development begins before a hotel is built; it begins with the first meeting of the developer of the project and the architect. Marketing strategy is endemic to the successful result of the overall planning process.

Let's look at an example. Last year, when a developer was going to construct a hotel in Cancun, Mexico, marketing people were called in to review the competitive environment, the location as a destination, the area market condition and the preliminary architectural plan. After the review, decisions were reached on the major positioning objectives of the hotel; i.e., "… the liveliest and most exciting hotel on the island, a unit known for activity and entertainment capability; a hotel that would attract other hotel guests in the evening …"

To achieve that positioning, a major marketing objective, required a product capable of delivering that objective. The key product strategy stated: "… the hotel must create an entertainment lounge environment featuring live show groups attractive to both singles and couples." Up to that point in the planning, no lounge had been contemplated. Now that a marketing strategy was agreed on—to implement a marketing objective—the owner did not hesitate to revise the plan to ensure compliance.

Unfortunately, this example of preconstruction strategy development is not typical. Most marketing strategy is created after the hotel has been constructed or while it is being constructed. Let's deal next with strategy development in such instances.

Strategy delineation begins after clear, concise and agreed-upon objectives are established in the marketing plan. Jon Canas, executive vice president of Dunfey Hotels, developed the term, "Mission Statement." A Mission Statement for every hotel and motel should document succinctly the description, the location and the position of the establishment, and what is required for the hotel or motel to be successful in finance, operations and marketing.

The Mission Statement tightens the unit management into a neat framework from which one can draw objectives for all the elements in the planning process. Although Mission Statements vary from company to company, depending on the input of those around the planning table, a sample for the Ala Moana Americana in Honolulu is presented [on pages 94 and 95].

The Mission Statement

Mission statement work is the key point of annual marketing review meetings. After this statement is complete, objectives are developed for:

1. Positioning the unit

2. Room revenue

3. Food and beverage revenue

4. Other income

Financial objectives are usually spread to three years to help create product development strategies far enough in advance to anticipate capital spending requirements.

Strategy development takes place when your team agrees on objectives (goals) in each of the revenue categories: occupancy, average rate, covers, average checks, number of drinks to be served, etc. It might surprise you when the greater part of the marketing planning process takes place before strategy development. It takes more time to agree on mission, positioning and objectives than on how to achieve goals. Don't let it worry you if strategies take little time to put on paper. You'll spend plenty of time making them work.

When objectives for all elements in the marketing plan are complete, you can begin strategy planning. Determine for each objective which of the elements of the marketing mix can effect the objective; then, for each element, develop the key strategies to achieve. For example:

Objective: Increase occupancy by 2 points over 1979.

A discussion now takes place on what markets or segments are desirable or available to generate that increase. The group reaches the decision that the increase should come from the corporate meeting business segment to improve Sunday night or Thursday night occupancy. Once that decision is reached, the checklist works this way:

Applicable marketing elements to obtain objectives:

Case Example

MISSION STATEMENT
ALA MOANA AMERICANA, HONOLULU

The Ala Moana Americana is a first-class hotel located between Honolulu's business section and the Waikiki tourist area. There is no first-class hotel closer to the business section and Honolulu's special event areas. The hotel is adjacent to Hawaii's largest shopping center with 155 stores.

To be successful, the hotel must be No. 1 to Honolulu's business traveler, airline crews, Japanese special campaigns, Kamaaina individuals, and Kamaaina groups. These markets should be supplemented by Japanese package series business, government employees, special events, and one-shot group business.

The Ala Moana must have authentic Hawaiian atmosphere, entrance, decor, and uniformity. It should be known for its Hawaiian style service (language, dress, fruit, flowers, and special touches).

When Japanese and U.S. F.I.T. demand slackens in the Waikiki area, the hotel is vulnerable to competition and loses significant business to the first-class Waikiki hotels. During these periods, it must depend on its major market segments and get one-shot group business. The hotel's rooms product must be designed and maintained to meet the needs of its four major market segments. There is a potential F.I.T. market of frequent Hawaii visitors and stopover business.

Because of the hotel's difficult competitive position for tourist room business and its high vulnerability to tourist fall-off, the food and beverage outlets offer the only major opportunity for revenue growth. These outlets must appeal to its local community; however, they must be flexible enough to meet its room guest requirements as well.

The Ala Moana must be known by its employees as the "best hotel in Honolulu to work in." Its employees should have the Aloha Spirit and should communicate that spirit to each other and to the guest.

Financial Goals

	Occupancy	Avg. Rate	Room Revenue
'79	86.4%	$30.16	$11,357,300
'80	87.0%	32.14	12,186,000
'81	87.0%	35.00	13,270,400

	Food Revenue	Beverage Revenue
'79	$5,757,000	$2,194,000
'80	6,670,000	2,632,800
'81	7,670,000	3,036,000

Assumptions:

1. **Major Market Segments**—The sales and marketing efforts of the hotel are geared toward the following market segments:

    a. Airline Crews

---

    b. Japanese Special Campaigns

    c. Yes We Cana

    d. Government

    e. Kamaaina

2. **Rooms Rehab Program** will continue as planned.

3. **Food & Beverage Department**—A master plan to reconceptualize total Food and Beverage outlets is being prepared in order to update and gear the operation toward the markets identified. This effort, in connection with increased sales and marketing efforts, will increase the growth in the Food & Beverage Department over the next several years.

4. **Room Supply**—Additional hotel rooms in the area are planned as follows:

1978
440 Rooms   Cinerama Reef Hotel-Waikiki Tower

1979
650 Rooms   Hawaiian Regent
360 Rooms   Ala Wai Sunset Seaside Towers
630 Rooms   Hawaiian Princess
495 Rooms   Pacific Beach Hotel

---

a. Direct Sales   Yes
b. Advertising   Yes
c. Public Relations   No
d. Sales Promotion   Yes
e. Research   No

Following each—if they are applicable—strategy development takes place at the team level. When each strategy is completed, a measurement and benchmark tracking system is set up. If a strategy can't be tracked, it shouldn't be there.

A Case Example

When at the Dunfey Hotel Company, I found a difficult marketing problem with Dunfey's resort at Hyannis, a 200-plus-room unit located in Cape Cod, Massachusetts. The unit had meeting room facilities far greater than sleeping rooms could utilize. For years, occupancy was lower than required because trade associations and transients came at the same time. This left wide mid-week gaps in the seven shoulder season months and the three off-season months.

The marketing objective developed from the mission statement read: "To be successful, the unit must be known as catering to individual vacationers on weekends and during the height of the season. But it must establish itself as a corporate meeting center in New England." Occupancy objectives were set at the low 70's (from the high 50's a year previously). Strategic development began:

Case Example

STRATEGIES AND OBJECTIVES
Rooms Business, Ala Moana
1980

Market Segment: *Special Events*

DEFINITION: Any one-shot event taking place in Honolulu in a city, state or public facility or area; i.e., state fair, high school/college or professional athletic events and trade shows that create a demand for lodging for either the participant or spectator.

OBJECTIVE: The Ala Moana Americana will be first choice because of location, facilities, service and price.

PERSON RESPONSIBLE: Group Sales Manager.

QUOTA: 3,100 Room Nights

Jan.	300	July	500
Feb.	200	Aug.	450
Mar.	250	Sep.	150
Apr.	150	Oct.	450
May	150	Nov.	150
June	150	Dec.	200

KEY STRATEGIES

1. Develop leads through the following facilities:

   a. Aloha Stadium

   b. Blaisdell Center

   c. University of Hawaii

   d. Department of Planning & Economics

2. Maintain list of special events in the city. Source: Newspapers, HVB (Hawaii Visitors Bureau), monthly activities at Blaisdell Center.

3. Cultivate key personnel within these facilities to insure that we get the leads.

4. Identify and work the five key promoters using these facilities: (In the Strategies worksheet, names of five key promoters are listed at this point, with affiliations and telephone numbers.)

5. Identify and solicit the major studios and producers filming in Hawaii: (In the Strategies worksheet, the names of five producers are listed at this point, with major movie studio affiliations.) Use other sources—newspaper (close) in business.

MEASUREMENTS

1. Source of Business Report.

2. Site inspection quotas met.

I. POSITIONING OBJECTIVE

Strategy: Change name to Dunfey's Hyannis Resort and Conference Center. Elements of marketing mix applicable: advertising, sales promotion and public relations.

Strategy: Advertising

a) Name to be on all media advertising to impress reader that resort and conference center caters to both markets.

b) Small space campaign to be developed in meetings trade magazines so regional meeting planner awareness will be created.

c) All in-house and external sales collateral material to be redone with new name (rack brochures, directory of services, meeting brochure, calendars, etc.)

Strategy: Public Relations

a) Writers from meetings publications, business and newspapers to be invited to resort to generate business oriented articles.

Note: Direct sales, research and sales promotion are not applicable to promoting this objective.

II. OCCUPANCY-INCREASE: OBJECTIVES

Objective is to sell 20,000 midweek corporate meeting room nights to be booked and consumed in the next 12 months.

Strategy: Direct Sales

a) Increase sales force from two to four and change location of outside representatives to four district territories.

b) Free up director of sales to sell the business by establishing convention service department to handle site inspections and group details.

c) Set up incentive program based on the 20,000 room-night target.

Strategy: Advertising

a) Meeting magazine campaign

Strategy: Sales promotion

a) Set up complimentary weekend stay package for New England area site planners; target three per weekend, "Be Our Guest" theme.

b) Set up two familiarization weekends for meeting planners.

Note: Public relations and research strategies not necessary in this case.

Obviously, the entire strategic plan developed for the hotel in the case example is not exposed here. What you need to understand is how and why objectives were stated and strategies developed. Strategies were executed and monitored and success, in meeting objectives, achieved. A year later, strategies were once again changed to meet the changing needs of the unit.

Strategy Execution & Measurement

Surprisingly, the lodging industry seems to handle the marketing planning function fairly well. Few hotels stand out as marketing white elephants or Edsels. Interestingly enough, most people in our industry are capable of adequate strategy development, even if we don't follow a process as comprehensive as the one just discussed.

So where do we fail? I feel that where we fail is in the execution of plans. Thus, we find an inordinate number of aborted marketing plans. Advertising agencies with hotel accounts confirm this judgment. What happens is this: the failure to adequately execute a strategy causes more often than not—a change in objective and premature denial of what might have been a progressive step. Besides the wasted dollars, we have wasted human resources. People blame themselves for the wrong reason—for poor planning instead of poor execution. The hotel does not make its fiscal goals.

If nothing else, we should ensure that strategies are being worked prior to changing anything. This requires monitoring on a regular, scheduled basis. We need to monitor to ensure measurement of what is happening today, not just what happened last month.

The Ala Moana

Consider, for example, the Mission Statement of the Ala Moana Hotel in Honolulu. The hotel previously had a significant occupancy problem. Occupancy objectives were set and strategies were developed to radically change the mix of business from a resort to a commercial base. The result was to be a commercial hotel located in a resort area.

This approach involved commitment to a new marketing position. One of the key strategies involved increasing the semi-permanent airline crew room base. A monitoring system was set up to test strategy execution and results on a weekly, then monthly, basis where call reports on the segment decision makers, proposals and decisions were reviewed by the general manager and his director of sales. This system continued until long after the strategy had been fully executed and was successful.

Follow-up strategies to ensure that the hotel keeps business are developed annually in a similar way. A combination of monthly written reports and weekly sales meetings reviews all segments to guarantee execution of this or other key account strategies.

Had no one monitored execution, the strategy might not have been successful. The business would surely not have showed up on its own. Failing in the new approach, management might have changed objectives. They might even have returned to the resort marketing approach where the product had had little competitive strength. Marketing dollars committed to that endeavor would have failed and the hotel would have operated at a significant dollar loss.

Strategy execution is the primary responsibility of the executor. But as managers, our primary responsibility is to monitor that execution. Systematic strategy monitoring is essential all through the marketing disciplines.

No strategy should be created, agreed upon, and put in any plan without the ability to monitor its execution. The best way to do that is to have the measurement system already in place in the plan. (See insert story on Ala Moana.)

The measurement system I recommend forces the responder to write in, on a scheduled basis, performance results vs. goals—either daily, weekly, or monthly, whichever is applicable. Let's return to the Hyannis example (above) for a moment. You'll recall that an objective was 20,000 corporate meeting room nights over a 12-month period and that one strategy was to increase the sales force to four people. What had to be monitored was:

1. Number of sales people in the field.

2. Number of leads generated.

3. Number of site inspections.

4. Room nights booked.

5. Room nights consumed.

There is no way the strategy could work without this monitoring. Forms (for reporting) were divided so that each key area was reported in the appropriate time frame. The 20,000 room nights were divided into target dates. By each date, sales people entered statistics that measured performance against ideal performance goals. This "paper work" was execution insurance. No attempt would be made to change anything until we knew a strategy wasn't working due to lack of response rather than lack of execution.

Changes in Strategy

Two circumstances warrant a change in strategy:

1. The strategy has been executed according to a prescribed plan, monitored for results, given time to grow and mature—and then has failed. Failure under these conditions gives you the right to sit down and create new strategies, or

2. The strategy has achieved the desired result and continuation is not necessary to maintain the result.

As a matter of policy, we review marketing strategies at least twice a year at formal meetings. In resorts with multiple seasons, we review more often. Once at a resort strategy review in Acapulco, we determined that food and beverage revenue objectives had been met at the expense of guest satisfaction. A projected decline in repeat business resulted. Specifically, forecasts indicated that our February and March occupancy projections would not be met. Since our occupancy plan represented our major objective, a number of strategies were discussed to beef up advance room sales; strategies that included:

1. Advertising in major markets.

2. Cooperative promotions with carriers and suppliers.

3. Direct sales programs.

4. Rate policy changes.

After full analysis, we decided on the key one: to change compulsory Modified American Plan to optional M.A.P. Sub-strategies chosen related to execution, mailgrams, telephone calls, sales calls, etc. Due to the timing, the new strategy gave us several advantages: a three-week lead time before competitors could react; a better chance to reach the occupancy objective in February or March; and a higher degree of guest satisfaction, which we know was a trade-off for food and beverage revenue. Benefits of the trade-off were minor compared to the potential damage to profit from lower occupancy.

Incidentally, this strategy was for 1980. At this writing, our measurements and benchmarks (daily reservations over the 800 number, weekly forward occupancy forecasts) have improved dramatically. Apparently, we are reaching goal. Here is an example of a planned review of a strategy creating a change because the strategy—which had worked—developed new circumstances not anticipated at the time of creation.

Although I do not recommend rapid changes to well-thought-out tactics, I do think it wise to set up a formalized, frequent review of marketing strategies due to rapidly occurring market changes and demands. Even annual marketing budgets should have contingency provisions to allow the flexibility to spend or hold back expenditure if objectives are not being met. The only way to know your strategy is correct is to note that the objective is being achieved. There is no law against reinforcing your commitment to a working strategy. The risk is to change for change's sake. This could result in the destruction of what is an already-sound foundation.

Conclusion and Summary

1. Marketing strategy begins as early as the purchase of the site for a hotel. Objectives set then create strategies in the product directly related to later financial and product success.

2. Normally, however, marketing strategies take place after the unit is built, or during construction. Strategies should never be agreed on until tight marketing objectives are fixed. A "mission statement" for every entity is necessary to help focus objectives.

3. Objectives are always set before strategies. No strategy can exist without an objective.

4. A strategy is an action/decision designed to initiate activity to achieve a specific marketing objective. Strategies are not objectives; objectives are ends, strategies are means.

5. Strategies are flexible. They should be reviewed periodically with corrections or additions in mind. Objectives should be in cement. They should be adjusted only when major changes in the product or the environment take place.

6. Strategies create sub-strategies. Sub-strategies are tactics to ensure that the strategy is executed.

7. Strategies are living things. They involve daily work. Objectives are shelved—that is, looked at in longer time frames, and rarely reviewed. Strategies put life into the corporate or unit planning process.

8. The number of strategies depends on the diminishing financial return and human investment necessary to achieve results. Too many strategies result in dispersion of effort over non-key areas and minimized capability of achievement.

9. Objectives are changed and plans fail more often than not because strategies are not properly executed, not because the objectives were wrong or the plans faulty in the original.

10. Monitoring systems should be regarded not only as a device for measuring results but also as a necessity for measuring strategy execution; they are vital to ensure compliance.

11. The key results expected from a strategic success and the key steps to implement the strategy should both be measured and reported.

12. Changes should take place only when strategies fail after execution, or when, even though they are successful, better or different results need to be obtained.

In addition to the 12 points listed, there is another ingredient—an elusive ingredient—to marketing success; that is, marketing intuition. Some people sense more, or feel more, than others. But in all cases, the successful strategist has, either by written design or mental past experience, logged a carefully organized path to strategy development.

He or she creates first the unit objectives. The rest has to do with understanding the unit capability, the competitive environment, the location conditions, the economic factors, the elements of the marketing mix—these and countless other input data. This data bank solidifies the objective planning and provides the foundation for strategic development.

But let there be no mistake about this: no intuitive genius ever achieved marketing objectives without a systematic approach to the execution of his strategies and measurement of their results. Creativity and intuition are no guarantees of success. Careful plodding, on the other hand, often sounds less exciting—less dramatic—but produces more effective results.

REVIEW QUIZ

When you feel you have covered all of the material in this chapter, answer these questions. Choose the *best* answer. Check your answers with the correct ones found on the Review Quiz Answer Key at the end of this book.

True (T) or False (F)

(T) F   1. Businesses that practice strategic planning are in better competitive positions than businesses that drift strategically.

T (F)   2. Strategic marketing planning and opportunistic thinking are almost identical ways by which to organize the marketing efforts of a company.

T (F)   3. Generally, the notion of strategy implies that short-term profitability is more important than long-term considerations.

(T) F   4. Preparing a mission statement is the first phase of strategic marketing planning.

(T) F   5. The objectives stated in a strategic marketing plan should be consistent with the property's mission statement.

(T) F·   6. Mission statements provide concise statements of the business's current product-market position as well as clear guidelines on where an organization's resources should be applied.

T (F)   7. Strategic planning objectives should be stated after the appropriate strategies and tactics have been formulated.

(T·) F   8. Strategies are statements about what should be done in order to achieve objectives and reach desired goals.

(T·) F·   9. Strategies tend to be ongoing in nature, while tactics are relatively short-term and flexible.

T (F)   10. Once objectives, strategies, and tactics have been integrated into the marketing plan, they should not be altered.

T· (F)   11. A market share philosophy seeks to increase business by expanding into new markets.

Multiple Choice

12. Without a strategic foundation, decisions made throughout an organization will:

   a. nearly always be successful.
   b. not differ from decisions made from a strategic foundation.
   (c) lack coherence and internal consistency.
   d. always fail.

13.   Preparing a mission statement helps a lodging operation to:

   a. differentiate its products and services from those of the competition.
   b. target specific customer groups.
   c. focus management's attention on opportunities that coincide with the company's business purpose.
   d. all of the above.

14.   The objectives of a strategic marketing plan should be:

   a. as general as possible.
   b. consistently checked against the mission statement.
   c. abandoned if immediate results are not achieved.
   d. reformulated every six months.

Chapter Outline

Sources of Threats and Opportunities
Environmental Threats
Environmental Opportunities
Timing of the Strategic Planning Process
Strategic Adjustment
Tourism: The Current Opportunity

Learning Objectives

1. Define environmental threats and opportunities.

2. Identify three sources of environmental threats and opportunities.

3. Explain the importance of timing in the strategic planning process.

4. Explain what is meant by the term "strategic window."

4

Analyzing the Environment

ALL HOSPITALITY ORGANIZATIONS must look beyond their immediate situations and recognize the changing conditions in the environment that affect their operations. Inflation, energy shortages, government legislation, and high interest rates are but a few of the environmental problems that have plagued the lodging industry in recent years. Along with problems, however, have come opportunities, such as increased spending by the baby-boom population and economic growth in regions of the sunbelt.

The major goal of strategic marketing planning is to counter environmental threats while achieving an optimal fit between the organization's resources and the opportunities in its changing environment. In this chapter, we will examine: (1) the sources of environmental threats and opportunities, (2) a system for classifying threats and opportunities, (3) the timing of the strategic planning process, and (4) the concept of strategic flexibility.

Sources of Threats and Opportunities

Environmental threats and opportunities can come from at least three sources: the government, the economy, and demographic and lifestyle trends.

Government. Government regulation can create incentives that encourage growth as well as create obstacles that hinder growth. Whether or not proposed regulations have a high probability of becoming a reality is always a debatable issue at the time they arise, but their potential severity usually warrants preparation of a contingency plan which specifies what strategic changes the hospitality operation needs to consider.

Economy. Evaluation and selection of some marketing strategies will be contingent on judgments made about the economy, such as projections of inflation and general economic conditions. Heavy investment in a fixed-asset-intensive industry like the lodging industry needs to be carefully timed to coincide with a strong economy in order to avoid a damaging period of losses. For example, a hotel firm may want to carefully time the construction of new facilities in order to open when the general economy is robust and business and pleasure travel are high. Similarly, investment by multi-national lodging companies in foreign countries should be carefully evaluated in light of the economic conditions in the nations where they are already doing business or are considering doing business. The increase in worldwide terrorist activities in the mid-1980s constituted an enormous threat to many overseas hospitality operations.

Demographic and Lifestyle Trends. Demographic and lifestyle trends can be strong forces creating major threats and opportunities. Demographic variables include age, income, education, and geographic location. An example of an emergent demographic trend with great potential impact on the lodging industry is the woman business traveler. In the United States, over 31% of business travelers are women—and this percentage will grow in the future.[1] Lifestyle trends include increased concern about food quality, diet, and physical fitness. Many lodging firms are already capitalizing on these "opportunities" by including more "natural" food items on hotel restaurant menus and many properties now offer spas and gyms as part of their service packages.

Should hospitality marketers pay more attention to threats than to opportunities? There is no easy answer to this question. On the one hand, threats can seriously undermine the viability of a hospitality operation and must therefore be identified and countered whenever possible. On the other hand, a great opportunity may only exist for a relatively brief period of time. To identify and capitalize upon it, a hospitality operation must have effective monitoring systems in place—systems that might not produce results for extended periods of time.

Environmental Threats

An environmental threat can be defined as "a challenge posed by an unfavorable trend or development in the environment that would lead, in the absence of purposeful marketing action, to the erosion of the company's position."[2] Threats can be classified according to their seriousness and according to the probability of their occurrence.

Seriousness. A firm's ability to cope with an environmental threat varies with the severity of the threat. When the threat is relatively minor, the firm can adapt by modifying its marketing plans or by making relatively minor tactical changes. When the threat is severe, however, the capacity of the operation to continue competing effectively may be seriously threatened. Related to the seriousness of a threat, is a firm's ability to do something about it. For example, currency fluctuations may seriously affect a lodging company's profitability, but the ability of the firm to stabilize or reverse currency fluctuations may be negligible. Another factor influencing a determination of seriousness is distance in the future; a threat with a high probability of occurrence ten years from now is less "serious" than an imminent threat.

Probability of Occurrence. Probabilities are a combination of many variables, not all of which are evident except in hindsight. One method for evaluating the probability of occurrence is to poll experts. This can be done systematically by surveying their opinions in the trade press and professional journals, or by interviewing them via telephone or through informal questionnaires. Cooperation can be gained in many cases by offering to share study results with them. Another method of gaining expert opinion is by group discussion. Here, the personal interchange of experts' opinions stimulates ideas and is a good way to discover underlying causal variables.

Environmental Opportunities

A marketing opportunity can be defined as "an attractive arena for company marketing action in which the particular company would enjoy a competitive advantage."[3] Marketers can classify environmental opportunities in much the same way that environmental threats are classified. Opportunities can be classified according to their attractiveness and the probability of success that the hospitality operation might have with each of them.

Attractiveness. The ultimate, bottom-line test of attractiveness is the potential profitability of an investment opportunity. Usually this is measured in terms of the return on investment (ROI). Other criteria for evaluating attractiveness include enhanced market standing or increased market share, and acquisition of undervalued resources such as the acquisition of a chain of bankrupt hotels.

Success Probability. The probability of a hospitality firm's success in regard to a new business venture or opportunity depends on whether its present business strengths match the requirements necessary to succeed in the new business area.

To compete successfully in the lodging industry, for example, firms need to possess specific business strengths such as the ability to conduct consumer, brand-oriented marketing. In a highly competitive marketplace, the ability to identify consumer needs and develop specific products to satisfy those needs is critical. Another business strength for multi-unit properties would be a well-known name supported by quality standards. Because services are difficult to evaluate before they are consumed, recognized quality standards go a long way toward reassuring guests that they will be satisfied each time they stay at any property in a chain. Multi-unit operations also need a strong network of well-located properties. To capitalize on its marketing skills and its image in the market, a lodging firm needs to have properties where customers want to stay. Otherwise, customers will switch to other hotel "brands."

Additionally, multi-unit properties possess a business strength in regard to important economies of scale such as being able to spread advertising costs over a large base of properties. This points to perhaps the most important business strength that multi-unit properties need to operate successfully in the lodging industry—financial resources. Compared to an industry like oil exploration, competing in the lodging industry requires relatively low capital investment. However, dramatic escalation in real-estate and construction costs as well as new-product development costs have raised the financial requirements for development for expansion-minded companies. Additionally, the development cost and costs of operating a national or international reservations system are high. Clearly, hotel companies with large financial resources by which to support state-of-the-art equipment, facilities, amenities, and services have a distinct competitive advantage in the lodging industry.

Another key success factor for lodging operations is to offer outstanding food and beverage operations. According to an analysis of the lodging industry's top 400 performers in 1984–85 (based on occupancy percentage, total sales per room, total revenues, and other factors), food and beverage sales were a key ingredient for success: 38% of the top 400's sales came from food and beverage outlets.[4]

Other important key success factors are the ability to identify good hotel sites, effective employee recruiting, selection, and training, and management development. For a summary of key success factors, see Exhibit 1, "Lodging's 400 Top Performers." It is important to keep in mind that key success factors differ from one sector of the hotel industry to another. For example, upscale food and beverage operations are not important in the economy/budget sector but are in the luxury sector.

Timing of the Strategic Planning Process

Highly successful companies do not wait until the environment has changed drastically before they respond to threats or opportunities. They anticipate major environmental changes and prepare plans either to influence those changes before they occur or to readily adapt to them after they occur.

One study of strategic planning systems concluded that planning systems could be classified in terms of the type of decisions being made.[5] A one-cycle system is typically little more than a sales forecasting and budgeting process for the following year. Major strategic decisions about the business are not explicitly dealt with. In a two-cycle system, budget preparation is preceded by the preparation of functional plans such as marketing plans and research and development plans. In a three-cycle system, functional planning and budgeting are preceded by strategic marketing planning.

Although there is a need for some kind of formal, scheduled strategic marketing planning, there is increasing recognition that some kind of strategic decision-making needs to take place outside the normal planning process. The phrase "strategic window" was coined to indicate that there are often only limited time periods during which there is an optimal "fit" between the "key requirements" of a particular market and the strengths and abilities of a firm.[6] Investment in product development, or in a particular market area, needs to be timed to coincide with periods in which a strategic window is open (i.e., when a close fit exists).

In order to capitalize on strategic windows, there has been a trend away from a rigid planning schedule toward a more continuous "on-line" system of information gathering, analysis, and decision-making. To facilitate this process, new approaches to strategic planning have been developed, including contingency planning, environmental scanning, issue management, and enhancement of the entrepreneurial thrust of the organization.

Issue management refers to continuously monitoring and reacting to a set of "issues"—forthcoming developments inside or outside the organization that could potentially affect marketing strategy. Strategic flexibility involves strategic options that allow quick and appropriate responses to sudden changes in the environment. Contingency planning involves the preparation of alternative plans for likely, or possible, developments resulting from implementation of the main strategy. Environmental scanning, like issue management, refers to the identification of components of the environment that could cause the most trouble and/or generate the greatest opportunities for the firm.

Exhibit 1   Lodging's 400 Top Performers

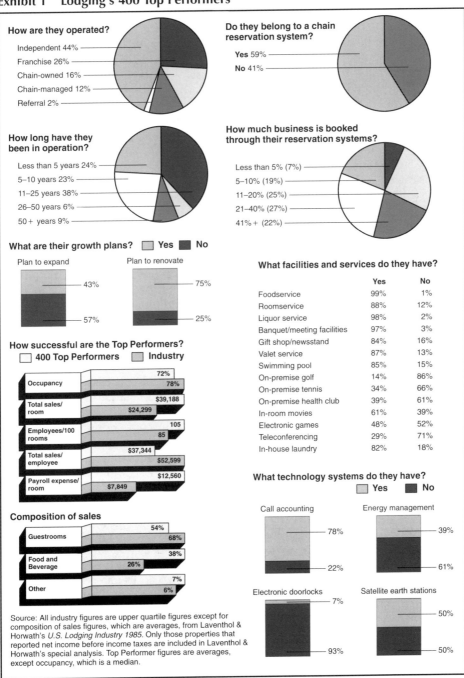

How are they operated?

Independent 44%
Franchise 26%
Chain-owned 16%
Chain-managed 12%
Referral 2%

Do they belong to a chain reservation system?

Yes 59%
No 41%

How long have they been in operation?

Less than 5 years 24%
5–10 years 23%
11–25 years 38%
26–50 years 6%
50 + years 9%

How much business is booked through their reservation systems?

Less than 5% (7%)
5–10% (19%)
11–20% (25%)
21–40% (27%)
41%+ (22%)

What are their growth plans? ☐ Yes ■ No

Plan to expand
43%
57%

Plan to renovate
75%
25%

How successful are the Top Performers?
☐ 400 Top Performers ☐ Industry

	400 Top Performers	Industry
Occupancy	72%	78%
Total sales/room	$39,188	$24,299
Employees/100 rooms	105	85
Total sales/employee	$37,344	$52,599
Payroll expense/room	$12,560	$7,849

Composition of sales

Guestrooms	54%	68%
Food and Beverage	38%	26%
Other	7%	6%

What facilities and services do they have?

	Yes	No
Foodservice	99%	1%
Roomservice	88%	12%
Liquor service	98%	2%
Banquet/meeting facilities	97%	3%
Gift shop/newsstand	84%	16%
Valet service	87%	13%
Swimming pool	85%	15%
On-premise golf	14%	86%
On-premise tennis	34%	66%
On-premise health club	39%	61%
In-room movies	61%	39%
Electronic games	48%	52%
Teleconferencing	29%	71%
In-house laundry	82%	18%

What technology systems do they have?
☐ Yes ■ No

Call accounting
78%
22%

Energy management
39%
61%

Electronic doorlocks
7%
93%

Satellite earth stations
50%
50%

Source: All industry figures are upper quartile figures except for composition of sales figures, which are averages, from Laventhol & Horwath's *U.S. Lodging Industry 1985.* Only those properties that reported net income before income taxes are included in Laventhol & Horwath's special analysis. Top Performer figures are averages, except occupancy, which is a median.

Source: Patricia Askin, "Lodging's 400 Top Performers," *Lodging Hospitality,* August 1985, p. 47. Reprinted with permission.

Strategic Adjustment

One of the dangers of strategic planning in any industry is the tendency for managers to stay with the plans they have personally had a stake in developing—to the exclusion of all other possibilities. While managerial pride of authorship is understandable, there are times when even a successful strategy must be altered and priorities rearranged. A strategy that worked well in the past may need to be changed to reflect changing conditions in the environment.

For example, a hotel may be successfully employing tactics for achieving the objective (set forth in the strategic marketing plan) of generating business from the national association market. However, this objective may constitute only one part of the overall strategic marketing plan. It may turn out that another market segment, projected in the strategic plan to be a strong source of business, is producing considerably less business than the plan called for. In this case, the firm might need to adapt its strategy and shift sales and marketing resources to the already strong national association market.

The need to adjust marketing strategy when conditions change is illustrated by a major challenge to the Canadian convention hotels during the 1970s. At that time, United States tax laws were changed to make it more difficult for U.S. companies to hold conventions outside the United States. It became clear to Canadian firms that owned convention hotels that they would either have to change their strategies to focus more on domestic business or sell to the U.S. market by using a totally different approach. Not surprisingly, some firms shifted marketing funds from U.S.-based media to Canadian-based media in the group field, and began advertising to the domestic market.

In general, this strategic adjustment met with great success. On the other hand, some hotels chose to keep their focus on the U.S. market and redesigned their marketing programs to minimize the impact of the new tax laws. One firm, for example, provided U.S. guests with assistance in completing their customs forms and used testimonial advertising that featured U.S.-based organizations that held very successful meetings in Canada. During this difficult era, the most successful Canadian convention hotels were those that used a combination of both the strategies just described.

Not all Canadian hotels did well, however. Generally speaking, these were the properties that ignored the new environmental conditions. They stuck with their traditional image advertising, followed traditional sales call patterns, and, as a consequence, suffered greatly. Ironically, these hotels even lost their market share of the U.S. convention business that came to Canada. Clearly, the U.S. companies that were going to Canada for conventions were enticed to use those properties that made it easy and attractive to do so, rather than those that pretended the tax law problem did not exist.

Tourism: The Current Opportunity

Perhaps the greatest opportunity facing the hospitality industry is the domestic and international growth of travel and tourism. The tourism boom reached such proportions as to seem almost unbelievable to many people. In the United States, tourism is second only to grocery store sales in terms of retail expenditures and ranks among the top three industries in almost every state—and is number one in Florida, Hawaii, and Nevada. Though the hospitality industry is the direct benefi- ciary of tourism, many other segments of the economy also benefit from tourism. Some authorities estimate that, for every dollar spent in lodging properties by a tourist, three dollars are spent elsewhere in the community.

The tourist dollar finds its way into so many pockets that it is difficult to iden- tify a clearly defined set of businesses and organizations that constitutes a tourism industry. Airlines hotels, motels, and restaurants obviously serve the traveling pub- lic. But local shopkeepers, supermarkets, and even taxi cabs also provide products and services for people visiting their communities. Although many local businesses benefit from tourism, few consider themselves part of a tourism industry. This makes it difficult for a destination area to coordinate its tourism efforts and gather political support for the development, management, and marketing of tourism.

Businesses and organizations must look beyond customers who walk in their front doors. They must stop reacting to changing patterns of tourism and begin an- ticipating changes by organizing tourism plans for their areas. The first step in this direction is to view tourism not as a loose aggregate of consumers, products, and services but as a system composed of interrelated parts. Viewing tourism as a sys- tem will help businesses, organizations, and even an entire community under- stand the ways in which everyone can benefit from tourist activity in their area.

However, jobs are not created without incurring certain costs, and these costs affect the amount of income generated by tourism development. An employment/ output ratio calculates the cost per job created by dividing the number of workers by the contribution of tourism to the national income. Some research indicates that, for the most part, the cost per job created through tourism development is about equal to the cost of creating jobs in other sectors of an economy. This is mainly due to the high costs of providing the necessary infrastructure (water, power, commu- nication, transportation, etc.) in order to meet tourists' needs. This high capital/ output ratio may decrease at a certain stage of tourism development and the cost per job created may decrease as well.

In 1983, 21.7 million foreign tourists visited the United States and spent $13.9 billion in this country, while 24.9 million U.S. tourists traveled abroad and spent nearly $19.5 billion.[7] Small wonder, then, that governments at all levels—from the national to the municipal—are actively promoting travel and tourism. Although, in truth, any industry generating such dollar figures might understandably expect greater economic and political recognition and support from the government and the general public than it often receives in America. The U.S. government currently spends only about 3.5 cents per capita per year to promote foreign tourism to the United States, an amount which stands in stark contrast to the $85 per capita per year spent by the Bahamas.

Considered on a large scale, tourism can have a dramatic effect on interna- tional and domestic economies. In the 1980s, the U.S. economy suffered from a tourism gap. Notice that the figures for 1983 previously cited reveal that Ameri- cans spent $5.6 billion more abroad than foreign visitors spent in America. In fact, with 1981 being the only exception, the years from 1960 to the present have seen this spending discrepancy grow to become a significant component of the total U.S. balance of payments deficit. In recent years, the major deterrents of foreign travel to America were the economic recession and the strengthening of the U.S. dollar against several major foreign currencies. Foreign tourism to the United States actually declined in 1982 for the first time in twenty years. The strong dollar is also largely responsible for the fact that U.S. travel overseas continues to rise. Efforts to eliminate this gap must focus on developing tourist packages to meet the needs of the highly price-sensitive foreign tourist market and on increasing the government's role in promoting America as a tourist destination.

The U.S. federal government uses national interests as guidelines in preparing legislation and regulations that affect tourism. However, tourism affects the culture and economy in so many ways that government committees and regulatory agencies do not always give sufficient attention to tourism when adopting legislation or setting regulations. Domestic and international travel acts are often structured without sufficient regard to other legislation or programs of federal agencies. Also, there are many federal agencies whose primary functions relate only indirectly to tourism. This leads to problems in coordinating a national tourism plan and often produces a lack of cooperation among committees and agencies. The sheer number of government committees and regulatory agencies makes coordinating their efforts a formidable task. The "red tape" of government bureaucracy often prevents government committees and agencies from acting with the speed required by the public sector.

In order to have the desired impact on the government, the disparate elements of the travel and tourism industry may need to unite to present a clear and forceful case to the public. Cooperation will be highly beneficial. It should not be long before the American Hotel & Motel Association, the National Restaurant Association, the American Society of Travel Agents, Discover America Travel Organization, and other related organizations get together and bring tourism into the spotlight.

Endnotes

1. U.S. Travel Data Center Report, Washington, D.C., 1984.
2. Philip Kotler, *Marketing Management: Analysis, Planning, and Control* (Englewood Cliffs, N.J.: Prentice-Hall 1984), p. 41.
3. Ibid.
4. Askin, Patricia, "Lodging's 400 Top Performers," *Lodging Hospitality*, August 1985, pp. 46–84.
5. Peter Lorange and Richard F. Vancil, *Strategic Planning Systems* (Englewood Cliffs, N.J.: Prentice-Hall, 1977), Chapter 2.
6. Derek F. Abell and John S. Hammond, *Strategic Market Planning: Problems and Analytical Approaches* (Englewood Cliffs, NJ: Prentice-Hall, 1979), p. 63.
7. "Recap of International Travel to and from the United States in 1983," Office of Research, United States Travel and Tourism Administration (Washington, D.C.: U.S. Dept. of Commerce, 1984), pp. 1, 5.

REVIEW QUIZ

When you feel you have covered all of the material in this chapter, answer these questions. Choose the *best* answer. Check your answers with the correct ones found on the Review Quiz Answer Key at the end of this book.

True (T) or False (F)

(T)   F   1. Inflation and general economic conditions can affect the timing of the opening of a new hotel.

T   (F)   2. Only after the environment has changed drastically should companies respond to threats or opportunities.

(T)   F   3. "Strategic window" refers to the period of time during which there is an optimal fit between the key requirements of a particular market and the strategies and abilities of a business.

T   (F)   4. Viewing tourism as a system would have little or no effect on lodging operations.

Multiple Choice

5.   Which of the following can be a source of threats and opportunities?

   a. government
   b. economy
   c. lifestyle trends
   (d) all of the above

6.   What should a company do in order to capitalize on strategic windows?

   a. stick to rigid planning schedules
   b. identify good hotel sites
   (c) keep the strategic plan flexible
   d. none of the above

Chapter Outline

Type
    Executive Floor Hotels
    Bed and Breakfast
    The Conference Center
    All-Suite Hotels
Size
Service Level
    Economy/Limited Service Hotels
    Mid-Range Service Hotels
    World-Class Hotels
Location
    City-Center Hotels
    Airport Hotels
    Highway Hotels
    Suburban Hotels
    Destination (Resort) Hotels
Affiliation
    Independent Hotels
    Chains

Learning Objectives

1. Describe the special-purpose concept of executive floor hotels.

2. Describe the special-purpose concept of bed and breakfast operations.

3. Describe the special-purpose concept of conference center operations.

4. Describe the special-purpose concept of all-suite hotels.

5. Explain what is meant by a mega-hotel.

6. Explain what is meant by an economy/limited service operation.

7. Explain what is meant by mid-range service hotels.

8. Explain what is meant by world-class hotels.

9. Describe the major categories which structure the lodging industry in terms of the location of properties.

10. Define what is meant by independent hotels and chain hotels.

11. Explain what is meant by franchising.

12. State the advantages that independent hotels should evaluate when considering chain affiliation.

13. State the disadvantages that independent hotels should evaluate when considering chain affiliation.

14. Explain what is meant by management contracts.

15. List criteria that owners can use in selecting a hotel management company.

Analyzing the Product and the Competition

A<small>N UNDERSTANDING OF THE BASIC STRUCTURE</small> of the lodging industry contributes to a sound strategic marketing plan. Such an understanding can be a logical starting point in determining how an operation should compete in the marketplace.

Although each property has a personal style, it is possible to group lodging operations into five broad categories. The categories that this chapter discusses are (1) type, (2) size, (3) service level, (4) location, and (5) affiliation. This chapter will also examine newer concepts in lodging operations and the markets whom they are designed to serve. Keep in mind, however, that it is difficult to fit most hotels into clear-cut categories. Although lodging properties share many similarities, the industry is diverse and several categories may apply to individual properties.

Type

The lodging industry today is primarily made up of commercial lodging establishments that have traditionally been identified as hotels, motels, and resorts. A hotel is typically defined as a multi-story building with its own dining rooms, meeting rooms, and other public spaces. A motel is usually described as a "low-rise" building with no meeting rooms and limited dining facilities and other public spaces. A motel (sometimes referred to as a "motor hotel") is generally used by the motoring public and is located close to highways or freeways. Resorts are typically found near beaches, mountains, or deserts and may offer such recreational facilities as golf courses, tennis courts, ski slopes, and health clubs. Resorts are almost always located within tourist destination areas. Some resorts, such as the Boca Raton Hotel & Club, have become a destination in themselves.

Within the past two decades, there has been a blurring of distinctions among these types of lodging facilities. Today, some so-called motels more closely resemble hotels with substantial meeting and public facilities as well as restaurants. In the same vein, some hotels now resemble traditional motels and offer the traveling public fewer services but retain the ambience of a fine hotel.[1]

Compounding the structure of today's lodging industry are the newer types of special-purpose hotels. Before we examine these types of hotels and see what they offer and whom they are designed to serve, let's hear from an expert who has been following this trend toward special-purpose properties.

     66We believe that the market has evolved from largely homogeneous to quite heterogeneous in its needs. This market evolution has created business opportunities of several 'niches,' which has led to our introduction of Embassy Suites, the acquisition of Granada Royale, the introduction of Crowne Plaza, and the introduction of Hampton Inn hotels.

On balance, we are saying that no one brand and product can succeed at being all things to all people, although we do believe the middle-market products will continue to be attractive and appropriate for the majority of the traveler market. **"**

—James L. Schorr
Former President
Holiday Corporation Hotel Group

Special-purpose lodging facilities have evolved to reach out to newer market segments by meeting the wants and needs of certain guests. The lodging concepts which this chapter discusses are executive floors, bed and breakfast operations, conference centers, and all-suite hotels.

Executive Floor Hotels

Executive floor hotels represent one type of special-purpose facility and are also known as the "tower" concepts or "hotels-within-hotels." Sometimes they are the upper floors of properties such as a Hyatt Hotel and can only be reached by special elevator keys. Other times these operations might be upper stories of Sheratons (see Exhibit 1) or separate buildings adjacent to Westins or Hiltons. These luxury facilities are all reaching for the same market: the extremely affluent business traveler. People in this segment don't want the limitations of a budget hotel, and they seek more than what is offered by typical full-service hotels.

Executive floor hotels normally provide very large, deluxe guestrooms that may contain a number of amenities. Whereas some hotel rooms today might offer the guest hand soap, bath soap, a shower cap, and shampoo, tower concepts might provide such amenities as skin creams, bath-oil beads, mouthwash, scented soaps, special purpose soaps, shampoos and conditioners in fancy bottles, and so forth.

The luxury items offered by executive floors are not confined to the bath. Within the guestroom itself, many hotels-within-hotels provide a nightly turn-down service. At that time any number of extras might be left on or near the bed to provide a personal touch for the guest. In many cases, the towers or executive floors contain a private lounge area for the exclusive use of registered guests. Breakfast or bar service may be provided there.

Executive floors are very attractive, but their guests must be willing to pay significantly higher rates. Although it is very expensive to run an executive floor, many hotels find that they cannot compete effectively with the smaller, dedicated deluxe hotels in their area unless they offer this option. Many hoteliers feel that offering a premium product makes their standard product more appealing due to its ascribed status.

Bed and Breakfast

This "new trend" is really an old trend brought up to date. The popularity of "B&Bs" has grown rapidly in the United States. The concept is simplicity itself, and it generally takes one of two forms. A few rooms in an existing home are converted

Exhibit 1   Ads for Sheraton Towers

Courtesy of the Sheraton Corporation

to overnight facilities for transients who eat breakfast together in the home, perhaps with the family that owns it. Or, a small luxury building is converted into a B&B for tourists on relatively short stays. Again, limited food service is offered to guests.

While bed and breakfast operations are only modestly competitive with full-service hotels (or even budget hotels), they are a force within the broad spectrum of "hospitality," and their popularity is a contemporary phenomenon worth noting.

The Conference Center

Many hotels aspire to serve the conference or meeting market because it is another source of revenue beyond the transient market. As the term is used today, a conference center is much more specialized than a mainstream hotel with some meeting facilities. A conference center may be a fully dedicated property offering well-organized recreation programs in a sports center, an area conducive to quiet study, state-of-the-art electronics equipment, and, in some cases, teletechnology of the most advanced type. More and more, advertising for conference centers features the capability to bring educational materials into guestrooms through a closed circuit or cable system.

Personal amenities are not featured as often in the guestrooms of a conference center, since they are planned to meet the needs of organizers more than the desires of the attendees. However, they normally provide high quality and very ample meals.

Today, conference centers are marketed on the basis of where they are as much as on what they are. Usually, they are isolated and rather far away from the hustle and bustle of the city—which is what their market wants. Their oversized grounds provide a campus-like atmosphere as well as adequate space to house the recreational amenities. The availability of a recreational outlet such as an in-house sports and fitness center may also be among the features which are usually attractive to conference planners.

Conference centers are also increasingly marketed as places to escape for the weekend. This, of course, is in response to the reality that, no matter how attractive the facility, businesspeople are usually reluctant to conduct business during the weekend. Creative efforts to stimulate demand through non-traditional approaches include holding seminars on specific topics and social weekends (similar to those held for years in the Catskills). This is a marketing trend worth watching.

All-Suite Hotels

Among the fastest-growing lodging industry segments is the all-suite hotel. Whereas the typical accommodation in an American hotel features one room, an adjacent bathroom, a king-size bed or two double beds, a desk/dresser modular unit, and one or two chairs, a suite unit offers a small living room with a grouping of appropriate furniture and a small bedroom with a king-size bed.

Some suites even include complete galley kitchens. In exchange for the fancier living quarters, all-suite hotels offer less elaborate public spaces and fewer services, enabling them to charge prices comparable to first-class guestrooms at more traditional hotels. Some all-suite hotels invite guests to complimentary evening cocktail reception to which they may bring their own guests. Some properties take this concept one step further and offer guests a full complimentary breakfast as well. Such gatherings provide guests with the opportunity to socialize, which may be important for guests who are staying for extended periods.

Of course, an all-suite hotel can offer extras to set it apart from other all-suite hotels. For example, the Park Suite in Denver is a luxury all-suite hotel with restaurants and meeting rooms. Its operator stated, "The hotel is specifically designed for

The Las Vegas Hilton and Las Vegas Convention Center.

corporate travelers and businesspeople. It is not a convention hotel; instead, it is designed to meet the needs of people who want to fulfill business and social obligations in a setting rich with personal service and comfort."[2]

Suites appeal to several different market segments. For example, suites not only provide temporary living quarters for transferred executives searching for new homes, they also serve as "homes-away-from-home" for executives who travel extensively. Professionals such as accountants, lawyers, and consultants also may appreciate an all-suite hotel if they are in town for an extended assignment such as an audit or trial. In fact, Holiday Corporation has designed the all-suite Residence Inns specifically for long-stay travelers. Some executives may find all-suite hotels particularly attractive since they can work or entertain in an area which is separate from where they sleep. Suites are ideal for families traveling on vacation because they provide, in effect, two rooms for the price of one. Parents relocating with children may also find the concept appealing because a second room allows for a reasonable amount of privacy.

The facilities of all-suite hotels have become increasingly attractive to businesspeople attending company training programs. Normally, corporations find it difficult to require their personnel to stay two to a room if they are not related, or at least friends. However, businesspeople are more willing to accept double accommodations in an all-suite hotel because they offer more living space and greater privacy.

The all-suite hotel also has many advantages for the operator and owner. By making the guestroom slightly larger and relocating the bathroom, developers can provide "suites" instead of "rooms" with only a 20% to 30% increase in construction costs. In addition, by including a kitchen in each unit's design and construction, the property may become relatively indistinguishable from luxury apartments in a condominium building. Should the local lodging market weaken, all or part of the suite hotel can easily be converted to apartments, condominiums, or even offices. Similarly, condominium projects completed in weak real-estate markets can often be converted to suite hotels, either permanently or until the condominium market improves. These factors often make all-suite hotels easier to finance than traditional hotels.

Despite these advantages, the all-suite concept does have some drawbacks. A special design criterion is necessary to ensure that the kitchen can be cleaned rapidly and thoroughly. The typical guest on a longer-than-average stay demands greater personalized attention from management and perhaps additional services like laundry facilities, cooking utensils, and transportation to and from grocery stores. Because suites generally cost more to build than standard guestrooms, operators must be extremely attentive to operating costs and occupancy percentages in order to enjoy equal or greater profitability than hotels which charge similar rates. Finally, hotel operators should keep in mind that a large portion of all-suite facilities are newly constructed. Therefore, it may not be as easy as it appears to convert an existing standard hotel room to a suite.

Days Inns of America was one of the first lodging chains to offer a suite concept with its subchain of Days Lodges which were targeted at vacationing families on a limited budget. At the opposite end of the all-suite spectrum, most properties in the Guest Quarters chain offer luxurious suites, restaurants, 24-hour room service, and meeting rooms. Interestingly, 85% of Guest Quarters' guests stay three days or less.[3] Among the largest suite-hotel operator is Holiday Corporation, which purchased the Granada Royale chain (now Embassy Suites) and Brock Residence Inns to complement its internally developed Embassy Suites. The corporation has developed a standard design and guestroom layout both to sell as a franchise concept and to build and operate as company-owned units. While not every major lodging company is attracted to the concept, enough buyers are choosing such all-suite hotels to make them a viable alternative and growing force in the industry.

Size

A property's size, or number of rooms, also plays a part in the classification of hospitality operations. With the declining availability of sites for large multi-story hotels, size considerations have become increasingly critical in marketing planning.

Lodging properties range in size from small, intimate upscale hotels with a club-like atmosphere such as the 98-room Sheraton Plaza in Copenhagen to giant hotels like the 1,876-room Marriott Marquis in Times Square. Additionally, some larger hotels are often constructed as part of large "mixed-use" facilities that include shopping centers, civic centers, marinas, convention centers, or high-rise office towers. These developments often function as "cities unto themselves" and are known in the industry as "mega-hotels."

Mega-hotels generally contain in excess of 1,200 rooms and offer at least two different concepts within the same building. These properties are constantly looking to a variety of market segments to fill their many rooms. While their marketing may appear to be frenetic, it is very often among the most imaginative of any hotel category—for the simple reason that mega-hotels must be clever in their marketing in order to meet the enormous expenses of running these huge facilities.

At best, mega-hotels can be beautifully designed to serve specific markets; at worst, they can be extremely confusing places to visit. Management tasks become considerably more complex as a property becomes larger. In addition, the anonymity which comes hand-in-hand with a large hotel can be quite frustrating to guests. In some respects, mega-hotels may be at a competitive disadvantage since smaller hotels are better able to provide the personalized service many guests prefer. An example of ultra-personalized service available at more modestly-sized hotels is the Italy-based Cigahotels. In these properties, staff are required to recognize and greet guests by name by the second time they meet them. Obviously, this would be a difficult job for staff to master in a mega-hotel filled with over 2,000 guests.

Service Level

Another way of classifying lodging properties is by service level. Service level is a measure of the benefits provided to the guests and is comparable to the quality level of a manufactured good in the sense that its design and performance characteristics are specified.[4] Closely correlated to the service level a hotel offers are the prices which a hotel sets. For example, a hotel which provides concierge service, valet parking, and several restaurants will be more expensive than a hotel which offers a small room with Spartan furnishings and no amenities.

Conceptualizing and setting service levels is an important decision area for lodging operations. Managers and marketers need to understand the tradeoffs which may be involved in terms of cost and guest satisfaction when a certain level of service is decided upon. Among the many areas that require service-level decisions are staffing, food-and-beverage quality, and the hours which particular areas will be open.

Setting service levels can be a difficult process. Many of the benefits the guest enjoys such as security, comfort, and status are intangible and difficult to measure. Changes in service level which affect these areas can be critically important to the guest experience. "Value engineering" is the process of determining what elements are necessary in a service-delivery system to create the perception of value in the guest and what costs these elements may entail. One goal of the value engineering process is to determine what minor additions could greatly enhance the service.[5] A superb example of value engineering is the design and development of the Park Hyatts, Hyatt Hotels' new generation of 200- and 300-room properties.

Hyatt's market research showed that most guests didn't want suites as much as they wanted large, airy guestrooms with separate areas for sleeping and living. From a design standpoint, Hyatt had to measure the costs of restructuring their typical guestroom against the value they might receive by satisfying the wants and needs of a particular market. As a result, guestrooms in the new Park Hyatts were designed 20% larger than standard Hyatt rooms to accommodate the need expressed by guests for additional space. President J. Patrick Foley remarks:

> **"**Our major Hyatt Regency projects cost between $120,000 and $160,000 per room to build and in many secondary cities and suburbs it's impossible to get the rate needed to justify that type of capital investment.
>
> "What we set out to do ... was put together a product that we can build for about $85,000 a room that still has all the ambience and quality guests demand in a Hyatt. With this design, we've scaled down the building costs without scaling down Hyatt quality and service. These new properties will offer guests the same services and facilities of any Hyatt we currently operate.**"**[6]

Obviously, the level of service a property sets will affect its place in the structure of the lodging industry. For the sake of simplicity, lodging properties can be discussed in terms of three basic service level categories: economy/limited, midrange, and world-class service.

Economy/Limited Service Hotels

The level of service and price at an economy/limited service property is typically less than that of other hotels in other categories. In comparison to the early 1970s when the only amenity which may have been offered was a black-and-white TV, most economy properties now offer color TV (many with cable or satellite reception), swimming pools, limited food and beverage service, playgrounds, small meeting rooms, and other special touches. The size of the economy/limited service property has also increased from the 40- to 50-room hotel of the 1960s. Some economy properties now have as many as 600 rooms although managerial considerations keep most properties between 50 to 150 guestrooms. What economy properties don't usually offer is room service, bell service, banquet rooms, atriums, health clubs, or any of the other amenities that would push the room rate to midrange or world-class level.

Lodging accommodations are usually priced according to the competitive rate structure which exists in the local market. Ronald J. Rivett, Vice Chairman of the Board of Super 8 Motels, remarks:

> **"**We want to maintain our price below the average. For Super 8, this means 25–50% less than a comparable room at a Holiday Inn in the same market. Super 8's rates vary and in some cases may be twice as high as its usual rates, depending on the location.**"**[7]

Low design, construction, and operating costs are part of the reason why economy hotels can be profitable. They incorporate simple, economical, efficient designs that can be built quickly and cheaply, often in "cookie-cutter" fashion. Some are built from modular units to take advantage of cost savings realized through mass production techniques.

Economy hotels are usually two to three floor structures constructed from cinder block. Among other typical features are double-loaded corridors (corridors with guestrooms on both sides), since they are cheaper to build than the single-loaded corridors found in many large atrium hotels. Motels may also be constructed in a back-to-back guestroom fashion with external entrances that allow guests to enter their rooms directly from a lawn or parking area. The typical staff of an economy-level hotel consists of a live-in couple as managers plus room attendants, front desk clerks, and sometimes a maintenance person.

Economy hotels appeal primarily to budget-minded travelers who want reasonably priced rooms with all the amenities required for a comfortable stay, but without the extras they don't really need and don't want to pay for. The retired senior-citizen population with leisure time is a strong source of business for this type of property since a large percentage of this population travels on a fixed income.

Economy facilities are apt to be located near other types of hotels. It is not unusual at all to see an economy hotel close to a group of world-class full-service hotels, and often doing very well. For example, a Days Inn near an airport might be located next to a full-service Sheraton or Marriott because the economy property is reaching out for a different segment of the traveling public. Units that compete in markets dominated by world-class hotels tend to be upgraded (perhaps with better beds, drapes, and wall coverings) and charge a slightly higher rate than other properties in their chain.

In seeking out a more upscale clientele, some companies have de-emphasized the word "economy" and favor "limited service."[8] As budget hotels penetrate certain cities, move away from traditional highway locations, and begin to suffer more from cyclic swings in occupancy associated with certain kinds of destinations or certain days of the week, they may mount aggressive marketing campaigns to capture business traditionally held by their more upscale competitors. For instance, some budget properties, like the Super 8 chain, are mounting full-scale campaigns to capture a larger segment of the business market.[9]

Competition has steadily increased in the economy segment of the lodging industry with major players being Days Inns of America, La Quinta Motor Inns, Econo Lodges & Econo-Travel Motor Hotels, Red Roof Inns, and Super 8 Motels. Most of these now nationally recognized companies in the economy segment began as a regional group. In contrast, a few national and international chains have entered the economy system and have enjoyed success. These include Quality Inns with its Comfort Inns, and Holiday Corporation with its Hampton Inn hotels.

Forecasters have predicted an explosion in the economy field. New areas under development include resort destinations, health-care sites, city-center redevelopment areas, and high-tech industrial parks. As a result of this expansion, estimates are that 80% of the rooms in the economy market will be less than 20 years old in the next few years. As these new properties come on line, the impact will be felt by properties that have not updated their facilities and marketing approach to help protect their existing client base. Increased competition in a rate-sensitive market may force many companies to add services to enhance their competitive positions.

Mid-Range Service Hotels

Hotels offering mid-range service probably appeal to the largest segment of the traveling public. Mid-range service is modest but sufficient and the staffing level is

A familiar design for La Quinta Motor Inn.

adequate without trying to provide overly elaborate service. These properties generally offer uniform service, airport limousine service, and food and beverage service. The property may also house a specialty restaurant, coffee shop, and lounge that cater to local residents as well as to hotel guests. The typical hotel offering mid-range service is medium sized although some properties are slightly smaller or larger.

Guests likely to stay at a mid-range hotel are businesspeople on expense accounts, travelers, or families taking advantage of special children's rates. In addition, special rates may be provided for military personnel, educators, travel agents, senior citizens, and corporate groups. Conferences, training meetings, and small conventions may also be a source of revenue where meeting facilities are provided.

Mid-range properties continue to constitute about 50% of all industry lodging operations. However, this market is beginning to feel competitive pressures from hotels falling both in and out of this classification. Competition is being felt from upgraded limited service, downgraded world-class hotels, and the newer concept of suite hotels as they package themselves in such a way as to attract a similar clientele. New construction and renovation of existing mid-market properties are also increasing competitive pressures within this hotel segment.

World-Class Hotels

World-class hotels, which typically cost 35% to 80% more than other hotels to build, provide upscale restaurants and lounges, exquisite decor, concierge service, and opulent meeting and private dining facilities. Primary markets for hotels offering these services are top business executives, entertainment celebrities, high ranking political figures, and other wealthy people. To cater to this clientele, hotels may provide oversize bath towels and bars of soap, shampoo, shower caps, clock radios,

Exhibit 2   The Bostonian Hotel

and more expensive furnishings, decor, and art work in guestrooms. Bath linens are typically replaced twice daily and a nightly turn-down service is usually provided.

When world-class hotels are successful, they are very successful. Chain affiliation for a world-class hotel is not necessarily a prerequisite for success because many of these properties are independently owned. The Bostonian in Boston, Massachusetts, is a good example (see Exhibit 2). However, because of their high prices, these hotels have a limited market. This leads many developers to consider such properties high-risk ventures. As with all lodging operations, extremely thorough research and planning should be conducted before such properties are developed and built.

Despite these factors, the upper end of the lodging industry has displayed a high growth pattern in recent years. Achieving high profits in this segment usually means maintaining average room rates once occupancy moves above the typical breakeven point of 70%. However, this desirable situation is ordinarily in areas where there are comparatively few world-class hotels in comparison to the demand for luxury rooms. Such a situation will become more infrequent as world-class property development continues to grow.

Location

Another way to analyze the structure of the lodging industry is to focus on location. This section categorizes hotels in terms of their locations to cities, transportation facilities, suburbs, and in terms of tourist destination areas. Statistical information provided under each category is based on an analysis of 400 top lodging operations conducted each year by the accounting firm of Laventhol & Horwath.[10]

City-Center Hotels

City-center hotels are usually located in downtown or commercial districts and may be small, medium, or large. Although the primary market for these properties is the business traveler, many tour groups, individual tourists, and small conference groups also find these hotels attractive.

About one-third of city-center hotels are less than five years old, while one-fifth have been open more than 50 years. Most offer food and beverage service and provide space for banquets and meetings. Elaborate recreational facilities are not usually provided.

City-center hotels in larger cities typically report higher ratios of room revenues to total revenues than their counterparts in smaller cities. This is probably due to the fact that guests staying in larger cities have more options for food and entertainment outside the hotel.

Airport Hotels

Airport hotels are popular because of their convenience for travelers. In some instances, hotel-owned limousines or courtesy vans transport guests to and from the airport almost constantly. Signs which announce direct line telephone service to nearby hotels for reservations and pick-up are a common sight in most airports. Typical markets for these hotels include business clientele, airline passengers with short stayovers or canceled flights, wedding parties, and the airline personnel themselves.

More so than any other category of hotels, chain affiliation is characteristic of airport hotels. Eighty-six percent of the properties analyzed carry some type of chain identification. Chains own or manage 54% of the properties, while 32% are franchised or belong to a referral group. New hotels dominate this category. Forty-four percent are less than 10 years old and 94% are less than 25 years old. All of the properties analyzed feature food service, room service, banquet and catering service, valet services, and swimming pools. In addition, 88% of the properties have in-room entertainment features.

Highway Hotels

In contrast to airport hotels, highway hotels are the leaders among the surveyed properties in terms of their affiliation with franchises or referral groups. Sixty percent of these properties belong to a franchise while 18% are owned by chains. Among the typical features of a highway hotel are food and beverage service, room service, banquet and catering facilities, and a gift shop or newsstand.

Suburban Hotels

Among the suburban hotels surveyed, food and beverage services represent 45% of their sales, compared to 22% for the all-industry group of suburban hotels. These properties rate high in chain affiliation with over 60% being franchised, owned, or managed by a chain. As a group, suburban hotels rely heavily on central reservations systems, with 65% belonging to some type of toll-free reservation network. With an average of 206 rooms, the typical suburban hotel is slightly smaller than most other categories surveyed. One of the largest suburban hotels is the 580-room Radisson Hotel South in Minneapolis, Minnesota.

Destination (Resort) Hotels

Analysis indicates that the typical top resort has 248 rooms, but can range in size from the 15-room Mother Lode Cookhouse & Saloon in Wasilla, Alaska, to the 1,120-room Disneyland Hotel in Anaheim, California. Seventy-two percent of the destination hotels are independent properties. In contrast to the highway hotel, less than one-fourth of the destination hotels rely on a centralized reservations system to book business. Resort properties are service-intensive and average 145 employees per 100 rooms. Statistically, this works out to be significantly above the traditional one-to-one ratio of employees to rooms that typifies many world-class hotels. Fifty-three percent of the properties surveyed are planning to expand their facilities in the near future.

Resort hotel communities are one direction this segment of the lodging industry is taking in terms of expansion and development. These communities usually emerge through one of two ways. Existing facilities, such as many of the hotels at ski resort areas in Vermont and Colorado, may be sold as condominium hotel investments or as leased investments in condos at hotel destinations that have already been established. On the other hand, totally new resort communities may be developed.[11] Dick Erb, Chief Operating Officer of Grand Traverse Resort Village and a specialist in resort community development, agreed to share some of his experiences and expertise:

> ❝Years ago, I decided to learn about resort development community management, as it appeared that virtually all new resorts would emerge under this umbrella, while most existing ones would be wise to consider real estate projects in conjunction with their resort property. The rising costs of land and the compatibility of resort hotels with real estate made this approach a natural one. When we opened the Mauna Kea Beach Resort Hotel in Hawaii 20 years ago, I saw the values of the barren, lava-covered land around the hotel skyrocket overnight. I've never forgotten that.
>
> The resort development community product is usually a condominium. The condominium concept is relatively new in the United States, but hundreds of years old in other countries. There are many types of lodging condominiums, from a single room in a hotel to a luxurious villa with complete kitchens, bars, fireplaces, and garages. Resort condominiums can work in two ways. First, they may be purchased by individuals for various reasons and [then] rented out as ... hotel or resort rooms by a management firm whenever the owners don't need them. Second,

Marriott's Rancho Las Palmas Resort, Rancho Mirage, California.

a time-sharing plan can allow each condominium unit to have many owners. Each of the purchasers is entitled to a certain amount of time in that unit.

Condominium hotels and resorts often operate within a larger plan [for total area development]. One common version is the resort development community which offers various real estate and hotel products…[through a] complex marketing plan mix. In this case the market research must identify the potential resort/hotel guest and then go on to qualify the hotel guest as a potential condominium or real estate buyer.

Initially, existing resorts sold home lots around their golf courses or ski slopes, primarily to their guests. Real estate marketing occurred within the lobby. Now the role is reversed, and the new resorts exist primarily as a tool for selling the real estate product. Therefore, they try to attract resort customers who are potential buyers as well—usually [those] whose incomes exceed $75,000 per year.

Normally these resort communities are not a part of a chain but rather individually operated. In some cases, chains operate the hotel on a franchise basis but are not involved in the real estate.

Marketing of condominiums at these resort communities presents a challenge, as the product is perceived as something other than a hotel room. As yet, no national affiliation has emerged for central reservations, but one soon will as the tremendous growth of condominium resorts continues. **"**

—**Richard Erb**
Chief Operating Officer
Grand Traverse Resort Village

Affiliation

Another method by which to analyze the structure of the lodging industry is by ownership or affiliation. Two basic classifications are possible—independent hotels and chain hotels. The term "independent" refers to a single-unit operator whereas "chain" refers to a property which is owned or operated by a multi-unit organization.

Independent Hotels

Many independently owned and operated hotels do extremely well without chain affiliation. Smaller, established hotels in downtown districts, for example, often have a stable market of repeat clientele. Some "super-luxury" hotels that cater to an exclusive, sophisticated clientele prefer the image of an independent operation. Given the attractive nature of managing an independent and renowned property, there are a number of factors hotels may want to consider before dismissing chain affiliation.

Financing. It can be extremely difficult for a developer to find financing for a new property without affiliation. Debt-service coverage and resale value may also increase with chain affiliation.

Nationwide or International Reservations System. Virtually all chains utilize a computerized toll-free telephone reservations system. In times of reduced occupancy, a reservations system may fill guestrooms that would otherwise remain empty. Days Inns of America claims that approximately 35% of the average franchisee's occupancy (70%) is produced through its centralized reservations system.[12]

Cost Benefits and Operational Expertise. These factors are especially critical during the start-up phase of a new hotel project. For example, Best Western, the world's largest association of "independent" hoteliers, gives its members not only brand name recognition, but also a comprehensive system to help members refurbish their properties easily and at reasonable costs. The system includes professional design help, centralized purchasing, and a flexible system of financing through a national financial organization. Best Western's Supply Division is also available to help members with refurbishing and furnishing needs. With the mass purchasing power of over 2,000 members, cost savings and discounts can be substantial. Among other benefits to members of Best Western are low credit card discounts, professional development and training programs, and insurance coverage at low rates through Best Western insurance.[13]

Despite these opportunities, there are several reasons why an independent property may decide against affiliating with a hotel chain.

Membership Fees and Marketing Assessment. Franchise fees and marketing assessments are usually based on total rooms revenue, including business that the independent operator would have enjoyed without chain affiliation. Affiliation typically affects a property's reservations system. Independent operations usually receive reservations directly through their front office. Under chains, some of these direct reservations would be placed through a reservations network—thus incurring additional reservation fees. Although fee structures vary, an owner may expect expenditures in the range of 5% to 8% of rooms revenue for fees covering the name, advertising, collateral material, the reservations system, and periodic inspections.

Conformity. Most lodging establishment owners are entrepreneurs or entrepreneurial companies. Their self-images may not conform to the standardization which affiliation usually requires.

Capital Cost. To protect the quality of the brand image, affiliated properties are required to maintain certain quality standards. In some cases, this may require renovation and modernization of a facility. In many cases, if operators don't invest in the changes stipulated by the chain, they risk losing their franchises.

Chains

Chain operations have a number of distinctions. The forms which will be discussed in this section are franchise agreements and management contracts.

Franchising. Conceptually, the franchise agreement is a long-term contract wherein an entity (the franchiser) agrees to lend its name, goodwill, and back-up support to a property (the franchisee) that agrees to maintain required quality standards for design, decor, equipment, and operating procedures. The franchiser receives income in the form of fees as its main benefit.

Although the franchiser imposes a number of controls on the franchisee, the franchisee maintains a degree of independence. Both parties may benefit from the agreement since the franchiser is able to rapidly penetrate a new market while the franchisee gains association with a company's logo, name, and expertise.

Through franchising, a franchiser may expand by using the capital or borrowing capacity of the franchisee. As an added benefit, a company may draw on a franchisee's knowledge of local markets and real-estate situations and acquire the best sites for future properties. From the side of the franchisee, the property may have greater motivation if equity is invested in the venture. This so-called "sweat equity" becomes a form of self-induced control and motivation. The major drawback to franchising is that companies may have problems maintaining quality control in their franchised units and that franchisees sometimes resist refurbishing their facilities.

Most companies with substantial franchise operations also operate some company-owned units. These units often serve as research and development locations as well as showcase operations of the "concept" that can be used to good advantage in establishing credibility with potential franchisees.

Management Contracts. Another type of chain organization operates properties whose form of ownership may range from individual businesspeople to partnerships to large insurance companies. In other words, management contract companies are hired by a hotel's owner to manage the property on an ongoing basis.

Management companies fall into two groups: (1) hotel chains such as Marriott, Sheraton, or Hyatt, and (2) independents such as single or small, multi-site operators that are usually regionally oriented. A management contract sometimes includes the rights to proprietary names and trademarks, but usually does not include the reservations network fees or marketing assessments. Unlike franchise or referral fees, management contract fees are highly negotiable, vary in structure, and may incorporate equity participation, fee limits, allocation of management company overhead, and other factors.

Hotel chains have found the use of management contracts to be a low-cost, low-risk method of expanding their markets. With considerably less investment per property than direct ownership, a management contract may, in some cases, also exempt a chain from loss or liability should a property fail. Independent management companies also enjoy the benefits of such arrangements as new lodging properties are regularly seeking their services.

Management companies are most often selected by the hotel's entrepreneur, institutional investor, syndicator, or developer. The following guidelines are criteria which some properties may use when evaluating and selecting a management company.[14]

1. **Experience.** Has the management company operated hotels similar in type and size to the subject property?

2. **Location.** Where is the management company's home office and current operational base? Geographic proximity to supervisory support staff is very desirable.

3. **Brand Familiarity.** Has the management company operated hotels affiliated with the same brand under consideration? Different hotel chains utilize different quality standards.

4. **Recommendations.** Can the management company provide recommendations from past and current clients?

5. **Current Performance.** How well is the management company performing with its current portfolio of properties?

6. **Fees.** How much does the management company charge for services? As pointed out, management contracts do vary.

7. **Services Provided.** Management companies often provide services in the area of sales and marketing, reservations, accounting controls, design, engineering, food and beverage, purchasing, and energy auditing. Additional service areas may include assistance in development, planning, construction, and preopening activities.

8. **Equity Investment and Guarantees.** Shortfall guarantees, working capital loans, or purchase of an ownership interest can sometimes be secured from the management company. In general, however, such investment usually results in tougher contractual terms.

9. **Termination.** Usually, the management company takes the position that if the property is doing fine under its control, then the company should maintain its role. However, should a hotel decide to terminate the contract and operate without outside assistance or hire another management company, hefty cancellation penalties can result.

Formulation of an effective marketing strategy must be rooted in a sound understanding of the nature of the competition that a firm faces. An important component of marketing strategy is understanding the different types of lodging facilities that exist. This chapter has examined the various categories that can be used to classify lodging operations in order to provide marketing strategists with a wider perspective of the lodging industry than that provided by the positions of their own hotels. By viewing the lodging industry in this way, unique insights can be gained that may help a property develop a marketing strategy that strengthens its competitive position within the industry.

Endnotes

1. The following definitions are from D. Daryl Wyckoff and W. Earl Sasser, *The U.S. Lodging Industry* (Lexington, MA: D.C. Heath and Company, 1981), p. xxiii.

2. Masgood Kahn, quoted by Barry Trader in "Denver's Park Suite: An All-Suite Star in the Heart of Downtown," *The Travel Agent*, February 27, 1984, p. 42.

3. Brian Hickey, "All-Suites Concept Prospering in Today's Economy," *Hotel & Resort Industry*, June 1985, p. 52.

4. W. Earl Sasser, R. Paul Olsen, and D. Daryl Wyckoff, *Management of Service Operations: Test, Cases, and Readings* (Boston: Allyn and Bacon, Inc., 1978), p. 18.

5. Dan R. E. Thomas, "Strategy is Different in Service Businesses," *Harvard Business Review*, July–August 1978, in *Strategic Marketing Planning in the Hospitality Industry*, ed. Robert L. Blomstrom (East Lansing, MI: Educational Institute of the American Hotel & Motel Association, 1983), p. 23.

6. Edward Watkins, "The Secrets of Hyatt's Success," *Lodging Hospitality*, October 1985, p. 74.

7. Brian Hickey, "Budget Chain Continues Phenomenal Growth," *Hotel & Resort Industry*, July 1968, p. 68.

8. Jay Ferguson, "Budget Hotels Luring Business Travelers by Emphasizing Value," *Corporate and Incentive Travel*, July 1984, p. 87.

9. Ibid.

10. Patricia Askin, "Lodging's 400 Top Performers," *Lodging Hospitality*, August 1985, pp. 46–84.

11. For additional information, refer to *Condominiums and Timesharing in the Lodging Industry: A How-To Manual on Operations and Management*, published by The Educational Institute of AH&MA.

12. Presentation by Henry Silverman, Chairman of Days Inns, to Economy Lodging Conference sponsored by Laventhol & Horwath, Chicago, September 9, 1985.

13. John Spina, "Best Western's Blueprint for the Future," *Hotel & Resort Industry*, November 1984, p. 18.

14. "Management Companies Sell Expertise, Efficiency, Control," *Hotel & Motel Management*, April 1985, p. 65.

REVIEW QUIZ

When you feel you have covered all of the material in this chapter, answer these questions. Choose the *best* answer. Check your answers with the correct ones found on the Review Quiz Answer Key at the end of this book.

True (T) or False (F)

T   F   1. A hotel is typically defined as a multi-story building with its own dining rooms, meeting rooms, and other public spaces.

T   F   2. The term "special-purpose lodging facilities" refers to hotels, motels, and resorts.

T   F   3. Bed and breakfast operations are designed primarily for business travelers.

T   F   4. The location of conference centers is relatively unimportant to the markets they serve.

T   F   5. All-suite hotels are usually more suitable for guests who need lodging accommodations for long periods of time.

T   F   6. A property's size should play a role in the property's marketing planning.

T   F   7. Forecasters have predicted that economy hotels will have all but disappeared from the lodging industry in the next ten years.

T   F   8. Economy hotels appeal primarily to budget-minded travelers who want reasonably priced rooms with relatively few amenities.

T   F   9. Hotels offering mid-range service appeal to the largest segment of the traveling public.

T   F   10. Location plays an insignificant role in the structure of the lodging industry.

T   F   11. The development of resort hotel communities may involve the sale of condominiums.

T   F   12. Affiliation refers to the political preferences of the owners of lodging properties.

T   F   13. Independent hotels are single-unit operations which are owned or operated by a multi-unit organization.

T   F   14. Hotel chains have found the use of management contacts to be a low-cost, low-risk method of expanding their markets.

T   F   15. In a typical franchise agreement, the franchisee does not need to maintain the quality standards of the franchiser.

Multiple Choice

16.   Conference centers are:

    · a.   usually located in major cities.
    b.   basically mainstream hotels with meeting facilities.
    c.   equipped with recreational facilities as well as areas conducive to quiet study.
    d.   usually busiest on weekends.

17.   All-suite hotels:

    a.   are among the fastest-growing segments in the lodging industry.
    b.   appeal to several different markets.
    · c.   can be converted to apartments, condominiums, or even offices.
    d.   all of the above

18.   Which of the following categories represents three basic levels of service provided
    by operations in the lodging industry?

    a. $30 and under, $50 and under, $90 and over
    b.   economy/limited, mid-range, world-class
    c.   independent, chain affiliated, managed by contracts
    d.   executive floors, conference centers, all-suite hotels

19.   Which of the following factors should owners consider when contemplating chain
    affiliation for their independent properties?

    a.   financing
    b.   reservations system
    c.   cost benefits and operational expertise
    d.   all of the above

20.   Management contract companies:

    a.   are hired by a hotel's owner to manage the property on an ongoing basis.
    b.   are generally less flexible than franchise agreements.
    c.   usually charge marketing assessments.
    d.   usually require greater capital investments than franchise agreements.

Chapter Outline

Basic Market Patterns
Criteria for Defining Useful Market
    Segments
Geographic Segmentation
Demographic Segmentation
Behavioral Segmentation: Occasion-Based
      Business Travel
      Pleasure Travel
Behavioral Segmentation: Benefit-Based
Behavioral Segmentation: Usage Rate
Behavioral Segmentation: Loyalty Status
Psychographic Segmentation
      Lifestyle Trends
      Psychocentric/Allocentric Personality
        Types
      Consistency and Complexity
Market Coverage Strategies
      Undifferentiated Marketing
      Differentiated Marketing
      Concentrated Marketing
      Criteria for Choosing a Market
        Coverage Strategy

Learning Objectives

1. Define market segmentation.

2. Identify three basic market patterns.

3. Define the criteria which determine the usefulness of market segmentation variables.

4. Explain what is meant by geographic segmentation.

5. Explain what is meant by demographic segmentation.

6. Explain what is meant by occasion-based behavioral segmentation.

7. Identify major segments of the business travel market.

8. Identify major segments of the pleasure travel market.

9. Explain what is meant by discretionary income.

10. Define leisure time.

11. Explain what is meant by benefit-based behavioral segmentation.

12. Describe behavioral segmentation that is based on usage rates and loyalty status.

13. Explain what is meant by psychographic segmentation.

14. Define psychocentric and allocentric personality types.

15. Identify three basic market coverage strategies.

6

Analyzing Markets

❝If you asked 100 hotel or resort marketing and salespeople if customer needs play an important role in the marketing of their product, everyone would probably say, 'Yes, of course they do,' and then wonder why you asked such a question.

I guess what I'm trying to figure out is, if we all think we are relating to customer needs in our marketing, then why does just the opposite appear to be true in so many cases?

A canned sales presentation that tells a motor coach broker about a hotel's meeting room for 1,000 people. A form proposal letter to the executive secretary of a professional society of nuns that describes the hotel's new disco in great detail. Advertising directed towards training directors that emphasizes romance in the tropics. These are just some examples of the overwhelming evidence that, while we may sincerely think we are relating to customer needs in hotel marketing, we really aren't doing a very good job of it.

Our problems in this area can be solved if we go back to a fundamental concerning customer needs that we must use every day of our business lives to be successful—Show customers how we can fulfill their needs better than the competition. In order to do this, we must know what customers' needs are, and then show them via personal selling, media advertising, direct mail, internal promotion and publicity that we are aware of their needs and have the means to fulfill them better than the competition.

This would be very simple if all customers had the same list of needs. However, we must recognize that, although there are certain needs that all customers have in common, other needs vary from market segment to market segment, organization to organization, and from one person to the next. Even though it's difficult to be totally aware of every customer's every need, we can make some pretty accurate assumptions if we look at four basic areas of needs.

First, there are needs that a customer has in common with all other hotel customers. These include needs such as a clean room, a comfortable bed, proper room temperature, hot water, good food and a hassle free atmosphere.

Secondly, there are needs that are shared in common with other customers within the same market segment. Motor coach tour operators have a common need for a place to park the bus, while a corporate meeting planner doesn't care where you park the bus. The meeting planner has a need for meeting space and wants specific information about it, while the family on vacation selects a hotel based on needs that certainly don't include meeting space.

Then there are specific needs a company or association has that are unique to that organization, such as needs for a specific number of meetings of certain sizes in specific locations.

Finally, we have the personal needs of the customer. The voluntary meeting planner who is arranging [his/her] first meeting has the need for direction from

Exhibit 1   Market Patterns

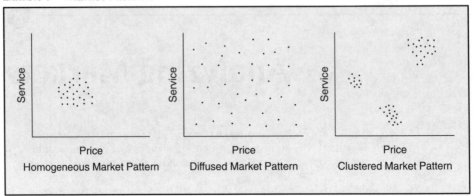

Adapted from Philip Kotler's *Marketing Management: Analysis, Planning, and Control* (Englewood Cliffs, N.J.: Prentice-Hall, Inc., 1984), p. 253.

the hotel to help [him/her] learn the rudiments of meeting planning. The full-time professional meeting planner who is on thin ice with [his/her] boss has a personal need to arrange the best meeting in the company's history.

The bottom line is that a customer's needs are very important to him or her. You turn customers on if it's obvious to them that you've given thought to those needs when you make a sales presentation, write a letter or advertise to them through a magazine. On the other hand, you turn them off when you are obviously not aware of their most basic needs."[1]

Basic Market Patterns

Market segmentation is a means of analyzing demand. Consumers with similar needs and wants are grouped together for the purpose of better focusing on and serving the market. The idea behind market segmentation is that the market for a particular product or service is really made up of groups of consumers with distinctive needs and preferences. These groups are called "segments" of the market. Through the process of market segmentation, lodging properties identify customer groups that differ from other customer groups in terms of certain variables such as needs, income, geographical location, buying habits, and other characteristics as well. Exhibit 1 reveals three different market patterns which could result from segmenting the lodging market according to just two consumer preference variables—price and service level.

The first graph reveals a homogeneous market pattern which discloses no natural market segments. Consumer preferences all fall roughly into one recognizable category. Lodging companies entering this market would strive to position themselves in the center of consumer preferences and offer mid-price rooms and a moderate service level.

The second graph reveals a diffused market pattern which also discloses no natural market segments. Unlike the consumer preferences of the homogeneous market pattern which fall into only one recognizable category, the consumer preferences in a diffused market pattern are so random that there are no recognizable categories whatsoever. Consumers differ so widely in their preferences regarding price and service level that no market segments exist—only individual buyers.

Although the diffused market pattern seems to be the opposite of a homogeneous market pattern, the marketing strategy of a lodging company entering a diffused market would probably be very similar to the strategy of a company entering a homogeneous market. In both instances the companies would try to position themselves in the center of the consumer preferences. This would be the strategy for a company entering a diffused market because the company would attempt to appeal to the majority of consumers while minimizing the degree of dissatisfaction that consumers at the higher or lower ends of the preference scale may experience.

A major difference between the homogeneous and the diffused market patterns arises in relation to competitors. Competitors that follow a company into a diffused market can not only position themselves in the center of consumer preferences, they may also position themselves at either the higher or lower ends of the consumer preference scale and so try to win over consumers that are dissatisfied with the mid-price and moderate service level offered by the first company to enter the diffused market. This latter marketing strategy is not an option for competitors within a homogeneous market. In our example of a homogeneous market, there are no customers at either the higher or the lower ends of the consumer preference scale.

The third graph in Exhibit 1 reveals a clustered market pattern which discloses natural market segments that are clearly recognizable. A lodging firm entering this clustered market has at least three strategic marketing options. The firm could position itself in the center of consumer preferences (that is, equidistant from all three market segments). This marketing strategy is called **undifferentiated marketing.** Or, the firm could position itself squarely within the largest of the market segments. This strategy is called **concentrated marketing.** The final option open to a firm is to develop three different price/service level concepts and position each squarely within each of the market segments revealed in the clustered market pattern shown in Exhibit 1. This marketing strategy is called **differentiated marketing.** Clustered market patterns also offer competitors more options than either the homogeneous or diffused market patterns.

Most lodging firms realize that it is impossible to serve all markets equally well. Customers are either too widely scattered geographically or too different in their buying habits. Furthermore, the particular resources and distinctive competencies of each lodging firm usually place the organization in a position to serve some market segments better than others. Consequently, most properties do not direct their marketing efforts toward the entire lodging market. Instead, they identify the most attractive portions of the market which they can serve most effectively. The final section of this chapter will address market coverage strategies in more detail.

Market segmentation is useful not only to lodging companies which are considering the possibility of entering into new markets, but is also useful to lodging companies which are evaluating the viability of offering new products or services at already existing properties. This is because market segmentation reveals important insights that averages often hide.

For example, let's assume that a lodging company is considering a new restaurant concept as part of its strategic marketing plan. The company polls 100 people and finds that the new restaurant concept receives an overall, or average, rating of only 3.2 on a 5-point scale. Given this information, the new restaurant concept might be dropped. However, the lodging firm's evaluation of the new restaurant concept might change drastically if the results of the poll were broken down in terms of the usage rates of the 100 people who were polled. If the people were **segmented** into such groups as light, medium, and heavy users, an entirely different conclusion could be drawn from the research. If, for example, light users rated the new restaurant concept 2.1, medium users rated it 3.3, and heavy users 4.7, then the average would still be 3.2, but the commercial viability of the new concept would appear much more positive.

Criteria for Defining Useful Market Segments

There is no single set of variables by which to segment a market. Each property must select those variables appropriate to its own resources and distinctive competencies. However, there are general guidelines, or criteria, which define how useful certain variables may be in segmenting a market. No matter which variables are used to segment a market, the resulting market segments must be measurable, accessible, and substantial.

A market segment is useful only if it is possible to measure the size and purchasing power of the consumer group(s) comprising that segment. It must also be possible to effectively reach the consumer group(s) through advertising and promotional campaigns. A useful market segment must also be substantial, that is, large enough and potentially profitable enough to justify a marketing strategy directed toward it. A perfectly useless market segment would be a consumer group of left-handed male business travelers who prefer shellfish in the hotel dining room on Thursday nights. While this market segment may be identified by observation and its purchasing power calculated in terms of an average guest check, the consumer group is inaccessible and unsubstantial.

Two other criteria also help to evaluate the usefulness of any market segment. Market segments should be durable and defensible. They should be durable in the sense that, given consumer trends and changing market conditions, the variables which define market segments today, must continue to be important tomorrow. Market segments should be defensible in the sense that it is possible for a property to actually formulate effective marketing programs by which to attract and serve them. A small lodging company may, for example, identify several market segments, but may not have sufficient staff or other resources by which to develop separate marketing programs for each segment. The defensibility of market segments may also be affected by the existing competitive structure of the industry. It may not be possible for a property to successfully compete against existing properties that already attract and serve a particular market segment.

Markets can be segmented in relation to geographic, demographic, behavioristic, and psychographic variables. The most commonly used variables for segmenting a market are geographic and demographic characteristics. These sets of variables offer the best way of determining how to reach a particular market segment. However, in a rapidly changing society, it may be unwise to base a marketing strategy solely on geographic and demographic data. Just because a segment of the market is within a particular age or income group does not guarantee that the consumers within that group will have similar lodging preferences. Geographic and demographic analyses of demand do not provide sufficient information regarding the likes and dislikes of the market segments which they define. Therefore, they may often need to be supported by a segmentation of demand in relation to behavioristic and psychographic variables.

Geographic Segmentation

Geographic segmentation is often the most useful starting point for a marketing analysis of demand. Geographic segmentation divides the market into different geographical units such as zones, countries, regions, domestic travel zones, districts, states, counties and Standard Metropolitan Statistical Areas (SMSAs), and cities. These discrete geographical areas are then assessed in terms of their growth potential which is often measured in terms of economic activity, competitive environment, and population growth.

Large international lodging firms divide the world into geographic zones such as the Southeast Asian Zone, or the Eastern European Zone. Domestic lodging firms divide the country into regions and domestic travel zones. Regions are often defined by natural boundaries such as the Rocky Mountains. Since, travel between cities within regions accounts for over 65% of all travel in the United States, geographic segmentation by region may be extremely useful to lodging marketers.[2] For example, in the western region, Los Angeles is a feeder market for such cities as Palm Springs, Las Vegas, Phoenix, and San Francisco. These cities are also feeder markets for Los Angeles. Marketing efforts within this region may, therefore, concentrate on both the primary feeder market (Los Angeles) as well as the markets which feed Los Angeles (for example, San Francisco).

Domestic travel zones are smaller than regions and they typically designate a sales or marketing area. For example, Albany to Syracuse to Rochester might be classified as a domestic travel zone. Domestic travel zones are frequently combined to form marketing districts. A district encompasses a geographic area with a concentration of customers.

Counties and Standard Metropolitan Statistical Areas (SMSAs) are other types of geographic segmentation. SMSAs tend to identify the population core within one large county or a number of small counties. For example, the New York City SMSA, which is a huge area in terms of population, encompasses counties in three states and Long Island. Counties and SMSAs play an important role in the marketing of hospitality services. Both print and broadcast media exposure are measured in terms of SMSA markets. Also, in the United States, 24 SMSAs generate approximately 50% of the overnight travel.[3] These SMSAs, which include Los Angeles, Atlanta, Chicago, St. Louis, and Denver, constitute key strategic markets. Heavy travel patterns between pairs of SMSAs (such as between Boston and New York, or between Washington D.C. and New York) are important concerns for large domestic lodging firms because marketing efforts and resources can be directed to those pairs that generate higher volumes of travel.

Geographic segmentation provides helpful guidelines in terms of media purchases such as television, radio, magazines, and newspapers; however, it fails to provide much direction in terms of the specific design of the advertising. This kind of direction is provided by demographic, behavioral, and psychographic methods of market segmentation which are more concerned with causal variables that attempt to explain *why* consumers behave in the ways that they do.

Demographic Segmentation

Demographic segmentation divides a market into customer groups on the basis of such variables as age, gender, family size, marital status, income, occupation, education, religion, race, and nationality. Demographic variables are one of the most common bases for distinguishing among customer groups. This is because there are often high correlations between demographic variables and consumer wants, preferences, and usage rates. For example, the 35 to 44 year age group shows a very high propensity to travel and to stay at lodging facilities when they do travel.[4]

Demographic variables are relatively easy to measure and demographic statistics are easy to obtain. Demographic statistics are compiled not only by independent market research firms, but by federal, state, and local governments as well. Also, since demographic data on readers, viewers, and listeners are readily available for most media vehicles, demographic segmentation provides direction for efficient and effective advertising decision. Even when a market is segmented in non-demographic terms (e.g., behavioral or psychographic variables), there must always be some link back to demographic and geographic characteristics in order to determine the size of the target market and how to reach it most effectively.

Behavioral Segmentation: Occasion-Based

In the lodging industry, occasion-based segmentation portions the market into categories in terms of the purpose for traveling. However, the concept of a "travel market" is so ambiguous that it is of little help to lodging properties in identifying their customers. It is much more practical for properties to distinguish two distinct travel markets on the basis of the purpose for traveling—for business or for pleasure.

Business travel accounts for approximately 45% of the room nights sold each year, while pleasure travel accounts for approximately 40%. Personal travel is another category of occasion-based segmentation. Personal travel accounts for about 8% of travel and includes such purposes as job seeking, funeral attendance, and other non-pleasure related travel. The remaining 7% comes from international travel. We will focus here on the two major purposes for travel—business and pleasure.

Business Travel

The business travel market is extremely important to many lodging properties. Approximately 18 million people (12% of the adult population) take business trips in any given year. They average six trips per year and, because business travelers are less likely to share rooms or stay in the homes of friends or relatives, they account for the bulk of lodging demand.[5] The business travel market can be divided into three broad segments: regular business travel, business travel related to meetings and conventions, and incentive travel.

Regular business travel is an important source of business for many lodging properties. Within the last few years, airlines and hotels have targeted specific products and services toward the business executive traveler. One of the fastest-growing segments of regular business travel is the traveling businesswoman whose needs may often differ from those of male business travelers.

Business travel related to meetings and conventions is commonly classified in terms of two markets: the institutional and the corporate/government markets. The gatherings held by the institutional market are usually open to the public. Examples of institutional gatherings would be the national conventions held by the American Hotel & Motel Association and the National Restaurant Association. The gatherings held by the corporate/government market are usually closed to the public because they often deal with specific corporate or government business matters which are private in nature. Examples of corporate gatherings would include management meetings, regional sales meetings, new product introductions, national sales meetings, training seminars, professional/technical meetings, and stockholder meetings.

Incentive travel is a "hybrid" segment of the business travel market. Although incentive trips are financed by businesses as work incentives, the persons on the incentive trips travel for pleasure as well as for business. Another version of this hybrid travel segment is emerging as business travelers tack vacation days on to their regular business trips.

Two components of business travel, conventions and smaller meetings, are critically important to the vitality of much of the lodging industry. They result in considerable expenditures not only for guestrooms but for banquet and meeting-room facilities as well. Furthermore, they can often be induced to stay at a hotel during off-peak periods. While meetings and conventions can attract hundreds, even thousands, of people, the decision of where and when to have a meeting is made by only a few meeting planners. Sales and marketing efforts that would otherwise be directed to attracting dozens of smaller segments can be more efficiently focused on these meeting planners.

Associations and other large convention groups have a great deal of bargaining power by which to negotiate low room prices. With so many hotels competing for easily identified convention business, it is not surprising that some hotels are targeting their marketing efforts toward the smaller meeting group market. Success in this area may often depend on the property's ability to meet the specialized needs of this market. Randy Lindner, executive director of the Society of Company Meeting Planners, sees new trends in hotel construction that cater to the needs of the small meeting groups: "By isolating conference facilities for small corporate meetings and offering separate catering staffs, small meetings now don't have to compete with larger meetings going on at the same time."[6] Many individual properties are trying to lure customers with special services. For example, Inter-Continental offers an Advantage Plan to meeting planners which includes an office complete with copier, typewriter, phone, message center and supplies. Also available to the meeting planner is a chauffeured limousine, and a twenty-four-hours-a-day meeting aide, who responds via a mobile paging system.[7]

Hotel marketers should realize that serving business travelers (no matter what their purposes for traveling) offers a tremendous opportunity for repeat business. Satisfying business travelers may not only convince them to return for the same business purposes, but may also convince them to bring their spouses, or even to revisit the property with their families during their next vacation.

Pleasure Travel

The pleasure travel market has not been segmented as thoroughly as has the business travel market. Consequently, there is a great deal of overlapping among segments of this market. The specific segmentation of the pleasure travel market often depends on the attractions, products, and services offered by the destination area of a lodging property. Typical market segments include: specialized resort travelers (for example, those seeking health spa facilities or sport instruction such as tennis, golf, etc.), family pleasure travel, travel by the elderly, and travel by singles and couples.

Pleasure travelers are probably among the more fickle of the travel industry market segments. They are generally price sensitive and the volume of pleasure travelers is highly correlated with general economic conditions such as fuel shortages, and national economic recessions. Futhermore, in contrast to business travel which is considered a "necessary" expense, vacations and related lodging accommodations are competing not only for the traveler's discretionary income, but for the individual's leisure time as well.

Income is an important inhibiting factor in shaping the demand for pleasure travel. An individual's personal disposable income is the amount of income left after taxes have been paid. An individual's discretionary income is the amount of disposable income left after expenditures for basic, maintenance living needs. This discretionary income directly affects pleasure travel because it is income that can be spent for leisure activities.

The amount of leisure time is another important factor in shaping the demand for pleasure travel. The way that individuals spend time can be broken down into three categories of activities: work activities, maintenance activities (eating, sleeping, shopping for food and necessities), and leisure activities. Since the total amount of time available to individuals is fixed, any change in one category of activities affects the amount of time available for the other two. As the workweek declines, more time is freed for maintenance and/or leisure activities.

Leisure time can be divided into three categories: weekdays, weekends, and vacations. The form of leisure time affects the opportunities that people have to travel. A further reduction in the workweek would certainly have consequences which affect the demand for lodging facilities. However, the specific effects would depend on the way that the workweek would be reduced. A shorter workday would increase weekday leisure time, a four-day workweek would probably increase weekend leisure time. The workweek could also be reduced by increasing workers' vacation time. These different kinds of reductions would have quite different consequences for the lodging industry.

Behavioral Segmentation: Benefit-Based ————————

The principle underlying this segmentation strategy is that the benefits people seek in consuming any product or service are the true determinants of buying behavior and that benefits actually determine behavior much more accurately than do geographic, demographic, or lifestyle characteristics. Benefit segmentation requires determining the major benefits that people look for in lodging accommodations, and the kinds of people who look for each of those benefits. Properties can then position themselves toward specific customer groups which seek similar benefits from staying at lodging facilities.

It is important to note that individual benefits are likely to have appeal for several segments. In fact, research suggests that most people would like as many benefits as possible. However, the relative importance they attach to individual benefits can differ markedly and, therefore, can be used to effectively identify market segments.

Behavioral Segmentation: Usage Rate ————————

Many markets can be segmented into non-users, ex-users, potential users, first-time users, and regular users of lodging facilities. High market share companies are particularly interested in converting potential users into actual users, while smaller firms will try to get users of competitors' properties to switch their loyalties.

Volume segmentation divides regular users into light-, medium-, and heavy-user groups. This approach can produce interesting results. For instance, it may be the case that heavy users, often the smallest portion of a market, account for a relatively high percentage of total sales.

The so-called "heavy-half" approach to marketing expenditures is effective in directing advertising dollars toward the most important segments of a market. However, the problem with this approach in relation to usage rate segmentation is that not all heavy-users are seeking the same benefits from a property's products or services. Furthermore, because of the law of diminishing returns, advertising dollars may be better spent targeting ex-users, potential users, and first-time users.

Behavioral Segmentation: Loyalty Status ————————

A market can also be segmented by consumer loyalty patterns. Lodging guests may be loyal to particular brands (e.g., Hyatt), or to particular properties (e.g., the Hyatt in Atlanta). If we assume that there are five brands, or five properties, (A, B, C, D, and E) for customers to choose among, we can segment the market demand into four customer groups according to their loyalty status.[8]

Hard-Core Loyals. These consumers buy one brand all the time. Thus, a buying pattern of AAAAA represents a consumer with undivided loyalty to brand A.

Soft-Core Loyals. These consumers are loyal to two or three brands. The buying pattern ABABA represents a consumer whose loyalties are divided between A and B.

Shifting Loyals. These consumers shift their loyalties from one brand to another. The buying pattern AABBB suggests a consumer who is shifting brand loyalty from A to B.

Switchers. These consumers show no loyalty to any brand. The buying pattern ABCDE suggests a switcher who is either deal-prone (buys only the brand on sale) or variety-prone (wants something different every time).

Brand loyalty can be explained in a number of ways:

- Habit
- Maximization of value to price
- Costs of switching brands
- Availability of substitutes
- Perceived risk associated with the purchase
- Past satisfaction with the product or service

Because of the difficulty in obtaining reliable pre-purchase information about services in general, consumers may be reluctant to change brands because they are uncertain whether the change will actually increase their satisfaction. Obtaining reliable information about alternative brands may be costly for a consumer in terms of both time and money. For instance, in order to "comparative shop" for services, consumers must visit various service establishments in person. This is not the case with comparative shopping for manufactured products where consumers generally shop in one or more retail stores which display competing products in close proximity. Also, consumers often perceive greater risks in purchasing services than they do in purchasing manufactured products. This increases the likelihood of customer brand loyalty when a lodging property succeeds in satisfying its guests.

Another reason why guests may become brand loyal is their own recognition that repeat patronage may lead to greater satisfaction of their needs. This can be an important factor in the lodging industry, especially in the luxury sector of the market. Becoming a "regular" customer allows the hotel staff and management to learn the guest's tastes and preferences, and this may encourage more interest on the part of the staff to satisfy the regular guest's needs. Therefore, a guest may exhibit greater brand loyalty in order to cultivate a satisfying relationship with the property.

One factor mitigating brand-loyalty in the lodging industry is the availability of individual brands in certain locations. For example, some consumers may prefer staying in Hyatt hotels, but are unable to locate a Hyatt in a particular city where their business takes them. Consequently, they may decide to stay in a Westin (or Sheraton, Marriott, etc.). In this way, they learn about competing brands and if the competing brand is roughly the same quality level (or higher), their loyalty to a particular hotel chain may diminish. Availability factors are one of the reasons why hotel chains want to expand as widely as possible.

A property can learn a great deal by analyzing the loyalty patterns in its market. For example, by studying soft-core loyals, shifting loyals, and switchers, a property can pinpoint which brands are most competitive with its own as well as identify its own marketing weaknesses. The property may be able to convert these groups into hard-core loyals through implementing a number of appropriate marketing strategies and tactics.

Psychographic Segmentation

Psychographic segmentation divides a market into customer groups on the basis of their lifestyles, personality characteristics, or the attitudes, interests, and opinions they may have relating to leisure time and lodging accommodations. Psychographic data is richer and more descriptive than demographic data because it often provides reasons which may explain certain forms of consumer behavior. In this section we will discuss two approaches to psychographic segmentation and their implications for the lodging industry: lifestyle characteristics and psychocentric/allocentric personality types.

Lifestyle Trends

The Value Analysis and Life-Styles program (VALS), developed by SRI International in Menlo Park, California, classifies the adult population into three major groups: needs-driven, outer-directed, and inner-directed.

Needs-Driven. These groups of individuals are driven by basic human needs. For the most part, these groups are composed of *survivors* which may include poverty-stricken individuals in the most disadvantaged segments of a society, and *sustainers* which include other disadvantaged, and mostly young individuals, who are struggling to get ahead economically.

Outer-Directed. These groups of individuals conduct their lives according to what they believe others may think. There are three distinct subgroups: (1) *Belongers* who are traditionalists, and are typically characterized as low or medium income and low to average educational backgrounds; (2) *Emulators* who are young and ambitious, live flamboyantly, are upwardly mobile and status-conscious with good incomes and above average educational backgrounds; and (3) *Achievers* who are generally success-oriented, materialistic, and have high incomes and excellent educational backgrounds.

Inner-Directed. These groups of individuals live according to their inner wants and pleasures. They include: (1) *I-am-me* types who are mostly in their late teens and early twenties, impulsive, faddish, and somewhat narcissistic; (2) *Experiential* types who are usually in their 20s and 30s, and are seeking a rich inner life, direct and immediate experiences, and intense involvement; and, (3) *Socially-conscious* individuals who are aware of social issues such as environmentalism, and attempt to pursue socially responsible lives.

VALS has begun to research the specific purchasing behaviors of these lifestyle types. Preliminary findings suggest, for example, that each group has a favorite kind of restaurant. Sustainers and survivors use fast-food services, whereas belongers favor family-type outlets. Emulators and socially-conscious types patronize fast-food restaurants when eating alone, but will go to a fine dining establishment when dining with someone else. I-am-me types are heavy fast-food users.

Some qualifications need to be made regarding these findings. First, as individuals mature and as their values change, they will pass through two or more of these lifestyle types. Second, lifestyle groups are not necessarily homogeneous in their make-up. The incomes of the experiential lifestyle group may be on the high-end for couples that bring home two paychecks and on the low-end for college students. Third, social and economic conditions have much to do with the ascendancy and decline of value systems. For example, a recessionary economy tends to adversely affect the I-am-me group, forcing them back to the more traditional belonger class.

While the VALS approach uses a relatively fixed classification system of lifestyle groups, the lifestyle types defined by Yankelovich, Skelly & White are revised as their annual survey of public attitudes discloses new information regarding social trends. Current lifestyle types include: (1) *Classic values*: An older age group tending toward more traditional values; (2) *Aimless values*: A younger age group, hedonistic and essentially without goals; (3) *Idealized*: Individuals oriented to self-fulfillment through personal achievement; (4) *Detours*: Individuals trying to pursue the good life, but thrown off the track by recent economic instability; and (5) *Balanced*: Individuals trying to balance new and traditional values.

Analysts at Yankelovich, Skelly & White also believe that economic conditions are the greatest determinants of lifestyle roles. That is, lifestyles may give the urge to travel, but the economy dictates the ability to travel. Daniel Yankelovich, founder and head of the firm, addresses what happens to choice when economic growth slows:

> **"**Almost everyone concerned with self-fulfillment stresses how directly their plans hinged on their economic prospects. From the late 1940s into the 1960s, Americans cherished the new freedom their affluence secured for them. Then, abruptly, came a stunning reversal of the economy and the culture. The economic reversals of recent years have disoriented Americans…. In the past ten years, a significant shift in attitudes has taken place—from an optimistic faith in an open-ended future to a fear of economic instability. **"**[9]

The analysis of lifestyles has important implications for hospitality marketers. First of all, a knowledge of lifestyles gives advertisers a better picture of the potential customers they are trying to reach. Lifestyle analysis also provides insights into the appropriate tone of voice to use in advertising. Advertisers can gain a sense of whether the tone should be serious, humorous, authoritative, cooperative, contemporary, or traditional. Psychographic information is also useful in identifying the rewards people seek in their activities and interests. Finally, lifestyle segmentation is extremely useful in understanding the roles that potential customers actually define for themselves.

Ruth Ziff, executive vice-president of the New York advertising agency Doyle, Dane Bernbach, notes that one of the most significant findings of the firm's latest survey of the lifestyles of the "middle" generation (from 25 to 49 years of age) is "the acceleration in the move away from material awards to personal experiential goals, that is, activities that contribute to physical and emotional well-being, things such as leisure and recreation. More than half (56%, up from 48% a year earlier) feel a vacation is no time to cut corners and that they'd rather spend money on leisure activities than on material possessions."[10]

Psychocentric/Allocentric Personality Types

Lifestyle analysis is not the only kind of psychographic segmentation tool. Personality analysis can also provide valuable insight into consumer behavior. Personality is a complex psychological phenomenon, and the terminology used to describe it is sometimes ambiguous and esoteric. Perhaps the simplest way to define the term "personality" is to view it as a constellation of traits, attitudes, and habits that direct a person's perception of and interaction with his or her environment. As such, "personality" is the underlying determinant of an individual's lifestyle. The following section reviews one aspect of personality and travel behavior through the dimensions of psychocentric and allocentric personality types.

Psychocentric Personality Types. Psychocentrics are detail-oriented, concerned primarily with themselves, generally anxious, somewhat inhibited, and usually not very adventuresome. Because they are somewhat passive, rest and relaxation are among their strongest travel motives. They have a strong need for predictability in their lives and typically visit familiar destinations within easy driving distance. Psychocentrics prefer activities, hotel accommodations, restaurants, and entertainment, which are consistent and predictable. Consequently, they are likely to visit the same vacation spot year after year, indicating a need for travel in terms of a change of scene rather than a desire for novelty. Psychocentrics avoid any "real" adventures because they fear the unknown.

Allocentric Personality Types. Allocentrics are adventuresome, self-confident, curious, outgoing, and eager to reach out and experiment with life, even at some risk. Allocentrics have a strong need for novelty and change in their lives. Allocentrics are active individuals, preferring out-of-the-way vacation destinations and meeting people with cultural backgrounds which differ from their own. They are extremely flexible and take every opportunity to escape from predictability and sameness. Another way of describing psychocentric and allocentric personality types is in terms of consistency and complexity.

Consistency and Complexity

Consistency can be understood as a need for balance, harmony, sameness, the absence of conflict, and predictability. According to theorists, inconsistency produces psychological tension in much the same way as thirst or hunger would. Under such circumstances, an individual is expected to seek out things which are predictable and consistent in order to reduce the tension. For example, travelers may learn to make advance reservations, or to use a travel agent, or to fly only on scheduled air carriers.

Complexity, on the other hand, can be understood as a need for novelty, unexpectedness, change, and unpredictability. According to theorists, complexity is pursued because it is inherently satisfying. Individuals seeking complexity might choose to drive on back roads and to patronize out-of-the-way inns and restaurants.

The Hyatt Regency at Hemmeter Center. (Courtesy of Wimberly, Whisenand, Allison, Tong, and Goo Architects)

An individual's need for consistency or complexity is greatly modified by his or her job and home life. The consistency (or complexity) that people find in their lives at home and at work must be balanced with some degree of complexity (or consistency). For example, prolonged exposure to a monotonous environment will cause most people to become bored and understimulated; this could lead to depression, paranoia, and hallucinations. An assembly-line worker, who performs the same tasks five days a week, fifty weeks a year, needs to counter the psychological tension brought on by extreme consistency by stimulating change. Likewise, prolonged exposure to a highly demanding environment will lead to overstimulation, producing tension and stress that can lead to ulcers, heart attacks, and premature death. Top executives work in an environment of extreme unpredictability, variety, and complexity. Each day executives deal with different problems, different people, and different work settings (e.g., the office, the hotel lobby, the airplane, etc.).

It should be clear that well-adjusted people need a mixture of consistency and complexity in their lives. Furthermore, the amount of novelty and change that is needed will vary from one individual to another. This need is usually fulfilled by seeking consistency in certain domains of experience and complexity in others. For the great mass of people, consistency is usually provided by the organized routine that they find at home and sometimes at work. At home, individuals may prefer to

Pago Pago Intercontinental. (Courtesy of Wimberly, Whisenand, Allison, Tong, and Goo Architects)

eat at precisely the same time each day, and to prepare their eggs, steaks, and martinis always in the same way. They may mow their lawns at the same time each week and look forward to watching the same TV show from their easy chairs. However, extreme consistency (especially if it is reinforced by consistency in the job) can lead to a great deal of psychological tension. To reduce psychological tension individuals may decide to travel.

Travel represents one of the most popular forms of stimulation for people seeking to escape boredom and consistency. More than most other forms of escape, travel frees us from boredom because it allows us to leave behind the attitudinal and behavioral restrictions that prohibit us from "playing" at home. There are no domestic roles to act out, no household jobs to be done. Joffre Dumazedier, a French social scientist, refers to travel as a kind of game that allows us to escape temporarily into a secondary reality. There we play for a time at being rich, primitive, or daringly brave—things which may be utterly at variance with our everyday lives.[11]

Individuals with strong psychocentric personalities will normally be attracted to destinations like Coney Island, Miami Beach, and Monterey—destinations which are well known, offer no surprises, and have been visited by thousands of others. Individuals with strong allocentric personalities, on the other hand, will normally be attracted to unusual destinations like the South Pacific, Africa, and Antarctica. The so-called mid-centrics—who are neither really adventurous nor fearful of travel—represent the mass market for pleasure travel. They are attracted to destinations that are foreign and unfamiliar, but not completely so such as Hawaii, the Caribbean, Europe, and Mexico.

Likewise, psychocentrics would tend to patronize only well-known restaurants as well as familiar lodging chains offering standardized accommodations and services. Allocentrics, on the other hand, might choose to patronize independent lodging facilities instead of chains offering standardized (or Americanized) accommodations and services. They would also patronize local, independent restaurants specializing in indigenous (and sometimes unusual) foods.

As people travel, they tend to become more receptive to new experiences, more active and adventuresome, perhaps in response to an established routine that they suddenly perceive as boring. Travel itself serves to make psychocentric people less so, and makes mid-centric persons more allocentric. The attitudinal change that travel brings about is normally a long-term process, but it is not unusual to see people who have visited the Caribbean or Mexico later traveling to the Orient, Russia, or Africa.

Non-allocentric individuals might tend to mitigate the threatening aspects of traveling to a relatively unknown destination by traveling with a large group or being escorted by a professional tour guide. The group itself might consist of a large number of acquaintances—fellow workers, fellow members of a church group, or a fraternal organization. Such a move would provide familiarity, consistency, and security. Club Med attempts to reduce the risk of traveling to relatively exotic locations by advertising their properties as self-sufficient villages.

Destinations, as well as people, change over time. At first, it is the allocentric personalities that are attracted to the less well-known, out-of-the-way vacation spots. As the destination becomes more well-known through publicity or word-of-mouth, people of a more psychocentric nature arrive. As the destination becomes more popular and more people arrive, the destination becomes more commercialized—standardized lodging facilities, fast-food restaurants, and gift shops quickly appear. Hawaii is a case in point. It differs markedly from what it was fifteen or twenty years ago. Today's visitor to Honolulu may spend a week in a Holiday Inn or Sheraton that is not too different from those in their hometowns. They can sip an exotic Polynesian drink, order fresh seafood, and buy a floral-print shirt, but unless they take a trip to one of the outer islands, it is unlikely that they will discover anything dramatically new or unusual.

Consistency and complexity can be achieved by mixing the elements of the vacation package. Consider the consistency-oriented business or pleasure traveler, who frequently journeys to the same destination and who regularly stays at the same hotel because it offers him or her standardized accommodations and services. In order to offset this sameness, the same individual may choose to balance his or her need for consistency with a more unusual experience—dining out at one of the local restaurants. Marketers need to identify the types of amenities and activities which offer a balance of consistency and complexity such as offering regional specialties in the restaurant, or an unusual decor. Conversely, marketers in relatively exotic locations need to identify activities which provide some measure of consistency such as bridge tournaments, home movies, and formal cocktail receptions.

There are some cautions to the use of psychographic segmentation. First, lifestyle segmentation greatly increases survey costs. Second, even where lifestyle segments have been identified, it is sometimes difficult for marketers to know how to effectively reach the identified segments. Segmenting a market in terms of lifestyle, or in terms of personality types, is of practical importance only if the identified market segments can be reached. It may be necessary to identify the geographic or demographic characteristics of psychographically defined market segments in order to effectively reach the target markets.

Despite these cautions, psychographic information can add a useful dimension for understanding consumers and their preferences. William D. Wells, Senior Vice President for Needham, Harper and Steers advertising agency offers some useful advice:

> **"**To be useful in making real-world marketing decisions, psychographic data must be in some middle range between being almost totally redundant and being entirely unrelated to the behavior being studied. They must contain just the right amount of surprise. When that is the case, they can be very useful indeed, even when correlations are not high and even when questions about reliability and validity cannot be completely answered.**"**[12]

Market Coverage Strategies

Once the market segmentation analysis is completed, the hospitality marketers must determine how many markets their property wishes to serve and how many products it wishes to offer. There are three basic types of market coverage strategies: undifferentiated or mass marketing; differentiated or multiple-segment, multiple-product marketing; and, concentrated marketing.

Undifferentiated Marketing

With this marketing strategy, a lodging firm targets an entire market or the largest segment of a market with a single product/service offering. Undifferentiated marketing focuses on what is common among the needs of consumers rather than on what is different, and designs a marketing program that will appeal to the broadest number of potential guests.

Undifferentiated marketing can usually achieve cost economies. The single product/service offering keeps down production, inventory, and advertising costs. Also, the absence of market segmentation research or sophisticated marketing planning lowers the costs of marketing departments and research and development departments as well.

However, the problem with undifferentiated marketing is that populations are diverse with respect to benefits and needs and it is difficult to design a product that appeals to all people. In fact, the very act of attracting one segment of a market may automatically alienate others. For example, a mid-priced motel with a moderate service level may not appeal to price-sensitive customers or to customers who seek the amenities and services offered by luxury properties. Competing firms with products designed for particular segments of the population may erode the market base of a firm that practices undifferentiated marketing. Also, larger market segments may be less profitable because they attract heavy competition.

Differentiated Marketing

A differentiated marketing strategy targets several segments or possibly even all the segments of a market and designs separate product/service offerings for each of them. By offering product and marketing variations (including variations based on price), a lodging firm hopes to attain a higher volume of sales and a more solid position within each market segment than it would if it offered only one product to all segments. It also hopes for greater repeat purchasing because the firm's offerings match customers' needs and wants, rather than the other way around.

While there may be some valuable synergies in this strategy, there are also disadvantages. When a firm operates in multiple market segments, scale economies may be lost and administrative functions may become fragmented. Potential cost increases for lodging firms include:

- Product-Modification Costs: Modifying a product (or designing an entirely new product) to meet different market segment requirements usually involves additional research, development, and design costs.

- Administrative Costs: The firm has to develop separate marketing plans for the separate segments of the market. This requires extra marketing research, forecasting, sales analysis, promotion, and planning management.

- Promotion Costs: Multiple-segment, multiple-product marketing involves trying to reach different market segments with different advertising. This leads to lower usage rates of individual media and the loss of quality discounts. Furthermore, since each segment may require separate creative advertising planning, promotion costs are increased.

Concentrated Marketing

Through a concentrated marketing strategy, a lodging firm seeks to achieve a strong market position in the few segments that it targets and plans to serve. Success in concentrated marketing strategies often comes about through a firm's knowledge of the segments' needs and the special reputation it acquires among that particular customer group. Generally, these firms enjoy many operating economies because of specialization in product design, advertising and promotion, and administration. Also, if the market segment is growing, the firm can earn a high rate of return.

Concentrated marketing can entail substantial risks. The particular market segment which the firm serves can be adversely affected by environmental, political, or economic conditions over which the firm has little or no control. For example, the market for highway motels may decline as oil shortages push up gasoline prices. Also, changes in the competitive structure of the industry may seriously affect firms that practice concentrated marketing. For example, a competitor may decide to enter the same market segment, taking sales away from the original entrant.

Criteria for Choosing a Market Coverage Strategy

In choosing a market coverage strategy, lodging marketers usually consider the following factors:

- Company resources: When the firm's resources are limited, concentrated marketing may make the most sense. A lodging firm with limited financial resources, trying to obtain a certain position within a particular market, may limit itself to serving one segment usually in one geographic region.

- Product/market homogeneity: Mass marketing may be best suited for firms producing commodities, or for reaching markets in which buyers have the same tastes or react the same way to marketing stimuli. Service industries that offer products and services which are capable of design variation may get better results with concentrated marketing strategies.

- Competitive marketing strategies: When competitors practice refined techniques of market segmentation, mass marketing or undifferentiated marketing strategies may be suicidal. Conversely, when competitors practice mass marketing, a firm may be able to gain market share by implementing concentrated marketing strategies.

A thorough analysis of the markets, the environment, the product and the competition gives hospitality marketers the necessary knowledge for effective strategic marketing planning. Hospitality marketers also need to understand the tools of marketing—what they are and how to use them most efficiently in the implementation of strategic and tactical marketing plans.

Endnotes

1. This material was excerpted from a column by Thomas T. McCarthy, Jr., "Keeping the Customer's Needs in Mind," *Hotel & Resort Industry*, May 1981, p. 34.
2. Ronald A. Nykiel, *Marketing in the Hospitality Industry* (Boston: CBI Publishing Company, Inc., 1983), p. 12.
3. Ibid, p. 13.
4. Daniel R. Lee, in a marketing study by Drexel Burnham Lambert, 1984, p. 53.
5. Carol Greenberg, "Focus on Room Rates and Lodging Demand," *The Cornell Hotel & Restaurant Administration Quarterly*, November 1985, p. 11.
6. Patricia Askin, "Sometimes Smaller Is Better," *Lodging Hospitality*, June 1985, p. 79.
7. Ibid.
8. This loyalty status classification is adapted from George H. Brown, "Brand Loyalty—Fact or Fiction?" *Advertising Age*, June 1952–January 1953, a series.
9. Thayer C. Taylor, "How Life-Style Shifts Will Shape Our Future," *Restaurant Business*, May 1982, p. 194.
10. Ibid.
11. Joffre Dumazedier, *Toward a Society of Leisure* (New York: The Macmillan Company, 1967), p. x.
12. William D. Wells, "Psychographics: A Critical Review," *Journal of Marketing Research*, May 1975, pp. 196–213.

REVIEW QUIZ

When you feel you have covered all of the material in this chapter, answer these questions. Choose the *best* answer. Check your answers with the correct ones found on the Review Quiz Answer Key at the end of this book.

True (T) or False (F)

(T)   F   1. Market segments are groups of consumers with distinctive needs and preferences.

(T)   F·   2. A homogeneous market pattern discloses no natural market segments.

T·   (F)   3. Diffused market patterns and homogeneous market patterns require entirely different marketing strategies.

(T)   F   4. A clustered market pattern offers competitors more options than either the homogeneous or diffused market patterns.

T·   (F)   5. Geographic segmentation is primarily concerned with causal variables that attempt to explain why consumers behave in the ways they do.

T   (F)   6. Demographic variables are difficult to measure and demographic statistics are difficult to obtain.

(T)   F   7. In the lodging industry, occasion-based segmentation divides the market into categories in terms of the purpose for traveling.

(T·)   F   8. Business travel and pleasure travel account for the greatest amount of travel.

T   (F)   9. Regular business travel is a relatively small source of business for most lodging properties.

(T)   F   10. Income and amount of leisure time are important factors which shape the demand for pleasure travel.

T·   (F)   11. Benefit-based segmentation requires determining the frequency with which a consumer uses a product or service.

T   (F)   12. The analysis of lifestyles is not very important in relation to the advertising functions of marketing.

T·   (F)   13. Psychocentric personality types enjoy challenging and unpredictable sorts of vacation experiences.

(T)   F   14. Travel represents one of the most popular forms of stimulation for people seeking to escape from boredom and consistency.

(T)   F   15. Hospitality marketers use market coverage strategies to determine how many markets their property will serve.

Multiple Choice

16. A homogeneous market:

    a. is characterized by random consumer preferences.
    b. discloses numerous natural market segments.
    c. gives competitors many options for positioning.
    d. is characterized by consumer preferences falling roughly into one recognizable category.

17. To be useful, variables which are used to define market segments must be:

    a. benefit-based.
    b. demographic.
    c. measurable.
    d. psychographic.

18. Demographic variables:

    a. include age, income, and education.
    b. are based upon the benefits consumers seek when purchasing a product or service.
    c. cannot be measured.
    d. are based on the reason for purchasing a product or service.

19. A psychocentric personality type would be most likely to vacation at/in:

    a. a country where a foreign language is spoken.
    b. a well-known location, such as Miami Beach.
    c. an independent lodging facility.
    d. a relatively new and exciting location.

20. Which of the following is *not* a market coverage strategy?

    a. undifferentiated marketing
    b. differentiated marketing
    c. homogeneous marketing
    d. concentrated marketing

Part III

The Tools of Marketing

This section focuses on activities that are important components of marketing programs at individual properties. Chapter 7 begins with a discussion of the typical structure of a hotel's marketing and sales division. The chapter also looks at how a hotel may develop a research base and use positioning techniques to establish and maintain a unique identity in the marketplace. From these two strategic activities, the focus turns to such tools of marketing as sales, advertising, public relations, promotions, and merchandising. Chapter 8 explains the selling process and what goes into successful sales plans. The use of advertising to support a positioning statement, a mission statement, and a strategic plan is discussed in Chapter 9, as well as what a hotel should consider when developing a public relations program. Chapter 10 highlights the importance of keeping promotions consistent with the overall strategic plan and includes a general discussion of pricing. Each chapter is followed by supplemental readings which center on particular applications or considerations for a specific marketing activity.

Chapter Outline

Departmental Organization
Interdepartmental Relationships
Line Level
Research
    Internal Research
    External Research
Positioning

Learning Objectives

1. State the departmental functions which are typically the responsibility of the director of the marketing and sales division in a large hotel.

2. Identify techniques for developing a marketing orientation at the line level of organization.

3. Explain what is meant by situation analysis.

4. State the difference between internal and external research techniques.

5. Explain the function of a focus group.

6. Describe the limitations of guestroom questionnaires and how to overcome them.

7. Explain how data bases may provide properties with valuable marketing research statistics.

8. Define positioning.

7

Integrating the Marketing Concept at the Property Level

For hotel marketing to equal or surpass the marketing practices of product industries, a marketing plan should be rooted in a strong foundation at the property level. Key to developing and maintaining this base is the organizational structure of a hotel's marketing and sales division. Hoteliers desiring a marketing orientation at their properties should also recognize the benefits of research as a strategic marketing activity. By gathering information on markets, competition, guests, and the property itself, marketers may determine how to create and project an image of a hotel's products and services that is attractive and distinct from the competition.

This chapter looks at integrating the marketing concept at the property level by examining the organization and structure of a typical marketing and sales division. Several approaches to research and their application in the development of a marketing plan are also presented. The last subject addressed involves using research data and other elements to shape how guests perceive a hotel in relation to the competition. This concept of positioning is basic to establishing and maintaining a unique identity for a property and works hand-in-hand with various marketing tools.

Departmental Organization

The specific organizational structure of the marketing and sales division (or department) will depend upon the specific needs of the property. Exhibit 1 illustrates one possible organization of a marketing and sales division in a large hotel. As illustrated in this exhibit, the director of the marketing and sales division reports to the assistant general manager and, in turn, supervises personnel with four functions:

- **Sales manager.** The sales manager supervises sales representatives (increasingly called account executives) and clerical staff. This department is responsible for generating group business such as conventions and meetings from associations and corporations, tour/travel business (frequently through interaction with travel agencies and tour companies), etc. When meetings are booked without food and beverage services and without associated guestroom sales, the function is managed by the convention services department. If guestrooms and/or food and beverage functions are sold, the sales department must interact with other divisions within the hotel.

- **Convention services manager.** This official is responsible for managing meeting rooms needed for group business accounts sold by the sales department.

161

Exhibit 1 Sample Organization of Marketing and Sales Division in a Large Hotel

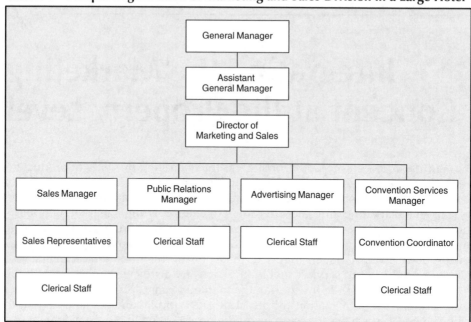

Frequently, this department is responsible for all contacts with the new account after the sale has been booked. In other properties, the responsibilities of the convention services director do not begin until setup work for the meeting begins. When the meeting involves food and beverage services, this department must work closely with the food and beverage division.

- **Advertising manager.** This official is responsible for developing the advertising budget, determining which media will be the most effective outlets for the property's advertising efforts, and developing advertising messages and/or working with the hotel's advertising agency.

- **Public relations manager.** This manager is responsible for developing and implementing short- and long-range plans to ensure that the hotel's preferred image is constantly and consistently portrayed to the community and to the markets being served by the hotel.

Very large hotels may have a fifth department, entertainment, organized within the marketing and sales division. You can imagine the need for someone with expertise in selecting, securing, and arranging for entertainment when budgets may exceed hundreds of thousands of dollars per year.

Interdepartmental Relationships

The hotel marketing and sales division must closely interact with many other departments and divisions within the lodging operation. This only makes good sense since, of course, a primary mission of the division is to sell the products and services offered by the hotel. Several common situations require close interaction, coordination, and communication. For example, suppose the sales manager and staff sell a group meeting which is to have food and beverage services. In a large hotel, the sales manager or sales representative may contact the catering manager whose sales staff may then work closely with the new account to arrange the events. Alternatively, sales representatives in the marketing and sales division may work out arrangements with clients using staff assistance as necessary from the catering department.

A close working relationship is needed between the marketing and sales division and other divisions within the hotel. Planning is critical to the successful execution of a special event of any size, and, from the customer's perspective, it is obviously very important to have that "special" function be right. This can only happen if the marketing and sales division—which makes initial contact with clients—can effectively communicate the customer's needs to affected departments. When communications break down within a hotel, the managers begin to suffer from role ambiguity and role conflict. They don't know what their roles are or how to perform them successfully. When managers are given the responsibility for certain functions without the corresponding authority to perform those functions, their frustrations filter throughout their departments and affect not only their staff, but eventually the guests as well.

Line Level

Besides developing an effective organizational structure at the property level and an efficient communication network among departments or divisions, hospitality operations also need to develop a marketing orientation at the line level. This is critically important because of the high degree of interaction that can take place between line employees and guests. Two effective approaches to instilling a marketing orientation at the line level are the use of internal marketing and the standardization of control through procedures manuals.

Internal marketing refers to those techniques used by some large service organizations to motivate employees and supervisors to adhere to desired performance standards. The techniques are similar to many of the marketing tools directed towards current and potential customers. Employees' preferences and concerns relating to the work environment are identified and addressed in much the same way that the property identifies and addresses the needs and wants of its target markets. Explanations of company policies or attempts to achieve consensus on performance standards are most successful when they take place in open, two-way communication situations. This kind of internal marketing is perhaps best summed up by William George: "The successful service company must first sell the job to its employees, before it can sell services to its customers."[1]

A second technique for integrating the marketing concept at the line level is control by procedure manuals. Operations manuals, found in almost every lodging firm, detail procedures and systems for performing the multitude of tasks found in a lodging operation. Through research and customer feedback, a hotel or motel can identify the "key success factors" and incorporate these into standard operating procedures to be followed by operating personnel.

For example, a number of lodging properties have expanded their manuals to include procedures for how service personnel should interact with customers. These procedures can specify such factors as the maximum time that guests should be allowed to wait before being served, key phrases that should be used in conversing with guests, and the need for service personnel to make eye contact with guests and, where appropriate, when to smile.

G. M. Hostage, former President of Restaurant Operations at Marriott Corporation, addresses many of these points while explaining the "Marriott Bellman" booklet:

> **"**The 'Marriott Bellman' is designed to convince our uniformed doormen that they represent an all-important first and last impression for many of our guests, that they must stand with dignity and good posture, and they must not lean against the wall or put up their feet while sitting. Bellmen are often looked at subconsciously by guests as being 'Mr. Marriott himself' because many times a guest will speak to and deal with the bellman more often during a visit than with any other employees of the hotel.... They are coached to smile often and do all they can to make the guest feel *welcome* and *special*.**"**[2]

Research

Research at the property level usually begins with a situation analysis. This analysis can be seen as an extremely focused form of strategic marketing planning that meets the needs of individual properties. In answer to an industry wide need for a practical guide to marketing planning at the property level, the Foundation of the Hotel Sales and Marketing Association, International, and the Educational Institute of the American Hotel & Motel Association have jointly published *Situation Analysis Workbook*, authored by Julia Crystler.

> **"**The hospitality industry has become increasingly concerned, in recent years, with the concept of strategic marketing planning. Competition is stronger than ever before, and chains continue to grow and dominate the industry. Consumers are more fickle in their buying preferences, and the costs of servicing their needs continue to escalate. Marketing planning is a means of survival and growth in the hospitality industry, and properties are using it in an effort to ... control an increasing competitive and rapidly changing environment.
>
> Situation analysis is the foundation of any good marketing effort. It is the determination, through systematic research, of a property's current market position and projected opportunities for promotion. In order to properly plan, you first need to know as much as possible about the business, the marketplace, and the environment in which the business operates.**"**[3]

—Julia Crystler
Lecturer
School of Hotel, Restaurant and Institutional Management
Michigan State University

Situation analysis is *not* based on hunches, intuition, or lucky guesses. Instead, it is accomplished by thorough, careful research and analysis of five basic components.

1. **The Product.** This is what the property has to offer in terms of accommodations, facilities, and service. Product involves both tangible and intangible aspects. Not only do you have to consider features such as the number of guestrooms in the property, you must also study psychological factors such as the image your property has or the atmosphere created by the furnishings in the lobby. Current marketing efforts, including marketing objectives and how well the property is accomplishing desired goals, should be evaluated. Analysis of the product takes into account both the strengths and the weaknesses of the property as a whole.

2. **The Market.** What types of business does the property currently attract and why? Identification and analysis of past and current guests for group and individual transient markets should be conducted. Market analysis involves a demographic profile of your guests in terms of 'what they look like' and a psychographic/sociographic profile of 'what they think and do.' This process of guest identification should be completed for the property as a whole and for each separate facility in the property.

3. **The Competition.** The same kind of product and market analysis should be conducted for your competitors, both in the local market area and in other cities and locations. What are your competitors' strengths and weaknesses? How is the competition different from or similar to your property? Which of the differences will be significant to what markets?

4. **Market Segmentation.** This portion of the situation analysis is based upon matching your property's needs to your guests' needs. First, determine your property's needs by identifying specific profit areas (rooms, food, beverage, other income areas) that require additional sales activity. Evaluating guests' needs takes into account their preferences for physical facilities, like meeting rooms, and also their personal needs, such as their desire for luxury, convenience, or security. Once property and guest needs are determined, market segments can be categorized and the appropriate target markets can be chosen to fulfill property needs.

5. **Evaluation.** Situation analysis is not a one-time activity. It is an ongoing process for monitoring your property's progress and opportunities in the marketplace. The marketing plan which is developed from your situation analysis must be continually updated through persistent research efforts. Objectives must be compared with actual results, and new strategies for achieving objectives should be developed as necessary. Research that monitors changes in the market and the environment and that evaluates your property's fit with the current situation should be a constant or frequent practice to maintain your competitive edge.[4]

While most people in the industry are familiar with the basic research techniques involved in situation analysis, very little specific emphasis is currently placed on externally conducted research or sophisticated internal research. "An in-house data base can record critical data such as guests' geographic location, SIC code number [standard industrial classification], length of stay, and average folio charge."[5] In view of the knowledge good research can provide, why are hotel companies and individual hotels still following what has been known for the last 30 years as the "Coffman Process"[6] This process of product analysis, competitive analysis, and market analysis, followed by a marketing plan, is still what most hotel people consider the state of the art of research.

Dr. Robert C. Lewis, Professor of Marketing in the School of Hotel, Restaurant, and Travel Administration at the University of Massachusetts, admonishes hotels for relying on descriptive data, rather than attempting to understand why consumers act as they do. On analysis, it is apparent that Dr. Lewis is correct.

> **❝**Descriptive data can identify consumers and classify them into market segments, but it does not make known their preferences and perceptions. Descriptive data can be a valuable management tool; however, it does not tell how consumers will behave.**❞**

> **—Robert C. Lewis, Ph.D.**

Elizabeth D. Kelly, former Director of Corporate Advertising for the Marriott Corporation and for the Ramada properties, describes the research conducted by a typical hotel company this way:

> **❝**Corporately the company has ongoing research. [An] annual tracking study, as well as consumer product and competition studies, is deemed necessary. It involves tracking study results, changes in the marketplace, the economy, etc. At the property level, a system has been developed to assist ... management [with] research in various areas of activity such as food and beverage, transient business, and so forth.**❞**

> **—Elizabeth D. Kelly**

Another corporate director of marketing stated that his company bends over backwards not to impose corporate or industry research too heavily on its properties. His company is careful to respect the local manager's knowledge of his or her marketplace. This corporate marketing director restricts his involvement to providing individual properties with the tools to sample their marketplace, and he does not look very carefully at the data they obtain.

If hotel marketing is to graduate to the level of sophistication already attained by product industry marketing, it must progress in terms of its research sophistication. Hotels must begin to use research generated by outside marketing firms and/or pay professionals to conduct research through focus groups, telemarketing, or consumer attitude surveys. Hotel managers must realize that the era in which they could rely on the data in their reservations system or reservations department, coupled with the Coffman Process, is over. Without this realization, their hotels are in great danger of having their markets taken away from them.

Why is there so much resistance to sophisticated research? The intangibility of the cost/benefit relationship associated with research may be the biggest stumbling block to its application in our industry. If one pays a salesperson, the salesperson covers a certain number of accounts. Likewise, if one buys an advertisement for a specific purpose, the advertisement runs for a certain length of time in identified media, and its effectiveness can be measured by readership appraisal, increased number of customers, or in a variety of other ways. Similarly, the extent to which a promotion attracts attention can be readily seen.

But the benefits of research cannot be directly measured. Research can only be used to make the other marketing tools more effective. The payback for the effective use of well-gathered data is a tangible return linked to one or more of the other marketing functions. Therefore, the value of research is that it contributes to the fulfillment of strategic needs and provides low-cost tactical support. While this may be difficult for some hospitality marketers to accept, it is even more difficult for them to sell to their respective companies' senior executives who lack a marketing orientation. The pervasive attitude, particularly in larger corporations, is that research is something owed to the company by its advertising agency. This is curious, since there is no guarantee that the staff of the advertising agency are effective researchers! Some are; others are not. More important, the need for research currently exceeds what our present suppliers of advertising can provide, so over-reliance on ad agencies is a mistake.

Perhaps the best reason for using good research techniques is that because of the industry's current lack of sophisticated research, the opportunity exists for a hotel to move far ahead of its competition. The manager who has more information than competing managers may be able to surpass these competitors, even if the hotel itself is not superior to those of the competition. Knowledge is power.

Internal Research

Hotels have at their disposal a tremendous amount of statistical data that is seldom considered a part of the research base they use in analyzing their business potential. Since the advent of in-house computers, managers are able to gather far more information on their properties and use it as part of the decision-making process.

For instance, in the food and beverage area, not only can we analyze cover counts in each outlet for each meal period, including banquets, but we can also abstract the checks. That is, we can compile records of which menu items have sold during that meal period. By recording which items are selling and which are not selling, management can see if patterns of customer preferences are emerging. Obviously, this information provides the intelligent manager with guidelines for adjustments in menus. If it is carefully used, it can also provide demographic and psychographic data about the clientele frequenting an establishment.

In the rooms area, most lodging operations that do any research at all analyze reservations information for geographic data only. Others, however, are using reservations data in more creative ways. For example, some hotels can track differences in geographic origin as well as differences in the type of room purchase (full-priced transient rooms, corporate-based rooms, or package plans) according to the day of the week.

The most difficult aspect of internal research is selecting the types of information to be gathered *before* the tracking mechanisms are set up. In most larger operations, computers are used to track many types of information. The hotel's computer system can be designed to receive input directly from the electronic cash registers at the various points of sale around the hotel. However, if management has not decided what information should be recorded and compiled by these machines before they are programmed, then the results are likely to be disappointing. Only the types of reports specified by the programmer will be forthcoming, and these may or may not meet the needs of the ultimate user of that data: the hotel manager.

If you think carefully about what you would like to know about your guests, you will be able to have a research mechanism that provides much more than a simple guest history. For instance, consider how invaluable it would be to know that the customers who purchased your rooms-only package were or were not high potential customers for your restaurants or bars. And wouldn't it be interesting to know whether these clients were responding to your newspaper advertising, or coming to you because travel agents were informed of your package and your commission policy, or whether both factors were involved? A well-designed internal research system can tell you the spending habits of your guests, their average length of stay, and the channel of distribution most often chosen by your guests to purchase each type of service you offer.

Trend analysis might show you that guests who are attracted by a low room price spend freely if promotions are occurring at the hotel during their visit. If this were the case in your hotel, simply putting an invitation or possibly a discount coupon into the registration packet provided to such guests could produce a significant increase in outlet traffic. Of course, to be most effective these actions would have to relate in some way to your property's strategic marketing plan.

Similarly, if a reconciliation of occupancy figures with cover counts indicates that your restaurant volume is lowest when your house count is highest, an internal merchandising program—well planned and executed to stimulate greater usage of the outlets—could be exactly what is called for. A manager's cocktail party on a Monday night, for instance, followed by an offer of complimentary house wine for all attendees who choose to have dinner in your dining room, might be a very successful step. (Of course, it would then be necessary to compile data as to how many of the guests actually went on to have dinner. Research is an ongoing process!)

External Research

This section examines some of the more common methods of externally conducted research currently being used by advanced marketers in the hospitality industry. External research is simply information which is gathered in various ways by hotel marketers themselves or contracted research firms to obtain new marketing data or data unavailable in internal records. External research methods include focus groups, questionnaires, telephone surveys, and data bases.

Focus Groups. The focus group research method involves gathering in one place people with one or more characteristics in common (for instance, they may all be traveling marketing executives in their mid-thirties, with incomes of more than $50,000 per year). Researchers ask the group members to discuss a topic or to view a particular advertisement and respond to it honestly and openly, without any inhibitions. As focus group members give their comments, researchers observe the interactions with an eye toward finding a "unique selling proposition" or USP for the product in question.

When properly conducted by trained, skilled researchers, focus groups can help to (a) pinpoint proper positioning, (b) identify the types of media such consumers use, and (c) clarify the attitude changes they are undergoing which may affect their buying patterns. To see how a focus group could be used for a hotel, let us assume the hotel management is contemplating a new advertising campaign to broaden its appeal to the woman business traveler. By bringing together a group of men and women business travelers of approximately the same age and asking them to preview the ad campaign, the hotel management may be able to gather several kinds of information. First, does this approach really appeal to the business woman who travels? (Frequently, well-meaning attempts to reach out to specific market segments are seen as patronizing.) Second, if the ad campaign is likely to succeed in attracting a new audience, will it do so at the cost of an existing market? (Some businessmen may feel that the advertising campaign excludes them and, therefore, may resent it.) Obtaining this input in advance can help the hotel spend its advertising dollars wisely. There are other benefits, too.

> Focus groups are particularly attractive because they are more economical and less time-consuming than large quantitative surveys. The cost of an average group session (not including travel) is estimated at between $1,800 and $2,500, and results can be obtained in as little as two weeks. An average study uses five groups. In contrast, the cost of a quantitative survey can easily run between $50,000 and $100,000, or more. Perhaps the greatest lure of focus groups, however, is the realization that advertisers can tap consumers' emotions and find a unique position for their product.[7]

Depending on the skills of the researchers and the suitability of the participants, focus groups can be a relatively low-cost, relatively high-benefit form of research. Yet, it is surprising that so few hotels take advantage of this research opportunity.

Questionnaires. For many years, guestroom questionnaires have been a staple of hotel research, particularly in chain-affiliated properties. Examples of questionnaires are shown in Exhibits 2 and 3.

Although guestroom questionnaires provide general information about the guest's attitude toward the stay, they are not representative of guests as a whole. Because participation is voluntary, those who do respond are usually either very happy or very disappointed. Therefore, most of the completed questionnaires received by management are extreme responses, not typical responses. True, the sum and substance of guest comments can be invaluable in examining the quality of the hotel's offerings. However, because the primary purpose for guests completing these questionnaires is to express their response to the facility (rather than to provide information about how it can be better marketed), such questionnaires are

Exhibit 2 A Holiday Inn Guestroom Questionnaire

HOLIDAY INN REPORT CARD

DEAR GUEST:

Thank you for choosing a Holiday Inn® hotel. We want you to feel welcome … and comfortable. That's why we give you this "No Excuses" room guarantee.

- Your room will be right. It will be clean, everything will work properly, and you'll have enough of everything you need.

- Or we will make it right.

- Or you stay free that night.

"No Excuses!" If you are not satisfied with your room, call the manager on duty. He will make every effort to correct the problem, or give you another room. If we are unable to correct the problem, and you believe it's serious enough to warrant a refund, tell the manager. Should you have any questions or problems, call 800/238-8000 and ask for Guest Services.

Again, thank you for giving us the opportunity to take care of you. I hope you will have a pleasant stay.

Sincerely,

JAMES L. SCHORR
President, Hotel Group
Holiday Inns, Inc.

P.S. I'd very much appreciate your taking a moment to fill out the attached "report card." Your opinions are a big help to all of us in making this hotel the way you want it to be.

BSA 1957

1. Overall how would you grade *this* Holiday Inn? EXCELLENT A B C D F BAD 1

Now, please grade:

2. **YOUR ROOM:**

	EXCELLENT				BAD	
Appearance	A	B	C	D	F	2
Cleanliness	A	B	C	D	F	3
Comfort	A	B	C	D	F	4
Furnishings	A	B	C	D	F	5
Bathroom	A	B	C	D	F	6

3. **RESTAURANT:**

| Food Quality | A | B | C | D | F | 7 |
| Service Quality | A | B | C | D | F | 8 |

4. **PRICE/VALUE:** EXCELLENT VALUE — BAD VALUE

| Of Your Room | A | B | C | D | F | 9 |
| In the Restaurant | A | B | C | D | F | 10 |

5. **FRONT DESK PEOPLE:** EXCELLENT — BAD

| Friendliness | A | B | C | D | F | 11 |
| Efficiency | A | B | C | D | F | 12 |

6. **SERVICES:** (Messages, Wake-Up Calls, Bellman, etc.) A B C D F 13

7. **OTHER FACILITIES:** (Pool, Lounge, Lobby, Parking, etc.) A B C D F 14

8. If you were to return to this area, would you stay at *this* Holiday Inn or look elsewhere? **Stay here** ☐ **Look elsewhere** ☐ 15

9. Number of people staying in room: **One** ☐ **Two** ☐ 17 **More than two** ☐

10. Have you stayed at *this* Holiday Inn before? **Yes** ☐ **No** ☐ 18

Comments: _____

Date of Stay _____ Room # _____
Your Name/Address _____
(Please) _____
Zip _____

Location of Inn: **Binghamton-Hawley St.-Dwtn., NY 1301**

TELL US HOW WE'RE PLEASING YOU.

Courtesy of Holiday Inns

Exhibit 3   A Grand Traverse Resort Village Guestroom Questionnaire

Traverse RESORT VILLAGE   GUEST COMMENT CARD

Please give names wherever appropriate.

(Rating columns: EXCELLENT / FAIR / POOR)

Reservation
Was your reservation handled promptly and effficiently? _____

Hospitable Reception
Was our staff friendly and helpful? _____
   Doorman/Bellman _____
   Desk Clerk/Cashier _____
   Telephone Operator _____

Accommodations
How would you rate your room? _____
   Cleanliness _____
   Housekeeping Service _____
   Other Comments _____

Restaurants and Lounges
Please give us your impressions.
Hannah Lay _____
   Food Quality _____
   Service _____
Orchard Room _____
   Food Quality _____
   Service _____
Deuce Bar & Grill _____
   Food Quality _____
   Service _____
Sand Trap _____
   Food Quality _____
   Drinks _____
   Service _____
Room Service _____
   Speed and Quality of Service _____
   Food Quality _____
Afterdeck Lounge _____
   Drinks _____
   Service _____
   Entertainment _____

Wild Cherry Lounge _____
   Drinks _____
   Service _____
   Entertainment _____

Sports and Recreation
How did we handle your "free" leisure time?
   Sports Desk Attendant _____
   Facility Cleanliness _____
   Availability of the various activities _____

Meeting and Convention Arrangements
   Attention to Detail _____
   Banquet _____

Highlights
What services or facilities did you enjoy the most? _____

Did a member of our staff provide extraordinary service? _____

Helpful Hints
Did we disappoint you in any way? _____

How did you hear about us?
☐ Friend   ☐ Return Visit   ☐ Newspaper, TV or Radio (Name) _____
   Source _____
☐ Travel Agent ☐ Auto Club   ☐ Other _____

Date _____ Room No. _____
Name (optional) _____
Address _____

Courtesy of Grand Traverse Resort Village

not, strictly speaking, marketing research. Although some marketing information can be derived from questionnaires, it is not considered highly accurate because responses are approximated, not based on research.

Given the limits of guestroom questionnaires, it is fair to say that the best results are obtained when the questionnaire is used so as to reveal what a cross section of people feel about the property, not merely what the extreme attitudes are.

There are several ways in which to obtain more representative results when questionnaires are used:

1. During a limited number of days, all guests can be surveyed at the front desk upon check-in or check-out. Another way to obtain a random sample of opinions is to ask every *n*th (5th, 10th, 3rd) guest checking in or out to fill out a questionnaire.

2. Questionnaires can be completed by a researcher who interviews each guest (or a random sample of guests) either at check-in or some time during the

guest's first day in the hotel. This is a very effective way to gather information on the hotel's "typical guest." It also allows management to focus on some categories of guests more than others. For example, in your hotel, you may want to know more about the long-term-stay guests than about the one-night-stay guest.

3. Questionnaires can be left in the guestrooms or distributed at the time of check-in, but with a specific inducement offered for completion. This increases the response rate from the middle-of-the-road guests.

Questionnaires can also be effective when aimed at specific categories of people who are not guests. For instance, if you wanted to know more about group customers who represent a specific category of business, you might administer a questionnaire to members of Meeting Planners International (MPI) chapters in a given community. Your survey of these people, whether they are customers or not, can tell you a great deal about their perceptions of your property, its facilities, and whether they are appropriate to this type of market segment. Again, these surveys are generally more successful if they are conducted face to face by a researcher than if respondents are allowed to complete the surveys on their own.

Telephone Surveys. Telephone surveys, whether of previous customers or of potential customers, can be effectively used by hotels. Such surveys produce a factual response, and from time to time they also produce an emotional or attitudinal response.

Americana Hotels conducts telephone surveys for specific purposes. Executive Vice President Mike Leven has developed the telephone blitz technique into an art form. He has found that an amazing amount of data about a specific subject can be obtained by putting a group of telephones into a room, gathering a group of people (either students or hotel employees) together in that room, and having them ask a very specific set of questions to a very well-identified target audience. This technique was used in conjunction with the University of Massachusetts School of Hotel, Restaurant and Travel Administration, under the direction of Dr. Robert C. Lewis. The purpose was to study the effectiveness of a golf-tennis package weekend at Americana's Canyon Hotel Racquet and Golf Resort in Palm Springs. The objectives were to determine:

1. Should the package be run again?

2. Could the package stand a price increase?

3. What forms of advertising would be effective?

Other hotels may want to use telephone surveys to test public perceptions of their property. For instance, you may view your hotel as a very friendly place, but may be uncertain as to whether this perception is shared by the public. A telephone survey can help you find out. Similarly, a resort hotel operator may know that she has a modern resort with every conceivable recreational facility within easy reach of a major city, but does the public know this? To find out how well the resort is communicating what it has to offer, she may decide to use a telephone survey of a random sample of citizens in that major city to find out how well the resort is communicating what it has to offer.

Several excellent examples of surveys and survey formats are presented in the book, *Strategic Marketing Planning in the Hospitality Industry*. One article by Robert C. Lewis and Abraham Pizam, entitled "Guest Surveys—A Missed Opportunity," is laden with excellent research formats and methods of analyzing the data provided through these research formats.[8]

Data Bases. While your research may begin with your hotel's own guest base, it certainly does not have to end there. The traditional approach to additional research is demographically oriented. For a fee, a professional list house or a credit card company will provide a list of individuals in certain economic strata or certain age groups which are similar enough to provide statistical validity. American Express, for example, provides excellent demographic information about their card users. While their lists are expensive, they offer a very high degree of accuracy.[9]

Similarly, directories of lists are maintained by most of the reputable direct mail houses around the country. These directories pinpoint the people who are listed very effectively. If one wishes to mail only to lawyers who work for large firms in greater Boston, for instance, such information can be obtained through list houses.

Recently, the Claritas Corporation of Arlington, Virginia, developed a market segmentation and targeting tool called PRIZM. Claritas has grouped all the postal zip codes in the United States into 40 statistically homogeneous cluster groups. These zip-clusters can be linked with national market research data bases from many other sources, including client-based information, to enable the marketers to know exactly how large their markets are, where they are located, and how to reach them most effectively by distribution, media, and promotions (see Exhibit 4).

While PRIZM is effective for many markets, it is particularly effective at reaching markets not normally associated with research. That is, PRIZM allows us to study the buying behavior of lower socio-economic groups as well as upper-scale consumers.

Positioning

Determining your hotel's position is the next logical step after you have carefully researched your markets, your competition, your property and its guests. By this time you should have a clear picture of your hotel's identity based on your research and analysis. Is it a luxury hotel that appeals to the upper five percent of the market? Is it a roadside family hotel? Is it a honeymoon retreat for newlyweds of the lower or lower-middle income groups? Within the wide range of lodging properties, your property has a position that must be identified and clearly presented; otherwise, you will fall short of your potential to penetrate key markets.

The position of a product or service depends upon consumers' perceptions or beliefs about the product or service in relation to similar products or services that are available. Positioning is concerned with image and is the attempt by management to establish, in the minds of the customers, a certain image of the company's product or service. It is one thing for management to say, "We're number one" and quite another for consumers to say, "You're number one." Therefore, strategies

Exhibit 4   PRIZM Profile Summary by Zip-Cluster Groups

	STAYED IN ANY HOTEL/MOTEL/LAST YEAR VS. BASE—TOTAL ADULTS (MRI WAVE 7–10)				
CODE	**CLUSTER GROUPS** **DESCRIPTIVE TITLE**	**BASE** **% COMP**	**MARKET** **% COMP**	**%** **PEN**	**INDEX**
S1	Educated, Affluent Executives & Professionals in Elite Metro Suburbs	4.55	7.03	45.483	154
S2	Pre- & Post-Child Families & Singles In Upscale, White-Collar Suburbs	6.80	8.41	36.413	124
S3	Upper-Middle, Child-Raising Families In Outlying, Owner-Occupied Suburbs	11.90	14.28	35.343	120
U1	Educated, White-Collar Singles & Couples in Upscale, Urban Areas	6.56	7.00	31.428	107
T1	Educated, Young, Mobile Families In Exurban Satellites & Boom Towns	8.81	9.90	33.066	112
S4	Middle-Class, Post-Child Families In Aging Suburbs & Retirement Areas	7.96	8.54	31.564	107
T2	Mid-Scale, Child-Raising, Blue-Collar Families in Remote Suburbs & Towns	9.97	10.45	30.883	105
U2	Mid-Scale Families, Singles & Elders In Dense, Urban Row & Hi-Rise Areas	6.87	5.93	25.420	86
R1	Rural Towns & Villages Amidst Farms & Ranches Across Agrarian Mid-America	9.17	9.14	29.358	100
T3	Mixed Gentry & Blue-Collar Labor in Lo-Mid Rustic, Mill & Factory Towns	8.98	6.92	22.679	77
R2	Landowners, Migrants & Rustics in Poor Rural Towns, Farms & Uplands	11.16	7.62	20.097	68
U3	Mixed, Unskilled Service & Labor In Aging, Urban Row & Hi-Rise Areas	7.27	4.78	19.377	66
TOTAL		100.00	100.00	29.445	100

Reprinted with permission. For restricted use by Sunset Magazine. ©Copyright 1984, Claritas Corporation, 1911 N. Fort Myer Drive, Arlington, Virginia 22209. Source: MRI Wave 5/Wave 6.

must be developed that will create and maintain the image and ranking (comparison with competitors) that is desired.

The positioning of that product in the market has little to do with what is done to the product. Product design is important, of course. But name changes, refurbishing, redecorating and design changes are largely cosmetic in nature, although they are done to influence consumers' perceptions. More important than what is done to the product is what is done to the minds of consumers. In other words, products are not positioned in physical markets. Products are positioned in the minds of consumers. What is the most desirable position in the minds of consumers and how does one get there? The most desirable position is to be number one, and the most effective way to get there is to be first.

How is this number one rank achieved? The most effective way is to be first with a high-quality product that satisfies the needs and wants of a well-defined market segment. People tend to remember firsts and forget seconds, thirds, and fourths. For example, what was the name of the first company to introduce a chain of standardized, high-quality lodging accommodations located along major highways? Holiday Inns. What was the name of the second company? Few people know.

Being first implies innovation, doing new things, introducing new concepts. It implies in-depth knowledge of market segments, knowledge of needs and wants and the ability to recognize needs and wants that are not being satisfied. It further indicates the ability to provide products and services that will give satisfaction.

In summary, the position a hotel or restaurant holds depends upon what consumers think of it. The position depends upon customers' perceptions of how well the product satisfies their needs and wants.

> ❝Don't let an advertising buzz word like **positioning** confuse you. It can be defined simply as 'the perception of a hotel by its guest or potential guests, as being different from or better than its competition.' Perception is a key word in that definition. A good positive perception can make a hotel successful. A poor one will lead to red ink.
>
> Determining the most effective position for a hotel isn't easy. It takes a good measure of hard work. It doesn't come from hunches or wishful thinking [or] from a general manager's pet theory or when an owner says, 'My wife thinks....' None of these lead to proper positioning.
>
> Determining the correct position starts with good research. Here are a minimum of five basic areas about which you should get as much information as possible:
>
> 1. Your target markets
>
> 2. Your competition
>
> 3. Your guests
>
> 4. Your own property's strengths and weaknesses
>
> 5. How people perceive you …
>
> The important point is to base the position of your property on sound, accurate research.
>
> Most frequently, research will reveal that a major reason a hotel is less profitable than it should be is low awareness combined with a lack of a clear perception in the marketplace.... The solution is clear-cut: establish a perceivable, readily identifiable position and sell it with an aggressive marketing/advertising program. When properly executed, this course of action will normally produce increased business.❞[10]
>
> **—George B. Frank**
> Former Executive Vice President
> Gardner, Frank, and Stein

What, then, is your position? It is a clear presentation of exactly what your hotel is, to whom it is best suited, and the conditions under which those people would most likely enjoy its services. Positioning can be achieved with a picture, a word, an expression, or anything that clearly says to an audience, "This is what we are all about. You are the right audience for us. Let's come together!" Of course, much of the business booked by a hotel may come through travel agents—one of many channels of distribution. Therefore, the hotel must position itself effectively in advertisements aimed at the travel industry.

One way hotels may effectively advertise to travel agents is to take a position or create a point of view about themselves. For example, a property interested in tour and travel business makes its positioning statement by including such informative details in its advertising of IT (inclusive tour) packages as: proximity to tourist attractions, family rates and facilities (such as suites or double doubles), recreational facilities, and more.

An excellent example of a property communicating a resort orientation is Omni Classic Hotels' advertisement for the Royal Orleans in New Orleans (see Exhibit 5). This advertisement presents the Royal Orleans' position by devoting one full page of its two-page spread to detailed, diverse package information, including rates and IT numbers. Excellent four-color photographs followed by concise, bold-faced listings of accommodations, restaurants and lounges, and recreational and meeting facilities communicate the property's emphasis on upscale amenities and ambience.

Because travel agents book resort accommodations more than any other type, Omni's decision to use a double-page ad format was a wise one. In addition to commanding the attention of agents, this large ad allows the Royal Orleans ample space to include package information which will be essential to the agents' decision-making. Obviously, every advertisement must include reservation information, but this ad also provides representatives' computer access codes (more on this shortly) and lists other properties in the Omni group to promote cross-selling. (Agents impressed with this particular property's ad might be expected to attribute many of the same characteristics to other Omni hotels.) While the advertisement clearly targets tour and travel business, it mentions the hotel's meeting facilities in an effort to appeal to other types of business as well.

Precise positioning is also evident in an advertisement for the Westin Bonaventure in downtown Los Angeles (see Exhibit 6). As a commercial property in the city center, the Bonaventure's ad gives location information. It quickly tells the business traveler that the hotel is in the heart of downtown L.A., near the financial district, music center, convention center, and so forth. Because business travelers look for rooms in which they can work as well as relax, guestrooms receive greater emphasis in advertisements for commercial hotels than they do in advertisements for resort-oriented properties. In this case, the Westin Bonaventure communicates that it has the in-room amenities which its management thinks business travelers want: 24-hour room service, free cable TV, and HBO movies.

Convention and recreational facilities are copiously noted, as are the Bonaventure's ten restaurants and lounges. Notice how the photography shows the hotel's many faces, ranging from leisure-oriented and relaxed to business-minded and orderly. For the benefit of travel agents, computer access codes are listed in the Westin Bonaventure ad, along with the usual reservation numbers.

Exhibit 5   Omni Classic Hotels' Ad for the Royal Orleans

Courtesy of *Hotel & Travel Index* and Omni Classic Hotels

Probably no one in the travel industry is better qualified to discuss the ways that hotels can most effectively advertise to travel agents than Melinda Bush. As publisher of *Hotel & Travel Index*, the largest hotel directory in the industry, and Vice President of the Business Publications Division of Ziff-Davis Publishing Company, Melinda has made a concerted effort to thoroughly understand the elements that contribute to successful hotel-travel agency communications.

❝Travel agents will never have the opportunity to personally visit the majority of the hotels they book for their clients. Consequently, they rely on hotel

Exhibit 6 Ad for the Westin Bonaventure

THE WESTIN BONAVENTURE
Los Angeles

Location: In the heart of downtown Los Angeles. Near financial district, marts, Music Center, sports facilities and Convention Center. Thirty-five minutes from airport. Designed by architect John Portman.

Accommodations: 1,500 guest rooms including 90 suites. Oversize beds, free cable TV and HBO movies, spectacular views, 24-hour room service. Magnificent six-story atrium, 5-level Shopping Gallery. Outside pool and garden deck, 8 tennis courts adjacent, and free health club facilities.

Convention Facilities: 24 meeting rooms for groups from 30 to 3,000. California Ballroom, West Coast's largest. Independent exhibit facility to accommodate 160 8×10 exhibits.

Restaurants: Ten restaurants and lounges, including rooftop restaurant and revolving lounge. Sidewalk Cafe. Live entertainment and dancing in the Cabaret. Beaudry's for gourmet specialty dining.

Reservations: In U.S. and Canada call 800-228-3000 and give your ATC or IATA number. Europe: London (01) 408 0636; Toll-free, ☎ Amsterdam 47 30 64; ☎ Düsseldorf 49 00 06; ☎ Frankfurt 2 07 84; ☎ Hamburg 44 25 54; ☎ Munich 18 50 64; ☎ Paris (6)079 15 33; ☎ Zürich 302 08 15. Or book through Apollo (WI25), Sabre (WI50), Pars (WILABON), Datas II (WI25), System I (WDLAXLAB), or Reservac II (WILAX011). Or call Westin Hotels in your city. The Westin Bonaventure, 404 South Figueroa, Los Angeles, California 90071. Telex: 67-7628. Cable: LABON.

Tariff:	Standard	Medium	Deluxe
Single	$110	$118	$126
Double	$130	$138	$146
Twin	$130	$138	$146
Suites	from $220		

Third person in room is additional $20 per day. Rates subject to change without notice. All accommodations subject to 10% city and state tax.

Policies: Children 18 and under free when sharing parents' room. If more than one room is required, the single rate applies.

Complete cooperation with travel agents. Prompt payment of 10% commission. Group rates available upon request.

Courtesy of *Hotel & Travel Index* and the Westin Bonaventure directories for carefully positioned, accurate information about hotels. This information should include everything the agent will need to tell the client about the property: location, accommodations, facilities, rates, packages, meeting space, and convention space.

City maps are highly useful in facilitating the booking process and are one of the most effective tools in improving hotel-travel agency communications. Along with effective advertising, locator maps in directories are helping to maximize agency-generated business for hotels, already estimated at $4 billion a year.

In any advertising showing facilities, hotels should take advantage of the subjective, qualitative gain associated with good, four-color photographs. By comparison, golf courses and swimming pools pictured in black-and-white are not nearly as appealing.

Directory advertising should also sum up services, sports activities, and other sales points in quick-reading paragraphs. Nearby attractions (theme parks, shopping, beaches, and so forth) should also be identified. I strongly recommend the inclusion of a map in the hotel's ad.

Ads should include regular rates and specials, for example, 'Children under 18 free.' Include toll-free numbers (prefix with 800 in the U.S.) or regular phone numbers with the words 'call collect.' *Hotel & Travel Index* augments booking information contained in hotel advertising by including symbols for the airlines' computer systems in the actual listings ('A' for United's Apollo, 'P' for Delta's Pars, and 'S' for American's Sabre). This is used by agents as a handy reference guide. It helps to go one step further and supply computer access codes. Travel agents may use this booking option, which takes them beyond the regular airline reservation systems, when the codes are provided. The listing of computer access codes is a growing trend, which is especially useful in the case of commercially oriented properties.

Finally, in addition to information for their clients, travel agents look for assurances that the hotel will be responsive to them. Statements such as 'Agent reservations are positively honored,' are helpful. A clear statement of the hotel's commission payment policies is also most welcome. Moreover, any special commission rates for low-season or weekend packages should be included in ads.

It would be difficult to overemphasize the role of accurate, carefully formulated information in expediting and expanding travel agent bookings. **99**

—Melinda Bush, Vice President
Business Publications Division
Ziff-Davis Publishing Company
and Publisher, *Hotel & Travel Index*

Thus far, this chapter has dealt with hotels that are well positioned for the transient guest and hotels that are marketed primarily through the travel agency channel of distribution. However, many hotels serve the corporate market, so the channels of distribution they use to reach corporate meeting planners are different. We asked Bob Rosenbaum, associate publisher of *Corporate Meetings and Incentives*, to select some examples of ads for very well-positioned convention hotels and to comment on them. He chose the ads appearing in Exhibits 7 and 8.

The ad for the Sheraton Tucson El Conquistador tells the meeting planner exactly where it is, what it is, how good it is, how big it is, and how attractive it is—all in a partial-page format. It succeeds because it positions the hotel against the

Exhibit 7 Sheraton Tuscon El Conquistador Ad

THE SOUTHWEST'S NEWEST, MOST COMPLETE LUXURY MEETING CENTER.

The Sheraton Tucson El Conquistador Resort.
In the tradition of Sheraton's contemporary resorts.
The Southwest's newest and most completely
self-contained meeting center. Open now.
With more of everything to make your next meeting or convention a dazzling success. More space.
More facilities. More activities. And Sheraton luxury
that pleases your budget.
For additional information and special introductory
group rates, contact our Director of Sales.

Sheraton Tucson El Conquistador
Golf & Tennis Resort
Sheraton Hotels & Inns, Worldwide, 10000 N. Oracle Rd., Tucson, AZ 85704
(602) 742-7000 or our toll-free GRAB number **(800) 343-6320**

Courtesy of *Hotel & Travel Index* and the Sheraton Tucson El Conquistador

mountains and thereby emphasizes the hotel's grandeur. The attractive ad for Arrowwood, an executive conference center in Westchester County, New York, also succeeds in communicating its message. The ad positions this beautiful facility as exactly what it was designed to be and is: an extremely opulent executive retreat with marvelous accommodations, a fabulous mix of meeting and recreational facilities, and the kind of seclusion that is conducive to productive business meetings.

Positioning a hotel properly means more than providing adequate information to agents or advertising in magazines read by meeting planners. Most hotels also need to establish their unique identity in the minds of individual guests who may make their own lodging reservations. In the following comment, Neil W. Ostergren, CHSE, Director of Advertising for Americana Hotels, approaches positioning from this consumer-oriented perspective. His statements serve as a summary and amplification of points presented in this chapter. They also remind us that positioning affects all the other sales tools.

> **"**With rising costs and increased competition, advertising dollars today must be spent more carefully and according to plan. Step one in developing a good plan is to position the property. Simply stated, this is identifying the customer benefits that the property offers. Identifying is positioning.
>
> To position the property, it is first necessary to analyze ... its advantages and disadvantages vis-à-vis the competition. This analysis should include the location of the property, its age, facilities, and general condition. What perception would a potential customer have seeing the property for the first time? What is the size of the hotel (the number of rooms or keys)? How many restaurants and

Exhibit 8   Arrowwood Ad

Arrowwood of Westchester.
The executive conference center
that stands alone.

Arrowwood of Westchester stands alone because of what it stands *for*. Arrowwood is a true executive conference center. Our main business is hosting conferences. So everything you need is right here—including a thoroughly professional staff at your service.

Arrowwood also stands for luxurious accommodations, superb cuisine and an executive sports and fitness center second to none.

Even *where* Arrowwood stands, helps it stand alone. We're on 114 acres of wooded, rolling hills, just 23 miles from Manhattan.

So make your next conference a success. Get away to Arrowwood of Westchester...the executive conference center that stands alone.

Call **(914) 939-5500**, or write: Arrowwood of Westchester, Anderson Hill Road, Rye Brook, New York 10573.
Managed by Conference Environments Corporation./"ARROWWOOD OF WESTCHESTER and the Arrowwood Design is a registered service mark of Citicorp."

Courtesy of *Hotel & Travel Index* and Arrowwood

lounges are there? What are the meeting and banquet facilities, and what is their capacity (theater-style, classroom-style, etc.)? Does this property have a reservations system? Is it franchised or part of a chain, or is it independent? What is the rate structure and the business mix? Is business seasonal or year-round, and what about weekends and holidays? These and other questions have to be answered.

It is also necessary to examine the business mix coming into the area, [the] transportation available, and the distribution system for sales and reservations.

Some of this information will be obtained easily, but some will be more difficult to obtain. After studying the market, [the next step is to] develop a demographic and psychographic profile of current guests. This is important so the advertising message to be developed can be scheduled in the correct media to reach the target audience. With the answers to these and other questions and with the assistance of the property's advertising agency, [management must] select one feature or benefit that the property offers. This becomes the Unique Selling Proposition (the USP)—also known as the Key Customer Benefit—around which the property's advertising message will be developed.

Good positioning may well result in potential guests and customers selecting one property over another. It will also affect the property's media advertising [and] collateral advertising. [Positioning] should also be long term—[intended to last] for an extended period of time—but reviewed regularly to stay on target. Remember that if the positioning should change, everything else will change as well. **"**

> **—Neil W. Ostergren, CHSE**
> Director of Advertising
> Americana Hotels

While positioning is discussed in this chapter in terms of advertising, positioning also underlies other marketing tools: sales, public relations, promotions, merchandising, and pricing. For example, the sales effort must be consistent with the position taken for the property. On the one hand, casually attired sales representatives would not convey the Ritz Carlton's message to its market. On the other hand, it would be equally incorrect to try to represent a resort hotel at a trade show while wearing a three-piece suit. These examples show that every tool of marketing must properly convey the position of the hotel.

Endnotes

1. William R. George, "The Retailing of Services—A Challenging Future," *Journal of Retailing*, 53, No. 3, Fall 1977, p. 90.

2. G. M. Hostage, "Quality Control in a Service Business." *Harvard Business Review*, July–August 1975, p. 102.

3. *Situation Analysis Workbook* (East Lansing, Mich.: HSMAI Foundation, 1400 K. Street NW, Suite 810, Washington, D.C. 20005, and the Educational Institute of the American Hotel & Motel Association, 1983), p. 1.

4. Ibid., pp. 2-3.

5. This comment was made during an interview with Laurel J. Walsh, Director of Market Research, the TIMA Corporation.

6. For more information on the process, see C. DeWitt Coffman, *Marketing for a Full House* (Ithaca, N.Y.: Cornell University School of Hotel Administration, 1972), chapters 2 and 6.

7. Sandra Levy, "Listening to America Behind See-Through Mirrors," *Ad Week Magazine*, January 24, 1983.

8. Robert M. Blomstrom, ed., *Strategic Marketing Planning in the Hospitality Industry* (East Lansing, Mich.: The Educational Institute of the American Hotel & Motel Association, 1983), pp. 159-166.

9. American Express offers properties who honor their card the opportunity to purchase a "lodging market analysis." This is a study of the hotel's repeat business, indicating geographic feeder cities and market share data. Additional information about lodging market analyses can be obtained directly from American Express.

10. George B. Frank, "Positioning as a Problem Solving Tool," *Marketing Review*, Summer, 1982, pp. 8–12.

Supplemental Reading ───────────────────────────────

The Positioning Statement for Hotels

by Robert C. Lewis, Ph.D.

> *It is fairly simple to create an image for a hotel—but images may be good or bad, persuasive or not persuasive. Does your positioning statement include the three elements required for effective marketing?*
>
> Robert Lewis is Assistant Professor of Marketing and Management in the Department of Hotel, Restaurant, and Travel Administration at the University of Massachusetts, Amherst. He received his doctorate from the University of Massachusetts, where his areas of concentration were communication theory and marketing.

Although the concept of positioning has been widely accepted in a range of industries, by most appearances it has largely escaped the attention of hotel marketers. Whereas positioning relates to a property's *subjective* attributes (and how they differ from competitive properties' subjective attributes), hotel advertising has traditionally emphasized such objective product characteristics as number of rooms, prices, facilities, and amenities—characteristics in which competing facilities are generally quite similar.

The concept of positioning in a marketing strategy calls for the creation of an image—the consumer's perception of the subjective attributes of the property vis-à-vis those of the competition. This perception may be radically different from the property's physical characteristics. The distinction between the perception and the reality is especially important for hotel marketers.

The Purchase Decision for Services

A hotel's offerings comprise a bundle of goods and services ranging from tangible to intangible.[1] Because the lion's share of the hotel product—services—is at the intangible end of the continuum, it is often difficult to determine which attributes are most important in the consumer's purchase decision. Indeed, the intangibility of services makes the decision difficult for the consumer: he cannot taste, touch, feel, see, or try a service before making the decision; in fact, he "consumes" the service at the same time it is produced. Moreover, because every hotel property offers a heterogeneous range of services, the consumer's risk in the purchase decision is high. Finally, because service offerings are easily duplicated, the consumer cannot always draw clear distinctions among competitive offerings.[2] Thus, while a consumer can objectively measure, compare, and evaluate tangible products, and can actually consume them, he can measure and compare intangible services only subjectively; he finds it difficult to assign a monetary value to a service, and can consume it only passively. Services are critical to the consumer's perception of a hotel

───────────

This article was originally published in the May 1981 issue of *The Cornell Hotel and Restaurant Administration Quarterly*, pp. 51–61, and is reprinted here with the permission of the Cornell University School of Hotel Administration. ©1981.

property, however, and generally have a long-term cognitive and affectual impact on that perception; the impact of tangible products is generally short-term.

Hotel marketers who recognize the influence of intangible attributes on consumers' decision-making often react by advertising the abstract: the ineffable ("escape to the ultimate"); the euphoric ("surround yourself with luxury"); the euphuistic ("capture the spirit"); the ephemeral ("make any occasion special"); and the antithetical ("get away to it all"). The problem with such an approach is that the consumer will not buy a service, no matter what its intangible attributes are, until a certain minimum threshold of *tangible* attributes has been reached. In fact, a halo effect is possible: the existence of certain tangible characteristics is assumed to signify that a certain level of quality (an abstraction) also exists. Recognizing this, many goods-producing companies imbue their recognized tangible goods with abstract qualities in their advertising. For example, Charles Revson of Revlon Cosmetics reportedly said, "In the factory, we make cosmetics; in the store, we sell hope"—and this strategy is still apparent in Revlon advertising.

It is difficult to employ a similar strategy in hotel advertising because hotel products have a high degree of sameness and hotel services *are* abstract. To emphasize the concrete in advertising is to fail to differentiate oneself from one's competitors, while to compound the abstraction is to dilute the reality one wishes to represent. Thus, hotel marketers should focus on enhancing and differentiating a property's abstract realities through the manipulation of tangible clues: "The degree to which the marketer will focus on either tangible evidence or intangible abstractions for (positioning an entity to its target market) will be found to be inversely related to the entity dominance."[3] Compare, for example, the intangibility of Merrill Lynch services to the tangibility of its bull strolling through a china shop.

The Most Common Failing

Hotel marketers who have adopted positioning strategies sometimes fail to incorporate one basic marketing concept into otherwise good positions: they forget that any positioning statement must be directed to the needs and wants of the consumer. Many who have written about marketing strategies also make this mistake. Stating that positioning is the first of three steps in cultivating an image for a restaurant operation, Sill suggested establishing "an explicit statement of the type of restaurant (management) *wishes to present to patrons*"[4] (emphasis added). In the same vein, Tissian stated that after a hotel's management has "identified the property's competitive strengths and weaknesses, the results of this analysis are articulated in the form of a positioning statement. The positioning strategy reflects a conscious decision … to communicate to the market a definition of the property as a particular type of hotel … this definition must be consistent with the property it describes."[5] The *next* step, according to Tissian, is to select the target audiences. The concepts set forth by Sill and Tissian are essential to effective positioning and may lead one to develop a fine positioning statement. However, they may just as easily lead one to formulate a position corresponding to the image that management wishes to project or believes it projects, rather than one that differentiates the property from the competition in a manner reflecting the needs and wants of the target market.

The Three Elements

True positioning entails three elements. First—and least important—*it creates an image*. Why is this least important? Because images may be good or bad, persuasive or not persuasive, inspiring or uninspiring. It is relatively simple to create an image of some kind (although many hotel ads fail to do so), and images alone do not incline the consumer to buy.

The element that does influence buying behavior is the most important of the three: the perceived *benefits* of the product or service. Positioning a product or service along *benefit dimensions* in an attempt to reflect consumers' attitudes forms the basis of an effective strategy. Once the benefit dimensions have been defined, the marketer can isolate those target markets consisting of consumers who hold similar attitudes about a bundle of benefits as they relate to a particular hotel or hotel class.

The third essential element of the positioning statement is that *it differentiates the brand* from the product class—in other words, it distinguishes the hotel from other hotels, whether they are truly different or (as is quite likely) offer essentially the same products and services. To combine these elements, the positioning statement should be designed to create an image reflecting the perception of the property that management wishes its target market to hold and reflecting promises on which the property can deliver and make good. The desired perception must be based on consumer benefits—first, on needs and wants, and second, on differences between the property and its competition. Consumers don't buy products or services; they buy expectations. Statements that both promise the consumer something and give him a reason to believe in the promise are most persuasive because they let the consumer know what he can expect and why he should stay at a particular hotel.

The three bases of persuasion set forth by Aristotle—ethos (credibility), pathos (emotional appeal), and logos (logic and reasoning)—are still the best tools we have; but first, said the philosopher, you must know your audience. The positioning statement cannot be developed until the strategy has been established, and the strategy must be based on the target market.

The Differentiation Element

One differentiates a property through the positioning statement by demonstrating the property's unique attributes to the consumer. The positioning decision is the most important factor in developing successful advertising, but "most brochures (and the properties they describe) look alike;"[6] few advertisements and brochures reflect any attempt at differentiation or positioning. When products or services are similar, the benefits unique to a property must provide the positioning differentiation.

Yesawich stressed this point in noting that lodging properties must become competitor-oriented to be successful in the '80s; knowing what one's guest wants is of little value if five of one's competitors are already serving his needs.[7] Identifying a property's unique attributes or benefits means not only knowing its strong points but also locating the weak points in the positions of competitors. Ideally, of course, the hotel marketer could discover an unoccupied position in which his offering could generate new business or lure customers away from competitors.

The task of the hotel marketer is to develop the desired consumer perception of the property's benefits as opposed to those of the competition—keeping in mind that the consumer seeks *tangible* clues to distinguish among the benefits of intangible services offered by competing properties. Research and self-examination should indicate how one property can be set apart from others, what its unique advantages are, and what positions remain to be filled.

A few hotels have developed positioning statements that differentiate them from the competition and that offer unique benefits. Some examples:

- **"A beautifully orchestrated idea in hotels"** (positioning a property in which every room is a suite)

- **"Soars 46 stories over Central Park"** (for a property featuring panoramic views not usually found in New York City)

- **"We think that vacation costs are outrageous"** (for a unique, inexpensive vacation experience)

- **"There *is* an alternative to high-priced hotels"** (directed toward the value-conscious business traveler; all the standard hotel amenities are mentioned, so the traveler can be sure that the low price does not signify low quality).

More often, however, hotel positioning statements fail to differentiate and to offer unique benefits. Consider the following:

- **"The flair and style of a Hyatt. The efficiency and courtesy of a Marriott:"** These phrases explicitly position the competition, but fail to define the position of the property they pertain to.

- **"The golden opportunity for the 80s:"** This approach is used by a chain that competes head-on with other "golden-opportunity" chains.

- **"We have room:"** This phrase simply announces an expansion that makes this hotel the largest in the state.

- **"We're the difference:"** This statement is weak because it is not accompanied by supporting evidence; the hotel looks like hundreds of others.

The Benefit Element

The benefits themselves are the real reason the consumer comes to a hotel. They *are* the image and they *are* the elements that differentiate a hotel from its competition. Benefits come in bundles, and it is the entire group of benefits offered that positions a hotel in relation to its particular target market. Benefits vary in the extent to which they are assigned importance by consumers, and their relative importance varies with different service levels.[8] Positioning the benefits means marketing the correct expectation—because, in the final analysis, it is the expectation that hotels have to sell to the selected target market.

The first problem is to determine the key characteristic of the various benefit segments (groups of consumers who attach similar importance to a bundle of benefits). Such procedures as conjoint analysis, multi-dimensional scaling, and discriminant analysis can be applied for this purpose,[9] but it is also possible to adapt some older, simpler concepts with a consumer-behavior application to services and hotels. Let us begin by considering the utility model developed by Lovelock to explain purchase behavior as it relates to services. Lovelock suggested that a consumer evaluates a service on the basis of its *form* utility, *place* utility, *time* utility, *psychic* utility, and *monetary* utility.[10] This model allows the marketer to classify benefits from a consumer's viewpoint, identifying the positive utilities to be emphasized and the negative utilities to be minimized. By applying the tools of the behavioral sciences to create an image and using tangible clues to support that image, the marketer can translate the utilities (which are intangible) into realities that define the property to various target markets.

Lovelock's model is useful in understanding how consumers evaluate services, and can be made even more useful if combined with the following modified marketing mix for hospitality operations, proposed by Renaghan:

(1) *The Product-Service Mix:* The combination of products and services, whether free or for sale, employed to satisfy the needs of the target market.

(2) *The Presentation Mix:* All components directed by the firm and used to increase the tangibility of the product-service mix in the perception of the target market at the right place and the right time.

(3) *The Communications Mix:* All communications between the firm and the target market that increase the tangibility of the product-service mix, that influence consumer expectations, or that persuade consumers to purchase.[11]

Lovelock's utility model and Renaghan's hospitality mix can be combined in a benefit matrix that helps the marketer understand the key characteristics of various benefit segments. The hotel marketer can complete the matrix simply by noting the property's benefits, management's capabilities, and the market's perception of the property and its offerings. (Exhibit 1 shows abstracts of some listings such a matrix might contain.) If a similar matrix is prepared to describe the competition's offerings, the marketer can perform an aggregated (non-segmented) positioning analysis. Even without a sophisticated knowledge of his target markets, the marketer is prepared from his own perceptions to develop that positioning statement, including the identification of the desired image, competitive differentiation, and consumer benefits. If target markets are identified, the marketer can also apply such techniques as conjoint analysis and discriminant analysis to evaluate the properties by benefit segment and determine the primary characteristics of the benefit segments. The benefit matrix can be used to identify the tangible clues that make the intangible benefits credible to the desired target markets.

The Positioning Statement

Communications used in the marketing effort should be both consistent and customized to fit the needs of individual target markets. Rather than attempt to crowd all information about every service into one campaign, the marketer should promote each service to its own target market, featuring the positioning statement in

Exhibit 1 Hotel Benefit Matrix

Utility	(1) Product-Service	(2) Presentation	(3) Communications
FORM	Food, room, pool, beach, lounge, room service, bed; performance	Physical plant (interior and exterior), employees, tangible presentations	Product-service; tangible attachments, tangible aspects of use and performance
PLACE	Convenience, ease of use, ease of buying, facilities, reservations	Location; nearby attractions such as business, shopping, arts; availability	Where available, where can be used, use- and performance-related aspects
TIME	Convenient times; when needed, wanted, or desired	Pleasant use of time, time-saving, service level, seasonal aspects	When available, when can be used, use- and performance-related aspects
PSYCHIC	Good feeling, social approval, prestige, reassurance, personal service, satisfaction, rest and relaxation	"Atmospherics": light, sound, space, smell; accoutrements	Tangible attachments to intangibles, dissonance reduction, nature of guests, prestige address, satisfied guests
MONETARY	Cost, fair value, save money, how much	Price-value relation, easy payment, psychological effect, quality	Value perception, quality connotation, risk reduction

Based on Lovelock's utility model for services and Renaghan's marketing mix for hospitality operations.

some form in every component of the campaign. This approach allows the hotel to implant its main services in the mind of the consumer, while giving each service its own image to, say, the businessman, the meeting planner, the travel agent, and the pleasure traveler.

The positioning statement is a unifying element: all subpositionings are promoted under one umbrella. Applied with this flexibility and consistency, the positioning statement creates an *image* that personalizes the operation; the customer who is buying an abstract service is reassured. It *differentiates* from the competition; the customer knows why he is choosing one hotel over another. It promises *benefits*; the customer is promised that his needs and wants will be fulfilled. Finally, positioning supports these elements with clues of tangible offerings that the consumer can observe with his five senses, indicating to him there is substance behind the promises....

Conclusion

Any hotel marketer can devise a positioning statement, and, as the concept of positioning has gained currency in the industry, many marketers have done just that. However, most hotel positioning still fails to incorporate the elements crucial to effective marketing: communicating a unique benefit image, supported by tangible clues, to a defined target market. The marketer whose positioning statement encompasses all these elements will have a marked competitive advantage in the years ahead.

Supplemental Reading Notes

1. It can be useful to think of these goods and services as lying along a bipolar construct of tangible dominant and intangible dominant offerings. See: G. Lynn Shostack, "Breaking Free from Product Marketing," *Journal of Marketing*, 41 (April 1977), pp. 73–80.

2. For a more substantive treatment of these and other unique aspects of services, see: John M. Rathmell, *Marketing in the Service Sector* (Cambridge: Winthrop, 1974).

3. Shostack, p. 78.

4. Brian T. Sill, "Restaurant Merchandising for the Independent Operator," *The Cornell Hotel and Restaurant Administration Quarterly*, 21, No. 1 (May 1980), p. 27.

5. "Advertising that Sells Hotels," *The Cornell Hotel and Restaurant Administration Quarterly*, 20, No. 3 (November 1979), p. 17.

6. Jane Maas, "Better Brochures for the Money," *The Cornell Hotel and Restaurant Administration Quarterly*, 20, No. 4 (February 1980), p. 21.

7. Peter Yesawich, "Marketing in the 1980s," *The Cornell Hotel and Restaurant Administration Quarterly*, 20, No. 4 (February 1980), p. 35.

8. Robert C. Lewis, "Benefit Segmentation for Restaurant Advertising that Works," *The Cornell Hotel and Restaurant Administration Quarterly*, 21, No. 3 (November 1980), pp. 6–12.

9. For application of these techniques in segmentation and positioning see: Paul Green, Yoram Wind, and Arun Jain, "Benefit Bundle Analysis," *Journal of Advertising Research*, 12 (April 1972), pp. 31–36 (conjoint measurement); Yoram Wind and Patrick J. Robinson, "Product Positioning: An Application of Multi-Dimensional Scaling," in *Attitude Research in Transition*, ed. Russell I. Haley (Chicago: American Marketing Association, 1972); Lewis, op. cit., pp. 6–12 (discriminant analysis); and Yoram Wind, "A New Procedure for Concept Evaluation," *Journal of Marketing*, 37 (October 1973), pp. 2–11.

10. Christopher H. Lovelock, "Theoretical Contribution from Service and Nonbusiness Marketing," in *Conceptual and Theoretical Developments in Marketing, Proceedings Series*, ed. O. C. Ferrell et al. (Chicago: American Marketing Association, 1979), pp. 147–165.

11. Leo N. Renaghan, "A New Marketing Mix for the Hospitality Industry," paper presented at the National Conference of the Council of Hotel, Restaurant, and Institutional Education, August 13–16, 1980, Dearborn, Michigan.

REVIEW QUIZ

When you feel you have covered all of the material in this chapter, answer these questions. Choose the *best* answer. Check your answers with the correct ones found on the Review Quiz Answer Key at the end of this book.

True (T) or False (F)

T F 1. The organizational structure of a hotel's marketing and sales division is important in developing and maintaining successful marketing practices.

T F 2. Good communications with other departments in a hotel is not necessary for a successful marketing and sales division.

T F 3. Internal marketing is a technique for positioning products in the minds of consumers.

T F 4. Situation analysis is an effective technique for analyzing industry-wide marketing efforts.

T F 5. The product analysis portion of a situation analysis does not take into account the strengths and weaknesses of the property as a whole.

T F 6. The marketing plan developed from a situation analysis should be continually updated through persistent research efforts.

T F 7. In the lodging industry, a great deal of emphasis is currently placed on sophisticated forms of internal research.

T F 8. The benefits of research cannot be directly measured.

T F 9. A manager looking for patterns of customer preferences by recording which items are selling and which are not selling is an example of internal research.

T F 10. External research involves compiling information from records maintained within a lodging property.

T F 11. Positioning is concerned with the actual appearance of a product.

T F 12. The position of a property depends on what consumers think of the property.

T F 13. Lodging properties do not need to position themselves to travel agents.

T F 14. Media and collateral advertising will affect a property's positioning.

T F 15. Sales efforts must be consistent with the positioning of a property.

Multiple Choice

16. A hotel's marketing and sales division:

   a. helps determine the image of the property's products and services.
   b. relies heavily on research.
   c. interacts closely with other divisions and departments within the hotel.
   d. all of the above.

17. Research at the property level:

    a. has been found to be ineffective for conducting successful marketing activities.
    b. has been universally accepted by hotel operators.
    c. produces benefits which can be directly measured.
    d. contributes to the fulfillment of strategic needs and provides low-cost tactical support of marketing efforts.

18. Which of the following is an example of external research?

    a. focus groups
    b. abstracting items on restaurant checks
    c. analyzing data gathered by the hotel's reservations system
    d. none of the above

19. The positioning of a hotel depends on:

    a. what hotel marketers think of the hotel's products and services.
    b. what consumers think of the hotel's products and services.
    c. what hotel employees think of the hotel's products and services.
    d. none of the above.

20. Which of the following would help to effectively position a property to travel agents?

    a. city and locator maps of the general area surrounding the hotel
    b. good photographs of the hotel property
    c. computer access codes
    d. all of the above

Chapter Outline

Who Are Your Customers?
The Corporate Market
Other Resources to Help Sell New Markets
Sales Administration
Sales Training

Learning Objectives

1. Explain in detail why professionally run hotel sales offices group their potential customers into market segments.

2. Describe four major market segments within the corporate market, and identify each in terms of the decision-maker responsible for making reservations.

3. State what a hotel can do to promote sales from each of the three major sources of reservations made in relation to the transient business traveler segment of the corporate market.

4. Explain why close communication and teamwork are necessary between a particular hotel's sales force and outside hotel representation firms.

5. Define a sales action plan and state what should be included within a typical job description for salespersons.

6. Describe three filing and tracing systems found in well-run hotel sales offices.

7. Define "lost business" reports and state at least three ways in which they can be useful to a hotel's management.

8. Describe the procedures of the sales cycle that all hotel salespersons should complete.

9. Describe four sales training devices which hotel sales directors can use to ensure quality control within the hotel's sales staff.

8

Sales

ALL HOTEL MARKETING is based on selling. In the absence of a successful sales program, a hotel cannot be fully successful because the most important ingredient of its marketing program is missing. On this point there is complete agreement among the senior marketing executives who participated in our survey. Here are some sample responses:

> 66The sales function is our most important function in marketing planning. We are a sales-intensive company and [we] believe that, unless our salespeople are in the marketplace every day ... our marketing for that day is incomplete.99

> —**Michael A. Leven**
> Former Executive Vice President
> Americana Hotels

Others express it differently:

> 66Once the positioning statement is formulated, the most important aspect [of] the marketing planning is the sales action plan. Nothing happens until something is sold. The sales action plan is [an] integral part of the marketing plan. Advertising and public relations support the sales action plan which, in turn, is designed to obtain the revenue goals and objectives set forth for the property.99

> —**John Russell**
> Senior Vice President of Marketing
> Days Inns

Sig Front of The Sheraton Corporation writes:

> 66The sales function ranks among the most important activities in all marketing planning. Each hotel must obtain its maximum amount of group ... and transient business. The sales function should contribute at least 30% of room[s] business, and in many cases 50% to 60%.99

Clearly, these senior marketing executives consider sales the basis for the marketing programs in their organizations. Their success suggests that this sales-oriented approach to marketing has merit. Yet, in their eagerness to be a part of the expanding hospitality *marketing* field, many who have been successful as sales executives abandon the selling function. Although selling today is very much different from what it was in the past, it is still fundamental to marketing and cannot be ignored, particularly by those who are best acquainted with sales.

It would be considered illogical if an individual became a general manager because of tremendous ability in the front office, and then spent all day every day in the kitchen. Yet, more good sales programs are ruined by sales executives being called marketing executives than by any other single cause. Time and again salespeople who have become directors of marketing have forgotten that selling is not only a part of marketing, it is the single most important part. They also forget that what earned them the title of "marketing director" was their professional skill in and knowledge of the selling function.

Similarly, those who have become general managers after working as sales executives a decade ago are often the worst kind of general managers salespeople have to deal with. Because they have not adapted to the changing times and the changing tools of salesmanship, they cannot accept the way selling is done today.

The first section of this chapter on sales deals primarily with identifying customers and markets. In the second half, techniques for sales and the proper administration of a sales office are discussed.

Who Are Your Customers?

The customer for whom you organize your sales effort is a multi-dimensional prospect. For example, the person you are attempting to attract to your hotel as an individual business traveler may be a member of a social group which is planning a group meeting and may also have part-time responsibility for planning company meetings. Taking the example one step further, the same person who is an individual business traveler one day and a meeting planner or convention decision-maker the next day may be, on a third day, the decision-maker within a family planning a vacation trip. Therefore, you have the opportunity to sell to this prospect in all of his or her various roles.

How can this be accomplished? Professionally run hotel sales offices avoid scattering their fire by grouping their potential customers into market segments. Then a sales plan can be developed to address each of these market segments. The professionally run sales department includes group sales activities and transient sales activities under the same umbrella plan, but it uses very different action steps and even different targets within the same business organization to approach these two markets.

Furthermore, the hotel with a professional sales effort recognizes that it must sell the entire hotel, not just its guestrooms. For this reason, a sound sales action plan should be developed for catering and even for each of the food and beverage outlets. In the following section, the corporate market is analyzed, and approaches to the various market segments it contains are suggested.

The Corporate Market

Corporations are sources of business for hotels and for all their facilities. Corporations need transient guestrooms in their home city for incoming field executives or for vendors coming to call on their operation. They also need transient accommodations outside of their home city in the various marketplaces where they do business. Corporations usually book guestrooms in one of three ways.

1. **The secretary in a given department makes the reservations.** The secretary who is placing reservations for a particular department is an employee of that

department. Thus, the secretary's requirements reflect the various needs associated with that department. In an organization that has many departments, the people who make reservations may use several different approaches. Some may be structured, while others are casual; some may need one extremely nice room, while others reserve multiple rooms, all of the same quality; some may be motivated by a desire to impress the guests, while others are concerned about price. Therefore, it is important for the salesperson to identify the department's need when making the first sales call in order to approach the call in an appropriate manner.

2. **A central person, either a secretary or a traffic manager, is designated to handle all or most of the hotel arrangements.** In this case, the individual decision-maker may be harder to get to but, once the salesperson has broken down that barrier, the sales calls are generally easier to make and more successful.

3. **A travel agency, either as part of the organization or as an independent, contracted agency, places all airline and hotel reservations requests.** Here the buyer may be motivated to achieve goals: (a) to make the very best selection for the client, and (b) to protect the business interests of the agency. In this case, the salesperson should recognize that, to the travel agency, the prompt payment of commissions and recognition of the agency's role is very important.

Obviously, the hotel sales staff must determine which method of making reservations is used in order to determine what sales and promotional efforts ought to be made and to whom these marketing tools should be directed. Only then can the appropriate steps be taken:

1. If all secretaries in an organization make reservations for their own departments, the hotel sales staff or the reservations manager should make personal sales calls to each secretary. Or, a hotel chain's regional sales representative can do the sales calls for out-of-town reservations. Special promotions, such as hotel-hosted parties for these secretaries, can also help the sales effort.

2. If a central secretary or traffic manager makes the reservations, then the hotel's sales director or corporate sales manager can make personal calls, host luncheons or dinners, or invite the person to share in the specific property benefits (pool privileges, fitness club, catalog gift program, etc.).

3. If reservations are placed through a travel agency, the hotel's director of sales or general manager can call periodically to make sure the commissions are flowing properly and that the agency has all of the appropriate promotional material on the hotel. The director of sales or general manager may also make courtesy calls to present any gifts the hotel has to offer. At the same time it may be possible to learn whether the total potential of the agency (not for this particular corporation alone but for all other corporate customers) is being realized.

The corporate market is also the source of group business. Many corporations have sales training classes, motivational meetings, personnel conferences, stockholder meetings, and even an annual convention. Some companies, either directly or through a third party, offer incentive travel programs to reward outstanding employees—especially salespeople—and others who may not be employees but have performed valuable services to the company. This group business may be outbound if the company is highly centralized. But if the company has many out-of-town representatives and the headquarters city is an attractive vacation destination, traffic may be inbound instead.

It is essential that all of the types of business that come from a corporation be filed separately. Without this separate tracking, the various types of business from a given company are all lumped into one file, the proper trace dates for following up on the individual pieces of business are often missed, and that business is lost as a result.

While many corporations now have central meeting-planning departments—and many corporate meeting planners are members of Meeting Planners International (MPI) or the Society of Corporate Meeting Planners (SCMP)—far more do not. Because the independent meeting planners are reached only by dogged sales work in the field, some hotel salespeople ignore them. They take out allied memberships in MPI, SCMP, or meeting planners' groups within particular industries. This is understandable, because these groups offer a new and exciting avenue through which to reach the best prospects. Organizations such as the Insurance Conference Planners (ICP) and the Society of Government Meeting Planners (SGMP) give hotels that specialize in a certain kind of group business an excellent opportunity to expand their customer base rapidly. However, concentrating on these groups to the exclusion of independent meeting planners is a mistake. A hotel with a good selling program covers all meeting planners, not merely the ones that are easier to find.

Corporations are also excellent sources of business which revolves around special events. This type of business is called function business, whether related to overnight accommodations or not. Quarter-century club meetings, company Christmas parties, departmental going-away parties, and similar events should be sought out and sold aggressively and effectively.

Again, if the catering department has its own individual sales action plan, the hotel is more likely to get all there is to get from the corporate social market. Of course, any corporation located near a hotel is an excellent target for promoting frequent use of the hotel's food and beverage retail outlets. Every effort should be made to promote among personnel at various levels within the corporation the use of the outlets which are best designed to serve them. Consider these examples:

1. If the hotel has a luxury dining room, the senior officers of the corporation should be invited to frequent it. If management decides to make it a private luncheon club in the day and a public dining room in the evening, then corporation officers should be the first prospects contacted for charter membership in the private club.

2. If the hotel's main dining room offers a proper environment for business conferences, then the heads of various departments within the corporation should be invited to use this facility as an appropriate site for doing business. The main dining room can be presented as an extension of the working space

available in their offices. Dining room personnel who have served these department heads before should know their likes and dislikes in regard to table placement and attentiveness of service.

3. If the hotel has a coffee shop and there is a large secretarial base or junior executive base in the corporation, special promotions could be offered to bring in these people, because they would probably find the coffee shop the outlet most in line with their daily budget.

Corporate buyers become prime prospects for weekend business as well when they are viewed as members of social groups and households. Several approaches to the corporate-employee-as-family-member can be used, depending on the type of property. If the facility has a pool and a nice dining room, the approach to use might be: "What better place could there be for a weekend getaway than the XYZ hotel right here in your own area?" Personnel departments of corporations are frequently very willing to display promotional materials on recreation-oriented programs, particularly when employees of the company are given special "employee discounts" not available to the general public. If the lodging property is an economy hotel, then fewer elements of the recreational weekend are available; but the fact that these elements can be provided for a very low price should be attractive to a portion of the market. Therefore, price would be the benefit to feature.

In this chapter one market has been used to illustrate the wide range of sales opportunities available to any hotel that is making a serious effort to achieve its sales potential. Similar sales opportunities can be developed by thinking about each of the following markets:

- Strictly social local clubs

- Fraternal/religious/ethnic organizations

- Government offices and military installations in the area

- State and regional conventions

- National association conventions

- Travel agents

- Tour operators

- Motor coach companies

- Airlines

- Hospital personnel and medical organizations

- University/school faculty and staff members

- Professional sports organizations

And the list goes on. In order to realize the potential of each of these markets, the sales staff must be committed to the same painstaking process described for the corporate market. While this demands more energy and creativity than some are willing to give, the payoffs make the extra effort worthwhile. For example, most hotel managers tend to look at sports teams as being sources of seasonal business only. However, one wise hotelier in the Northeast makes it a point to go after all the off-season rooms business from the local professional teams in his area. This business includes long-term stays of new players relocating to the area, business travelers in town for owners' meetings, and all out-of-town journalists coming in to do preseason features on the sports teams. For this hotelier, professional athletic organizations are a source of business throughout the year.

Other Resources to Help Sell New Markets

Many hotel chains employ regional sales offices to assist the sales departments of their individual properties. Hundreds of hotels that are not affiliated with a chain (and even some that are) use hotel representation firms to generate more sales in specific marketplaces. In effect these firms become corporate sales offices for the various properties that use their services. The Krisam Group, David Green and Associates, Robert F. Warner and Company, and many other very good representation organizations provide excellent sales support. Exhibit 1 shows typical guidelines which may be furnished by such a representation firm for use in a hotel's sales department.

Any hotel with a good sales program includes these outside resources in its sales action plan. For instance, if support for a hotel in the Chicago marketplace is available from either a corporate office or a representation firm, the action steps involving that outside office should be factored right into the Chicago hotel's sales plan. Furthermore, these outside action steps should be tracked just as if they were the responsibility of on-site personnel. To be effective, the use of outside resources demands close communication and teamwork. Outside sales support arms are only as good as the hotel's own sales and follow-up efforts. If a regional office generates a lot of leads but the property does not respond to them for some reason, this failure will hamper the regional office's future dealings with that client for this hotel and for other hotels as well. If corporate sales offices and representation firms are not seen as an effective, quick means of gathering information and making reservations, then the public will by-pass them. If this happens, an important part of your sales arsenal will be wasted.

> ❝You have to separate the sales function into two categories. You have individual hotel sales functions, and you have the corporate sales function which supports them.
>
> We allocate substantial sums of money to regional sales offices and to corporate sales personnel in key cities, which should indicate their importance [to] the company as a whole. Input from the sales function, both from property salespeople and regional salespeople, is extremely important in marketing planning. It allows us to make broad but nevertheless key assumptions about where the business is coming from and what opportunities still exist for growth and new business. Then we can go out and test in individual marketplaces.
>
> In marketing planning, the ability to have a company-wide program that is implemented at all levels in a supportive and effective way is ideal. We may not be perfect, but we've come a long way in achieving that consistency. Regional sales offices allow us to present a consistent face to key buyers of our product in

Exhibit 1 Example of Major Account Coverage Progam Summary and Spread Sheet

TIMA corporation

David A. Troy
President

One Grove Street
P.O. Box 367
Wellesley, MA 02181

Wellesley (617) 237–3391
Boston (617) 227–5515

TO: All 1984 TIMA clients

FROM: David A. Troy

SUBJECT: Major Account Coverage Program—Your Hotels

It has been suggested by some clients that we prepare a brief summary of the Major Account Coverage Program recently discussed with some of you.

Objectives of the program

The program is designed to increase the efficiency of your sales team and to provide more frequent coverage of your most important accounts and less frequent coverage to your lower priority accounts.

Further, it will help you to identify any existing markets which are not currently covered adequately and help you to determine the proper actions to take to improve that coverage.

It will also provide a method for establishing better quotas and tracking the performance of your field sales team in an equitable and professional manner.

It will also help you to determine what, if any, reallocation of your sales resources or redeployment of your sales people could yield greater results.

Procedure

1. Each salesman should evaluate each and every account assigned, and indicate on a spreadsheet the following information: (see spread sheet, page 1a).

2. After this sheet is completed through Column 5, the director of sales should review the work with each salesperson. At this time, Column 6 and 7 should be completed, jointly indicating revised call frequency in Column 6, and account priority in Column 7. I suggest that you weight the accounts 1 through 4 with the most important accounts being level 1 and the least important accounts being level 4. These could be

— Marketing Management Services To The Hospitality Industry —

TIMA corporation

–2–

color coded, if you wish, according to your own choice (red for level 1, blue for level 2, green for level 3, yellow for level 4, etc.). If you so choose, account file folders can match this color code.

3. The total number of sales calls now assigned for 1984 is the total of Column 5. If this account load does not equal an appropriate work load per salesperson (for example, most sales people can make approximately 30 calls per week, approximately 40 weeks per year, making a total of 1200 sales calls), several things can happen.

First, we can assign additional accounts to the salesperson to bring the estimated load up to par. Second, we can assign a greater share of the prospecting responsibilities to this individual by market segment.

Accounts should be totaled not only for the grand total per person, but should also be evaluated by market segment to see whether or not we have the proper number of accounts to give us the yield we expect from each market segment. This can be done by adding an additional column to the summary sheet or by doing a separate tabulation for each market to be prospected for 1984.

Once this work has been completed, quotas for each salesperson should be agreed upon for the first quarter. These quotas can be adjusted each quarter to meet the new priorities for the hotel and may or may not, depending on your needs, be structured against room night objectives alone. You may, for instance, with a salesperson who is assigned a heavy prospecting mission, wish to evaluate their performance more in terms of new accounts opened and account potential, rather than an actual account yield.

Please modify, in any way you see fit, this program and use it only if you see that it will be helpful in reaching your objectives. My honest opinion is that once you go through it, you will have more effective quotas for your team, more time free for new prospecting, a much greater call frequency on your most important accounts, and a much clearer picture as to the appropriateness of the size of your sales force and the resources they are given to work with.

Good luck with your new account evaluation work. Best regards.

Column 1	Column 2	Column 3	Column 4	Column 5	Column 6	Column 7
Name of account	Account contact(s)	How often these accounts were called on in 1983	How often we expect to call on them in 1984	Estimate of the account room night value	Revisions after review	Account priority (1 through 4)

Courtesy of TIMA Corporation

key markets. Whether it's a corporate meeting planner, an association executive, or a corporate travel department representative, regional salespeople can act in behalf of individual hotels who become aware of an opportunity in a distant location and engage the nearest corporate salesperson to act in their behalf. Or they can go out and show a broad product line of more than 50 great hotels. **"**

> **—Bill Newman**
> Senior Vice President of Marketing
> Westin Hotels

What Bill has said here about Westin's approach is just as true of independent properties who work properly with their outside representation firm. There is constant communication between the two sales arms, the results of which are more business for the property and more marketplace credibility for the regional office.

Knowing your markets and the customers in your markets is basic to a successful sales operation. The next section of this chapter discusses the tools and techniques you will need to master in order to maximize the potential from your markets. This section also explains how to identify major accounts and plan an account coverage program.

Sales Administration

When older hotel executives criticize a hotel salesperson, they often say, "He is more of an administrator than a salesman." By this they mean that the salesperson is more concerned with having the details of office administration running perfectly than he is with actually contacting prospective customers. Of course, it is possible to err on the other side by spending too little time on sales office organization.

Experience has shown, however, that the best sales offices are those that have both extremely good administration *and* very active sales programs. These strengths are certainly not mutually exclusive.

> **"**A well-run sales office is not a frantic place. It is active, to be sure, but the activity is organized, and the people move from function to function in a prescribed manner. There is a sense of urgency but not a sense of panic, and the feeling of organization is apparent despite the pace.
>
> Without a solid administrative plan, no sales office will bring in its maximum potential business. In fact, it may … , through disorder, lose the priority business because it is too busy handling that which has come in without much assistance. **"**

> **—Buck Hoyle**
> Executive Vice President
> HSMAI

What is required for sound administration of a sales office? Basically it involves being organized. A well-administered sales office begins and ends each week with a sales action plan prepared in advance for each salesperson. The action plan contains the names of only those accounts for which the particular salesperson is responsible. The action plan outlines the objectives to be achieved by that salesperson during a certain sales week. Each salesperson should be allowed to see and agree to the plan prior to the start of that sales week. Then the individual salesperson should refer to the plan frequently throughout that sales week in order to stay on track. Exhibit 2 shows a typical format for a weekly sales action plan.

Exhibit 2   Typical Format for a Weekly Sales Action Plan

Salesperson: _____		Week Ending _____	
DATE	PERSONAL CALLS	TELEPHONE	SPECIAL ACTIVITIES

In addition to individual sales action plans, the department as a whole should have a key accounts list. Because the key accounts list includes a hotel's top accounts, an extremely large share of the business booked for the hotel comes from this relatively small client base.

A well-administered sales office should not only have clear market segment breakdowns; it should have clear-cut job descriptions for everyone from secretaries and clerical personnel through the most senior member of the department. Job descriptions for salespeople outline what markets are to be covered, what supplemental duties go with the job, and how much time is to be spent on each type of activity. If quotas are assigned to the sales positions, these should be explicitly stated in the job descriptions for the hotel's protection. On the other hand, for the salespeople's protection, the job descriptions should note any regular, ongoing activities from selling with which they are required to involve themselves. For example, if sales personnel are expected to attend or participate in nonsales meetings, this loss of selling time can be pointed out to management by spelling out in the job description the amount of time required to prepare for and attend these meetings.

For every account assigned to a salesperson, there should be a file folder containing all correspondence and background on the account which will help the salesperson become familiar with the customer or prospective customer. Once the account has been contacted, however, an effective filing and tracing system is necessary to ensure that the proper follow-up action is taken on the account. Experience suggests that files should be traced for action on specific dates. The trace dates should be reviewed periodically to make sure they reflect the number of files each salesperson is assigned, the call frequency required by those accounts, and the decision-making cycle of the account as represented within the file. The filing and tracing system most favored in well-run hotel sales offices consists of three types of files: (1) an alphabetical master card file which contains one card for every account on file, regardless of trace date; (2) a trace file, which contains the same accounts sorted by the date they are to be contacted next; and (3) a geographic file containing the same accounts sorted by location of the decision-maker.

The geographic file may seem unimportant to managers of smaller properties; but because small properties have only a limited amount of sales time available, they can benefit most from a file sorted geographically. They can confine their sales activities to the size of territory they consider appropriate. It would not be necessary for a 100-room motor inn to have a breakdown of every major city in the United States, but it might be very important to have a breakdown of its state's capital city, for instance. A smaller hotel might only have accounts in two or three cities and it might have each of those cities broken down by (postal) zip code or some other guideline that makes sense for that particular hotel.

Of course, with so many hotel offices being automated, some hotel sales files are now stored in computerized data bases. The computer's ability to search for and identify accounts by particular type of business, geography, month of decision-making, month of meeting, or any other account characteristic makes it a most compatible tool in a hotel sales office. As with any computerized data processing system, the office that is very well organized is in a position to take full advantage of the computer's capabilities. Unfortunately, in many hotel sales offices, sophisticated equipment is simply taking up space. Perhaps the former director of sales who purchased the equipment had very good intentions but failed to document the reason for the purchase and its intended uses. Perhaps the current director of sales is too embarrassed to admit unfamiliarity with the equipment and to seek out advice on how to operate it to its full potential. Regardless of who is to blame, these sales offices are missing out on an opportunity to increase their efficiency and productivity.

A well-run sales office avoids confusion by putting its procedures in writing. The way bookings are to be entered, the process by which file data should be transferred to the various service departments, and rate concession policies should all be documented. High turnover in the sales department, combined with the long lead times involved with some types of business, makes written procedures essential. Function book policies also must be committed to writing if the hotel is to maximize its revenue. Naturally, the same policy need not apply to every function room in the hotel. There is no reason why the lead time stated for a 1,000-seat ballroom should be the same as that stated for a 20-seat conference room. If the policies differ, however, it is important that all personnel understand these differences.[1]

One administrative technique that can be very helpful in increasing sales is the lead log system (see Exhibit 3). By logging tentative business and leads from all sources (convention bureaus, in-company sources, self-generated leads) according to the month for which the business is booked, a director of sales can help all sales department personnel keep track of what happens with each of the hotel's business prospects.

Exhibit 3   Lead Log System

Hotel Name _____	Potential Business For _____	19 ____				
GROUP/CONTACT/FILE #	SOURCE/ OFFICE/DATE	MAX RMS	TOTAL RM NTS	DATES	SALESPERSON ASSIGNED

DATE: ACTION:
DATE: ACTION:
DATE: ACTION:
DATE: ACTION:
DATE: ACTION:
DATE: FINAL DISPOSITION:

Another very helpful administrative procedure is the proper completion of "lost business" reports on every piece of business the hotel tries but fails to book. If these lost business reports are filed according to the date for which the business was booked, they can be used three ways:

1. If the business had to be refused because other bookings blocked the space, but later one or more of the other bookings are cancelled, the prospect can be easily retrieved.

2. In building a sales plan for the following year, the director of sales can review the lost business reports to see if the hotel missed more profitable business that normally books later because it had already taken less profitable business that typically books earlier.

3. If a number of lost business reports indicate that an operational or physical shortcoming of the property caused the loss of business, the sales department may be able to persuade management to correct the problem by showing convincing evidence that the problem is a serious liability.[2]

Sales Training

The hotel business is an extremely competitive one. Selling for a hotel is, by its very nature, a competitive activity. To compete on an athletic field, an athlete needs training and conditioning. No less than the athlete, the hotel sales professional needs training and, yes, conditioning as well. First, salespeople in hotels require training in the mechanics of booking business. Second, salespeople must know the proper procedure to follow at each stage of the booking. A hotel salesperson has certain responsibilities to a prospect from the time that prospect is booked through the consumption of the hotel's services to the follow-up call. The cycle is complete when the salesperson recontacts the customer to determine how satisfied the customer was with the function and to try to book the next function. The rhythm of this cycle becomes more familiar and comfortable as the salesperson gains sales experience. However, sales trainees must be taught these procedures step by step.

Some managers resent the task of training; they consider it an intrusion upon their already busy workday. Granted, it is not easy to find time on a regular basis for ongoing sales training. However, training is such an important activity that time must be found for it, even if it is after normal business hours.

As explained earlier in this chapter, salespeople must know their markets. In particular, hotel salespeople who are new must be taught the characteristics of the market segment assigned to them. Salespeople must learn how to analyze and respond to interactions between themselves and the customer, taking into account the nature of the customer's market segment. The well-trained salesperson considers all of the following factors before, during, and after a sales presentation:

1. What is the customer's role in the buying organization?

2. How does the customer perceive your hotel in relation to the buying organization?

3. What is the customer's attitude toward you as a representative of your hotel?

4. How does the customer feel today about the job, about the event to be booked, and about the time that you are involved together? Is it an important event or a routine booking? Are you solving a major problem by booking the customer's event, or are you simply assisting an experienced buyer who makes such purchases frequently?

It is important that sales training not be limited to new members of the sales team. Experienced salespeople need refresher training in customer attitudes, in hotel policies, and in the basic selling process. As new competition arises, experienced salespeople should be brought together to share ideas about how the market perceives the new competition. Also, various policy changes occur as the circumstances and personnel of the hotel change, so training in the new priorities may be needed.

Finally, salespeople need to keep selling skills and good sales techniques fresh in mind. Because salespeople tend to acquire bad habits over time, sales call situations recorded on videotape equipment can be extremely helpful. Many sales organizations that care about the quality of their sales presentations reqire salespeople to participate periodically in sales role plays. These simulated sales calls are videotaped so they can be played back and evaluated in a critiquing session.

If videotaping is not available, however, the supervised sales call is still an excellent form of quality control. It would seem that sales directors are spending less and less time "double calling" with their salespeople to see how they perform under fire. While the double call can be somewhat awkward, it can also be extremely educational. For instance, the senior salesperson may detect a flaw in the salesperson's delivery of a presentation which would probably not show up in the written call report. Similarly, by observing the subordinate's sales call, the sales

Exhibit 4   Market Segment Analysis—Corporate Transient Market

Characteristics	Suggested Sales Tactic
1. Buyer tends to be young and relatively inexperienced.	1. Buyer reacts positively to personal attention.
2. Buyer is not high up on corporate ladder.	2. Buyer is receptive to attention in the form of promotion parties, gifts, etc.
3. Buyer is not the ultimate user of the product.	3. Positive feedback from the user is a major influence on the buyer's decision-making process.

director may notice a mannerism or speech habit that is distracting to the buyer and ought to be corrected to increase the salesperson's effectiveness.

Sales training can bring both new and experienced salespeople together for market segmentation drills. In these exercises, a group of salespeople discusses a particular market segment in an informal setting. Even though some of the salespeople have not had experience covering this market segment, an open discussion is held on it. Gradually, the discussion moves toward analyzing characteristics of the market segment. A flip chart or chalkboard is divided into two columns, one for the market segment's characteristics and the other for the sales tactics these characteristics suggest. In this way, ideas for new and different sales approaches are developed for various segments and can then be tested in the field. Exhibit 4 shows an analysis resulting from a typical market segmentation drill.

If the discussion of the market segment stays on track, a certain pattern of buyer characteristics and tactics to use with the buyer emerges. Because the same exercise can reveal radically different characteristics for different market segments, it is important to review segments individually. There are too many buyers and too many differences to try to reduce all of the hotel's customers to a single profile.

Finally, the case study is another very effective sales training exercise. The trainer can either borrow the facts from a competing hotel or use the characteristics of another hotel that is less likely to be recognized. Some trainers use existing cases that have been published in marketing textbooks or industry publications. This exercise challenges a hotel sales team to put together a sales action plan for a property very different from its own. Participants learn to interact and, more important, they are better prepared for the time when they will be asked to contribute to their own hotel's marketing plan.

A well-administered hotel can surpass its competitors, regardless of some physical advantages or disadvantages it may have. Salespeople who have taken a sound sales training program and who have a thorough knowledge of their market and the characteristics of the buyers within their market are likely to do better than most.

Endnotes

1. The section on sales administration is partially based on the comments of Thomas T. McCarthy, Jr., CHSE, of Thomas McCarthy Associates, made in his column,

"Administrative Support—A Must for Sales Success," in *Hotel & Resort Industry,* July 1982, p. 62. His assistance is gratefully acknowledged.

2. Excellent examples of sales call report forms, trace systems, and other administrative support systems for a well-run sales office are given in the *Situation Analysis Workbook,* published jointly by HSMA International's Foundation and the Educational Institute of AH&MA.

Supplemental Reading ——————————————————————

Some Thoughts for the New Salesperson

by Thomas T. McCarthy, Jr.

More than once over the years, I've noticed that new salespeople who have just been promoted from other departments in the hotel to sales take a lot of kidding from their old co-workers. The recurring theme of the kidding is that you really have it made in sales. The impression is given that sales is a glamour job that really doesn't require hard work. After all, what does it take to shake a few hands, entertain clients at lunch, and take prospects on tours of the hotel?

While the kidding is good natured on the surface, there are many who honestly believe that the most important decision a salesperson makes is where to entertain the client for cocktails tonight, and the most difficult task, the filling out of the weekly expense account. Unfortunately, many new salespeople arrive on the job on the first day with the same misconceptions about sales that their co-workers have, only to find that sales isn't the bed of roses they thought it would be.

As a new salesperson you soon realize that it's kind of lonely out there making sales calls day after day, it's tough to get out and going on days when you're not really in the mood, there's a lot more paper work than you expected, and it's frustrating not to have the answers to all the questions the prospects ask.

The next highlight of your career as a new salesperson is the terrifying realization that your efforts are resulting in few, if any, bookings. It's at this point that you often become discouraged and wonder if you really were cut out for sales in the first place. This is the point where some counsel and advice can help you through a very frustrating point in your life.

The first thing that you must understand is that every successful salesperson has experienced the same kinds of frustrations early in his or her career. The real fun in selling is the booking of business resulting from your hard work. Unfortunately, in the first few months of selling there's plenty of the hard work but not much of the fun. This is what leads to temporary, understandable discouragement in most cases. It's a little like playing golf. After taking a couple of lessons from the pro, the new golfer goes out every day and seldom gets a good shot. Usually this leads to discouragement, but we know that if he keeps at it, the good shots will start to come with more frequency and encourage him on to even greater success. Remember, most salespeople look back on their first few months in sales as an interesting, work-filled period but not as one of the most fun-filled times of their lives.

When I think back about advice for new salespeople, I have to think back to some seminars that I had the pleasure of moderating for the Worldwide Sales people of Holiday Inns. Within that group were some of the finest salespeople I have ever met. They were hard working, articulate people whose experience in sales ranged from one to twenty-five years. We discussed the challenges faced by new salespeople and I asked them to give me the answer to the question, "If you were

This article is reprinted with permission from *Hotel & Resort Industry,* February 1982, p. 36.

asked to help a new salesperson by giving one short piece of advice regarding sales, what would that piece of advice be?"

The answers that these successful salespeople gave me to that question dealt with many aspects of the salesperson's job and, hopefully, will help you or someone within your organization who has just started a sales career. The following are twenty-five of the answers I received:

- There are good days and bad days, but always the overall feeling of accomplishment.

- Everyone makes mistakes. Don't dwell on them. Use them to help you do better the next time.

- Even the most successful salesperson with years of experience continues to use the most basic of proven sales techniques.

- The more sales presentations you make, the more you will sell.

- The effort you make today will show up a few months from now. Don't be frustrated because the results aren't immediate.

- Know your product and show confidence when selling it.

- Obtain complete information from the client regarding needs.

- Know how your product fits your client's needs.

- You must believe in your product to sell it successfully.

- In order to sell your product and services, sell yourself to the client first. If the client believes in you, it's a lot easier to sell your product.

- Always remember the importance of planning, product knowledge, persistence and creativity.

- Don't promise anything you can't deliver.

- Never try to bluff a client when you don't know the answer to a question. Don't be afraid to say you don't know the answer. Offer to get the answer, and get it.

- Have perseverance.

- Show clients that you can be of assistance to them in doing their jobs better.

- Be enthusiastic. Enthusiasm can be the deciding factor in many selling situations.

- Show your sincerity.

- Be honest.

- Never ridicule the customer, competition, or your fellow workers.

- Try to keep energy level high at all times. The key is good health habits.

- Have the strong desire to succeed.

- ABC—Always Be Closing.

- A client will pay any amount for a product if dollar for dollar it is the best value.

- Do your homework and follow up.

- Don't get discouraged because of denials or rejections.

All of us can learn from this advice from 25 salespeople who have all weathered the frustrations of the new salesperson to become successful sales professionals who enjoy their work.

As a closing thought, keep in mind that new salespeople will always fondly remember the people who helped them through their early days, and who doesn't like to be fondly remembered?

REVIEW QUIZ

When you feel you have covered all of the material in this chapter, answer these questions. Choose the *best* answer. Check your answers with the correct ones found on the Review Quiz Answer Key at the end of this book.

True (T) or False (F)

T   F   1. All marketing is based on selling.

T   F   2. An individual may be a member of several markets and market segments which a hotel attempts to reach.

T   F   3. Professional sales efforts should recognize a responsibility to sell the entire hotel, not just guestrooms.

T   F   4. Professionally run hotel sales offices avoid scattering their efforts by grouping their potential customers into market segments.

T   F   5. A single sales plan is developed to address every market segment.

T   F   6. A professionally run sales department uses very different action steps and even different targets when selling to different market segments within the same business organization.

T   F   7. It is important for the salesperson to identify the needs of a corporate department after making the first sales call.

T   F   8. It is essential that all of the types of business that come from a particular corporation be filed together to allow for separate tracking and easy follow-up.

T   F   9. All meeting planners may be reached through Meeting Planners International (MPI) or the Society of Corporate Meeting Planners (SCMP).

T   F   10. The marketplace credibility of outside hotel representation firms is not the concern of any individual hotel.

T   F   11. Experience shows that good administration and active sales programs are mutually exclusive.

T   F   12. A sales action plan outlines the objectives to be achieved by a particular salesperson and is not given to the salesperson until the start of a particular sales week.

T   F   13. High turnover in sales departments, combined with the long lead times of some types of business, makes written procedures essential.

T   F   14. Only inexperienced salespersons benefit from simulated sales calls, supervised sales calls, market segmentation drills, and case study exercises.

T   F   15. Participation in market segmentation drills should be limited to those sales persons who have had direct experience with the market segment to be analyzed.

Multiple Choice

16. The corporate market is a source of:

    a. transient guestroom business.
    b. group business.
    c. function business.
    d. all of the above.

17. The booking sources of guestroom business from the transient business traveler segment of the corporate market are:

    a. secretaries.
    b. personnel managers.
    c. meeting planners.
    d. travelers themselves.

18. The corporate meeting segment of the corporate market includes:

    a. sales training classes.
    b. personnel conferences.
    c. stockholder meetings.
    d. all of the above.

19. Job descriptions for salespersons should outline everything *except:*

    a. what markets are to be covered.
    b. a sales action plan.
    c. supplemental duties.
    d. the amount of time to be spent on each activity.

20. Well-run hotel sales offices have which of the following file systems?

    a. an alphabetical master card file
    b. a trace file
    c. a geographic file
    d. all of the above

Chapter Outline

Advertising
    Setting Advertising Objectives
    Advertising Agencies
    Types of Advertising
    Budgeting
Public Relations
    Publicity and Media Relations
    Consumer/Guest Relations
    Employee Relations

Learning Objectives

1. Compare advertising and public relations in terms of their similarities and differences as tools of marketing.

2. Correctly identify how the setting of advertising objectives enters the overall sequence of strategic marketing planning.

3. State what factors a hotel should consider in selecting a good advertising agency.

4. Identify the distinguishing characteristics of each of the four major types of advertising: collateral material, print media, broadcast media (radio and television), and out-of-home media.

5. State what initial concerns a hotel should have when budgeting for its advertising program.

6. Identify a variety of programs which public relations in the hospitality industry could involve.

7. State the features that distinguish a hotel's promotional publicity program from simple publicity-seeking.

8. List and describe the basic press kit materials that a public relations department should have on file.

9. List the specific responsibilities of a publicity coordinator who serves as the public relations spokesperson for a hotel.

10. Itemize what a hotel can do to direct a positive public relations campaign toward the consumer who is a guest of the hotel.

9

Advertising and Public Relations

As MARKETING TOOLS, advertising and public relations can be viewed as investments in a hotel's future. Both are designed to build, enhance, or maintain an image of a hotel in the public's eye or to solve a particular image problem a property may have. A successful advertising or public relations campaign can help to increase revenues by projecting a media-based message that is positive, in line with your position, and which attracts a profitable or identified market to your hotel.

Although similar in orientation, advertising and public relations are distinct and sophisticated marketing tools. The difference lies in the extent of control a property may have over the message being heard, read, or viewed by a particular audience. In advertising, a hotel must buy the media space or time, and the hotel controls the message content and presentation. Public relations announcements, however, are accepted by the media when they consider them newsworthy items likely to be of interest to their readers, listeners, or viewers.

The first part of this chapter focuses on setting advertising objectives and developing an advertising approach which is suitable to your property. The second half identifies areas which are generally the target of public relations campaigns and touches upon what a hotel can do to develop a positive public relations plan.

Advertising

Until about 26 years ago, the hotel industry viewed advertising programs rather skeptically. Although advertising was included in the annual budget, if profits did not develop in the first half of the year, management would reduce or eliminate advertising in the last half of the year to balance the budget.

Over the last 20 years, however, the foolhardiness of this approach to advertising has become apparent. Because marketing planning is playing a larger part in the business cycles of hotels and hotel companies, advertising is receiving more attention and support. In fact, the advertising plan has become an integral part of the marketing plan; thus, it is viewed as an ongoing marketing process and not simply an expense to be eliminated. Consequently, hotels have been doing more consistent advertising. Furthermore, this advertising has exhibited much better positioning and has been more closely linked to the other elements of the marketing mix. As a result, the entire lodging industry has been enjoying a much better image in recent years.

⁶⁶Hotel advertising today is becoming more and more market-sensitive and reflective of the type of hotel that it represents. The audience focus of hospitality advertising today is a far cry from what it was a few years ago. Advertising to the travel trade, for instance, indicates the change in attitude on the part of hoteliers to treat agencies as an extension of their sales arms rather than as interlopers in the booking process. ⁹⁹

—**Alan Fleschner**
Publisher
Travel Weekly

In listening to several marketing executives from different corporations talk about advertising, one need was repeatedly expressed: management needs to participate not only in the budgeting for advertising, but also in the determination of the creative message. Although this opinion was not commonly held just a few years ago, it is certainly typical of marketing thought among senior marketing executives today.

Michael Leven, former Executive Vice President of Americana Hotels, states:

⁶⁶Advertising is planned by the advertising agency as an outgrowth of the marketing planning meeting. After the plan is submitted, those of us with fiscal responsibility review the plan to determine the amount of money we are able to spend within the budget limitations. ⁹⁹

Setting Advertising Objectives

Advertising, like other elements of the marketing program, requires objectives. These can only be set when the hotel's position has been determined. (Remember, a hotel's advertising, and indeed its total marketing program, must be consistent with its position.) Just as it is important for all the key decision-makers to agree on what the hotel's position should be, it is equally important to reach a consensus on what the objectives of the hotel's advertising program should be. This agreement can be achieved in a group meeting. Alternatively, those involved with the advertising program can be asked to submit written statements of objectives which are then analyzed by the final decision-maker. (This is usually the marketing director or the general manager working in concert with an advertising agency.) Once the decision is made, all who had input should be privy to and in agreement with the chosen objectives.

The type of advertising objectives selected has a major impact on the budget required for advertising. For example, if a long-established property has a well-defined image and proven results with certain media, then a maintenance program and a maintenance budget would probably suffice. If, however, the advertising objective is to introduce a brand new product at a unique destination to a whole new audience, then a traditional advertising budget would be both inappropriate and unusable.

Setting objectives is not an exact science, but to the extent that the objectives contain specific numerical targets, they will be useful guides to proper ad placement and budgeting. Let us assume a high-rise Holiday Inn, which has had a stable occupancy over a four- or five-year period, is located in the middle of a small city in upstate New York. Here is a sample statement of objectives for this hypothetical hotel:

> ❝The Holiday Inn-Center City enjoys acceptance as the best hotel to stay in for a 'no surprises' guest experience. We serve fine meals and well-poured drinks. Our objective in the next year is to maintain our position in the marketplace, while adding four or five occupancy points and increasing food and beverage volume by 15%. Because we have a new enclosed swimming pool and a new emphasis on recreation and fitness, the market most likely to deliver this improved occupancy is the weekend guest market.❞

Once the key contributors to the Holiday Inn-Center City's advertising program agree to this statement of objectives, it should be relatively simple for the decision-makers to see where their advertising ought to be placed. By calculating what the probable improvement in occupancy would mean in terms of revenue, the marketing manager can calculate what the increase in the hotel's advertising budget should be. Again, there is no magic formula, but this approach allows management to estimate what the budget ought to be in this case.

Now consider a radically different situation. Suppose a hotel that was at the bottom of the market and then closed for several years is being repositioned at the top of the market and is seeking out an audience it has not enjoyed for decades. This was the challenge actually faced by the Belz family of Memphis, Tennessee, when they bought the Peabody Hotel at a foreclosure sale in the summer of 1975.

First opened on September 1, 1925, the Peabody had been one of the preeminent convention hotels in the southern United States from the mid-thirties until the sixties. However, it began to show signs of aging after World War II. The Peabody's position was also eroding due to the combined effects of a general decline in the downtown area and the rise of motels (particularly Holiday Inns, headquartered in Memphis). These problems were just too much for the Peabody's management to cope with alone. In 1965 the Sheraton Corporation bought the Peabody and spent $2 million in renovation. However, despite its efforts to save the refurbished property, which was reopened in 1968, the Peabody went into bankruptcy in March 1975.

In the summer of 1975 new ownership began to change the picture. Three generations of the Belz family planned the physical restoration of the hotel, which was executed over the next six years. With an extremely complex financial package, the owners spent more than $25 million before they were through with the restoration. In a clever move designed to capitalize on its historic prominence, the Peabody was officially reopened on September 1, 1981—exactly 56 years after it first opened its doors to the public. Since then, it has been listed on the National Register of Historic Places and has been cited by the U.S. Department of the Interior as one of the most outstanding preservation case studies in the nation.

During the restoration project, the new management also set about the monumental task of repositioning the hotel in the minds of its public. What was perceived as old and tired needed to be repositioned as grand and restored. Furthermore, the public had to be assured that once it was reopened, the hotel would be there to stay. Fortunately, the people of Memphis had a sentimental attachment to the Peabody and wanted it revived. Hundreds of supportive letters were received from citizens interested in seeing the hotel reopened and its long-standing traditions reinstated. The new owners capitalized on their restoration project in their advertising by using the slogan "Again and forever, the South's grand hotel."

Each facet of the Peabody's marketing program had to be better than the norm because the marketing team had a dual challenge: creating positive new thoughts in the minds of the audience and eliminating negative old thoughts. Although it would not be easy to accomplish such a turnaround in the property's image, there was complete agreement on the objectives of the advertising program, which made everyone's job easier.

Three of the advertisements the Peabody used successfully to upgrade its image appear in this chapter. Note the mallard ducks which have played a key role in the Peabody's marketing program. The hotel's daily parade of ducks has been used effectively to separate the Peabody from its competition. By using ducks as a logo on everything from its collateral to the candy placed on each pillow at night, the Peabody's unique identity has been reinforced. The ever popular mallards have even been featured on network TV morning news programs. This publicity has been an added help to a hotel that formerly suffered from public relations problems.

Advertising Agencies

With very few exceptions, today's hotel advertising is generated by advertising agencies. A few companies have an in-house advertising production staff. Some smaller hotels have their advertising designed and produced by the medium in which it will run. For the most part, however, it would appear hotel advertising dollars are spent through advertising agencies.

What is an advertising agency? Quinn Johnson of BBDO, a Boston agency, says:

> **“**An advertising agency is a consulting agent generally assigned ... the primary charge of creating, producing, and placing advertising for its clients in return for some form of compensation. **”**

Quinn's statement explains what an advertising agency does, but how can a hotel person tell a good advertising agency from a bad one? Obviously, results have a lot to do with the judgment, but most hotels cannot afford the time or money a trial-and-error approach would require. Therefore, it is helpful for hoteliers to have a few criteria to guide their selection of an ad agency.

Choosing an Agency. First, good advertising agencies are outspoken. When agency representatives meet with hotel staff members to discuss advertising issues, the agency's ideas should be strongly held and clearly stated. After the discussion, the hotel management makes the final decision. If the hotel chooses not to heed the agency's advice, the client's decision is made with a clear understanding of the agency's opinions. Having had the opportunity to express its views loudly and clearly, a good agency runs the program the client considers best for the hotel.

EACH DAY AT 11 AND 5
THE WILDEST THING HAPPENS.

It's The Peabody Ducks. There are five of them. Mallards. Twice a day they parade to and from this magnificent marble fountain. On a red carpet.

We have 454 elegant and generously proportioned guest rooms and suites. Some of the finest dining anywhere. 65,600 square feet of well-managed function space in 20 exquisite meeting and banquet rooms.

But ask anyone about The Peabody, the South's grand hotel, and you know what they'll tell you about first? Call toll-free 1-800/ 238-7273. Or write: Director of Sales, Union at Second, Memphis, Tennessee 38103.

The Peabody

Member, Preferred Hotels Worldwide

Courtesy of the Peabody

Second, good advertising agencies are effective budget managers, on behalf of both the client and themselves. The position of a hotel can be beautifully presented through four-color advertising; but if the advertising budget does not justify using color in the media scheduled, the agency must find less expensive alternatives with high impact. Similarly, if a spectacular ad campaign aimed at one segment of a hotel's market precludes the hotel from reaching another important segment, the advertising program is not in balance. The agency must exercise proper control so that ad dollars are spent wisely. The hotel manager using the services of an agency should be able to rest assured that the hotel's advertising is affordable as well as attractive.

Finally, good advertising agencies are prompt. If the hotel has developed a good comprehensive plan with the help of its agency, and if the agency is anticipating the hotel's needs in advance, there is no need for expensive last-minute creative and production work, which is frequently blamed for cost overruns. Of course, the client must allow the agency sufficient time to do the job well. Agencies have enough legitimate deadlines to meet without being put under the additional pressure of unfair deadlines. Hastily prepared ads are more likely to contain errors, and correcting these errors at the last minute is costly. Many a hotelier has had to learn the difference between changing an artist's pencil sketches and changing finished art. Early in the ad development process, changing whole paragraphs of typewritten copy costs nothing but a little frustration on the part of the copywriter. But later, when the ad is about to be printed, changing a single comma on an offset plate can cost upwards of $50. The rules which follow were adapted from guidelines developed to help clients of agencies control advertising costs:

1. Communicate your advertising needs to your agency early (for example, when you have finalized your marketing plan).

2. Make all content changes on typewritten copy, before it has been typeset for printing.

3. Change art in pencil and layout forms, not on finished compositions ("comps").

4. To reduce the cost of creative work needed for your advertising, share the product and the fee with other properties that have similar problems but different markets.

5. Avoid last-minute rush work. Think ahead and save money.[1]

Types of Advertising

Whether your hotel develops its own advertising, uses an agency, or relies on the media for assistance, you need to be aware of the various advertising alternatives available. This section discusses collateral and the three major forms of paid advertising: print, broadcast, and out-of-home media.

Collateral. All hotels use what is called collateral material such as brochures, fact sheets, tent cards, signs, posters, and folders. In fact, smaller hotels that spend very few dollars on paid media advertising may rely almost exclusively on collateral for their advertising. All of the rules of advertising presented in this chapter also apply to collateral material.

Despite the heavy use of collateral in the hotel industry, much of what is produced for collateral is not usable or effective. Jane Maas, now President of Muller Jordan and Weiss Advertising in New York City, said in addressing a 1977 HSMAI convention that over 34% of the one billion dollars worth of collateral material sent to travel agencies each year is discarded because it is misleading, dull, and doesn't give the facts. In her speech, Ms. Maas presented 24 tips on how to develop better collateral material.[2] Tips based on her recommendations are presented in Exhibit 1.

Exhibit 1   How to Develop Better Collateral Material

1. Decide on your positioning. Orient your product a certain way in the consumer's mind.
2. Understand the new consumer. Talk to important segments such as people who like the outdoors, culture seekers, fishermen, single women, etc.
3. Agree on a creative strategy. Put in writing what you will say and how you will say it.
4. Set your objective. Identify your target audience. Include a consumer benefit(s) and support the benefit(s) with proof.
5. Set yourself apart. Give your product a distinct personality.
6. Demonstrate how your product differs from the competition.
7. Keep your collateral consistent with your paid media advertising; all of your advertising should have the same feeling.
8. Put the selling message on the cover like a headline in an ad.
9. Put your positioning on the cover.
10. Put a benefit on the cover.
11. Use one striking illustration on the cover instead of many small ones.
12. Avoid clichés, both visual and written.
13. Use photographs rather then drawings.
14. Show activity, not just scenery.
15. Show food close up.
16. Caption your photographs.
17. Don't be afraid of long copy.
18. Highlight the important facts.
19. Tell the truth.
20. Be helpful, not clever.
21. Use maps, which tend to get high readership.
22. Don't skimp on quality.
23. Include several pieces in the mailing.
24. Break all of the above rules, but only for a good reason.

Adapted with permission from a speech by Jane Maas, then Vice President of Wells, Rich, Green, to HSMAI, Nov. 19, 1977.

Print. The most common type of paid media advertising used by hotels is print. It may take the form of a black-and-white ad in the local newspaper announcing a new act in the hotel lounge or a glossy four-color full-page advertisement in *National Geographic* for a group of trendy resorts. The biggest advantage of print advertising is that the people who read the publication can be clearly identified geographically and described demographically. Virtually all the print media in which a hotel would be likely to place substantial amounts of advertising have their circulation audited. From these audits, profiles can be produced of the people who subscribe to or purchase the publication.

Unfortunately, without a great deal of careful, expensive research, the percentage of subscribers or purchasers who actually read and understand a particular ad is not known. Therefore, it is very important for a team involved in developing print advertising to agree that the message presented in the ad will get through to the readers of the particular publication in which the ad is to be placed. Too often hotels have attempted to "save production costs" by using advertising developed for one medium in another medium. Often this cost-cutting measure ends up negating the effectiveness of the ad. For example, a four-color plate that looks beautiful in a full-page magazine ad may not be appealing when it is translated into a small, black-and-white newspaper ad. Usually details that are vivid in color do not look good when the color highlight is lost. Conversely, a well-executed black-and-white newspaper advertisement is generally not appealing if it is used in media where color is the norm. If the competition is using color as the accepted standard, showing a hotel in black-and-white makes the hotel look stark and cold by comparison.

Broadcast. An increasing number of hotel advertisers are using the broadcast media (radio and television) to reach their target audience. Hotels have advertised on radio quite frequently in the past. Because of the excellent information available about the audiences tuning into various radio stations, advertisers can be selective. For example, a daytime audience for ads about a specific kind of vacation retreat can be pinpointed. The radio audience is responsive, particularly when the correct time-slot for an ad is identified. "Drive-time" slots, for example, are best for reaching the business traveler.

Radio advertising is generally quite efficient; that is, most of those who receive the messages are potential customers. The advertising is not "wasted" on those who will never respond. Furthermore, radio stations generally support hotel advertisers with free publicity (called "editorial" exposure), particularly when the hotels have done a good job of selling to as well as buying from the station. Obviously, it is in a hotel's best interests to see that all local radio personalities, talk-show hosts, reporters, and announcers are knowledgeable about and favorably impressed by the hotel. The best way to accomplish this is to invite them to be guests of the hotel.

In short, radio offers a range of audiences to choose from, cost efficiency, and favorable identification with popular local personalities. It is not surprising that radio has been so frequently used in the hotel field for years.

Another broadcast medium not used much in the past, but very much in use today, is television. Unfortunately, most of the early hotel advertisements on TV were poorly done. Now, however, hotel marketers are more accustomed to the costs associated with TV advertising, and many excellent commercial messages for hotels are being produced and run. Also, thanks to the development of the hand-held camera (or "mini-cam"), it is possible to videotape commercials on-site at a much lower cost than ever before. Therefore, attractive, action-oriented hotel ads can be made, even on relatively low budgets. Furthermore, multiple commercials can be produced from a single videotaping session to save on production costs. For example, acceptable one-minute, thirty-second, and ten-second ads can be taken from the same body of work.

Because television stations have many reasons to use the facilities of a hotel, TV time is very often bartered. (Bartered arrangements are also called "trade-outs.") Bartering is the practice of exchanging goods or services for other goods or services without the use of money. A barter can be arranged through a third party such as a

IF YOU DON'T STAY AT THE PEABODY, IT DOESN'T MATTER WHERE YOU STAY.

The guest rooms and suites are so spacious and elegant you might actually feel spoiled. There are 454 of them.

But you see the legendary lobby first. There's only one of them. With its carved pillars and stained glass. The classic marble fountain. And, of course, The Peabody Ducks.

We offer 65,600 square feet of well-managed function space in 20 exquisite meeting and banquet rooms. And it comes with some of the finest cuisine you'll experience anywhere. Plus a level of personal attention and commitment to detail equalled by no one. If you go somewhere else, you might as well go anywhere else.

Call toll-free 1-800/238-7273. Or write: Director of Sales, Union at Second, Memphis, Tennessee 38103.

The Peabody

Member Preferred Hotels Worldwide

Courtesy of the Peabody

barter company. In most cases, however, a fair barter agreement can be worked out by direct communication between the TV station and the hotel.

A new form of TV advertising has sprung up with the spread of cable TV. It is now possible to "narrow-cast" on TV by using commercial cable channels that reach very specific audiences. For example, restaurants on Cape Cod frequently use the local cable station's late afternoon news broadcast, particularly the weather report, to air their messages. The target audience is vacationers who are visiting the Cape for a short period of time. The commercials are intended to acquaint vacationers with a particular restaurant and its features. The underlying premises of these narrow-cast ads are: (1) most vacationers will tune in the local cable TV channel to find out what the next day's weather will be; (2) most of the people who tune

A FRESH APPROACH.

The fresh look and feel of Dux Restaurant. Open, bright and promising. The freshest ingredients in America in a new and innovative menu. Mesquite-grilled oysters. Blackened redfish. Prime beef. A surprising and unique all-American wine list. A fresh approach for Memphis and the Delta just where you'd expect it. At The Peabody,   the South's grand hotel, 901-529-4199.   *dux*

Courtesy of the Peabody

in will be disinclined to cook at their Cape Cod home because they are on vacation; and (3) most of this audience is not familiar with the local restaurants.

Out-of-Home Media. Out-of-home media include billboards, signs, and airport displays that are located off the advertised property. This form of advertising is difficult for many hotels to use and can be even more difficult to cost-justify. Yet it can be more valuable than all other forms of advertising to a property with problems that fit the solutions that out-of-home media provide. For example, hotels are not always easy to find. Those that have this problem need to find extremely effective ways of bringing the traveler to their doors. A billboard can do wonders to bring people to a particular location.

However, due to their scarcity, outdoor signs are expensive. Also, their audience is extremely difficult to analyze with any scientific reliability. Nevertheless, if a hotel can obtain billboard space and deliver a clear message, the cost may be justified. Most hotel people can recall at least a few examples of effective hotel billboards they have seen and wished they were able to obtain for their own property.

Airport signs and hotel telephone identification signs are not used as heavily as they were a few years ago. This is because airports in major cities have expanded from one main terminal to many satellite terminals. Therefore, the one sign that might have sufficed in the past is now inadequate since many such signs are required. However, in certain cities these displays can still be quite important.

If you decide that out-of-home media can be effective for your hotel, it is absolutely imperative that you remember three points: (1) the message must be simple; (2) the copy must be extremely limited; and (3) your positioning must be absolutely clear. In other words, with out-of-home media advertising you must get your point across the first time because you won't get a second chance!

Budgeting

Since advertising is an investment in the future of the hotel, its budget should be planned like any other investment. Managers must ask themselves, "What is the potential return if we increase our stake?" In producing the advertising budget for a hotel, each market segment included in the occupancy and business mix of the hotel needs to be considered. Management may ultimately decide to advertise only to some of these segments, but the question of advertising to each of them should first be reviewed for potential return.

Suppose, for example, a hotel with fabulous meeting facilities has just been constructed. As the new director of marketing, you are attempting to introduce the hotel to the convention market. You recognize that the market for such facilities would most likely be associations and corporations that hold national or regional meetings. For your advertising, you choose the association trade literature because, even though it is relatively expensive, it reaches the very audience that most needs to know about your new facilities.

Because your product suits the convention market best, you don't waste your advertising dollars on lots of ads for transient guests. You know that if your advertising strategy works, and the targeted audience responds, the potential return on your advertising investment may be enormous. If your ad is enough to convince a meeting planner to consider your property, you may bring in conventioneers by the hundreds, rather than transients one by one. Your substantial investment in advertising is, therefore, justified by the very substantial improvement in revenues you expect to generate. Conversely, a newly redecorated coffee shop may be an attractive feature that makes a guest's stay in your hotel more pleasant, but because the coffee shop is not a high-profit outlet and its improvement—in and of itself—is not much of a people magnet, you would not want to focus your advertising program on this feature.

What does a completed ad budget look like? Exhibit 2 shows the advertising expense portion of a recent advertising and promotion budget for the Wilmington (Delaware) Hilton Hotel.

As you can see, this small hotel has budgeted wisely to do only the amount of advertising it can realistically afford. This plan shows the Wilmington Hilton spending its dollars primarily to reach the corporate and state business markets. It is also reaching out to the travel industry through *Hotel & Travel Index*, to the surrounding

Exhibit 2   Excerpt from Wilmington (Delaware) Hilton Hotel's Advertising and Promotion Budget for 1983

	Advertising Expense		
Market: Segment	**Advertising: Rooms**		
1-1 & 1-2	Business North Carolina (Meetings & Convention Special Edition)	1 × $^1/_6$ pg.	$ 350
1-2	State Magazine	2 × $^1/_4$ pg.	250
1-2	North Carolina Association of Women's Clubs (Annual Directory)	1 × $^1/_4$ pg.	175
1-3	State Magazine	1 × $^1/_4$ pg.	125
2-1 & 2-2	Pace Magazine	3 × $^1/_6$ pg.	2,900
2-1	Business North Carolina	2 × $^1/_6$ pg.	700
2-2	Chamber of Commerce (Annual Directory of Accommodations)	1 × $^1/_4$ pg.	400
2-4	State Magazine	1 × $^1/_4$ pg.	125
2-5	Raleigh News & Observer	10 × 8 column inch	650
2-5	3 Military Newspapers	1 insertion per week × 18 weeks	1,700
3-1	Hotel & Travel Index	4 × $^1/_4$ pg.	3,300
3-4	Chamber of Commerce (Bus Tour Manual)	1 × 1 pg.	200
			$ 10,875
	Billboards	(2 highway & 2 airport)	10,300
	Total Rooms Ad Budget		$ 21,175
	Advertising: Food & Beverage		
	Star News	(3) 8 column inch ads per week	$ 9,000
	Star News	Holiday promotions	1,500
	Local Radio	40 spots per month	3,000
	Total Food & Beverage Ad Budget		$ 13,500
	Total Rooms, Food & Beverage Ad Budget		$ 34,675

military community through military newspapers, and to the general public in its local area through print advertising in local newspapers.

Like advertising, public relations is a budgeted expense which uses the media to project a message to the public. The next section contrasts public relations with advertising and discusses its application as a tool of marketing.

Public Relations

When advertising, a hotel must buy the media space or time to present information to a reading, listening, or viewing audience. In public relations, however, the media accepts and uses a hotel's press releases and announcements when they consider these items newsworthy and of interest to their audience.

Many people confuse public relations with publicity, which is the gratuitous mention in the media of an organization's people, product, or services. Although publicity is important, public relations embraces much more than publicity. The American Hotel & Motel Association sponsors an annual competition focusing attention on public relations in the industry. Hotels and motels entering the competition are asked to state a problem they faced, describe a program they designed to solve the problem, and tell how the program worked out. Entries for the AH&MA Gold Key Public Relations Achievement Awards are accepted in the following five categories:

1. Community service
2. Crisis public relations
3. Employee relations
4. Guest relations
5. Special events (accepted for both one-time only and ongoing events)

This chapter focuses on public relations primarily in terms of promotional publicity. However, this chapter also touches on guest relations, employee relations, and special events since, coupled with publicity, these categories usually receive most of the emphasis in marketing planning.

> ❝I can't think of any aspect of the marketing discipline that can be as cost-effective for the hotels as public relations, and yet, of all of the marketing tools available to us, it is the most misunderstood, misused, and underused. It is time we got away from the hokey, contrived 'events' and started developing meaningful publicity plans. We need to employ PR professionals, either in-house or consultants. The publicity business is no place for amateurs.❞
>
> **—Robert D. McGrail**
> Senior Vice President of Marketing
> Lincoln Hotels of Dallas, Texas

Since public relations is dependent on the discretion of the media, there are no guarantees that public relations announcements, or press releases, will actually reach the public. (This element of risk separates public relations from advertising, but risk is an essential element of any successful marketing program.) However, when a hotel's public relations announcements *are* considered newsworthy and are picked up by the news media, they help to create an impression of the hotel in the minds of the public. More importantly, what the media say about a hotel—good or bad—is generally believed more than paid advertising. If the public relations professional who distributes a property's materials has done his or her job properly, the hotel will be mentioned favorably. On the other hand, negative publicity is worse than no publicity at all.

An effective public relations program can create a positive image of a new property or alter the image of an existing property by presenting it in a different way. A recent example of an extremely successful publicity-seeking event was the grand reopening of the Royal Sonesta Hotel in Cambridge, Massachusetts. This important hotel was reintroduced to the Boston area with one of the cleverest promotional events staged in recent years. By Greater Boston standards, the hotel was perceived as relatively small though of high quality. Recently, however, the

Royal Sonesta had added significantly to its room capacity and function space to increase its appeal. Now, the objective of the hotel was to make the public see the Royal Sonesta as a part of the Greater Boston hotel community, and not merely as a suburban Cambridge hotel. A public relations campaign was needed to change the public perception of the hotel.

For this reason the Sonnabend family, who owned the hotel, in concert with Managing Director Michael M. Schweiger, Director of Public Relations Laurie Nagler, and their consulting firm, Irma Mann Strategic Marketing, decided to stage a colossal, once-in-a-lifetime fireworks display as a gift to Greater Boston. The spectacular event would be promoted along with the hotel's grand reopening. The hotel contracted the renowned Grucci family to design and execute the fireworks display. George Plimpton, the noted writer and commentator who has had a long-time interest in fireworks, was secured to serve as narrator.

Excellent pre-opening press kits were assembled for distribution to the media. These kits included a comprehensive fact sheet about the Royal Sonesta, the hotel staff, and the Sonesta International Hotels Corporation. (It was, after all, a corporate promotion as well as a hotel promotion.) Additional information about the hotel's grand reopening event included background on the Grucci family and George Plimpton, the celebrity participants.

The most eye-catching element in the press kits was a photo of the Boston skyline with fireworks superimposed (see Exhibit 3). This photograph made it clear that the hotel's opening celebration was not just for a few selected guests but for the whole metropolitan Boston community. To support the public relations effort, other publicity materials were used. A press release from the corporate office (see Exhibit 4) announced the kick-off meeting of Sonesta's sales blitz team operating in the Boston area prior to the hotel's grand reopening and in other cities later in the year.

The reopening was successful because it was newsworthy and well promoted, and because the advertising program for the event worked hand-in-hand with the publicity. Approximately one month prior to the hotel's grand reopening, a general advertising campaign was launched with the theme, "On June 16th, the Royal Sonesta Hotel, Cambridge, will light up the Boston skyline." And light it up they did. Some 150,000 metropolitan Boston citizens turned out for the free spectacle.

The net effect of this tremendously successful promotion was that the hotel was recognized for completing its new construction project while it was lauded as a good community citizen and neighbor. The hotel had done something good for its city and for its neighbors, and the media publicized it widely. There were no negatives attached to this event and none of the usual press cynicism. The media covered the celebration as a positive contribution to Boston's calendar of summer events and as a novel way of presenting new information about a familiar hotel with a fine reputation.

In this case, a hotel's positive story was effectively presented by professionals who knew what their objectives were and how to achieve them. However, many hotel managers are reluctant to attempt any bold, new public relations programs for fear that they will backfire. Poorly conceived publicity schemes may seem contrived and, thus, may be treated with suspicion. This is particularly true when the hotel has had a poor reputation or has not cultivated a good working relationship

Exhibit 3   Royal Sonesta's Press Kit Photo

FIREWORKS BY GRUCCI—The new Royal Sonesta Hotel in Cambridge, MA, will celebrate its grand opening on Saturday, June 16, with the largest fireworks show in the history of New England. This massive display will be produced by the Grucci family, America's "First Family of Fireworks."

Photo credit: Ken Clark

Courtesy of Royal Sonesta Hotel, Cambridge, Massachusetts

with the media. If, however, the hotel has been a good community citizen, has introduced itself properly to local journalists, and has been cooperative with the media whether the news was good or bad, the risk of negative publicity is probably minimal. A hotel that has earned a positive media image is generally treated well by reporters and editors. On the other hand, a hotel with a poor reputation among journalists can use a well-organized, ongoing public relations effort to develop a more positive media image. A positive media image leads, in turn, to a positive public image.

As in other industries, a few "brand names" are instantly recognizable. For example, the names Boca Raton, Waldorf-Astoria, and Greenbrier are sure to conjure up images of impeccable service and the highest level of hospitality in the minds of

Exhibit 4   Royal Sonesta's Sales Blitz News Release

SONESTA HOTELS
NEWS RELEASE

FOR IMMEDIATE RELEASE   contact: Laurie Nagler
May 31, 1984   617-491-3600
(Complete in caption)

READY, SET, BLITZ -- Eager to begin a major sales blitz of the
Boston metropolitan area and anxious to spread the word about the
Royal Sonesta Cambridge's June 16 gala opening, more than 30
enthusiastic Sonesta employees gathered together for a recent
Sales Blitz Kick-Off Meeting at the new hotel. Pictured here
with posters, sales literature and assorted give-aways in hand
are (l. to r.) Michael M. Schweiger, vice president and managing
director, Royal Sonesta Cambridge; Susan Schrade, director of
sales, Royal Sonesta Cambridge; Stephanie Sonnabend, vice
president of sales, Sonesta International Hotels Corporation;
Joseph Phillips, director of marketing, Royal Sonesta Cambridge;
Nancy Wexler, Bermuda sales manager, Sonesta Beach Hotel; Mary
Zazzaro, director of sales, Portland Sonesta; and Carol Schoeni,
national director of industry sales, Sonesta International Hotel
Corporation. The meeting began with a hard-hat tour of the new
facility, followed by a slide show of all ten Sonesta hotels, and
sales briefing for those people with less sales experience. The
Boston blitz is one of many scheduled to take place during 1984.
The first was held in New York in April. Others are planned for
California in June, N. Carolina in July, Philadelphia and New
Jersey in September, and London in October.

                              # # #

Sonesta International Hotels Corporation
200 Clarendon Street, Boston, Massachusetts 02116
Telephone: 617-421-5437 Cable: Sonesta Telex: 94-0593

Courtesy of Royal Sonesta Hotel, Cambridge, Massachusetts

the American traveling public. Such brand awareness generates public relations
support that is invaluable to these hotels. Hotels that aspire to earn the image of
these fine properties but lack their credentials should do all they can to build their

reputation by continuously generating publicity announcements about them-selves. In fact, any hotel can benefit from taking an organized approach to public relations, including publicity. Yet we have only rarely seen hotels spend as much as ten percent of their total marketing investment in this neglected area. Because it is so drastically underbudgeted, publicity is the major focus of this section.

Publicity and Media Relations

Most of us think of publicity in connection with special events such as the Sonesta fireworks and opening celebration already described. However, good publicity can be generated without staging any event at all. For instance, in some communi-ties a list of who is meeting in a hotel is considered newsworthy. In most cases, the media are interested to learn that a celebrity is staying or has stayed at a hotel. Of course, some celebrities ask that their stay not be publicized, either during or after the visit. However, in situations where publicity is allowed, celebrity visits lend additional status to a hotel.

Similarly, the achievements of a hotel's employees can be newsworthy. Their accomplishments either for the property itself or for civic organizations are a re-flection on the hotel as a whole. For example, an employee who competes athleti-cally and wins honors contributes to the image of the hotel as "a winning property" by his or her association with it.

It may take some experimenting before you learn what types of information a newspaper or magazine or radio or TV station is most likely to use. Generally, however, your chances of getting positive publicity are enhanced to the extent that you succeed in building an image (either as a good community citizen or as a place that makes it easy for reporters to do their work) and by making the hotel known to key members of the media. Granted, these are not easy tasks, but they can pay enormous dividends.

This is particularly true if an emergency situation should arise at your hotel. In dealing with the press, the initial fear that the property will be cast in a negative light must be overcome by an understanding of the public's right to know what is going on. A publicity coordinator should be made available to the media to pre-vent unauthorized comments and rumors. Your hotel spokesperson's role is to present facts, which should then counteract negative notions of what is happening. The straightforward approach of your designated spokesperson can make a tre-mendous difference in the way the press perceives the crisis. Clear-cut information supplied on a timely basis can keep your hotel's image from being diminished by association with a negative happening.

Naturally, it also helps to be prepared in advance to supply basic information when it is requested. The American Hotel & Motel Association has published an excellent booklet entitled *Positive Public Perceptions: Media Relations for Hotel/ Motel Managers.* The following recommendations are quoted from that "how-to" publication:

Basic Press Information You Should Have on Hand

In assembling basic press or publicity materials for the hotel or inn, start by put-ting together one or two fact sheets. They should describe the hotel/inn at a glance.

Exhibit 5   Sample List of Facilities

Facts About New Plaza Hotel
Anytown, U.S.

Size:
195-room, 14-story, convention hotel, 150,000 sq. ft.

Construction Cost:
Approximately $10 million
Solar System Cost: $375,000

Structure:
Post-tensioned concrete frame for hotel tower with steel structure lower levels and atrium.

Exterior Materials:
Insulated aluminum panels and insulating glass.

Interior Materials:
Exposed bushhammered concrete frame with carpet floors, acoustic ceilings and vinyl-covered gypsum board partitions.

Mechanical/Electrical Systems:
The building is heated with steam from central city steam system utilizing heat exchangers and fan coil units in the guest rooms and for air handling units in the public spaces.
The domestic water system and makeup ventilation system is supplemented by two solar systems.

Site:
Area Size: 30,000 sq. ft.
Parking: Incorporated in city-owned parking ramp
Features: Part of a major downtown Anytown development

Location:
Fifth and Main Streets; five miles from Metro Airport

Facilities:
Three restaurants, four bars, disco, ballroom (banquet capacity—800), health club

Source: *Positive Public Perceptions*, p. 28.

- General design and appearance
- Facilities (restaurants, banquet or function rooms and their capacities, shops, and so on)
- Location—if downtown, where located in city
- Neighborhood
- Distance in time and miles from airport
- Proximity to the beach, ski area, etc. (if a resort)
- Distance to business center, tourist attractions
- Any outstanding facilities or services that set your hotel/motel apart from the competition [see Exhibit 5]

You should also prepare brief biographical fact sheets [see Exhibit 6] and assemble a file of sketches and glossy print head-and-shoulders portrait

Exhibit 6   Sample Biographical Fact Sheet

Biography

Amy Carlson

Executive Chef   Anytown Hotel, Anytown, U.S.

Ms. Carlson joined the Anytown Hotel staff as a garde-manger in 1970. She was promoted to successively more responsible positions until named to her present post in 1977.

As Executive Chef, Ms. Carlson supervises menu planning, quality control, and food preparation for the Anytown Hotel's three restaurants as well as banquet service.

A native of Ypsilanti, Michigan, Ms. Carlson received her earlier training in food operations in several Detroit area restaurants and private clubs to prepare for admission to the Culinary Institute of America, Hyde Park, NY, where she graduated in 1969 with a degree in Culinary Arts/Hotel Management.

Ms. Carlson has authored a cookbook, *Delicacies for Dieters*, and is a recipient of the Escoffier Award from the Minnesota Chefs Association.

#   #   #

Source: *Positive Public Perceptions,* p. 29.

photographs of the manager, the director of sales, the food and beverage manager, and possibly other key department heads. Other fact sheets and news features based on the same information can be prepared covering:

- unique or unusual architecture and interior design …;
- the atmosphere, entertainment, and food of specialty restaurants, nightclubs, and lounges;
- furnishings in the presidential suite or similar deluxe accommodations.

These fact sheets and releases do not have to be written by a trained journalist. It's essential, though, that the information be committed to paper.… Here are some useful guidelines.

Stay away from liberal use of adjectives. Just describe (the facility) in simple, accurate language, or list the positive points of the particular property. For example:

- High quality food and beverage outlets (local or ethnic cuisine)
- Excellence of service
- Recreational facilities
- Parking facilities (capacity, type, enclosed garage, free to guests or rates charged)
- Tasteful decorations and furnishings (local cultural influence, if appropriate)
- Range of special facilities and services (types of shops, valet, laundry)
- Special art features (e.g., paintings, murals)
- Unusual architectural features

Distributing sales promotion pamphlets and brochures with press materials and to those who call for information on your property can be valuable to the media. Be sure that convention chairmen and others having meetings at your property are supplied with this kind of information, so that they may learn as much as possible about your facilities. In assembling your press materials, try to obtain good, sharp interior and exterior photographs of the property. If the hotel has become known for or is easily recognizable by any special design features, these should be shown prominently in some of the photos. Black and white glossy prints are generally most acceptable. In most cases, show people using the hotel or motel's facilities because this makes a more interesting picture.

Once you have prepared and collected all these materials, you should file items individually. Then you are ready to put together press kits when the occasion warrants—for example, [when you are] opening a new restaurant.[3]

It is easier to establish or maintain an effective, positive publicity program in a hotel when a director of public relations or director of publicity is a full-time member of the staff. If your hotel does not have a full-time spokesperson and publicist, however, it is very important to assign individual members of the hotel staff the responsibility of coordinating publicity for a particular aspect of the hotel. For example, the secretary to the director of sales may be responsible for sending a weekly events list to the news editors of the local media. Contacts with the media should be continual, but at the very least one publicity coordinator should be assigned to each special event at the hotel.

What are the specific responsibilities of a public relations spokesperson for a hotel? First of all, he or she should send the weekly activity schedule for the property and a list of any noteworthy events every week to all reporters (both print and broadcast journalists) who are responsible for covering activities in the area. Press releases should be written in the traditional "who, what, when, where, why" format. They should be sent to newspapers or broadcast media at least two weeks in advance of the target date of publication and at least six weeks in advance to magazines.

Additionally, the public relations coordinator should alert the staff of both the food and beverage department and the rooms department to the anticipated arrival at any time of media personalities who may be covering an event at the hotel or conducting an interview. How should the hotel deal with visiting press? In a very straightforward, helpful way. They are, after all, professionals with their own tasks to perform and their own set of responsibilities. Their interest is in the story that they are attempting to cover, whether it be your story or that of people who are meeting with you. Hotels that make it easy for these professionals to do their work are generally mentioned in a positive and supportive way. Those that make it more difficult for the press generally receive less than glowing comments. Here are some suggestions on how to develop a rapport with media representatives:

Who to Contact, How to Do It

Once press materials have been assembled, the publicity representative should get to know, and then maintain contact with, key news editors, photo editors, and news assignment editors at radio and TV stations. In larger cities, be sure to include the wire services (Associated Press, United Press International, Reuters).

Exhibit 7   Typical Deadlines

Morning newspapers	3 P.M. to break the following day. Reach the editor the morning before.
Afternoon newspapers	9 A.M. that day. Reach the editor the day before.
Sunday newspapers	Wednesday (some sections 1–2 weeks ahead)
Sunday magazines	4 weeks in advance.
News magazines Weekly newspapers (based on Thursday publication date)	Monday. (Stories are written or rewritten Tuesday; printing and delivery take place Wednesday.)
Monthly trade magazines	Either the 1st or 15th of the month preceding cover date.
National monthly magazines (e.g., National Review, Vogue, Atlantic)	Either the 1st or 15th of the month preceding cover date. However, these magazines generally work on a three-month lead time (so, in April, they're working on the July issue).
Television news	2 P.M. that day for 6 o'clock edition. Most TV news conferences take place at 10 A.M. However, they'll work a later schedule to make the 11 P.M. edition.
Television features, talk shows	Book 2–5 weeks ahead of time (except in case of extra big celebrities). Differs for each show so check with the producer.
Radio news	Anytime. Some are on the air 24 hours. All-news stations are a particularly good bet.
Radio talk	Roughly 2 weeks ahead but, again, it varies from show to show. Check with producers.

Source: *Positive Public Perceptions,* p. 11.

At an early date, it would be a nice gesture to invite media people, individually, to the property for a visit, a drink, or a meal.

Most newspersons work under deadline pressure, so it's possible you may wish to visit some of them in their offices instead. If so, you may be sure they'll appreciate this courtesy.

Ask when their deadlines are [see Exhibit 7] and what times and days of the week would be best for a getting-to-know-you visit. This is the kind of information that should be included on index cards in setting up your press contact file.

Personal visits with news media people will give the press contact person a chance to find out how best to serve their needs and the type of news in which they're particularly interested.

Besides establishing valuable contacts with media representatives, their comments and suggestions will help the inexperienced publicity person recognize what makes news.

Having a journalist over for lunch or just a drink also may serve to give the editor, writer, or broadcaster a better idea of the kind of news-making events that frequently take place in a hotel/motel, and [may communicate] the fact that you have a genuine interest in helping them do their jobs.

Also, when the occasion arises for you to phone them, chances are they'll remember you and be inclined to give favorable consideration to your news, photo tips, or suggested article idea, rather than give you the fast brush.

Having prepared basic press materials, established contact with the media, and prepared a current list of these contacts, the hotel/motel spokesperson should be ready to start producing. In other words, as soon as anything newsworthy happens, it's up to the contact person to relay this information promptly to the media people he or she had identified and cultivated.

Once you've made valuable news media contacts, you can expect occasional inquiries from them. And the most important thing to remember in dealing with the press is that you must respond promptly to their questions.

If you don't have the answer, say so, and offer to try to get the information right away.[4]

In dealing with the media, the main thing the director of public relations or publicity must remember is to keep sending them a steady flow of newsworthy items. If not every item is used, don't be discouraged nor angry with the media people you talk with. In many cases, they are not the final decision-makers regarding what is put on the air or into print.

Consumer/Guest Relations

Just as a hotel must keep a flow of positive articles going to the various media, it is very important that you direct a positive public relations campaign toward the individual consumer and, in particular, the consumer who is a guest of your hotel. Sending newsletters to previous guests, listing any upcoming events of interest to guests, giving out recipes from the hotel's chef, and highlighting features of the hotel and its personnel ought to help improve your occupancy and outlet revenue. These objectives are generally high on the list of goals for any publicity campaign.

Guests' perceptions of a hotel restaurant as a community citizen can be enhanced in some very simple but highly effective ways. For example, you can inform them of your restaurant's special holiday menu plans by providing good promotional material (such as display cards, which describe the holiday menu, placed at elevator landings). Try providing guests with daily news clips as they come into the restaurant, particularly at lunch time. Efforts such as these will encourage businesspeople to use your hotel more frequently because they will see the property as a positive part of the business community.

Employee Relations

Just as you need to keep the general public and, in particular, your consuming public informed about your hotel and its activities, you also want to keep your employees informed and involved. Clearly, an employee who has no idea of the purpose behind a particular publicity campaign will not be likely to help the hotel promote it very effectively.

If a hotel is scheduling an event in an attempt to gain additional publicity, the first people who ought to know about it are the employees. This event can be announced at a general employee meeting or in notices posted in the employee cafeteria, locker rooms, and other key employee areas. Fact sheets can also be added to the envelopes containing employee paychecks to be certain they receive the information. If a hotel's staff includes many employees whose native language is not English, it is highly advisable to have important messages printed in the first language of the majority of the non-English-speaking employee population as well as in English. Employee relations are an extremely important part of a hotel's marketing effort. If servers are unhappy with the meal they have just consumed in the employee cafeteria, they will probably not do an outstanding job of serving the hotel's guests. Conversely, goodwill breeds goodwill.

Because public relations is often an underbudgeted and underused marketing function, the hotel that does a good job in improving the public's perception of it can actually jump many places beyond competing hotels that are not sensitive to the contribution publicity can make to their marketing efforts. In short, hotel marketers have an excellent opportunity to become increasingly successful by fully utilizing a tool that the competition uses poorly or not at all.

Endnotes

1. These five points are used by permission of Dan Goldman, President of Dan Advertising Agency, Newport News, Virginia.

2. For additional information on this subject, readers are referred to Jane Maas, *Better Brochures, Catalogs, and Mailing Pieces* (New York: St. Martin's Press, 1984).

3. *Positive Public Perceptions: Media Relations for Hotel/Motel Managers* (East Lansing, Mich.: Educational Institute of the American Hotel & Motel Association, 1980), pp. 2–3.

4. *Positive Public Perceptions*, p. 3.

Supplemental Reading

Advertising That Sells Hotels

> *A veteran advertising practitioner discusses the principles of effective advertising for lodging properties*
>
> "*Advertising for hotels is still unsophisticated—but it's improving,*" observes one of the advertising industry's most accomplished practitioners. As executive vice president of Spiro and Associates, Norman R. Tissian counts among his responsibilities the marketing and advertising functions for more than 40 individual hotels and hotel operating companies. To complement his 25 years of experience in advertising for the hospitality industry, Tissian calls on the wide-ranging expertise developed by his firm in serving diverse clients, from the manufacturers of packaged goods to accounting firms and universities.

Begin at the Beginning

Hoteliers embarking on an advertising campaign make their most crucial—and common—mistake, Tissian maintains, when "they fail to realize that designing the ad is the last thing to be done, not the first." Effective advertising is the result of a careful analysis of a property's strengths and weaknesses; only after completing this assessment can management proceed to develop a strategy, which is then translated into an advertising message. Tissian enumerates the requisite steps to be performed before advertising is created:

1. Establish management's perception of the subject property.

2. Ascertain the market's perception of the property.

3. Develop a positioning statement for the property.

4. Select advertising's target audiences.

The rudiments of this approach are applied in various ways, depending on the property under analysis and the conclusions reached at the individual steps. To illustrate the process, Tissian cites examples drawn from his firm's numerous engagements.

1. Management's perception of the property. Deriving and expressing management's view of the subject property is not difficult, Tissian points out, but verifying its accuracy often is. Hotel managers hardly bear sole responsibility for their overestimations of a property's position in the market; in fact, the misconceptions typically commence with the developer, whose view of a property's potential is frequently colored by his personal commitment to the project. Developers' optimistic expectations are communicated to management and adopted without critical evaluation of their appropriateness to the type of property and the market it operates in. As a result, among the advertising executive's first responsibilities is to evaluate objectively management's perception of the property's position in the market, providing the impetus for management to reassess its strategy.

When analyzing the market segments they serve, many hotel managers fail to make full use of data available to them, relying instead on imprecise impressions regarding the origins of their business. Even managers who supplement firsthand observation with the review of registration requests, guest folios, and the pattern of commission payments to travel agents typically fail to define with accuracy the prime sources of their rooms business. Again, an orderly, objective review of the facts available will often yield a breakdown of the composition of the hotel's clientele that is divergent from management's view.

As an example of the difficulties management may face in correctly evaluating a hotel's status and appeal, Tissian describes the case of a downtown hotel located in a major U.S. city. A full analysis of the property's current position and its likely prospects in the future revealed that its primary market had become group business and that, based on the recent development of several luxury properties in the market area, the subject property could not hope to regain its former status as a rather exclusive transient hotel. Although management accepted some aspects of the plan developed to capitalize on the hotel's competitive strengths, Tissian observes, "the general manager believes deep down that the hotel can capture the top-rate, expense-account business traveler—and he's going to operate that way, all evidence to the contrary."

2. The market's perception of the property. Testing the market's view of a property frequently requires field research, but this need not be intricate or expensive, Tissian points out. A methodology used by Spiro and Associates to assist Chicago's Whitehall Hotel in discerning local residents' perception of the property offers a case in point.

To assure that the results of the research would reflect the views of members of the demographic group likely to frequent a hotel of the Whitehall's caliber, blind questionnaires were mailed to owners of late-model Jaguars and Mercedeses. Questionnaire recipients were asked to discuss their impressions of seven downtown Chicago hotels, including the Whitehall, five other exclusive properties, and—to test whether the respondent was able to distinguish a luxury hotel—a large convention property. The questionnaire results showed that many Chicagoans either thought the hotel was private (because the property also contains a private dining club) or that it served primarily "high-society dowagers." Since management and Spiro had determined that the hotel's location, amenities, and service positioned it to appeal strongly to top-level executives, evidence of the market's quite contrary perception was important information.

Similarly, a client operating a resort hotel was able to identify its ethnic clientele readily, but management needed to know the extent and nature of the property's appeal to a wider spectrum of persons in the same ethnic group. A telephone survey was conducted to poll both frequent guests and nonguests, asking for their impressions of the property. By comparing the responses from the two groups, the agency's personnel and the hotel's management were able to identify positive aspects of the guest's experience at the property that needed to be touted in the advertising subsequently developed. Conversely, both users and nonusers pointed to the negative images of the property that needed to be combated by advertising.

Finally, Tissian notes that there are two very simple forms of research that often yield important insights into the market's perception of a property. First, those responsible for developing a hotel's advertising should sample the guest experience, bringing to their evaluation of the property an objectivity management often cannot provide. Second, advertising executives can often provide helpful insights to management by discussing a property's position with other hoteliers. "After all," Tissian observes, "who's better qualified to help the GM analyze his property than another hotel manager?"

3. Developing the positioning statement. After management and its advertising agency have identified the property's competitive strengths and weaknesses, the results of this analysis are articulated in the form of a positioning statement. The positioning strategy reflects a conscious decision on management's part to communicate to the market a definition of the property as a particular type of hotel. Above all, Tissian emphasizes, this definition must be consistent with the property it describes, and it must be reinforced by advertising and management's delivery of the product promised.

A hotel's positioning statement is given full narrative treatment in its marketing plan, but a succinct version of it appears in the property's advertising....

4. Select your target audiences. Although management may be able to identify numerous market segments whose lodging needs, demographics, and tastes match the product it is offering, advertising efforts must be directed to those segments likely to yield the largest number of room-nights. The target audiences selected for advertising describing Americana Hotels' new Puerto Vallarta property, for example, were carefully chosen to maximize the response. Puerto Vallarta's location, although a perfect illustration of the "splendid isolation" theme carried through all the property's advertising, removes the hotel from serious contention for the convention and association meetings market. For incentive travel, however, the remoteness and tranquility of the location enhance its appeal. Group-business advertising was directed therefore not to the meetings and conventions market but to some 200 incentive houses. In a decision motivated by similar considerations, consumer advertising was virtually omitted in favor of advertising to selected travel agents, including those engaged in tour wholesaling and west-coast retail travel agents. It was reasoned that the latter would prove an efficient producer of business because of the modest air fares from west-coast origin cities and the greater likelihood of client familiarity with Puerto Vallarta. Travel-agent wholesalers were viewed as a means of generating business from the broad mass of consumers who, though unfamiliar with Puerto Vallarta, could be informed about the property by the travel agent.

Creating the Ad

Having defined the target audiences to which it will direct its advertisements, management and its advertising agency are prepared to develop the messages appropriate to each. Although there are subsegments within each target audience,

Tissian identifies three broad groups and suggests considerations to bear in mind when addressing each.

• **Consumer advertising.** The cardinal rule governing this category of advertising is, according to Tissian, "Create with the prospect—not the general manager—in mind." The most prevalent violation of this precept is advertising that uses, as its primary illustrative feature, a photograph of the exterior of the subject hotel. "Very gratifying to the general manager," Tissian observes, "but what can the prospective guest learn about the hotel from an aerial view?"

Architecture's dictum, "less is more," applies to consumer advertising as well, Tissian notes. The aim of advertising directed to the consumer is to motivate him to try the property—but advertising has achieved its maximum impact if the prospect stays *once* at the subject hotel. Too many hoteliers, Tissian argues, ignore this primary intent of hotel advertising, succumbing to the temptation to overload advertisements with distracting detail describing minutiae of the services offered. The "one image, one ad" rule of thumb may *appear* to give the hotelier less than his money's worth, says Tissian, but it sells more rooms.

Finally, consumer advertising should be custom-designed for the medium selected to carry it....

• **Advertising to travel agents**. Creating evocative advertisements that communicate a distinctive image for the hotel is a secondary concern in advertising directed to a travel agent. The primary, more utilitarian objective of travel-trade advertising is to impart essential information regarding the hotel's positioning, facilities, and rates. The basic task of informing does not require the same subtlety as the effort to influence....

Whenever possible, Tissian advocates the use of two measures of consumer and travel-trade advertising impact: coupons and packages. Although returned coupons are not necessarily converted to sales, they offer reliable feedback on advertising's ability to generate interest in the hospitality product. By offering packages in its advertisements, management can measure advertising's effectiveness directly by charting sales of the plans. Moreover, the pricing of packages constitutes an important positioning statement: travel agent and consumer alike are able to infer the price-value relationship of the subject hotel from the prices and features of the packages offered.

• **Advertising for group business**. The needs of this target audience are similar to the travel agent's: to derive an impression of the property's positioning and to learn the basic facts regarding its facilities. "Advertising for the group business market should be informational only," Tissian notes, "because personal selling consummates the sale."

[A] convention and meetings brochure designed by Spiro for Adam's Mark illustrates Tissian's emphasis on communicating essential facts. Eschewing the typical architect's rendering as the cover illustration, the brochure features a complete floor plan of the hotel's public rooms and meeting facilities. The brochure's interior pages are similarly functional and direct, providing more details of the layout and design of the hotel, describing the food and beverage outlets and the expertise of the meetings-services staff, as well as depicting the hotel's location in relationship to Houston's attractions and transportation facilities.

In Conclusion

Colorful and creative advertising can be very impressive, Tissian concludes, "but it won't necessarily sell the property." First the hotelier must take a hard look at his hotel, and then apply logic and experience to create effective advertising.

How to Select Advertising Media More Effectively

by Howard A. Heinsius

> *Howard A. Heinsius, president, Needham & Grohmann, Inc., advertising agency, is a former boy soloist in New York City choirs, World War II navigator, USO entertainer, Cornell University Glee Club tenor soloist, hotel barkeeper, night housekeeper, sales manager, vice president, treasurer, director; president of the Cornell Class of 1950; president of the Cornell Society of Hotelmen. He is the husband of Marilyn Heinsius, the father of Diane, Lee and Lynn, a sometime convention speaker or tenor soloist, and an occasional sensation at whatever performance he happens to be giving at the time.*

A competent advertising agency keeps abreast of marketing information and is certainly knowledgeable about the creative and media functions of advertising. It is important, however, for you as a hotel or motel marketer to also have a working knowledge of the various media at your agency's disposal so that there can be intelligent agreement with, or revisions of agency recommendations. This also helps in coordinating local and national efforts in advertising and promotion.

The most significant vehicles of the 20th Century are the electronic broadcast media: radio and television. In less than a half century, they have revolutionized communications, creating immediacy and shared experience on events, news and entertainments as they happen.

First radio and then television dazzled the world's population. Now they have become a daily habit (almost obsession). There is no question that these two electronic media dominate public interest. In fact, they have over 80% "share of mind" for major media (the exact amount depending on whose figures you believe).

Radio Advertising bureau currently puts "share of mind" of the major media at: television 45%, radio 41%, newspapers 8% and magazines 4%. The Television Bureau of Advertising states that television's share of the time spent by adults is 53%, radio 32%, newspapers 9% and magazines 6%. Either way, radio and television enjoy at least 85% "share of mind."

From *Lodging* (May 1977), pp. 33–35. Reprinted by permission of *Lodging*.

Let's briefly examine each of the major media, first, in terms of their statistics, and then how each might fit into your media mix locally. (Magazines are excluded because they are seldom local.)

Television

Television has blossomed into the ultimate advertising medium: sight-sound and color (in over 70% of U.S. homes) with an added boost from cable TV. Television now occupies about 25% of its listeners' 24-hour day—average of 6 hours, 14 minutes.

The growing popularity of daytime TV adds another dimension to this medium. However, as a "success medium," television suffers from too many spot announcements.

Radio

Radio has found a new niche which complements rather than competes with television coverage. Where once radio was a mass medium reaching out for a total audience group, it now has become a "personal medium" that speaks to individuals in specific segmented groups. Thus, there are all-Black radio stations, Spanish radio stations, classical music, rock, top 40 and country music stations, all talk (including news) stations, etc. Each of these forms of programming can deliver a defined audience group with excellent cost efficiency.

Besides this, radio has become fully mobile—battery-powered sets, auto sets—to reach an almost exclusive audience on the move. This "drive-time," 7 A.M. to 9 A.M. and 5 P.M. to 7 P.M., is a prime listening period for radio. Significantly, radio has grown as a medium along with television (rather than declined) which demonstrates the compatibility of the two electronic media.

Newspaper

Newspapers are the original news and advertising medium. They are primarily a local advertising medium with over 1,738 morning and evening newspapers reaching about 63 million circulation daily. As such, they dominate local advertising 72% (or $6,745 million) while having a 14.7% share of all national advertising ($1,165 million).

The local advertising dominance, however, is now under heavy attack from television stations who are aggressively seeking more local business. But newspapers provide an information medium that gives readers up-to-date news coverage in-depth and unmatched by any other media. Further, newspapers can cover local, state, regional, national and international news in a continuous manner.

Newspapers also offer excellent coverage of a wide range of special reader interests such as: business, finance, stock market, fashion, grooming, cooking, recipes, sports, hunting, fishing, science, society, television, other entertainments, travel and astrology and many others on a regular and continuing basis.

Newspapers enjoy a close identity with their community. They are, in effect, a "public utility"—a service medium for both readers and community. Besides this, newspapers, as a shopping medium, help create a market for products and services. Another important aspect of newspaper advertising is the structured format (and sections).

Newspaper advertising rates tend to favor local advertisers (particularly if on contract) with a rate differential of about 50% less for local advertisers. This has mitigated against the growth of national advertising.

Incidentally, our agency is one of the largest users of newspapers for travel advertising in the country. Over the years, we've sorted and sifted, analyzed and researched the newspaper as an advertising medium. We've developed 15 guidelines which are essentially error-proof.

I'm glad to share with you our 15 guidelines for publication advertising, and to add 12 essentials for media selection. The two checklists complement each other. I hope that, studied together, they will help make your advertising of your property and its facilities more professional and more profitable.

The 12 Essentials in Media Selection

- **Market focus.** Take a close look at your market by product category/brand, by areas/cities, etc., by identified product demand, by target market groups. In this context, how does your hotel fit in? How does it rank? And what do you want to advance?

- **Media focus**. Take a fresh look at the media in your market area. Get a current review/data on each newspaper, television and radio station, and outdoor plant. Keep an "open-door" policy for all media representatives, with "open eyes" and "open ears" for the facts. Be alert and watchful for changes, events, new programs, new editions for whatever opportunities they may offer you.

- **Periodic media update.** In terms of rates, costs per thousand, audience, circulation, etc., start with a new set of rate cards—and from there negotiate until you come to a firm market price. Constantly review new research data to see if it can deliver advertising more effectively for your hotel. Markets and media are in a constant state of change. Stay up with it.

- **Set basic media effectiveness yardsticks.** Set basic media yardsticks with which to measure the effectiveness of media advertising. Use such data as:

  Reach. How many households/persons (unduplicated) does a specific medium buy/deliver?

  Frequency. Weekly/monthly, etc., per buy? How often does your message reach?

  CPM. Cost per thousand readers/viewers/listeners.

  Target Market Group. Since it's too expensive to reach the broad public at large, it is best to focus on the best target market group by sex, age, ethnicity, etc. *Continuity* and cumulative effort are necessary to achieve an effective impact on the market.

- **Advertising by objective.** Set definite objectives for your advertising, including a sales forecast, consumer awareness (before and after), and exactly what you are trying to achieve. Is your media effort the best way to do it? What other supporting elements will you utilize?

- **Coordinate your advertising with marketing campaigns.** Since advertising is but part of the marketing mix, it should be coordinated with the other elements, such as sales, distribution, promotion, etc., to work effectively. Don't just run ads. Make the ads part of a marketing program.

- **Use your ad budget properly.** Start with what you can afford and then allocate it by subject (entertainment, weekend package, C & I, etc.) and by market. Make sure that whatever you budget is sufficient to do what you set out to do. Don't overspend, or underspend, and don't fritter away your budget over too many small buys. When you make a buy, make sure that it is enough to create an effective impact on consumers. Achieve the reach and frequency needed to get the proper action.

- **Plan your way around "Media pollution."** No one talks much about the fact that there are now too many products, in too many ads/commercials aimed at a very finite and weary audience. Clutter comes in many forms: 100-page newspapers that are chock full of ads, back to back. The same with many magazines.

    While radio and television have pushed back the "annoyance threshold" of listeners/viewers with the amount of commercial announcement that a person must be exposed to in a few minutes' timespan, clutter is still a problem. There is no simple cure for "media pollution," but a sensitive awareness can lead to stronger impact commercials/ads, and buys that sometimes are a little less cluttered. The smart advertisers are doing both and buying more spots to make sure that they get through.

- **Plan and coordinate local/national effort.** Make full use of national advertising as an "umbrella" of advertising on your market (this assumes your corporation runs a national campaign). Plan local advertising to work with it. Reap the harvest with well timed, follow-up effort. Also, coordinate sales and promotion efforts in such a way as to maximize the benefits of national advertising. It's a "tail wind" to drive home more sales.

- **Mix and match media.** Within the limits of budget and effective buy levels you should try various media combinations to see which works best and/or more economically for you. Using the proper mix of media is a fine art that pays big dividends in effectiveness.

- **Keep documented records of each advertising campaign.** This should fully document each advertising campaign, including: budget, media schedule, ad or commercial used; timetable, sales results (before, during and after). Thus, when you do something very successful, you have all the details to repeat it when desired.

- **Keep alert for special buys.** Radio and television time is a highly perishable commodity, somewhat like a block of ice on a warm, sunny day. It doesn't keep. There are times when radio stations (television less so) are anxious to sell time for a current, upcoming period. If you have the money, they have the time. Don't adopt the posture of a perennial "bargain hunter," but keep a sharp eye open and keep close contact with stations that you might want.

15 Guidelines for Publication Advertising

1. Color advertising has a 50 percent advantage over black and white.

2. Full-page ads have a 67 percent advantage over half-pages.

3. There is no distinct advantage for a lefthand page or a righthand page of advertising. Both get about the same readership.

4. Front, back or middle positions in a magazine or newspaper offer no significant advantage over each other.

5. The thickness of a magazine or newspaper has a moderate effect on readership—

    •   For 80 to 160 pages, readership scores are 45 to 35.

    •   For 40 or less pages, readership scores are about twice that high.

    •   For more than 160 pages, scores drop to below 35.

6. Ads on the back cover pull much higher readership than those inside the publication. The back cover pulls 65 percent more readers than the middle section.

7. Readership does not increase proportionately with ad size. Message and position within the publication make for efficiency quite outside the space unit.

8. Tall-column ads attract more attention than square ads. Vertical ads pull better; horizontal ads don't stop readers as well as vertical ads.

9. The meaningful headline, and the dominant focal point, are the most important characteristics of an ad in stopping readers.

10. Continuity of advertising is important. Assuming a readership level of 20 percent, it takes six insertions to reach 75 percent of the publication audience, 12 insertions to reach 95 percent.

    A 40 percent readership gets 78 percent after three insertions, and 95 percent after six.

    A good ad should be run at least three times. This allows it enough exposure to begin paying its own way.

11. There are three levels of readership: first, when a reader notes your ad; second, when he sees it and associates with it; third, when he reads it actively.

    The degree to which a reader will become a customer hinges on the readership he gives your ad.

12. The six points that generally attract high readership are: dominant attention-getter in headline or text; people in action around product; provocative claims; buyer benefits; specific and concrete offerings, and believable copy.

13. Readership scores drop slightly with length of copy. A poster-type ad (75 words or less) usually pulls slightly better than a text ad (more than 75 words), but the difference is small, and the sales message dictates what will be read.

    Though brevity is favored over wordiness, length of copy is a secondary consideration.

14. It is desirable to advertise in publications that have a built-in audience for your type of service or product, and in those publications, to advertise in sections appropriate to your offering.

15. Bizarre, attention-getting (but not thought-provoking) ads don't pull well. They may irritate instead of ingratiate.

    Beware of the cute ad that doesn't really say anything.

REVIEW QUIZ

When you feel you have covered all of the material in this chapter, answer these questions. Choose the *best* answer. Check your answers with the correct ones found on the Review Quiz Answer Key at the end of this book.

True (T) or False (F)

T   F   1. In the case of smaller hotels, the advertising medium itself often performs the functions of an advertising agency.

T   F   2. The effectiveness of an advertising program may suffer when hotels cut advertising production costs by using the material developed for one medium in another medium.

T   F   3. Public relations is the gratuitous mention of an organization's people, product, or services.

T   F   4. Public relations is just as risky as advertising in reaching the public.

T   F   5. Radio is the most common type of paid media advertising used by hotels.

T   F   6. The general public grants more credibility to what the media say about a hotel in terms of news than what a hotel says about itself in its own advertisements.

T   F   7. Advertising objectives should be set before a hotel's position has been determined.

T   F   8. Hoteliers should avoid advertising agencies whose representatives' ideas are strongly held.

T   F   9. Hotels rarely budget as much as ten percent of their total marketing investment for public relations.

T   F   10. In times of emergency or crisis situations, a hotel should appoint several spokespersons.

T   F   11. Most of today's hotel advertising is generated by advertising agencies.

T   F   12. The directors of a hotel's advertising program should first decide where its advertising should be placed and then formulate objectives for the program.

T   F   13. All materials for press kits should be filed together for easy access.

T   F   14. The type of advertising objectives selected should have little impact on the hotel's budget for advertising.

T   F   15. Improving consumer/guest relations is the job of a hotel's operations manager and not that of the hotel's public relations director.

Multiple Choice

16. The main thing the director of public relations or publicity must remember to do when dealing with the media is:

    a. to respond promptly to reporters' questions.
    b. to send reporters a steady flow of newsworthy items.
    c. to write fact sheets in a direct, plain style.
    d. to meet media deadlines.

17. Every hotel's advertising program:

    a. must be consistent with its position.
    b. should be the sole function of the advertising firm contracted by the hotel.
    c. should concentrate on collateral material.
    d. should use all available media.

18. The first people to know about any event scheduled by a hotel to gain publicity should be:

    a. potential guests.
    b. newspaper reporters.
    c. the hotel's employees.
    d. broadcast media reporters.

19. Effective out-of-home media advertising must be:

    a. simple in its message.
    b. limited in its copy.
    c. effective in immediately positioning the hotel.
    d. all of the above.

20. Good public relations work may push the hotel beyond its competitors because:

    a. it will increase the public's perception of the hotel.
    b. competitors may be insensitive to the contributions that public relations can make to their own marketing efforts.
    c. media representatives may be inclined to consider events at the hotel as more newsworthy than events held at competitors' properties.
    d. all of the above.

Chapter Outline

Promotions
    Self-Contained Promotions
    Promotions Involving Other Travel
      Partners
    Full Destination Promotions
    Tips on Planning a Promotion
Merchandising
Pricing Considerations
    Rack Rates
    Approaches to Determining Basic Rates
    Special Market Conditions
    Surveys by Dr. Shaw
    Other Approaches to Pricing
    MAP and FAP
A Word of Caution

Learning Objectives

1. Define promotions and state the ways in which promotions interrelate with other marketing tools.

2. List characteristic features of the three major types of promotions in the hospitality industry.

3. Define merchandising and state various ways in which a hotel can "sell up."

4. Define rack rates and state why pricing considerations must be unique to individual properties.

5. Define market mix and state its possible influences on hotel pricing considerations.

6. State how competition may affect a hotel's pricing considerations.

10

Promotions, Merchandising, and Pricing

ALL MARKETING TOOLS are essentially geared toward solving particular problems a hotel may have. These tools are carefully coordinated to consistently position the hotel in the marketplace while achieving the goals set down in the hotel's strategic marketing plan. The marketing tools this chapter addresses are promotions, merchandising, and pricing.

Successful promotions do not spring fully born from the imagination of marketers, nor are merchandising or pricing policies formulated overnight. Rather, each of these marketing tools is guided by the hotel's mission statement, and refined by an analysis of its markets, property, and competition. Such an approach ensures that each tool has a direct and immediate connection to the specific objectives of a hotel's marketing plan.

This chapter begins by defining promotions and moves on to discuss how promotions may interrelate with other marketing programs. Characteristic features of the three major types of hospitality promotions are also reviewed. Like promotions, merchandising is defined in terms of how it relates to and works within a hotel's strategic marketing plan. The third tool, pricing, is addressed more in terms of the various factors which influence and mold this major marketing tool into a unique consideration for individual properties.

Promotions

If promotions are the most hectic means of marketing a hotel, they are also the most enjoyable. Promotions have been defined as the tying together of a variety of normally unrelated elements around a central theme for the purpose of stimulating business. Some marketing professionals prefer to define promotion as a creative activity which involves one or more aspects of the hotel in solving a business problem. Strong promotional campaigns are characteristic of a hotel that works at being a good community member, markets aggressively, and watches trends in its environment. Such a hotel can realize benefits far beyond the solution of the particular problem the promotion is designed to solve. For instance, hotel companies that are seen as promotions-oriented usually find it much easier to attract bright, talented people as employees than hotels with stodgy or conservative images. Furthermore, the image of a hotel can be dramatically improved by running a series of successful promotions such as food festivals.

251

❝Promotions are one of our most effective ways of exposing our products to the market. There are many opportunities to use them, and overall costs can be shared by several parties, not to mention the greater exposure the joint effort provides. Promotions are effective for particularly weak occupancy times and are easily directed to specific markets. Effective promotions can be repeated year after year.❞

—**Richard Erb**
Chief Operating Officer
Grand Traverse Resort Village

How can promotions help you? Promotions can offset your hotel's low-occupancy periods by bringing in guests who previously had no desire for or awareness of your services. Promotions can fill restaurants on slow nights or liven up lounges that have never enjoyed much business. Even leased or rented shops at your hotel can participate in promotions and benefit from them.

Over the last 20 years or so, the promotion has been a way of life in the well-marketed hotel. Hotels in the Catskill Mountains originated the "singles weekends" which are now spreading into many urban areas. Special programs, such as computer education weekends and sports packages, have been used to attract special interest groups. The Hyatt Corporation has had a great deal of success with food-oriented promotions. In two recent years, the Hyatt Regency O'Hare has run a family-oriented "Ice Cream Weekend."[1] During 1983, 3,500 people were drawn to the event. This promotion included family films, magicians, jugglers, and a "Lana Turner Look-Alike Contest," in honor of the star who was discovered in Hollywood at Schwab's Drugstore in an ice cream trivia contest. Hyatt's "Chocolate Lovers' Weekend" was another very successful food-oriented promotion.

Promotions are not always big money-makers. Sometimes events or giveaways are created to gain additional exposure for a hotel. For years special theme promotions around the Christmas holiday were a feature at each Treadway Inn. The traditional "boars head ceremony" at which the innkeeper presided was very much a part of the Christmas season in communities served by the Treadway Inn organization. While the ceremony was not particularly profitable, it almost always received media coverage and added to the image of the property as an active participant in the community scene. Likewise, the St. Patrick's Day festival provided excellent media exposure and an opportunity for community involvement.

Many other similar promotions are continually executed by hotels individually or in tandem with travel partners or community groups. This chapter highlights the three most prevalent kinds of hotel promotions: (1) self-contained, internally controlled promotions; (2) promotions planned and executed in conjunction with another travel partner; and (3) full destination promotions in which a number of hotels participate.

Self-Contained Promotions

The largest category of hotel promotions may be called "self-contained" because they are planned and executed solely by the hotel staff. One very popular type of self-contained promotion is the theme weekend. Almost any hotel can run one of these events. Your hotel might well want to consider scheduling a theme weekend.

The theme could be an ethnic festival featuring the costumes, foods, wines, and entertainment of a particular country or region. Another theme weekend might be a classic film festival featuring great movies of a given period. Some hotels that have used this promotion have arranged for some of the stars of the films to appear in person during the weekend.

The theme a hotel chooses is not as important to the success of a theme weekend as is guest involvement. People attending the event must have the opportunity to be involved from beginning to end. One way to maximize your guests' involvement in a weekend event is to offer an insider's view of how your hotel operates. You could begin your weekend with a wine-tasting party on Friday night. Based on the preferences of the participants, you would then select the wines for the banquet on Saturday night. During the day on Saturday, guests could watch the kitchen staff prepare for the banquet. By seeing how the ice carvings are made, observing the chef at work cutting the meat, and receiving tips from the purchasing director on how to select good vegetables, your guests would gain a greater appreciation for the hotel's quality standards and its desire to please guests. The culmination of the weekend could be a Sunday brunch at which your hotel staff mingles with the guests to gather ideas about various aspects of the weekend event. An informal setting such as a brunch would allow guests to ask more specific questions about the hotel's operation, and staff members could share the responsibility of explaining their work in more detail.

Shangri-La, a resort complex in northeastern Oklahoma, uses musical celebrity weekends to improve its occupancy on winter weekends. These events also develop the resort's relationship with the many condominium owners who reside seasonally and on weekends in that part of Oklahoma. By providing these celebrity events, the resort enhances its community image while attracting regular summer guests to use the guestrooms and facilities on winter weekends when the rooms would otherwise be empty.

Of course, promotions need not be restricted to weekends. The Sheraton Plaza in Palm Springs wanted to bring in business seven days a week during the summer months—not the natural tourist season for Palm Springs. The hotel decided to run a "Summer's on Sale" promotion to counteract the off-season lull. Art Nigro, the General Manager, described the challenge he faced at that point: "I had less than a month to develop the project and its promotion before summer hit."[2] Despite the lack of time, Nigro developed a varied program of activities to be supervised by the hotel staff. A member of the banquet staff was appointed activities director for the summer. Certain other staff members were relieved of their regular assignments so they could be free to coordinate each of the special summer events. During the promotion all of these special workers wore distinctive uniforms to help guests identify them as activity leaders.

A seven-day series of supervised children's activities was repeated throughout the summer to enable parents to enjoy their own activities. Swimming lessons and tennis instruction were offered for children without additional charge. The two tennis pros who taught the children conducted tennis clinics for the adults, also without additional charge. Complimentary orange juice was available during both the children's and adults' tennis sessions.

Each day the hotel informed guests of the activities schedule by distributing color-coded program sheets to every room with the morning newspaper. The day's events were also listed on a poolside bulletin board. The Sheraton Plaza's pool (which is one of the largest in the desert) became a focal point of the hotel's summer activities. Aerobic water exercises, water games, and swimming races took place in the pool. Guests were invited to compete at poolside for awards.

"What we attempted to do was provide all the fun of a cruise ship without the seasickness." The results of all of this planning and promotion far exceeded Nigro's initial expectations. "We had hoped for a modest 10 to 15% increase over the previous summer, but wound up with a gain of 28%."[3] Obviously, promotions do not have to be held on weekends to be extremely successful.

Before you decide what kind of promotion to run at your property, it is important to determine what problems you would like the promotion to overcome (for example, low occupancy on specific days of the week, or lack of public awareness of one of your hotel restaurants). Then you can design your chosen promotional event to fully utilize the internal resources of your hotel. Keep in mind that the limitations of your hotel's resources will shape the final product you design. Some hotels have space limitations that keep them from staging people-intensive promotions such as an official ribbon-cutting ceremony in the lobby; others have staff limitations which prevent them from executing expertise-based promotions such as a food festival requiring the talents of a fine chef. If you plan a self-contained promotion to solve certain problems of your hotel, avoid multiplying your problems as a result of shortages and haste. Make sure you have adequate resources and allow yourself plenty of lead time to make all the necessary arrangements.

Promotions Involving Other Travel Partners

In addition to operating your own self-contained promotions, you can also join with other travel-related businesses in sponsoring a promotion. Some joint promotions with travel-related businesses are done on a very grand scale. For example, early in the 1980s airlines set the tone for expanded promotions with their frequent traveler programs. They invited rental car companies and hotels to participate in these campaigns, and millions of dollars were spent promoting and administering these massive multilateral promotions.

Smaller scale promotions, involving only modest investments by the individual hotel, can also work very successfully. All it takes is a little creativity to put together an attractive promotional package. Suppose, for instance, that your hotel is planning a week-long ethnic festival celebrating Portuguese culture. You could invite TAP (The Airline of Portugal) to participate by providing posters of Portugal and possibly some uniformed flight attendants. A drawing for a free trip to Portugal could be a special feature on the final day of your program. During the week you could ask Lancers, the wine company, to provide special wine incentives to increase their sales as well as the hotel's. Perhaps a Portuguese wine tasting party could be held one or more times during the promotion. Similar arrangements could be made to carry the Portuguese theme through your entertainment, decor, and menu.

In addition to the joint promotions planned by hotels, hotels are sometimes invited by other organizations to participate in their promotions. The personnel at

Grand Traverse Resort Village (located in Grand Traverse Village, Michigan) graciously agreed to share the story of a promotion in which they were involved with Polaroid and Meijer Thrifty Acres (a discount department store and supermarket). Director of Marketing Colleen Bagley explains the step-by-step process by which the joint promotion was worked out with the resort:

> ❝Polaroid contacted us in response to meetings held between Polaroid and Meijer regarding possible ways to heighten summer sales in 1984. Their proposal was that we offer some type of special value for Meijer customers who purchase a Polaroid camera (of a specific type) during a certain time frame. After many interactions, it was agreed that Grand Traverse Resort Village would offer $25 off a minimum two-night stay, redeemable within a certain time frame. This was our second promotion of this type with Polaroid and Meijer. [See Exhibit 1 for exact details.]
>
> For their part, Polaroid would offer discounts on certain cameras and act as coordinator for the promotion between Grand Traverse Resort Village and Meijer. Meijer would pay for the entire promotional campaign, which included the following:

- 156 30-second television spots airing throughout all of West Michigan plus Lansing, Jackson, Flint, Saginaw, Traverse City, and some cable plus 21 spots in Cincinnati, Ohio

- 388 radio spots in all of the Michigan and Ohio markets listed above and also including Adrian, Michigan, plus 108 radio spots in the additional Ohio markets of Marion, Newark, and Springfield

- 300 + posters to be hung near camera displays in all Meijer stores (four to five posters per store)

- Newspaper ads running on the following dates:

    April 29, 1984—four-color full-page ad in Grand Rapids, Kalamazoo, Lansing, Flint, and Saginaw

    April 30 and May 14, 1984—40-column-inch black-and-white ad running in seven major Meijer markets in Michigan.

> The TV spots … which featured some 13 seconds of videotape from our property, were produced … at absolutely no cost to us. We supplied the videotape to Meijer's advertising agency, and the spots they developed promoted us in a very positive light.
>
> The Polaroid/Meijer promotion is just one of a long list of promotional ventures that our marketing department has worked out with a variety of companies, ranging from shopping malls to radio stations to TV entertainment shows, etc. They are used:

1. to promote awareness of Grand Traverse Resort Village and heighten identification of our property and facilities;

2. to augment ad budgets in markets where the depth of penetration is not as great as is desirable;

3. and to serve as the **only** planned exposure (other than editorial coverage) in certain markets where there is no budget money allocated.

Exhibit 1   Ad for Polaroid and Meijer's Joint Promotion with Grand Traverse Resort

Courtesy of Grand Traverse Resort Village

As a final note, it should be made clear that these joint promotions are always an 'everyone wins' situation. No money changes hands; everyone exchanges existing products; no advertising agencies must be paid; and, as long as the customers of the companies you co-promote with have a demographic profile that matches your property's demographic profile, then joint promotions provide an added boost within a given market segment."[4]

If promotional partners do not flock to your hotel, don't rule out joint promotions. They are still worthwhile, even if you have to take the initiative to find promotional partners and arrange to use them in **your** promotion. For instance, if you are operating a hotel in the eastern United States and you want to run a California food festival, then contact the many trunk carrier airlines flying between your general area and California. At least one airline would probably be happy to participate in your promotion, and agree to fly in special fresh foods from California. Perhaps the airline would also provide promotional personnel and grand prizes for your drawings.

Your joint promotion could also be extended to include specific promotional organizations, such as the California Avocado Commission. Trade groups for various products—citrus fruits, strawberries, pork, beef, eggs, milk, and virtually any other product you can name—are eager to help increase sales of their product. Regardless of what you decide to feature in a food festival, there is probably at least one trade association devoted to its promotion. All it takes is a bit of ingenuity, careful planning, and a willingness to commit your people to the success of your promotional project.

Experience shows that the most successful joint promotions undertaken by hotel businesses are those in which all the participating companies assign coordinators to be fully responsible for their part of the program. Central coordinators who are delegated full authority to carry out a project tend to become totally immersed in it. They are far more committed to its success than are employees who work on isolated pieces of the project without ever getting "the big picture."

Very successful restaurant menu promotions can be done in department stores, particularly those with cookware departments. Since department stores are generally very heavy users of print and broadcast advertising, the return they receive for doing a hotel or restaurant promotion is usually greater than the return other promotional partners receive. Beyond the immediate benefit of a short-term sales increase, these promotions make more new friends for your hotel. One promotion can lead to other joint ventures, so it is well worth the effort to involve other members of the business community in your promotion.

Full Destination Promotions

Many hotels participate in total destination programs. The Sheraton at Steamboat, Steamboat Springs, Colorado, turned a hotel promotion called "Way It Wuz Days" into a very successful destination promotion. The hotel was smart enough to invite the community to participate, and the community (including competing hotels!) was smart enough to agree. Historic communities often attract tourists by promoting the destination as a whole. For example, Sturbridge Village in Massachusetts sponsors "Yankee Winter Weekends" and all the village merchants participate.

Destination promotions can also be geared to seasonal recreation. For instance, Montreal's Winter Carnival brings people into a cold climate at the peak of the snowy season for the express purpose of having fun with winter. Montreal's businesses cooperate to turn a liability into an attraction, and it works!

A total destination promotion has certain advantages over other promotions. From the tourist's perspective, this kind of special promotion allows tourists to immerse themselves in a community, seeing all of its attractions and features at a comfortable pace and often at a lower price than they would normally pay. Usually, airlines offer special rates, restaurants give discounts, and hotels put together attractive packages. Although competitors may appear in the same destination advertising, they participate in order to make a good destination better. The work involved in developing a destination promotion is actually fun because it draws members of the travel-related industries together. Any hotelier who does not take advantage of an opportunity to participate in a full destination promotion is missing out on both a good business opportunity and a fine personal experience.

Tips on Planning a Promotion

You must set your sights on exactly what you want to accomplish with the promotion. If your objectives are not clearly stated, you will not know how to allocate resources to meet the objectives and, therefore, the promotion will probably fail. To succeed, a promotion must be adequately budgeted and carried out according to plan. Unless you are committed to running the promotion according to an established schedule, don't start. Hotel promotions usually fail because those in charge prematurely cut off the necessary support and drop the project. Promotions are not for the faint of heart.

Having set firm objectives, you are ready to select your market. It is important to be honest with yourself in choosing a target market. For example, if your hotel is in a cold winter area and your objective is to build up winter weekend business, you must be reasonably certain that the people you intend to approach are predisposed to attend winter weekend events such as winter carnivals. If you target a market (for example, warm winter communities) whose basic behavior patterns would have to change in order for your planned promotion to work, then you have probably doomed your promotional project before it ever gets off the ground.

Once you have identified your target market, you must design your promotion to appeal to people from that marketplace. The desired business will never materialize to meet your objectives if the theme of your promotion does not fit the needs of the market you have targeted. For example, a fine wine promotion in a blue-collar neighborhood would be destined to fall short.

It goes without saying that promoting your event is the key to making it work. Whether your program is self-contained, a joint venture with your partners in travel, or a total destination promotion, adequate funding and a commitment to stay the course will largely determine the program's success or failure.

If the prospect of possible failure has you asking yourself why you should even bother with promotions, remember the potential benefits of a good promotion:

1. It often generates word-of-mouth advertising. Therefore, as your hotel's reputation grows over a period of time, it will be less dependent on paid media.

2. It can increase customer awareness in a broader market area as well as in the cities beyond your local market.

3. It can help the public see your hotel in a more positive light.

4. It can raise the morale of employees, particularly those who are intimately involved with the promotion.

5. If partners in travel join with you in running a promotion, your hotel's objectives can be accomplished at a relatively low cost.

6. If it is carefully planned, it can solve several problems at once.

Suppose a hotel's two largest business problems are low weekend occupancy and inadequate public awareness of the hotel's full-service restaurant. In this case a "gourmet weekend" could be just the answer. Both problems could be solved by offering a package of overnight accommodations and dinner in the restaurant. To help you start your own list of ideas for promotions to try in your hotel, consider the following interesting promotions that have been used by various hotels:

1. **Sports packages.** Participants receive tickets to a nearby college or professional game. Afterwards the hotel holds a reception featuring speakers connected with the team. Pennants and streamers highlight the decor.

2. **Theater packages.** Attendees receive tickets to a local theater production staged by a university drama department or a professional company in the community.

3. **Costume theme weekends.** Costumes for events such as Mardi Gras are provided to guests as part of the package.

4. **"Suite deals" weekends.** Travelers who normally do not use suites are encouraged to upgrade their accommodations to a suite for the weekend. The package is sometimes "sweetened" by combining it with champagne, gourmet dining, etc.

5. **Cultural weekends.** Authors (or other leading figures in the arts community) are invited to lecture, attend a reception in their honor, autograph the guests' copies of their books, and so forth.

The list of promotions your hotel can sponsor is endless. You are bound only by the limits of your imagination, so you would be wise to let it run free.

Merchandising

Merchandising requires the same level of awareness as promotions. Although merchandising is far more subtle and less dramatic, it can, nevertheless, produce even more profit in the long run than a promotion. Merchandising is "point-of-purchase" sales advertising and includes everything from lobby cards to directional signs, from menu clip-ons to suggestive selling of menu specials and wine by service personnel in the dining rooms.

Other businesses have used merchandising to increase sales volume at the point of purchase for years. By placing candy bars at check-out counters, cigarettes and gum at newsstands, and golf balls in pro shops, businesses stimulate incremental sales primarily of impulse items. The key to merchandising success is presenting these items in the right place at the right time. Hotels can also use "selling by suggestion" in all guest-contact departments and so add to their revenue. For example, merchandising-oriented hotels may encourage guests to use suite parlors on weekends by offering the parlors at prices that are lower than usual, yet still profitable. Here, again, everyone wins.

Hotel managers with a merchandising mentality apply its principles to every point of purchase in the hotel. The front desk staff is trained to "sell up." The food and beverage staff builds profits by constantly promoting attractive, highly profitable food and beverage menu items. Servers sell more wine at tableside and suggest more elegant desserts in hotels where merchandising is emphasized than in those hotels where merchandising is ignored.

A classic merchandising story in the hotel industry concerns Jim Lavenson, former President and Managing Director of the Plaza Hotel in New York City. The Plaza's luncheon waiters noticed that very few desserts were being sold at lunchtime. The main reason for the low dessert volume was believed to be increased weight-consciousness. It seemed that many people preferred to skip rich desserts at the midday meal. After Mr. Lavenson learned of the problem, he called a meeting of the restaurant staff. Underneath his suitcoat, Mr. Lavenson was wearing a T-shirt with a large strawberry printed on the front in full view. He used the theme "think strawberry" to encourage the restaurant staff to replace the usual variety of fattening desserts with a number of desserts featuring strawberries as their main ingredient. Needless to say, the number of desserts sold during lunchtime soon increased significantly. From that time forward, whenever a difficult marketing problem arose at the Plaza, they referred back to the "think strawberries" motto for motivation.

Pricing Considerations

Many marketing textbooks do not include any references to pricing, yet it is one of the most important factors in determining the profitability of any product or service.

> BToday, more than ever before, pricing is an integral function of hotel marketing. In an era when high inflation and fierce competition are the norm, the balance between average rate and occupancy is delicate, indeed. 99

> **—David Karpilow**
> Director of Marketing
> Treadway Inns Corporation

Determining the price at which a hotel should put itself into the marketplace is a very complicated process. Product analysis, competition analysis, market analysis, and market planning are frequently used in price-positioning a property. Market segmentation also has a bearing on pricing. In many cases, the market mix (the number and type of different target markets) chosen for a property at one price level might be unacceptable to some potential guests at another level.

You should therefore examine a variety of factors which are often pertinent in setting the prices for hotels. Bear in mind, however, that every situation is different.

No single source can or should tell a hotel how it should price its product or service: each hotel faces its own individual market conditions and has its own marketing and profitability goals. Moreover, the antitrust laws require that each competitor in the marketplace price its own product or service independently. For these reasons, this chapter does not recommend or even suggest that any members of the hospitality industry price or market their products or services in any particular way. Rather, in an effort to inform the reader, it reports marketing and pricing concepts which have been employed by members of the industry. Readers can then exercise their independent business judgment to adopt those concepts, if any, which will best achieve their individual business goals and objectives in their own market.

> ❝Hotel management is confronted almost daily with room rate pricing decisions. It is important that management consider the impact that demand, competition, and cost have on pricing decisions.❞
>
> **—Margaret Shaw, Ph.D.**
> Assistant Professor of Marketing
> University of Massachusetts—Amherst

Dr. Margaret Shaw conducted research which explored traditional hotel pricing strategies. She has graciously allowed us to present throughout this chapter excerpts from her thesis, "An Analysis of the Hotel Room Rate Pricing Decision."

> A one-price system was evidently the norm in the 1920s and 1930s. It is common today, however, to observe two-, three-, and five-tier published room tariffs. Additionally, reduced package, tour, corporate, and group rates are commonly offered to various demand segments to stimulate demand, especially in low occupancy periods. This is a direct result of hotel operators recognizing various segments of demand with various price elasticities within these segments.[5]

Rack Rates

The prices for all categories of hotel rooms are derived by many hotels from their established rack rates. The term "rack rate" originated in the days when the rate for a room was posted on a rack at the front desk. These days, very few hotels have racks, so rates may be listed on a computer screen, on the back of the guestroom door, or both. The rack rate can be defined here as the regular rate charged by the particular hotel for the given room in normal times. Before assuming that circumstances in a community warrant special pricing, hoteliers should check carefully for legal guidelines affecting their marketplace.

Special conditions can also cause prices to drop below the rack rate. In a perfect world, the rack rate would be the rate charged for the room each day to each market throughout the year. But in some hotels, the price charged for a room may at times be below the posted rack rate. After discussing how basic rates are determined, this section examines some of the reasons why a particular hotel may reduce rates.

Approaches to Determining Basic Rates

Various hotels have various formulas to determine their basic rates. Setting the rack rate for each room category and determining discount categories and rates are major decisions for the hotel's management. Management should take great care and consider several factors such as cost, inflation, and competition before setting rates that will ensure the hotel's profitability. Each hotel must determine its own room rates. However, the following process might be used when determining a particular hotel's rates.

Step 1
Estimated operating expenses

plus

Taxes, insurance, etc.

plus

Depreciation (standard rates on present fair value)

plus

Reasonable return desired on present fair value of property

equals

Total estimated expenses and fair return desired

Step 2
Total estimated expenses and fair return desired

less

Credits from sources other than rooms

equals

Amount to be realized from guestroom sales to cover costs and desired reasonable return on fair value of property

Step 3
Amount to be realized from guestroom sales to cover costs and desired reasonable return on fair value of property

divided by

Number of rooms to be occupied at estimated average occupancy

equals

Minimum daily rate per occupied room to cover cost and desired reasonable return on present fair value

Even given this "scholarly" method of determining room rates, one fact remains—competition sets the limit that a hotel or motel can charge for its rooms. The "proper room rate" is one that is large enough to cover costs, offers a fair return on invested capital, and is reasonable enough to attract and retain the operation's targeted clientele.

On the other hand, this approach to pricing may not work for a hotel if the hotel is located in a city that is "overbuilt"—that is, in a city with too many hotels for the amount of demand. (In the late seventies and early eighties, San Francisco, Atlanta, Dallas, and Houston struggled with excess rooms. They were joined by Boston and Seattle in the mid-eighties.) In order to survive, hotels in these cities were forced to compete in a variety of market segments other than those for which their facilities were originally designed. As a result, a hotel sometimes charged prices which were lower than a formula would indicate. The resulting diversification was intended to help the hotel capture an increasing share of the limited room-nights available, a larger piece of too small a pie.

Construction costs may be affected by construction timing, especially when a hotel is counting on business from sources it cannot control. For example, to serve the convention market, a hotel may be planned near the site of a municipal convention center that is being constructed (or expanded) to build up convention traffic. Such dual planning works well only when the two construction schedules match. There have been cases in which the private venture has met its timetable while the government project has fallen behind. Even though hotel rooms become available at the appointed time, the convention planner who would like to use the hotel cannot do so without access to meeting space at the convention center. Under these circumstances, the convention has to find another host city and the hotel booking has to be postponed until all construction is completed.

Now, in light of the lack of convention business, management has to either live with the gap in occupancy or, more logically, turn to other market segments. However, the only alternative segments reachable at a particular time may be price-sensitive. For example, if the convention hotel's most promising alternative market is the government market, whether for group or transient business, management must pursue this segment with the realization that maximum per diem rates limit the amount government employees can receive as a reimbursement for rooms, food, and beverages (see Exhibit 2).

Reducing the hotel's rates to meet the per diem rate may be justified by the fact that the lower rate should attract more business. If occupancy and, therefore, total revenues would be high enough to offset the lower rates being offered, this strategy could help to meet the hotel's financial needs until the convention center construction could be completed.

This example illustrates a key principle of pricing: a combination of market factors and special economic conditions determine how well a property is received at any given rate. There is no clear-cut formula.

Special Market Conditions

A number of conditions may cause a hotel's management to re-examine the prices the hotel is charging for various categories of business. The three major categories of business are transient, resort, and group.

Many hotels that enjoy steady full-rated business on weekdays do, nonetheless, offer exceptional rates to special categories of business within their major markets. For example, hotels frequently provide special rates to companies that are committed to using a given number of room-nights per week, per month, or per year. Similarly, special rates are sometimes provided to companies that transfer a lot of executives into the city. Here the justification is that these guests are likely to be using the hotel seven nights a week, rather than just part of the week as transients do.

Other categories of travelers have only so much money to pay for accommodations. Often military personnel, members of university faculties, and clergy are traveling on fixed budgets that limit their choices. The hotelier who wants to attract these segments must determine whether these people will be attracted to the hotel at the prices they are asked to pay.

Exhibit 2   Some Sample Government Per Diem Rates

High rate geographical areas (HRGA)	Prescribed maximum daily rates (in dollars)
Illinois	
Chicago (all locations within the counties of Du Page, Cook and Lake)	75
** Rockford (all locations within Winnebago County)	62
** Springfield (all locations within Sangamon County)	65
Indiana	
** Indiana Army Ammunition Plant, Charlestown (see also Louisville, KY)	75
** Ft. Wayne (all locations within Allen County)	70
** Gary (all locations within Lake County)	67
Indianapolis (all locations within Marion County, including Fort Benjamin Harrison)	75
** South Bend (all locations within St. Joseph County)	67
Iowa	
** Des Moines (all locations within Polk County)	65
Kansas	
Kansas City (all locations within the counties of Johnson and Wyandotte) (see also Kansas City, MO)	75
** Wichita (all locations within Sedgwick County)	75
Kentucky	
** Covington (all locations within Kenton County)	65
** Lexington (all locations within Fayette County)	75
** Louisville (all locations within Jefferson County and the Indiana Army Ammunition Plant, Charlestown, Indiana) (see also Indiana)	75
Louisiana	
Baton Rouge (all locations within East Baton Rouge Parish)	75
** Lafayette (all locations within Lafayette Parish)	69
** Lake Charles (all locations within Calcasieu Parish)	65
New Orleans (all locations within parishes of Jefferson, Orleans, Plaquemines, and St. Bernard)	75
** Shreveport (all locations within Caddo Parish)	74

One very common market condition is a fluctuation in occupancy according to a weekly cycle. Some hotels counteract the predictable drops in occupancy by offering lower rates to transient guests on slow days of the week. These special rates may be offered as packages or may simply be offered on a per-night basis by a wide variety of hotels. Traditionally, city center hotels have high demand Monday through Thursday and relatively low demand on weekends. The same is true, to a lesser degree, of airport hotels and certain roadside facilities. Conversely, resort hotels generally have heavier demand on weekends and lesser volume on weekdays. For this reason, the time restrictions on special price offers for resort hotels are often exactly the opposite of the time restrictions specified by city center properties.

Holiday periods also offer special pricing opportunities, and many hotels—both center city and resort—take advantage of them. If a hotel's offering is sufficiently attractive, many people who have a few vacation days to use up, or perhaps a three-day weekend, can be induced to spend that leisure time at the hotel.

Group business can be attracted by many factors, not the least of which is pricing. In this market, pricing must be used skillfully to meet the need of the particular organization. Association, convention, and meeting planners may be most concerned about the meeting costs directly chargeable to their organization. For example, meeting room rentals, security costs, and banquet prices will all affect the convention registration fee or the organization's out-of-pocket expenses. In the case of association board meetings, no registration fee is charged to the attendees, so the association must absorb the entire cost. Corporate meetings, however, are usually coordinated by a planner who is responsible for an overall meeting budget that includes the room rate as well as all of the other costs. Because the corporate meeting planner is concerned with the overall cost of the meeting, the room rate may be as important as any of the cost considerations.

Like transient and resort business, group business tends to fall on certain days of the week. For example, some conventions have *always* followed a Wednesday through Saturday schedule and they have always met in early May. Therefore, a hotel salesperson who knows the pattern a convention typically follows can easily evaluate the business based on the group's requirements. Given the group's expectations, if the business is still attractive to the property, the hotel salesperson can calculate the price for the convention. If the calculated price is too high for the group to pay, the hotel can either forget about making a bid or recalculate the price to equal what the other market segments are paying during the same time period.

Not all groups are this predictable, however. Some organizations are willing to be quite flexible about the days they will meet. In fact, fewer and fewer organizations today are bound to rigid guidelines or inflexible policies. Rather, they tend to stay with certain dates simply because these dates have been attractive to members and have worked successfully in the past.

Unfortunately, much of the data about the meeting patterns of organizations has suffered from computerization. As publishers of directories and other list organizations have transferred their accumulated knowledge from paper files to computer files, they have been forced to make the information as absolute as possible. In some cases, a group tendency may have become confused with a group requirement. For example, compilers may have assumed that because a group has held conventions Monday through Thursday in previous years, it will only consider those day in future years. The creative marketer should not be afraid to approach a group with an offer that is new and different, if the offer can be made sufficiently attractive.

Surveys by Dr. Shaw

In the course of preparing her thesis on pricing, Dr. Margaret Shaw contacted major multi-unit, domestic hotel firms. The hotel firms were, for the most part, made up of commercial hotels. On the basis of their marketing expertise, corporate executives holding positions of vice president or higher were selected and interviewed individually by Dr. Shaw. Then Dr. Shaw inferred from the interviews how the hotels in the five participating firms established their prices.

The range of responses indicated that some firms had rather rigid pricing policies while others were extremely flexible. Some firms said that they changed their pricing policy according to the economic climate: in good times, they let local managers determine pricing; in difficult market conditions, corporate guidelines are emphasized. One company stated the criteria it uses for setting prices at one of its hotels:

> **❝**What we want to know, really, is what is your anticipation of supply/demand relationship for the time frame you're looking at … anything else is irrelevant. Are you in a market where demand is greater than supply, or are you not? If you are in a situation when demand is greater than supply, you play a different kind of a game … than if you are in an opposite situation.**❞**[6]

Other Approaches to Pricing

Today many categories of hotels use pricing as their dominant marketing tool. Many of the economy hotels, for instance, do relatively little selling or advertising on the local level. Independent economy hotels merely put up a sign indicating a rate that is lower than its competition in the same area. If the economy properties are franchised facilities, they may also be listed by location in a chain's national ads (see Exhibit 3) The franchise organization's advertising campaign for its economy hotels generally conveys an overall message of their value. Ads invite the consumer to compare the rate and the quality of these accommodations with others in the area. On these premises, guests are expected to make a choice that, of course, the economy organization hopes will be in its favor.

A modern combination of all of the elements of pricing may be found in emerging facilities called "all-suite hotels." For example, Guest Quarters provides a guestroom, a living room, some type of breakfast, and frequently an evening cocktail reception, for one all-inclusive price. In addition to being particularly attractive to business travelers, in some markets these facilities reach out to special segments because their overall cost may bring them down into the range of the traveler on a fixed budget.

MAP and FAP

Many resort hotels still operate on the Modified American Plan (MAP), and a few still operate on the Full American Plan (FAP). The Modified American Plan includes two meals a day (usually breakfast and dinner), while the Full American Plan includes three meals a day. Some MAP and FAP resorts include at least some recreational amenities as part of the rate as well. Use of pools, skating rinks, and bowling alleys is usually included but use of tennis courts, racquetball courts, and golf courses is generally not included.

Hotels that are primarily resorts offering both of these pricing plans generally find that today the traveler is more likely to be away from the main dining room during the noon hour; thus guests tend to be more interested in the Modified American Plan than the Full American Plan. The European Plan (EP), which does not include meals, is beginning to be used at more resorts.

Exhibit 3   National Days Inn Ad

Days Inn® is a better place to stay. For less.

Stay with us on your next business trip and you'll see why.
At Days Inn hotels, you'll get clean, quiet accommodations with two double beds, color TV, direct dial phone, plus, a well lighted and appointed bathroom with separate dressing area. You'll also enjoy great food and friendly, quick service in our restaurants. And with over 320 convenient locations all across America, you're sure to find a Days Inn hotel close to where you're going. Try us. Just once. And compare. You'll see why we're a better place to stay...for less.

Try us. And compare.™ Call 1-800-325-2525

© 1984 Days Inns of America, Inc.

A Word of Caution

Pricing and positioning work hand in hand with market segmentation. In determining your market mix, it may be a poor strategy to consider pricing alone. Some markets cannot be successfully mixed. If, in your zeal to fill your hotel, you illogically reach out to market segment pairs that have very little in common (e.g., executive seminars and ski tour groups), then you may wind up serving both groups badly. This undercuts your marketing effort in the long run.

Each hotel must not only establish its prices so that they are satisfactory from a marketing standpoint but must also be sure that its prices are in compliance with the law. There are many legal constraints on pricing. For example, federal and state antitrust laws require that pricing and marketing practices be established individually by each hotel acting on its own best business judgment. Never confer with competitors about pricing or marketing practices.[7] Many federal and state laws also regulate the representation of prices to the public. There should be no misrepresentations when the public is advised of a hotel's prices. For example, if the special rate you are offering only applies to a limited number of days, be certain that your advertising makes this absolutely clear to the public.

Because of the many local laws and regulations which bear on pricing, it is not possible to outline here every legal constraint. Every hotelier, however, should be sensitive to the need to establish prices which will be both effective in the marketplace and legal. If there are any doubts about the legality of your pricing, legal counsel should be consulted. Pricing is important and, unfortunately, pricing is difficult. However, if your hotel sets a fair price, there is a good chance that your hotel may successfully induce some business through pricing considerations.

Endnotes

1. "Ice Cream Weekend: A Second Helping," *Travel Weekly,* July 23, 1984, p. 11.
2. "Summer's on Sale in Palm Springs," *Lodging Hospitality,* November 1982, p. 90.
3. Ibid.
4. This account was provided in writing at our request by Colleen Bagley, Director of Marketing, Grand Traverse Resort Village, Grand Traverse Village, Michigan.
5. Margaret Shaw, *"An Analysis of the Hotel Room Rate Pricing Decision,"* thesis, January 1984, p. 9.
6. Ibid, p. 110. We are grateful to Dr. Shaw for letting us borrow these comments made by her research subject.
7. See Jack P. Jefferies, *Understanding Hospitality Law,* 3d ed. (East Lansing, Mich.: Educational Institute of the American Hotel & Motel Association, 1995).

Supplemental Reading ————————————————————————

Upselling Rooms: Three Effective Techniques

by Marc Gordon, CHA

> *Choice-of-doors, door-in-the-face, and foot-in-the-door methods are de-scribed by educator experienced in practicing what he preaches.*

One of the most effective marketing tools available to a hotel is the upselling of guest rooms by the front office staff. Upselling, in this context, refers to the effort by reservationists and desk clerks to induce guests to buy medium-priced or deluxe rooms rather than standard accommodations.

Since hotels normally have several rate categories, based on such factors as decor, size, location, view and type of beds, the rack-rate difference between two given rooms can be substantial. With such a disparity of rates, a great opportunity for upselling exists.

The impact of upselling on total rooms revenue, average rate and operating profit can be tremendous. Remember, the costs of selling a deluxe room varies little if at all from that of selling a minimum-rate room. A deluxe room may have extra amenities that slightly increase the cost of occupancy compared to that of a standard room. But more often, 100% of the difference in rates is profit.

Here is the point: *the incremental revenue generated by the sale of deluxe accommodations will drop directly to the bottom line.*

Compute for yourself what this could mean to your hotel. Assume that you could upsell half the rooms you are selling to the extent of $10 or $20 per room per day. What would this amount to in revenue and profit? At hotels where I have worked, the dollar advantage has sometimes been dramatic.

To upsell rooms, front office personnel must be trained to be professional sales people rather than order-takers. This is seldom the case. More often, hotels don't regard front office activities as a part of the property's total marketing effort, and front office personnel simply ask the guest what type of accommodations he or she wants and then write down the order.

The reservationist and desk clerk must realize that they can upsell rooms in much the same way that a waiter or waitress can sell extra food items by suggestions to the customer.

So what does the so-called order-taker in the hotel front office need to learn to become a professional sales person?

- First, how to control encounters with the guest.

- Second, how to overcome natural inhibitions in dealing with the guest.

- Third, how to be enthusiastic in asking for the sale.

From *Lodging* (January 1986) pp. 64–65. Reprinted by permission of *Lodging*.

Controlling the encounter. The hotel reservationist or desk clerk should avoid such open-ended questions to the guest as, "What type of room do you wish?" This allows the guest to take control—to direct the negotiation from that point on.

The hotel clerk should instead ask specific questions (more later) that move the guest in the direction of selecting medium-priced or luxury rooms.

Getting rid of natural inhibitions. The hotel clerk often earns far less money than the guest who stays at his or her property. The clerk may regard the hotel's rate as very expensive, far beyond what he or she could afford to pay. It can be difficult for such a person, making a modest salary, to recommend a deluxe room rated at $100 a night.

In looking at rates from their own perspective, front office personnel may be inhibited from selling rooms at a rate higher than the minimum. They have to overcome such inhibitions before they can upsell effectively.

Asking for the sale. Once the reservationist or desk clerk has learned to control the encounter and overcome inhibitions to suggest better accommodations, he or she must learn to ask for the sale. And be enthusiastic about it.

Few guests will buy a better room—even if they would enjoy it—unless the hotel representative suggests it. Most guests will—many for reasons of conscience—take the minimum rate unless "pushed."

So all hotel salespeople should learn to ask for the sale.

After front office personnel are trained and encouraged to be professional salespeople, they are ready to learn special compliance techniques for upselling. Compliance techniques are either pressure or non-pressure.

High-pressure upselling is totally inappropriate for the sale of guest rooms. Hotel guests truly *are* guests and must be treated as such at all times. It is inconsistent to offer gracious service and then imply that only a fool would reserve a standard room or that the guest can reserve a deluxe room or else. No—hospitality doesn't work that way. Only non-pressure compliance techniques are appropriate in upselling at hotels.

Non-pressure compliance techniques exert little or no perceived pressure on the buyer to induce compliance. There are three non-pressure compliance techniques that are effective in inducing guests to reserve medium-priced and deluxe rooms instead of minimum-rate rooms. I call them:

- The choice-of-doors technique.

- The door-in-the-face technique.

- The foot-in-the-door technique.

Choice-of-Doors

In applying this technique, the desk clerk or reservationist gives the guest a choice of rate-category alternatives. He or she then asks: "Which would you prefer?" No pressure is put on the guest. The guest tends to put pressure on himself to choose a room in the middle of the range.

You see, people tend to avoid extremes. They think that a choice of the least expensive room would make them look cheap, whereas the choice of the most expensive room would make them appear extravagant. Thus, internal pressure is created to move to the middle rate to demonstrate to themselves and to others that they are reasonable and compromising.

The choice of alternatives or choice-of-doors technique is an easy and effective way to upsell guests to the middle rate when they might otherwise have chosen the minimum rate and were very unlikely to be susceptible to the deluxe accommodations.

Door-in-the-Face

The door-in-the-face technique is called "theory-based" because it has proved effective in various market areas. It begins with a large or unreasonable request from the sales person—a request so unreasonable that compliance is unlikely. After the original request is refused by the buyer, the seller makes a more moderate offer, which represents the intended compliance request.

Consider this example: A man needs $2 and the only person available for a "touch" is a chance acquaintance whom he knows is not likely to lend him any money at all. So he asks the acquaintance for $10, and receives a prompt turndown. He now asks if he could at least have $2. Research shows that his chances of getting the $2 are significantly enhanced because he has used the door-in-the-face technique. The acquaintance feels that $2 is a reasonable compromise. The success of the technique is based on the theory of reciprocity.

The door-in-the-face technique can be applied easily in selling hotel reservations or selling rooms to walk-ins. The application could be termed top-down, suggestive upselling. The hotel salesperson starts with a strong, enthusiastic recommendation of the highest room-rate category that fits the guest's situation; for example, a deluxe room with king-size beds for a married couple or a deluxe room with two double beds for two commercial travelers. One of two guest responses is likely from the hotel clerk's suggestion.

One, the guest might comply and take the room in the highest-rate category. After all, some guests are on liberal expense accounts with their own or client companies. Further, there are also guests who simply want the best room available.

Two, in a more typical situation, the highest room rate will be rejected. The desk clerk or reservationist will then go to the next highest rate with an enthusiastic recommendation of its merits. The hotel staff member will continue down in the same manner until the guest makes a decision.

This technique for upselling is used to get more guests to reserve middle and high-rate rooms than would otherwise have done so. Economy-minded guests on restricted budgets will still opt for minimum-rate rooms, but the majority will choose accommodations in the middle range. The theory of reciprocity will convince many guests that after rejecting the highest rate suggested by the reservationist, accepting a middle-rate room is a rational compromise. Even in the most expensive hotel, a $125 single sounds reasonable after the reservationist suggested the deluxe single at $165.

Foot-in-the-Door

This technique, by contrast, is applied by obtaining compliance for a moderate request initially, setting the stage for more likely compliance with larger, more substantial requests.

The technique can be illustrated by asking a homeowner to sign a petition requesting the local government to keep his city beautiful. If the homeowner signs the petition, he will be far more likely to comply with a second request, a week later, asking him to contribute $10 to the "keep the city clean" campaign than if he had been asked at the onset to contribute $10.

In the foot-in-the-door technique, people who comply with an initial request imply from their compliance that they are the sort of people who comply with such requests and are therefore more likely to comply with larger requests in the future. Compliance leads to further compliance, just as non-compliance leads to future non-compliance.

Consider how the foot-in-the-door technique can be applied to the upselling of guest rooms. A desk clerk is registering a guest who has a reservation confirming a minimum or low-rate category. The clerk might say, "For $10 more, you can have a king-size bed." Or, "For $20 more you could have a deluxe room with a view of the lake." Or, "For only $35 more, you could have our entire package, including a dinner and a breakfast for two."

Because the guest has already demonstrated a level of compliance (by making the room reservation), the larger request, during registration, represents not a total outlay but a small increase over the anticipated charge. Often, the guest will comply.

The choice-of-doors, foot-in-the-door and door-in-the-face techniques represent powerful, non-pressure upselling tools that every hotel can use to increase, significantly, total room revenues, average rates, and operating profits.

Hotels that train all front office personnel to be professional salespeople—in controlling the sale, being uninhibited, and being willing to ask for the sale—and to use upselling techniques, will enjoy much greater financial success.

Upselling should be an integral part of every property's internal marketing strategy.

REVIEW QUIZ

When you feel you have covered all of the material in this chapter, answer these questions. Choose the *best* answer. Check your answers with the correct ones found on the Review Quiz Answer Key at the end of this book.

True (T) or False (F)

T   F   1.   According to Richard Erb, promotions are effective for particularly weak occupancy times and are easily directed to broad markets.

T   F   2.   The most important element contributing to the success of a theme weekend type of self-contained promotions is the choice of the theme.

T   F   3.   According to Dr. Shaw, hotel management confronts pricing decisions almost daily.

T   F   4.   A "market mix" refers to the number and type of different target markets.

T   F   5.   The Modified American Plan includes three meals a day while the European Plan includes two meals a day (usually breakfast and dinner).

T   F   6.   Promotions are more subtle and less dramatic than merchandising.

T   F   7.   The computerization of data about the meeting patterns of organizations has worked to confuse tendencies with requirements.

T   F   8.   Promotions involving other travel partners form the largest category of promotions.

T   F   9.   Most successful joint promotions are those in which a single director oversees all participating companies and takes full responsibility for the entire program.

T   F   10. A "trade rate" is the regular rate charged by a particular hotel for a given room at all times.

T   F   11. Antitrust laws encourage hoteliers to confer with the competition when setting prices and when developing marketing strategies.

T   F   12. The most important aspect in planning a promotion is to have clearly stated objectives.

T   F   13. How well a property is received at any given pricing rate depends on a combination of market factors and special economic conditions.

Multiple Choice

14. The promotional ventures undertaken by the Grand Traverse Resort Village were designed to meet which of the following objectives?

   a. to promote awareness and heighten identification
   b. to augment advertising budgets in problematic markets
   c. to serve as the only planned exposure in certain markets
   d. all of the above

15. Full destination promotions:

    a. are often geared toward seasonal recreation.
    b. are the largest category of hotel promotions.
    c. are most effective merchandising techniques.
    d. never involve your hotel's competitors.

16. The "proper room rate" is one that:

    a. is large enough to cover costs.
    b. offers a fair return on invested capital.
    c. is reasonable enough to attract and retain the operation's targeted market segments.
    d. all of the above.

17. A potential benefit of a good promotion is:

    a. raised employee morale.
    b. a simultaneous solution to several of the hotel's marketing problems.
    c. increased customer awareness of the hotel in markets beyond the local area.
    d. all of the above.

18. There is no one pricing formula for hotels because:

    a. each hotel faces its own individual market conditions and has its own marketing and profitability goals.
    b. there are many local legal constraints on pricing.
    c. increased competition may force wide changes in any hotel's original pricing considerations.
    d. all of the above.

Part IV

Marketing Tools in Action

This section sets in motion the tools of marketing presented in Part III. Chapter 11 examines the elements involved in putting together a marketing plan. These principles and others are further illustrated in Chapter 12 as the focus shifts to pre-opening marketing activities that bring a new hotel into the marketplace. Current examples of how marketing techniques can be applied at the property level are featured in Chapter 13. The last chapter of this section provides four case studies which illustrate good marketing planning and execution. Supplemental readings follow Chapters 11, 12, and 14. These readings are intended to complement the chapters and give readers an added perspective.

Chapter Outline

Market Mix
    Trade Associations
    Corporations
    Travel Trade
    Other Markets, Other Characteristics
The Marketing Mix
    Trade Associations
    Corporations
    Travel Trade
Developing the Marketing Plan
Key Account Coverage Program
Food and Beverage Marketing Planning
    The Service Package
    Location and Visibility
    Advertising and Promotion
    Alcoholic Beverage Service

Learning Objectives

1. Define "market mix" and "marketing mix."

2. List the distinguishing characteristics of the following major market segments: trade associations, corporations, and travel trade.

3. List possible marketing mixes for each of the market segments you have distinguished in Learning Objective #2.

4. State the sequence of the five basic elements which the text recommends for any marketing planning process.

5. List the benefits that arise from key account coverage programs.

6. State strategies for marketing food and beverage outlets.

7. Outline several new approaches to marketing alcoholic beverage service.

11

The Marketing Plan

THE DEVELOPMENT OF A MARKETING PLAN revolves around understanding a hotel's product, competition, and the marketplace. In addition, it is critical to have a clear understanding of marketing tools when formulating a strategic plan. Developing a marketing plan essentially involves two overlapping functions: (1) determining which markets a hotel is going to compete for; and (2) determining which marketing tools a hotel is going to use to compete for those markets.

Of course, these decisions must be based on a reasonable familiarity with hospitality markets. This chapter, therefore, begins by describing the characteristics of various markets that may be included in your mix. Hotels may also use a variety of methods to identify the market segments from which they plan to receive a certain level of occupancy or business. These segments make up the market mix.

Following these descriptions of hotel markets are suggestions on how you can use the tools of marketing to reach particular segments. In some cases, a combination of tools can be used to bring your hotel into distribution within the marketplace. This is the marketing mix.

Whatever the final market mix and marketing mix of a hotel, it is important that management consistently follows a precise sequence of planning. This chapter therefore suggests techniques for putting together a coherent marketing plan that may work for your hotel. An overview of marketing hotel food and beverage operations is also provided in the last section, as restaurants are often a valuable asset to the success of a hotel.

Market Mix

"To determine probable market mix ... at the destination level, we make use of research and information from convention and visitor bureaus. We look at airplane arrivals and departures. We look at city pairs; we talk to corporate traveling departments and to anybody who is involved in the movement of people to and from that destination to determine what the potential is for that particular city. At the hotel level, we look at the competition to see what kinds of meeting space they have, how large, how attractive, and how likely it is to be used, to determine what kind of convention business we are likely to get.

We look at the strength of the corporate base in a city by calling on companies like the phone company or large companies which are headquartered there (like Boeing in Seattle), to find out what their requirements are for individual business coming to the city and what their expectations and requirements are for room rates.

If a hotel is already in place or analyzing its market mix geographically, we can also look to area code reports from our 800 number. Where are reservations of the hotel coming from? We also look at travel agency commission reports. Who is generating the most business for us?

Out of all this, we can make some reasonable projections about where our business is coming from or [is] likely to come from: 60% individual and 40% group, let's say, with 50% of individual business coming from the California area, 30% from Texas, 15% from Florida, and the remainder [from] all over the lot. **"**

—Bill Newman
Senior Vice President—Marketing
Westin Hotels

Marketers of consumer-oriented products or services should no longer attempt to reach the mass market with a single product. According to Laurel Kutler, Executive Vice President of Market Planning at Leber Katz Partners, "target marketing" is now the marketing thrust. Today "every market [is] breaking into smaller and smaller units with unique products aimed at defined segments."[1] What then are some of the "targets" of the hotel business?

As pointed out earlier, a hotel channels its marketing efforts toward specific market segments. To identify the segments which constitute your hotel's market mix, you should first recognize that the occupancy of every hotel is drawn from multiple sources of business. Normally, these sources of business are classified geographically as well as by other characteristics. For example, does your business come from one particular geographic location or from several? Does it come from nearby, a small geographic radius, or from distant, cross-country, or international locations? Does your clientele seek any particular benefit when they choose your property? For instance, your guests may be looking for the convenience of a city center location, spacious and well-appointed meeting facilities, or just the opposite—a quiet out-of-the-way spot offering sedate surroundings. Do you do a lot of volume, group or repeat business? Do your guests use your property for business or for pleasure, or a combination of both?

If you categorize your guests as a business market, more specific questions might look like this: Is the source of business corporate in nature? And does it primarily come from the major cities within 200 miles of your hotel? If so, what channels of distribution are best utilized to bring the business from these cities to you? What combinations of other businesses blended with this source give you the ideal market mix? Once these classifications or segments have been identified, management can begin to make intelligent marketing decisions.

It is extremely important to ask these questions for each market segment you are attempting to serve. Only then can you select the best mix of market segments. The wrong mix of market segments renders sales efforts nonproductive and results in overlapping demand for the same time periods. A carefully selected market mix can fill in the soft spots throughout your occupancy pattern and help your hotel to prosper. The next section of this chapter examines major market segments which may be part of your market mix.

Trade Associations

Generally, trade associations are professional organizations concerned with one or more aspects of a particular industry. Some trade associations are empowered to provide education and/or to certify professionals in their particular disciplines.

Others concentrate solely on lobbying efforts at various levels in order to enhance the industries which they serve. Trade associations can function at the international, national, regional, state, or local level. Each of these levels represents a different kind of opportunity for hotels.

Many people in the hotel industry make the mistake of assuming that trade associations only conduct one or two meetings per year. Actually, trade associations are an enormous source of business. While it is true that annual and semi-annual meetings are normally the most heavily publicized and best-attended, most associations sponsor other meetings, both large and small, throughout the year. Consider that almost every trade association has a board of directors which must meet on a regular basis. Practically every trade association has committees which also conduct meetings, in most cases, according to an agreed-upon schedule.

Many associations also receive visitors, such as field staff members and volunteers, who frequently travel to association headquarters. This subsegment of the trade association market may be virtually untapped today. For example, very few Washington, D.C., area hotels solicit the transient business associated with the headquarters of the Hotel Sales and Marketing Association International, even though many people who visit the HSMAI offices make their hotel reservations through the association's staff. Other associations in the Washington area and in other cities may also be experiencing this same lack of attention.

Trade associations normally have fairly rigid requirements for meeting space. Any hotel that cannot meet these requirements is simply not seriously considered for the larger group meetings. Before you spend a great deal of time, effort, and money to attract this segment, be sure you honestly evaluate whether or not your hotel meets the needs of the trade association market.

Corporations

This category is difficult to describe because corporate meetings vary widely and embrace every conceivable characteristic of a particular business. Some meetings, professionally run by outside organizations, involve elaborate stage shows, while others are very simple, across-the-table business meetings with no fancy frills. Many corporate meetings are not only meetings but are also company-sponsored incentive trips awarded for outstanding service to the company. These honored guests may not even be directly employed by the corporation; they could be distributors or retailers who handle the company's products and have generated sufficient volume to qualify for the trip.

Corporate meetings (with the exception of "planning" meetings) often tend to occur in reaction to major political and economic events. For example, for a brief time in the mid-seventies the energy crisis in the United States stimulated a tremendous number of corporate meetings. Of course, the energy consumed by those who traveled to meetings about the energy crisis was apparently no obstacle to their travels! Alert marketers have learned that studying not only competitive forces in specific industries, but also world conditions in general, helps them reach prospects ahead of the competition. Also, they can use facts gleaned from the news to make their sales solicitation more timely and effective. Consider the U.S. auto companies' response to changes in the harsh market conditions of the early eighties. When the

U.S. government acted to protect domestic auto companies by restricting imports, the U.S. car manufacturers began producing cars designed to meet the requirements of buyers who had previously relied on foreign car manufacturers. This turn of events in America has resulted in (1) more and splashier new car shows, (2) more executive meetings on how to further expand the U.S. car market, (3) more middle management meetings to discuss sales techniques, and (4) more incentive trips for individual car dealers who are selling more cars.

The corporate market is the most valuable of all markets because of its steady, high-volume, profitable repeat business. However, tapping into this valuable market is often complicated because corporate business can come from such a variety of sources: a company meeting planner, a company traffic department, individual operating departments (e.g., sales, personnel), or from secretaries in executive offices whose titles may not immediately suggest that they are likely to be sources of business. Therefore, prospecting may need to be handled differently for each corporation in a particular industry.

After you have determined which (if any) subsegments of the corporate market your hotel can serve well, you can build a solid corporate marketing program by: (1) honestly analyzing the geographic mix of your current business and your competitors' current business; (2) acquainting yourself with the characteristics of the major industries in those areas; and (3) prospecting company by company for those that are most likely to use your hotel.

Travel Trade

Like the two market segments discussed previously, the travel industry is multi-faceted, and this has created some confusion. Many hotel people fail to recognize the differences among tour operators, wholesalers, and travel agents. Some fail to differentiate a corporate travel department from a travel agent. Others fail to take advantage of opportunities to join with their "partners in travel" in selling similar destinations to similar markets. Therefore, it is no understatement to suggest that the key to marketing to the travel industry is to first identify the distinctive aspects of that industry.

Travel agents are the source of travel industry business that most hotel people find easiest to understand. Travel agencies typically do a mixture of corporate and social business and many even do some group business. They retail the packages put together by tour operators, and they may also function as wholesalers, selling their own product as well.

There are now travel agents who specialize in corporate travel. Commercial hotels that never received much business from travel agents before are now finding this new channel of distribution to be a significant source of corporate business. Some hoteliers have resisted this development on the basis that the corporate market segment has always come directly to them in the past and should continue to do so now. However, this attitude ignores the very real fact that over periods of time channels of distribution do change. If corporate business is being brought to a hotel in this new way, hoteliers need to recognize it and accordingly determine their policy in relation to these specializing travel agents.

A change taking place in the world of travel agents is the emergence of travel giants. These giants assume one of two forms: (1) multiple local outlets of the same large agency, or (2) travel consortia with which travel agents affiliate in order to improve their access to the latest technology, or in order to increase their market strength. In many ways consortia become their own reservations centers because state-of-the-art equipment from many airlines, hotel companies, and auto rental companies is at their disposal and available to their member properties. If they choose not to run their own reservations centers, they may function as a clearing-house for reservations.

A consortium of travel agencies may make special collective deals with certain designated hotels in cities frequented by business travelers. It may even be able to guarantee a specified level of volume to a particular hotel in return for rate consid-erations. For example, one very large travel consortium guarantees a New York City hotel a specified volume on a daily or an annual basis in order to obtain a rate below that which corporate clients could obtain on their own buying power. There-fore, it is important for hoteliers to investigate the potential of these travel giants for their own marketplace and their own hotel.

Of course, the unaffiliated retail agent who serves a local community will still exist and will continue to be a force in the marketplace, particularly for resort des-tinations and for international pleasure travel. However, when you realize that the fastest-growing segment of the travel agents' clientele is the corporate customer, it is not surprising that an increasing share of the corporate market is going to those travel organizations that can provide the fastest service and the greatest assurance of confirmed space to the corporation.

Hotels also market to two other elements of the travel industry: tour operators and wholesalers. Tour operators put together specific programs for specific destina-tions and sell them as travel opportunities either to groups or to individuals. Whole-salers offer tour packages to various destinations by direct solicitation and through retail agencies. Depending on the markets it serves, a hotel may find that tour opera-tors and wholesalers play a major role in bringing business to the hotel's market-place. If you are aware of tour operators and wholesalers who operate in a source market of significance to your hotel, get to know them and let them get to know you; otherwise, you will miss out on a great opportunity to build your business.

Your hotel can also explore marketing opportunities with your "partners in travel." This group includes airlines, motor coach companies, auto rental compa-nies, convention bureaus, and other bodies that have a common interest in bring-ing people from a particular source market to your destination. Here is one idea that progressive hotel marketers have used successfully: take the list of your ho-tel's best customers from a given city to an airline operating from the same city. Invite the airline to combine its best customer list with yours so you can make sales calls to these prospects as a team. The impact of joint sales calls can be significant. It can induce the customer of one company to be a customer of both.

Too often hoteliers leave it to the partner in travel to be the driving force in a program rather than assuming responsibility themselves. For instance, hotels react to familiarization opportunities created by others instead of taking an active role in the planning process. If your resort hotel needs exposure in a given marketplace, there is nothing wrong with approaching the airline that best serves your destination from that source market and asking its assistance in putting together a familiarization program. If you take an active role, your hotel's needs are more likely to be met.

Other Markets, Other Characteristics

The market segments already examined constitute a significant percentage of the business received by many hotels. However, other market segments may be important in your particular situation. As you consider the other market segments in this section, remember that any segment you consider serving should be examined as thoroughly as we have examined the foregoing segments. Thus, for each market segment you intend to have your hotel serve, you should spell out in detail what the characteristics of that segment are, and what makes that segment a potential source of business for your hotel.

For example, if your hotel's rate structure allows for it, the government market may be attractive to you. But what is the government market? It is a combination of federal, state, and local agencies that have specific purposes for using hotel rooms. Depending on your property's location, you may be in a position to develop a great deal of business from one of these government levels or you may, to a lesser extent, serve all three. It is unlikely that you would attract all three levels equally because the characteristics of the travelers at various levels of government can vary enormously. For example, international diplomats are government travelers with very different needs from those of employees from a state auditing department.

Similarly, the buying power of members in the military varies with their rank. In this case, it is easy to see that more than proximity to a military installation is necessary to ensure that the military will be a good source of business for a hotel. The type of work being done at the military installation affects the type of rooms demanded. A hotel near a major research and development facility may have the potential for room use disproportionate to the installation's size because much of its demand may come from private sector vendors who are calling on the military. If, however, the hotel is located near an artillery training center or an infantry basic training site, the potential for business from visitors to the military installation may be significantly lower. On the other hand, such a hotel might enjoy a great deal of business from soldiers on leave for brief periods of rest and relaxation.

Like the military market, the university market contains diverse subsegments. If the university is a major institution of higher education with most of its student body coming from distant towns and cities or from other countries, it will generate business from the normal academic, administrative, and private sector visitors. In addition, business is likely to be generated by parents visiting students and by prospective students visiting the campus. If the university happens to be in a state that requires its professional license bearers (e.g., doctors, lawyers, nurses) to fulfill significant continuing education requirements, the university could be a likely source of seminar business on weekends through its continuing education departments.

On the other hand, if the university is an urban commuter school attended primarily by local residents, it will generate relatively little room demand, even if it has a large student body. For example, the Massachusetts Institute of Technology generates a tremendous amount of business for hotels in the greater Boston area, while Northeastern University, which has a much larger student population, generates far less room demand.

Although they are not discussed here in full, social, military, religious and ethnic fraternities and associations; professional sports teams; attendees of local attractions; and leisure travelers can all contribute to the market mix of a well-marketed hotel. If you learn the characteristics of each market segment by carefully examining it without many preconceived notions, you will be more likely to attract a successful mix of market segments.

For planning purposes you should by now have identified the market segments which you expect your market mix to comprise. In all probability, however, none of these market segments will deliver exactly the amount of business you expect it to. Don't let this discourage you, though. The important thing is that you will be using your soon-to-be-developed marketing strategy on the right targets. The next section of this chapter examines how you can use and combine particular marketing tools in your marketing plan.

The Marketing Mix

The marketing mix or marketing tool mix is simply the way in which you select and apply the elements of marketing (research, positioning, sales, advertising, public relations, promotions, merchandising, and pricing) to your selected market segments. Just as a cook needs a recipe and a builder needs a blueprint, so you need a marketing plan. To prepare you for the discussion of planning later in this chapter, let's look at how the marketing mix might be applied in several market segments, beginning again with trade associations.

Trade Associations

Because they are oriented toward a particular profession, many trade associations are best reached by advertising through literature which serves the industry. For example, *The Insurance Conference Planner* is published for the insurance industry's benefit. Another good approach is to advertise in magazines that provide information to executives and managers of trade associations. For instance, *Association Management Magazine* is published by the American Society of Association Executives (ASAE) for the information of its members. Obviously, this would be a likely place to advertise if you have the kinds of facilities professional meeting planners would find useful. If your hotel is a likely place for a certain association to meet, salespeople from your hotel would probably be treated with courtesy during personal calls on trade association executives. This is because the meetings of professional organizations tend to be technical in nature and can require a great deal of careful planning within the framework of the hotel. Therefore, personal sales calls are often a most effective tool by which to reach the association executive. From time to time, trade association executives also take familiarization tours of destinations that are likely to fulfill the meeting requirements of their memberships.

Booths at trade shows can also be a very effective way to represent your facility to trade associations. Ideas are exchanged at trade shows such as annual ASAE meetings and at expositions sponsored by vendor groups. Attendees are likely to be looking for new ideas and new approaches at these shows. If you decide to go after the trade association market, select the most logical segments for your particular hotel and attack them accordingly.

As you can see, the marketing tool mix to reach trade associations is varied. The tools of advertising, personal sales, familiarization promotion, and trade show participation can all work together to bring this type of business into your property. These tools are all means of getting the word out—bringing a hotel into distribution in the marketplace.

Corporations

The corporate market segment also requires careful selection, subsegment by subsegment. Some corporations meeting in the local marketplace can best be reached by personal calls, promotional parties, and advertising in the local press. Sometimes you need to work through third parties such as travel agents who handle the outbound business for corporations and plan their local meetings. If the company has a member of Meeting Planners International (MPI) on its staff, your own membership in this body may be the best way to reach this corporation.

Travel Trade

The travel industry has an extremely active trade press and its literature is widely read by travel agents. However, travel publications penetrate the travel agency community in different ways and in varying degrees. It is important to learn which publications are most often read and, therefore, are most beneficial for your advertising dollar. One way this may be accomplished is through close contact with agents in your marketplace and in your major source cities.

More about how to "mix" the tools correctly to reach each market segment will be presented later in this chapter. However, the examples already given suggest that there is plenty of room for creativity in developing your marketing plan. In fact, the hotel marketer who demonstrates the most marketing imagination is probably the one who will win the battle with the competition. In a recent article, the Harvard Business School's marketing guru, Theodore Levitt, defined the marketing imagination:

> **❝**It's the starting point of marketing success, and it's distinguished from all other forms of imagination by the unique insights it brings to understanding customers, their problems, and the means to capture their attention and their custom.
>
> The marketing imagination—by asserting that people don't buy things, but buy solutions to problems—makes an inspired leap from the obvious to the meaningful ... Charles Revson's famous distinction—'In the factory we make cosmetics; in the store we sell hope—' showed imagination. And so did Leo McGinneva's famous clarification about why people buy $1/4$-inch drill bits: 'They don't want $1/4$-inch bits; they want $1/4$-inch holes ...'**❞**[2]

If you apply the spectrum of marketing tools to properly identified market segments along with all the marketing imagination (or customer-mindedness) that you can muster, then how can you go wrong? As you can see, the discipline of marketing produces far more than a series of educated guesses about where your business will come from; it results in a viable and effective marketing plan.

Developing the Marketing Plan

Once a hotel has identified its market mix and selected the tools for reaching that mix, it is important that management devise and follow an orderly marketing plan. The next section of this chapter focuses on the steps which may be followed in the planning process and presents techniques toward helping a hotel reach its marketing objectives.

> ❝The foundation of successful marketing planning is the development of a comprehensive situation analysis. This is true whether the marketing planning process be for a hotel corporation, an individual hotel, or even a cocktail lounge within that hotel. There are three basic elements that must be analyzed in a situation analysis/mission statement: your hotel, your competition, and your customer. Only after a thorough, objective study of these three has been completed can the development of objectives and strategies begin. This analysis is designed to point out your advantages and disadvantages, as they relate to your competition, and the many potential customer markets that you can serve. It will help you in identifying the market segments of greatest potential and how to effectively compete. The analysis will also help you identify your major point of difference.❞

—William Hanley
Vice President-Marketing
Radisson Hotels

There is a tendency in the hospitality industry to think that marketing planning is only for larger hotels and that writing a plan for a hotel with a very limited staff is a waste of time. However, because jobs are not as well defined in smaller properties, it may be even more vital for the small property to commit its marketing plan to writing. In a larger property, assignments are generally confined to a particular market segment. Here, the schedules kept by the markets tend to keep the staff's efforts on track. By contrast, in a smaller property the staff may find itself getting bogged down in activities not directly related to selling. Indeed, in small hotels there is so much cross demand for the salespeople's time, that even the most sales-minded of managers can end up spending far less time in sales and marketing than he or she intended. However, if a marketing plan has been put into writing, it can be used to check management's daily activities and to prevent the staff from getting off track.

Regardless of the size of a property, its marketing plan should be well-written. Furthermore, the marketing plan should be reviewed by the owner and senior management for two important reasons. One very obvious reason for the person preparing the plan to solicit support from all levels of supervision is that such a vote of confidence ensures that those supervisors will carry out the plan and that their activities can be judged against it. Another reason for obtaining agreement on the priorities of the program is that later, when funds are needed to carry out various parts of the program, requests can include a reference to the previously approved priorities. This should make it easier for the person handling the market-ing program to obtain the necessary funds from management.

Broad-based participation from key people in every department or outlet which the hotel intends to market will contribute to the plan itself and, more im-portantly, to the team spirit of the hotel staff. This camaraderie is essential if the hotel is to sustain itself through those dark days when occasional major setbacks (which no one could predict) occur.

Given the participation of so many people, the preparation of a marketing plan is bound to be a complex and time-consuming process. If the plan is simply written and filed away, rather than integrated into the day-to-day operation of the hotel, the commitment of all that time and effort will have been for naught. Ideally, the marketing plan is not merely one part of day-to-day operations; it is the most significant part, because all of the hotel's operating policies should flow from it.

In putting together the marketing plan for a property, it is important to use a logical planning process. The precise steps used in the process are, however, not as important as the consistency with which the selected process is used. The market-ing planning process followed in some hotels includes five basic elements:

1. **A statement of the position the hotel wishes to assume in the marketplace.** Regardless of whether it is called a mission statement or a positioning state-ment, the hotel management and the supervisors of all the marketable facili-ties of the hotel need to agree upon and clearly state what the hotel is, and what markets it intends to serve.

2. **A situation analysis.** This analysis includes analyses of the property, the com-petition, and the markets. Property analysis includes evaluation of internal research data compiled locally; competition analysis provides data on compet-ing hotels, based on public information; and market analysis describes, both geographically and by market segment, the potential markets for the hotel.

3. **Comparative statistics.** The next step is comparing the hotel's actual business volume during the current year with projections for the twelve months of the upcoming year. (If the current year is only partially over, it is acceptable to project results for the remaining months of the current year.) More specifically, statistics are needed on rate occupancy, rooms volume, food and beverage vol-ume, marketing overhead expenses, and, if possible, gross operating profit which is departmental profits minus overhead. Then management should do the best job it can of projecting how these statistics will change over the course of the next five years.

   It is also important for the hotel to project its mix of transient business and of group business for upcoming years. The current status of bookings can be judged by: (1) recording the amount of future business already on hand as of today's date, and (2) comparing it to the amount of business booked as of this same date last year. Gathering all of these data helps management to effec-tively analyze where the hotel can realistically expect growth and what must be done to produce this growth.

4. **Action plans.** Now the hotel needs to produce a monthly plan of sales activi-ties for each market segment (group, social transient, business transient, etc.).

Each plan should include target dates, an assignment of accountability to particular staff members, and standards of measurement and evaluation.

Next, a key account list should be compiled along with an action plan for attacking these key accounts during the upcoming year. More will be said about key account coverage later in this chapter. From this last step, management can develop each salesperson's sales travel schedule and sales quotas for the year.

Taking the results projected for the upcoming year (see step 3) management can develop a realistic budget for marketing activities. The *Uniform System of Accounts for Hotels*,[3] approved by the American Hotel & Motel Association, may be a useful guideline for preparing a marketing budget.

5. **A promotions schedule.** Finally, management should list in chronological order the schedule of promotional events to be held at the hotel. Next to each entry and calendar date the objectives of the promotion, the advertising media to be used, and any creative recommendations should be stated.

The classical approach to marketing planning just outlined is similar to approaches used by many of the major chains. Americana Hotels has graciously allowed us to describe its marketing planning process here. An Americana hotel begins by scheduling marketing planning meetings. Corporate staff, property personnel, and outside agency support personnel come to these meetings armed with facts and prepared to state their opinions as to the direction the property should take. The planning process begins with a discussion of how the business mix currently enjoyed by the hotel compares with the mix that had been anticipated. Pricing is reviewed, and the success or failure of the pricing plan is evaluated, market segment by market segment.

Once the team has decided whether to keep the current positioning statement or to modify it, a mission statement is generated. From this mission statement flow projections for rates, occupancy, and market segments to be served in the future.

After the probable occupancy and revenue yield of each market segment has been determined, the planning team decides when and how the business from each market segment should be solicited. The sales team's quotas, or targets, are set to ensure that business will be booked from each market segment. Bookings in the upcoming year are intended to meet that year's need and to contribute to fulfilling the following year's goals. Next, budgets for advertising, sales, and promotions are put together.

Approximately six weeks after the initial planning meeting, the Americana planning process is wrapped up with a final review meeting. At this meeting, detailed action plans, a detailed advertising program, a tight schedule of promotional events, and the budget are presented for final approval. (Incidentally, each promotional event is budgeted separately so that its success or failure can be judged by a yield analysis at the end of the cycle.) Finally, if this hotel is to provide a portion of the funding and input for any multi-property corporate tie-ins, these are discussed at this time. (This is yet another good reason to have corporate staff participate in these planning meetings.)

Exhibit 1 **Major Account Coverage Spread Sheet**

Column a	Column b	Column c	Column d	Column e	Column f	Column g	Column h
Name of the account	Account contact(s)	how often account was called on last year	How often account will be called on this year	Estimated total room night account value (for all hotels)	Account priority (1 = most important; 4 = least important)	Revised call frequency (see Column d)	Revised account priority (see Column f)

Key Account Coverage Program

An important part of any marketing plan is the key account coverage program. There are at least four good reasons why you need such a program. First, this program increases the efficiency of your sales team by providing more frequent coverage of your most important accounts and less frequent coverage of your lower priority accounts. Second, a key account coverage program helps you to identify and correct any inadequate coverage of existing markets. Third, it provides a method for establishing better quotas and for tracking the performance of your field sales team in an equitable and professional manner. Finally, a key account coverage program helps you to decide whether or not a reallocation of your sales resources or a re-deployment of your salespeople would yield greater results.

The following procedure is only one of many ways to set up an effective key account coverage program:

1. For each and every account assigned to a salesperson, the salesperson should complete the following columns on a spread sheet (see Exhibit 1):

    a. The name of the account.

    b. The name of the account contacts.

    c. How often the account was called on during the previous year.

    d. How often the account will be called on this year.

    e. The approximate total potential value of the account. (Note: This is not the booking value at this hotel alone, but the total potential value of the account in the entire marketplace.)

f. The priority of this account, as the salesperson sees it, on a scale of one to four with one being most important and four being least important.

Two additional columns should be reserved for revisions of columns d and f after the salesperson consults with his or her supervisor in the marketing department.

2. After the salesperson completes columns a through f, the director of sales should review the work of each salesperson. The director of sales should indicate whether the entries in columns d and f are acceptable at this time. If not, columns g and h should be completed to indicate the jointly revised call frequency and account priority, respectively. In addition to assigning numeric values or weights to the accounts, the salespeople may also want to color code the accounts according to some uniform, agreed-upon system. Four different colors of file folders can be used to code the accounts according to their assigned priority. Then, when the director of sales is discussing a particular account with sales personnel, the color of the folder will immediately alert them to the priority of the account.

3. Now the total number of sales calls to be made by the salesperson during the next year is calculated by adding up all of the figures in column d. If this salesperson's account load is not as large as the workloads of the other salespeople, the director of sales can: (a) assign additional accounts to the salesperson to bring this individual's workload up to par, and/or (b) assign this salesperson a greater share of the prospecting responsibilities by market segment.

4. Next, accounts in column a should be totaled to show the number assigned to each salesperson. Then the accounts should be evaluated by market segment to see whether there are enough accounts to produce the desired yield for each particular market segment. This evaluation can be facilitated by adding another column to the summary sheet on which the columns are totaled, or a separate tabulation can be done for each market segment in which the hotel needs to develop new prospects during the coming year.

5. Finally, quotas for the first quarter should be set by the director of sales and agreed upon by each salesperson. As the priorities of the hotel change, these quotas can be adjusted for the second, third, and fourth quarters. Depending on the hotel's needs, its quotas may or may not be pegged only to room-night objectives. For instance, if a salesperson is assigned a heavy prospecting mission, management may wish to evaluate the salesperson's performance on the basis of new accounts opened, account potential, and actual account yield, rather than on account yield alone.

While not all hotels have achieved this level of sophistication in their key account coverage programs, the program just outlined can be modified to help almost any hotel reach its objectives. The most important requirement of any key account coverage program is that it give salespeople a clear picture of what their task is and where that task fits into the overall business of operating the hotel. If your program is effective, you will have more realistic quotas for your team, more

Exhibit 2   Weekly Entertainment Plan

Room in which entertaining will take place (name of host)	Date	Name and Title of Guest	Guest's Affiliation	Reason for Entertainment	Amount of Check
The Left Bank (Troy)	8/6	Buck Hoyle, Executive Vice President	HSMA International	Site Inspection	
LeBar (Walsh)	8/10	Marge Conway, Branch Manager	American Express Tours	Familiarization Trip	

time available for new prospecting, and a basis for evaluating the adequacy of your present sales force and the resources with which it has to work.

Best of all, a good account coverage program will reduce or eliminate those ongoing philosophical debates over which market deserves how much emphasis from the other elements of marketing. Thus, your marketing staff will be able to focus on their real priorities without confusion. For instance, if your account analysis indicates that 80% of your corporate business (which is half of your total group business) can be expected to come from four cities remote from your own, this will justify the expenses associated with advertising in and taking frequent sales trips to those cities. On the other hand, failure to place that advertising and make those trips might eventually result in a disappointing performance in the corporate market segment.

Other subschedules can be added to your marketing plan to meet your hotel's needs. For example, many hotels complete a weekly entertainment schedule to help the director of marketing and the general manager keep track of who is being entertained as a representative of what company and why. A sample of a weekly entertainment form which a hotel might use appears in Exhibit 2.

In one sense an outsider can get a pretty good picture of how well a hotel is marketed by carefully reviewing its plan (including its budget), the market segments it has targeted, the travel schedule it has set up, and the level of entertainment and promotional events it is planning. A strong plan is characteristic of a well-marketed hotel.

However, as difficult and as time-consuming as the preparation of a marketing plan might be, developing it is only half of the battle. The real way to measure the strength of a marketing plan is to see whether it is being used! Many corporate marketing directors agree that some of the prettiest plans containing the most impressive goals are never even looked at after they are submitted to headquarters. Some hotels may actually bind their marketing plans in book form. Despite their attractive appearance, these plans are probably nowhere near as successful as those that are dog-eared, marked over, scribbled upon, and coffee-stained by the end of the year. Quite frankly, the marketing plan is only as good as its implementation. The best plan is the plan that is used as a road map and not treated as an end in itself. As the business environment changes, new paths are constantly being recognized so the map must be altered accordingly. As in the initial preparation of the marketing plan, broad-based participation in all revisions of the plan is extremely necessary if the revised plans are to be successful.

Food and Beverage Marketing Planning

Following the guidelines already presented in this chapter, you can (and should) put together a food and beverage action plan for each of your hotel's outlets. These can be combined with the rooms sales plans you have already developed for each of your primary market segments. For each outlet, you should follow principles of sound marketing planning and prepare a description of the outlet's market mix and marketing mix, the series of action steps to be taken, and a list of the supporting measures that will be necessary to make the action steps work.

Many hoteliers assume that a hotel's food and beverage operation exists primarily as a service to hotel guests in contrast to the freestanding restaurant which serves as a profit-maker for its owner. From this perspective, food and beverage operations are seen as "loss leaders"—or simply as amenities to entice guests through the hotel door.

An increasing number of hoteliers, however, believe that a hotel restaurant can be profitable and even serve as the keystone of a successful lodging operation. In fact, in many hotels food and beverage revenue is often equal to or greater than rooms revenue. For example, The Registry Hotel Corporation can be credited with running one of the most profitable hotel food and beverage operations in the country. Forty-two percent of total Registry profits are derived from food and beverage revenues as compared to the national average which ranges from 15 to 18%.[4]

Charles W. Lanphere, Chairman and President of the company, discovered early on that there were extraordinary profits to be made from a successful hotel food and beverage program. Throughout their success, the Registry did not overlook the fact that operating a restaurant requires different skills than managing hotel rooms. The Registry recognized the principle that if any department in a hotel is poorly managed, a property could easily lose its appeal to the very market it wants to attract. As Lanphere remarks:

> **❝**With one exception, every one of the general managers in our Registry properties is a European-trained chef.... In fact, all of our top management have extensive food and beverage backgrounds. These executives tend to be detail

oriented and can translate their expertise to the finer points of running a hotel—
and of providing guests with consistently excellent service. **"**5

In developing the first Registry hotel in a suburb of Minneapolis, Minnesota,
Lanphere and his staff spent time visiting well-rated restaurants in the Twin Cities
region to investigate local food preferences. He gambled that local residents would
frequent the restaurant at his 330-room property if it was top-quality and set out to
design a restaurant which would appeal to the area's market. As a result of these
efforts, the hotel's restaurant, Latour, was an unqualified success and attracted corporate dining groups, local clientele, and dining critics. Today, a significant portion
of food and beverage sales comes from local residents.

The Service Package

Since many hoteliers view hotel food and beverage service as an amenity, hotel restaurants typically offer meals at breakfast, lunch, and dinner. Some market research reveals that this three-meals-a-day approach may not be as necessary for all
hotel properties. A study by Days Inns indicates that 89% of its guests eat breakfast
at the hotel, 4% eat lunch, and 17% eat dinner. Such studies prompt debate as to
whether some hotel dining rooms need to be open for lunch and possibly even for
dinner. Considering these statistics, hotels may need to develop new approaches to
food and beverage service that are both cost effective and desirable to guests. One
alternative is to lease the restaurant to a food service expert like Burger King and
provide complimentary breakfasts in hotel lobbies.[6]

Another strategy being used by hotel companies which may lack either the
capital or management expertise to run a food and beverage operation is joint ventures with freestanding restaurants. Economy or limited-service hotels may find
joint ventures to be an effective way to compete with full-service lodging establishments. For example, new franchisees of Days Inns are not required to have their
own restaurant or interior dining room, but must be located within easy walking
distance of a restaurant serving breakfast, lunch, and dinner.[7]

The guest convenience provided by a quality restaurant next door tends to ele-
vate the image of an economy or limited-service lodging operation. Other benefits
a hotel may enjoy are an increase in room sales, and occasionally, higher room
rates. Joint ventures may also allow for shared or reduced development costs. For
example, the hotel and restaurant may agree to develop on a common parcel of
land as opposed to developing under separate contracts. This arrangement often
helps to keep the parcel's size smaller since a parking lot and routes for automobiles to enter and exit would be shared. Joint ventures may also allow for cost savings through shared advertising, repair and maintenance, and removal of trash
and snow.

Such ventures, however, are not without risks. The possibility always exists
that a poor working relationship may develop between the two facilities or that one
of the operations will fail. To be safe, a hotel should maintain a separate identity to
protect itself against unsatisfactory products or services which may be delivered by
the restaurant. Not all food and beverage operations are suitable for joint ventures.

Larger hotels have traditionally opted to meet guests' needs and expectations by having coffee shops, medium-priced restaurants, fine-dining sites, and specialty-theme outlets within their operations. Multiple outlets, however, usually require duplicate staffing, extra equipment, and expanded managerial control. In addition, multiple outlets generally increase costs by increasing the opportunity for dishes, utensils, and supplies to be broken, mishandled, or stolen.[8]

Many hotels are trying to limit the number of food and beverage outlets in their hotels by offering one full-range restaurant for all three meal periods. Where hoteliers cannot combine or otherwise eliminate outlets, careful planning should be used to reduce expenses. Other alternatives include lobby bars or delicatessens within the lobby. A deli, for example, can provide guests with both an early-morning breakfast and a place where a sandwich, cold drink, and potato chips can be picked up after all the property's other outlets are closed.[9] A lobby bar can serve several functions as well. For instance, it can provide a gathering place for businesspeople throughout the day; a comfortable environment for female travelers; and a pleasant site for people to relax after work that adds ambience to the lobby.

Location and Visibility

Hotel restaurants are generally constrained by the location of the hotel itself. A hotel site that provides excellent accessibility, visibility, and proximity to primary markets may not lend the same advantages to its food and beverage outlet. For example, a hotel located next to a research park usually generates a strong demand for rooms and a strong luncheon trade on weekdays. However, breakfast, dinner, and weekend food service may suffer, with little or no demand being made.

Situations related to location and visibility are sometimes difficult to resolve. One strategy which may help to improve a restaurant's revenue is to target local residents in a marketing campaign. The theory is that if guests learn that local residents patronize the hotel restaurant, they will be more inclined to dine at the hotel themselves rather than at one of the local restaurants. Lunches can be creatively designed and executed to attract the local business clientele including corporation executives, political figures, or media personalities. Fun-filled atmospheres can be created through such promotions as lounge fashion shows, hiring a disc jockey, and by sponsoring contests and games. One problem associated with this approach is that the same crowds won't necessarily come out for the same kind of promotion. Depending on the property, an alternative strategy may need to be considered.

Hotels can also improve the performance of their restaurants by updating their menus. Sensitivity to guest preferences, taste trends, and diet and health consciousness are important factors in menu planning. For example, the Waldorf-Astoria still serves its trademark salad, but also offers new items which appeal to modern tastes for seafood and poultry, light sauces, fresh vegetables, and high-fiber foods.

Competition requires that hotel food and beverage operations pay as much attention to theme, concept, and design as their local, freestanding counterparts. In order to attract local residents, lodging restaurants should be designed so that patrons can enter off the street without having to walk through the hotel lobby. Another touch which may promote a freestanding image is to provide guests access to a direct telephone line. Restaurants that appear independent also appeal to hotel guests since they can relax and dine without feeling trapped inside a hotel.

Advertising and Promotion

Most hotel advertising is devoted almost exclusively to selling rooms to potential out-of-town guests. However, advertising a hotel food and beverage outlet can also pay off if the restaurant itself is appropriate for the intended market.

Some of the techniques that can be used to promote the hotel's restaurant could be to place elegant miniature menus in guestrooms, mail menus to former hotel guests, advertise in the local media, offer VIP guests the opportunity to dine with the hotel general manager, and encourage small meeting and group business to use the hotel's food and beverage service.

Special promotions can generate publicity as well as revenues. The Westin chain has sponsored a variety of promotions which revolve around food festivals at a number of their properties. The Westin Galleria in Houston holds week-long tributes to the foods of Sweden, South Africa, and California, while Swiss cuisine is the featured bill-of-fare during three-weeks of festivities sponsored by the Westin Bonaventure in Los Angeles. In Detroit, the Westin Hotel/Renaissance Center has held both Swedish and German food festivals.

Catering services can also be part of a promotion to customize guest food and beverage service. For example, theme parties patterned after a South Sea Island luau or a Texas barbecue can give a business or association the opportunity to impress important clients and reward employees. Such activities also create a welcome change of pace for hotel employees who may need creative and entertaining tasks in addition to daily responsibilities.

However, as a stand-alone department of a hotel, catering needs to create its own sales action plan, which can then be integrated into the hotel's overall marketing plan. Unfortunately, many catering departments (in particular those with good reputations) are reluctant to use a structured prospecting program. There is no logical reason for this reluctance since catering and banquet selling are measurable activities. Hotels do not have to accept the customary resistance of catering departments to their legitimate participation in the marketing program. If a hotel has significant walk-in or repeat demand, then special attention should be placed on measuring business which is solicited as a part of a prospecting mission. Otherwise, this new business will be lost in the numbers that come in without stimulation.

Alcoholic Beverage Service

Foremost among the goals of a food and beverage outlet is meeting the needs of guests by providing quality, hospitable service. Whether guests come to a restaurant to relax, dine, drink, or socialize, concern for guests' needs lends a personal touch to each guest's experience and helps create a unique atmosphere of hospitality.

Concern for the well-being of the guest must today also extend to the service of alcoholic beverages. Americans are becoming increasingly concerned about alcohol-related traffic accidents. In 1984, 25,000 highway fatalities were alcohol-related and each day more than 70 citizens are killed in driving accidents in which alcohol is a factor. In addition, the leading cause of death for young people between the ages of 16 and 24 is alcohol-related traffic accidents.

Because of these factors and because of increasing health concerns, many guests are drinking less. Third-party liability issues have also prompted many hotel food and beverage outlets to discontinue "happy hours" as well as to monitor alcohol consumption.

With these new concerns in mind, hotel restaurants are developing new approaches to marketing alcoholic beverages. This section examines some of the new strategies a food and beverage operation may take.

Low Alcohol, Specialty Drinks, and Food. Some hotels may offer guests the option of purchasing low-alcohol beer or wine coolers, imported beers, cordials, and carbonated mineral waters. Specialty or high quality hors d'oeuvres such as shrimp, clams, and steamship rounds can also be a welcomed option in place of drink specials during happy hours.

Suggestive Selling. Proper staff training can transform servers from mere order-takers into true sales agents of the food and beverage operation. Servers can be helpful in prompting guests to try premium brands of alcohol. For example, when a customer requests a scotch and water, a server can suggest a premium brand which may prompt the guest to choose a drink that costs 25 to 50 cents more.

In all cases, a mature and careful approach should be taken when serving alcohol. The Educational Institute publishes an excellent training resource and produces a complementary video program which suggest guidelines on how servers may properly serve and monitor alcohol consumption. *Serving Alcohol with Care* is designed for both managers and servers and can be helpful in providing useful information which can make alcoholic beverage service a pleasurable experience for guests and staff.[10]

Wine Service. Guests today are tending to drink less so they may be inclined to be more selective about what they drink. This lends servers the opportunity to encourage guests to take an interest in the wine they order and to suggestively sell more expensive brands. Therefore, while the average guest check may turn out to be the same or greater, the amount of alcohol consumed per guest should actually be less with this type of approach.

Hotel managers may wish to consider upgrading the quality of their wine, beer, and spirits in light of this trend. With the advent of wine-dispensing machines, wines can be served by the glass and bottles can be kept open for up to one month. Guests dining alone or bar patrons who cannot afford to buy a $200 bottle of wine can now splurge on a $15 glass.

Wine and food festivals are another option to consider in the promotion of food and beverage sales. Examples of current festivals include the two-day Colony Spring Wine Fair at the Colony Beach & Tennis Resort in Longboat Key, Florida; the three-day Wines of America Festival at Harrah's Marina Hotel Casino in Atlantic City; and the three-day California Wine Lovers' Fest Weekend at the Hyatt Regency in Woodfield, Illinois.

Guestroom Service. Some hotels look to the guestroom as a source of beverage revenue by installing in-room refrigerators and mini-bars. In this approach, a hotel staff person checks the room daily and charges guests for the amount of alcohol consumed. Generally, bars are stocked with premium brands and wines as guests usually are not interested in the inexpensive wines, beers, or liquors they can purchase at their local liquor store.

Hotel managers should understand that hotel restaurants are competing against other restaurants in their areas that may be marketed aggressively. Recognizing this fact, hoteliers should start to think about strategically marketing and positioning their own food and beverage outlets. Market research can help to determine what type of food service concept will fit into a community and can include a tour of competitive establishments as well as an informal polling of consumers. By fitting all these techniques and information together, a hotel can usually develop and market a successful restaurant that works in the competitive mix.

In recent years marketing plans have advanced rapidly from what was accepted as state-of-the-art just a few years ago. As hotel managers and marketing executives learn to make better use of their computer-based data, the quality of marketing plans will continue to improve. The sophisticated pinpointing of marketing plans will increase, just as market segmentation has in the last few years. Because many hotels will vastly improve their marketing planning, competition will most certainly become even keener in the future.

Endnotes

1. Based on a cover story: "Marketing: The New Priority," *Business Week*, Nov. 21, 1983, p. 97.

2. Quote from Theodore Levitt, in *Ad Week Magazine*, Aug. 1983, p. MR 13.

3. *Uniform System of Accounts for Hotels*, 8th rev. ed. (New York: Hotel Association of New York City, Inc., 1986). Smaller properties may find similar help in *Uniform System of Accounts and Expense Dictionary for Small Hotels, Motels and Motor Hotels*, 4th ed. (East Lansing, Mich.: Educational Institute of the American Hotel & Motel Association, 1987).

4. Brian McCallen, "The Registry Hotel Corporation: An Expanding Group of Luxury Hotels," *Hotel & Resort Industry*, February 1985, p. 18.

5. Ibid, p. 17.

6. *Hotel & Resort Industry*, September 1985, p. 22.

7. Henry Silverman, Chairman and Chief Executive Officer, Days Inns of America, Inc. From a presentation to Economy Lodging Conference sponsored by Laventhol & Horwath, Chicago, Illinois, September 9, 1985.

8. Bjorn Hanson, "Hotel Food Service: Where's the Profit?" *Cornell Hotel & Restaurant Administration Quarterly*, August 1984, p. 94.

9. Dennis Lombardi and Richard Conti, "The Turnaround in Lodging Foodservice," *Lodging Hospitality*, May 1985, p. 43.

10. Van V. Heffner, *Serving Alcohol with Care* (East Lansing, Mich.: Educational Institute of the American Hotel and Motel Association, 1985). Readers who desire more detailed information on this low-cost alcohol awareness training program are encouraged to write the Educational Institute of AH&MA. A videotape component which complements this training program for owners, operators, and employees of the hospitality industry is also available.

Supplemental Reading ————————————————————

Developing a Balanced Market Mix

by Bill Parr, CHSE

Today's hotel executives face strong competition and ever-changing markets. New hotels and motels on both ends of the economic scale seem to force specialization. Shifting population patterns brought on by high unemployment and high energy costs have caused a decrease in the market for individual leisure travel, vacationers, and IT/FIT customers, creating high competition for group business.

Full service hotels have difficulty maintaining occupancy and average daily rate goals. If your marketing efforts have been geared primarily toward the convention industry, you already know that the average number of delegates per meeting in 1983 is projected to be 545 delegates compared to 725 two years earlier.[1] Corporate meetings, including sales meetings, annual meetings, training meetings, retreats, and new product showings, have declined in the last two years.

Whether you are in an area of declining population and business closures or in a fast growth area with an abundance of new hotels, you are dealing with essentially the same problem—an unstable marketplace.

The key to improving a disappointing financial statement is greater efficiency in marketing segmentation. "Every hotel cannot design itself to fit precisely the desire and needs of every possible market, but every hotel must design itself to please and satisfy the needs and desires of its principal markets," according to C. DeWitt Coffman in *Marketing for a Full House*.[2] This statement is as true today as it was when first written in 1972. It does not mean we should not make a strong effort to seek out new customers in areas previously thought to be out of reach. Sig Front has written that, "If you place too much emphasis on any one portion of the potential marketing mix of a hotel, it could be a mistake."[3] When you note your occupancy decreasing because delegate attendance at conventions has decreased and corporations have reduced their number of annual meetings, yet you find other hotels with little dependence on such business doing well, you should realize your marketing plan lacks balance. To reach your potential in today's business climate, you must develop a sophisticated plan of action in many market segments.

The purpose of this article is to review and categorize the variety of potential hotel guests. Midtown, country, suburban, and resort locations can benefit from aggressive and conscientious sales planning in each market segment. By creating a balanced market mix, hotel sales executives can be assured of a larger demand for guest rooms, seven days a week, year-round.

Positioning

Positioning can be stated simply: "The perception of a hotel by its guests, or potential guests, as being different from and better than its competition."[4] What kind of

This article is reprinted with permission from *HSMA Marketing Review,* Winter 1983/1984, pp. 25–30.

hotel image are you projecting? Convention hotel, resort, corporate hotel, expensive hotel? Are you catering to just certain travelers? In order to evaluate your current positioning, answer the following questions:

- What are your current market segment goals and target markets?
- Who are your competitors and what are their market segments?
- What are the best and worst features of your hotel?
- What do people think of your hotel?
- What do your competitors think of your hotel?

Once you understand your position in the marketplace, you can devise a plan for your hotel, creating greater appeal for the specialized guest markets of today. With proper technical support, your hotel can appeal to more types of travelers than you may have previously believed.

Key Market Segments

Listed below are the key market segments making up today's mix of hotel guests:

- Individual business travelers
- Corporate meetings
- Conventions
- Trade shows and expositions
- Tour groups
- Tourists/visitors/vacationers
- Government agencies and military personnel
- Incentive groups
- Sports groups
- Crowds attending special events
- IT/FIT and in-house packages

Keep in mind your hotel's limitations—size and location. The market segments will be analyzed, and suggestions will be made to help maximize the percentage of each segment available to you.

Individual Business Travelers

Most hotels and motor hotels consider themselves "commercial," i.e., the bulk of their business is the traveling businessperson. What are the members of this large segment looking for in a hotel? According to *Lodging Magazine*, in a recent survey,[5] location was the factor most often mentioned. Therefore, proximity to area business firms, hospitals, schools and universities, government offices, association headquarters, clubs, and unions becomes very important. As almost everyone has heard, E.M. Statler stated many years ago that he believed the three most important considerations for selecting a hotel were location, location, and location. Given that your hotel's location is nonnegotiable, you must develop a plan to capitalize on that location. You could develop a plan as a secondary optional hotel when primary location hotels are not available to business travelers. Having an opportunity to please guests on a referral basis, as an optional hotel, may create a new loyal customer—and loyal customers are, after all, our biggest source of revenue, no matter what segment they fall into.

It is interesting to note that in the same *Lodging Magazine* survey,[6] only 35 percent of those surveyed answered "yes" to the question: "Are you finding it easy, today, to get the kind of accommodations you want?" That response explains why today's most aggressive hotel companies, independents and chain affiliates, are creating clubs for their best and most frequent travelers. The benefits of joining such a club range from discounted room rates to fully stocked private bars in guest rooms, with round-the-clock maid and butler service. With proper research of guest needs and expansion of personalized services within any given hotel, such a club can be established and offered first to regular guests. If the club proves successful, an extensive advertising and direct mail campaign can be developed.

Corporate Meetings

Corporate meetings now produce more revenue for the hotel industry than conventions produce. That should not be too surprising when you consider that almost every company in America has meetings of some kind. They can include board, sales, educational, committee, and new product meetings; retreats; and incentives, which will be dealt with separately. The most numerous, by far, are sales meetings. Insurance and automobile companies plan the largest number of meetings and are potential customers for virtually every type of hotel. Variety in hotel selection has a relationship with new products or services. Not every hotel may be a candidate for the president's annual meeting, but there usually are several other meetings with varied attendance and budget requirements.

In terms of developing business, remember that most Americans who work, work for corporations. Many who stay in your hotel as individual business travelers may influence a future meeting site selection.

Unlike association conventions, corporate meetings often are planned on a short-term, as-needed basis—as little as one month in advance. Flexible in-house policies and procedures can influence a hotel's ability to attract short-term corporate business. You should know, too, that according to a 1980 TIME Marketing Services survey, "The importance of a travel agent, corporate travel department, or secretary appears to be minimal, leading to the conclusion that the business traveler should be sold directly." Hotel selections were made by traveler (86 percent), secretary (8.2 percent), travel agent (13 percent), and corporate travel department (6.9 percent).[7]

In another survey, conducted by Moore Diversified Services in 1982, hotel selections were made as follows: traveler (56.5 percent), secretary (17.3 percent), travel agent (16.8 percent), and corporate travel department (9.4 percent).[8] Also in 1982, the *Official Airline Guide* commissioned the Burke Company to survey its subscribers and determined that hotel selections were made by traveler (81 percent), secretary (12 percent), and travel agent (7 percent).[9] The importance of creating a responsive program with your existing individual business travelers and corporate meeting attendees becomes obvious. They are the ones making most decisions for future individual and group business.

Conventions

Much has been written about this segment, which is the most familiar to larger hotel sales department staff members. By far, HSMAI provides more and better information about selling and servicing conventions than any other source. Obviously a hotel must have appropriate meeting and banquet facilities to compete with other hotels. Unlike most corporate meetings, conventions meet on a regularly scheduled basis. "Almost anyone who is interested can find out when big conventions are scheduled through books, periodicals, trade publications, convention bureaus, or word of mouth."[10]

Conventions can have international, national, regional, or state origins. They can involve associations, societies, unions, and other organizations. They almost always commit a future meeting site one to five years in advance. Larger conventions, because they require less readily available larger facilities, must select sites further in advance to ensure quality meeting sites in approved locations. While corporate meeting sites and meeting arrangements generally are left to one individual, conventions usually are planned by a committee. Sometimes the responsibility falls into the hands of an incoming president. And if the organization is large enough, a paid, full-time executive director will handle the arrangements.

In reality, though, most conventions are scheduled and planned by inexperienced people, many of whom have never been involved with meeting planning and are quite vulnerable. Often, one of the greatest selling points a professional hotel salesperson has is the ability to help an inexperienced meeting planner with all of the arrangements.

To describe fully the convention industry in this report is impossible. The purpose here is simply to define this market segment. The three largest markets for conventions in the United States are New York City, Washington, D.C., and Chicago. More than 90 percent of all national associations are headquartered in these three cities. These headquarters advise about future convention plans on a national, regional, and statewide basis. They can provide the names of key decision makers within the associations and generally will give more information about a group than any other source. Because personal selling is the strongest sales tool for convention promotion, a hotel should consider using a sales person on an exclusive basis in this market segment. A convention salesperson should know as many influential people as possible on a local level. Most community leaders are involved in national associations and will heavily influence selection of a hotel site, often on the basis of a relationship with a hotel salesperson.

Trade Shows and Expositions

This segment most often is associated with a larger convention. To solicit this market segment, a hotel requires facilities for the exhibits themselves, in addition to the normal needs of a convention. In many cities non-hotel exhibit facilities draw large numbers of people, and nearby hotels benefit by providing overnight guest accommodations. The location of the hotel again becomes the most important consideration. Check with the housing chairperson associated with either the exposition or the operating body of the exposition facility, to find out how many guest rooms a hotel can provide.

Tour Groups

This segment, also known as bus tours or motor coach tours, can be a part of a well-balanced market mix only if certain considerations are met.

1. Is your hotel located at a tour destination point or en route to one? Overnight stops are made about 200 miles apart.

2. Is your hotel near shopping, entertainment, or other leisure-time activities? Because tour passengers have no personal transportation, this becomes an important consideration.

3. For the tours that arrive by train and plane, proximity becomes a factor. Assistance with ground transportation sometimes can influence a tour operator.

Locating potential business can be as easy as determining which operators use which hotels in a particular area. Tours, unlike conventions or meetings, cannot be drawn to an area that is not a resort destination or that lacks tourist appeal unless the area is an overnight stop en route to such a destination.

Perhaps the best source of information as to the viability of a specific area for tour business is the National Tour Association. Membership entitles the hotel to receive the annual *Motorcoach Tour Manual*. As stated by 1983 President R. Bruce Beckham, "This directory represents one of the most detailed compilations of North American tour operators' programs available today." A similar group is the American Bus Association. Deluxe, semi-deluxe, and economy tour operators have different clientele for different hotels. Finding the correct economic level of tour group for a particular hotel is very much like defining other market segments.

Tourists, Vacationers, Visitors

Perhaps the most broad based of all segments, tourists, vacationers, and visitors can include members of all other market segments at different times—one-time only visits, international travelers—literally everyone who travels. Experts consider this group, more generally called "individual room business," the heart of a hotel, motel, or resort anywhere, regardless of size, location, or facilities. More effort should be put into this area because, without exception, this customer generates the largest amount of revenue per guest room occupied. These people pay "regular" rates for the most part, and they help fill hotels on weekends and holidays and during summer vacation months—traditional times of low business and convention occupancy. Most hotel marketing publications itemize what a hotel operator must do to classify this group as a market segment. Special effort should be made to establish a positive relationship with the American Automobile Association and the American Association of Retired Persons. Both groups represent substantial blocks of leisure travelers.

The current recession and the compression effects of high unemployment have resulted in fewer individual room travelers, and hotel operators no longer can take this market segment for granted.

Government Agencies and Military Personnel

Almost 17 million people work for local, state, and federal government agencies, including the military. Government officials represent 7.6 percent of hotel/motel occupancy in the United States.[11] Per diem allowances vary depending on the area of the country and the level of the individual government official. In some cases, for both individual and group travel, there is no set per diem allowance, but rather an "actual and necessary per diem." While many hotel operators have traditionally viewed this segment as business requiring low rates, that judgment is not entirely true. Many meetings planned by government agencies and divisions of the armed forces work on a contract basis. The total cost of guest rooms, meals, meeting facilities, and support are "packaged" by the hotel. Although in many cases a hotel must offer lower guest room rates to be competitive, the government's ability to pay for support and meeting facilities can put the total expenditure in line with other types of group business.

Finding out about government business in a given area is as easy (or difficult) as picking up a telephone book and contacting department heads in the various agencies in a given location. There are 66 federal agencies and, depending on the area, fewer local and state offices. There is no central meeting planning system or travel office to deal with. On a national level, however, a small group, the Society of Government Meeting Planners, is developing in Washington, D.C. It is worth joining; it is not part of the federal bureaucracy. Remember that government agency meetings generally are short-term bookings that can be handled on a space-available basis. There is no need to hold meeting space at the expense of a more lucrative long-term convention booking.

Individual government business is basically the same as individual business travel. In most cases the hotel must provide a special government rate structure to fit the area's per diem requirements. A hotel's willingness to do this can open a very large market. Individual military guests are always available as hotel guests providing, of course, you are near a military installation and offer reduced rates. If interested, you can plan on regular weekend business year round.

Incentive Groups

Recently two famous western resort hotels did a survey. They determined that most corporate groups who visited the area came for a "business meeting," not an incentive trip—a perfect example of why true figures on the number of "incentive" vs. "business" meetings do not exist.[12] The reason is that companies do not want to lose the tax deduction of a meeting. (All incentives are income to the recipient and are taxable.) Regardless of this point, "incentive travel, unlike some other segments of the travel industry, is definitely on the upswing."[13] Because of the worldwide economic slump, incentive travel planners are turning their attention to domestic destinations.

What is incentive business? It is one way corporations and organizations motivate their employees through a system of rewards. Those awards can include travel to exotic or resort locations, including deluxe accommodations, cash, and other rewards. During the past few years, hotels have aggressively pursued this segment. Even more recently, hotels not previously considered premium incentive destinations have been selected by incentive planners. Companies are reducing the funds available for travel. Consequently, more hotels can now operate in this growing market.

Because many companies specialize in creating incentive group travel, it is necessary to develop a list. Contact *Incentive Marketing* in New York City or *Incentive Travel Manager* in Los Angeles to begin. Remember that incentive groups can range from 10 to 1,000 or more. And, because the current recession has brought on budget restrictions, locations not previously considered incentive destinations are now attracting business.

Sports Groups

Chances are that cities large enough to maintain a college or university host visiting basketball, football, baseball, and soccer teams. For larger communities with several institutions of higher learning, the possibilities are endless. For example, a traveling college football team will use about 50 guest rooms for one or two nights, usually over a weekend, and will require extensive catering service. Most hotels need this type of business. Professional teams, such as those in the NFL, the NBA, or major league baseball, generally stay longer and influence friends, fans, and booster clubs to use accommodations and facilities, too. Golf, bowling, and tennis tournaments bring many people to an area.

Literally thousands of travel sports organizations in America seek hotel accommodations at a variety of rate structures. Contacting local sports arenas, stadiums, and college and university sports departments to obtain copies of future schedules is the best way to begin a sales program in this market segment. Most sports groups return annually, increasing their value substantially in future years.

Crowds Attending Special Events

Many communities host annual rodeos, music festivals, and religious events that fill up stadiums, as well as visits by international celebrities, auto races, and other such activities. They all require large blocks of guest rooms at nondiscount rates. The Super Bowl and the World Series are two examples of high demand for accommodations, and guest rooms generally are sold at premium rates. The Summer Olympics is another event that creates a supply and demand problem. Such events are an important opportunity to establish high average daily rates. Remember, rate structures that exceed advertised levels are unethical and illegal in some states. Operationally, your reservation department should be aware of such activities at least one year in advance to ensure a minimum of discounting.

IT/FIT's and In-house Packages

The number of inclusive tours (IT) and foreign inclusive tours (FIT) has decreased over the past 18 months because of the worldwide recession and its effect on consumer leisure spending. Most airlines, many travel agents, national and international wholesale tour operators, and hotel companies are actively marketing "package" tours to consumers. Resort and traditional tourist destinations benefit more than other locations. Any hotel, however, can develop a package that might include two nights of lodging at a special rate, breakfast or dinner, optional car rental, and admission to local attractions. The package can be sold directly to the consumer through advertising and direct mail, or it can be distributed to retail travel agents on a regional or national basis and be sold to the consumer through their efforts. Similarly, a package including air fare can be created in conjunction with an airline and sold through the airline's reservation system as well as by travel agents. Keep in mind that travel agents receive hundreds of such packages from hotels, airlines, and wholesale tour operators, decreasing individual visibility. Travel agents have more opportunity to sell such packages, but 50 or more may be available in many major cities. Many hotels have found that they get the best results from a combination of direct selling to the consumer and regional distribution of package information to travel agents with whom they enjoy a professional relationship.

Another growth market is the domestic or international wholesale tour operator. Such companies put together interesting activities of a community, generally including ground transportation and air fare, and seek out hotels on three economic levels—deluxe, semi-deluxe, and economy. Wholesale operators sell their finished product to consumers through brochures distributed by travel agents. Major airlines operate their packages the same way, except that they have the added benefit of their own sales and reservation agents.

Many consumers would not be motivated to travel without the inclusive and foreign inclusive tours. These tours provide an opportunity to control spending, and the most popular attractions in a specific area either are included or offered as an optional expense. Tours are another way for hotels to fill guest rooms, most often over weekends and holidays and during summer months.

Conclusion

Active involvement in all available market segments for a specific area allows a hotel operator to create more demand for guest rooms. During high occupancy periods, the option to be selective exists. By carefully evaluating each segment at such times, the highest possible average daily rate can be established. When a hotel operator controls the type of guest, in-house food and beverage outlets can be balanced with meeting and banquet rooms. And, during low occupancy periods, more guest rooms can be sold to more guests because of a larger variety of market segments and guest room rates, as outlined in a hotel's marketing goals.

Remember, too, that active involvement in all markets exposes a hotel and its sales and marketing people to more travel industry leaders, presenting a greater opportunity for referral business than a narrower marketing plan.

Regardless of the level of occupancy achieved in a hotel, if future goals include maximizing a hotel's ability to serve more guests, then creating a selling plan in all market segments will prove worthwhile. Creating more demand for your product and services presents the ultimate opportunity to manage a hotel successfully.

Supplemental Reading Notes

1. International Association of Convention & Visitors Bureaus, 1983.

2. C. DeWitt Coffman, *Marketing for a Full House*, Ithaca, New York: Cornell University, 1972, p. 46.
3. Sig Front, *HSMA Marketing Review*, Summer 1982, p. 3.
4. George B. Frank, *HSMA Marketing Review*, Summer 1982, p. 8.
5. C. DeWitt Coffman, *Hospitality for Sale*, The Educational Institute of the American Hotel & Motel Association, 1980, p. 220.
6. Ibid.
7. TIME Marketing Services, *Guest Survey*, 1980.
8. Moore Diversified Services, *Rodeway Inns Survey*, 1982.
9. The Burke Company, *Official Airline Guide Survey*, 1982.
10. B.Y. Auger, *How to Find Better Business Meeting Places*, St. Paul, Minn.: Business Service Press, 1966, p. 13.
11. Jay Stencil, *HSMA Marketing Review*, Summer 1982, p. 25.
12. Connie Goldstein, *Corporate Meetings and Incentives Magazine*, May 1983, p. 4.
13. Lauren Yankus, *Hotel and Resort Industry*, April 1983, p. 21.

Bibliography

Coffman, C. DeWitt, *Hospitality for Sale*. East Lansing, MI: The Educational Institute of the American Hotel & Motel Association, 1980.

Coffman, C. DeWitt, *Marketing for a Full House*. Ithaca, NY: Cornell University, 1972.

Blomstrom, Robert L., ed., *Strategic Marketing Planning in the Hospitality Industry*. The Educational Institute of the American Hotel & Motel Association, 1983.

Hotel & Motel Management Magazine, May 1983.

Hotel & Resort Industry, April 1983.

HSMA Marketing Review, Autumn 1982.

HSMA Marketing Review, Spring 1983.

HSMA Marketing Review, Winter 1982–83.

Incentive Marketing Magazine, May 1983.

Jones, James E., *Meeting Planners International Travel Arrangements*, 1981.

Lodging Magazine, 1980 subscriber survey.

1983 National Tour Association Tour Manual, Lexington, KY, 1983.

How to Develop a Positioning Strategy on a Small Restaurant's Budget

by Roy W. MacNaughton

The small restaurant operator's market research and analysis lay the groundwork for a marketing plan that effectively sets the operation apart from other restaurants large and small.

This article was originally published in the February 1981 issue of *The Cornell Hotel and Restaurant Administration Quarterly*, and is reprinted here with the permission of the Cornell University School Hotel Administration. ©1981.

Roy W. MacNaughton is president of Hospitality Marketing, a consulting firm specializing in the international hospitality industry. A graduate in hotel, restaurant, and tourism administration from Ryerson Polytechnical Institute in Toronto, he received his M.B.A. from the University of Western Ontario.

Restaurateurs have begun to recognize the importance of positioning to success in the marketplace, but the independent operator—who generally lacks the time, expertise, and budget to develop a positioning strategy for his single outlet or small chain—is at a disadvantage when competing against large chain organizations with marketing departments capable of performing the analysis internally. The present article will help the independent food-service operator develop a positioning strategy for his firm.

The sequence of steps forming the marketing process is depicted in Exhibit 1. Although the discussion to follow centers on market segmentation (Step 3) and the development of a positioning strategy (Step 4), a brief discussion of marketing research is appropriate because the independent operator must systematically collect data to describe the essential attributes of his clientele: who they are, their food-away-from-home patterns, what they seek in a restaurant, and how they arrive at the operation.

Numerous sophisticated survey and analytical techniques are used by market researchers to answer these questions with a high degree of reliability, but the independent operator with limited financial resources must rely on less complex methods of market research. Nevertheless, he should not conclude that his data are necessarily less valuable for being obtained at a modest cost; if carefully gathered and objectively analyzed, the operator's in-house data can prove very useful in developing an accurate view of the firm's environment.

Basic market research might take the form of an in-house contest in which patrons are asked to complete entry forms with their names, addresses, and zip codes, thus permitting the operator to plot his customers' residences on an area map—and perhaps to use the information as a ready-made mail list when announcing special events. Informal after-meal interviews with randomly selected patrons can yield important information on such matters as their menu preferences, patronage habits, and basic demographics. Equipment currently available allows patrons to answer these and similar questions by punching their responses into a minicomputer placed near the cashier's stand or in the restaurant's lobby. These devices permit the operator to survey a large number of respondents cost-efficiently without compromising the objectivity of their responses—a potential problem when data are gathered through personal interviews.

Many data whose application has traditionally been limited to accounting and control functions—including sales by shifts, sales to labor-cost ratios, product mix, and average check—may also constitute valuable marketing information. Today's electronic cash registers make accurate and timely data of this type available to the operator at an extremely reasonable cost.

Finally, marketing research must include a survey of the operator's competition. It is especially important that this review be conducted and interpreted with objectivity; absent a realistic view of the marketplace, the operator cannot develop an effective segmentation strategy.

Exhibit 1   The Marketing Process

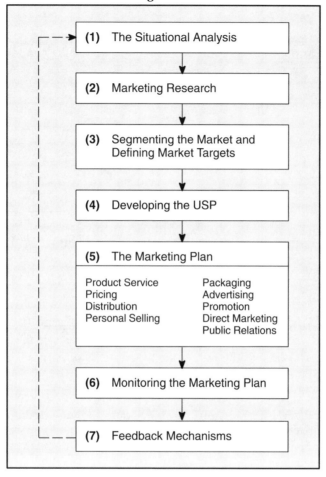

Market Segmentation

Market-segmentation strategies are based on the premise that all prospects are different, but not so different that they cannot be usefully classified into relatively homogeneous groups. Although it is possible to segment markets along psychographic dimensions (e.g., attitudes, opinions, preferences), it is more common to categorize prospects by such demographic variables as age, income, sex, education, ethnic background, marital status, and so forth. Segments of consumers residing or working in the overall trading area and described according to these variables can be isolated. Thus, instead of attempting to be all things to all people, the astute marketer can target his marketing efforts to distinct subsegments where consumer needs remain unfulfilled.

The operator can refine his definition of market segments by matching demographic variables to consumer preferences and behaviors. The matrix shown in

Exhibit 2   Market-Segmentation Matrix

Demographics	Food Product Types (e.g., chicken, burgers, pizza, Mexican food)	Group Composition (singles, couples, groups of people)	Eating Occasion (breakfast, lunch, dinner, special occasion)	Price Variations (average lunch or dinner check)	Convenience Variations (eat-in, take-out, drive-through)	Environmental Variations (theme restaurant versus family restaurant)
Age						
Sex						
Marital status						
Income						
Occupation						
Education						
Ethnic background						
Address						
Number of children						

Exhibit 2 suggests some of the numerous descriptions of patronage patterns that can be arrayed against demographic variables to help the operator develop a systematic description of market subsegments.

How it works. Based on research using mailed questionnaires (respondents' cooperation was enhanced by the use of a coupon offering them a free drink on their next visit) and personal interviews on the premises, an independent restaurateur found that 40 percent of his customers frequented his operation on pleasure occasions. In contrast to these patrons, who visited the restaurant primarily on weekends, more than 50 percent of the remaining traffic represented diners conducting business over lunch during the week. A review of the operation's accounting information revealed a well-known law at work: the smaller pleasure-oriented segment provided most of the restaurant's gross profits, while the larger business-lunch segment contributed only 20 percent of the gross profits.

Armed with this information, the restaurateur took action to increase the size of his more profitable segment—in this case, a drive-time radio campaign emphasizing his operation's appeal as an elegant dinner house. Simultaneously, he restructured his luncheon menu to reduce the number of labor-intensive items, and—because he reasoned that his luncheon patrons were on expense accounts and therefore somewhat price-insensitive—raised his menu prices. As a result of this strategy, the restaurateur increased the contribution margin from his lunchtime segment and, more important, experienced 50-percent growth in his more profitable dinner market.

Segmentation Guidelines

There are three major criteria for choosing a potentially profitable market segment. First, the segment must be of sufficient size to warrant the expenditure required to exploit that segment. Second, the operation must have the physical capacity to service the demand the restaurateur expects to create for the outlet. Last, it must be economically feasible to reach the chosen segment using media currently available. If the costs to reach a specific segment are prohibitive, further analysis may uncover another segment that can be reached cost-efficiently.

The USP

Having identified his target markets, the operator can position his outlet to appeal to those patrons most likely to respond to the image he has chosen to project. Although advertising is a critical component of any positioning statement, it is not, as many practitioners seem to think, the sole means of communicating an operation's attributes to consumers. An operation's *unique selling proposition*, or USP, comprises all the elements—price, style of service, quality standards, cleanliness, and so forth—that differentiate the operation from its competitors.

"USP" is perhaps the most celebrated set of initials in the marketing and advertising business. The concept is also one of the most imitated and most misunderstood. A USP is *not* puffery, a blind advertising headline, a closing line that fails to sum up the benefits of the service, or a clever statement designed to attract attention without explaining the attributes of the service or the restaurant. Especially today, when the restaurant industry is awash with many comparable offerings, the astute food-service operator must distinguish what he has to sell from what all the others are selling. Therefore, each element of the marketing mix and each advertisement must answer this basic consumer question: "Why should I patronize this restaurant rather than others?"

The development of a unique and relevant positioning strategy demands a great deal of logical and creative thought. To prepare a preemptive and effective marketing plan, the operator must ask himself a single question each time he contemplates employing a specific tactic in his overall marketing strategy: "Is what I am about to do consistent with my positioning strategy?" Moreover, he must ensure that all elements of the plan are consistent and feasible. The road to ruin is amply populated with food-service companies whose managements attempted to establish a preemptive position but failed to execute all the components of their marketing plan. Many of these restaurateurs ignored the basic rule—deliver on the promises made. The food-service industry is unlike the manufacturing industries in that the delivery of the dining experience occurs at essentially the same time as the production of goods the consumer purchases. It is therefore critical that the operator scrutinize the operational aspects of his marketing plan to ensure that his outlets can consistently deliver the goods, service, and ambience commensurate with his positioning.

Harvey's: An Illustration

Although McDonald's maintains a huge lead in number of stores and total sales volume, Harvey's, a 110-unit Canadian chain that predated the American giant's arrival, continues to operate extremely profitably. Harvey's has positioned itself to appeal to the market segment seeking an alternative to standardized, prepackaged burgers. The firm's slogan, "Harvey's makes a hamburger a wonderful thing!," distinguishes the product from its mass-produced counterparts—as do the chain's operational procedures, which include charcoal broiling to order and allowing the customer to see his own burger garnished to his specifications. Finally, consistent with the firm's position as offering highly personalized service, the Harvey's unit is smaller than most other chain stores, and its lower cost yields a greater rate of return on the firm's assets.

In Conclusion

For the independent restaurateur, the proper development of a positioning strategy lays the groundwork for an effective marketing plan. Lacking an understanding of his competitive position and a rationale for dealing with it, however, the independent operator is likely to become an endangered species.

REVIEW QUIZ

When you feel you have covered all of the material in this chapter, answer these questions. Choose the *best* answer. Check your answers with the correct ones found on the Review Quiz Answer Key at the end of this book.

True (T) or False (F)

T   F   1. A carefully selected market mix renders sales efforts productive and results in overlapping demand for the same time periods.

T   F   2. Written marketing plans are not particularly efficient for small hotels or motels with limited staffs.

T   F   3. In the marketing planning process, the success or failure of the current pricing system should be evaluated, market segment by market segment.

T   F   4. Since the travel industry has such an active press and since its literature is widely read by travel agents, advertising in virtually any travel trade publication will ensure reaching travel agents in a hotel's important source cities.

T   F   5. The most important requirement of any key account coverage program is that it give salespersons a clear picture of what their tasks are and where those tasks fit into the overall business of operating the hotel.

T   F   6. Channels of distribution for the hospitality industry seldom change over time.

T   F   7. Marketers of consumer-oriented products or services should attempt to reach the mass market with a single product or service.

T   F   8. It is only necessary to develop a single action plan for all food and beverage outlets in a hotel.

T   F   9. Tapping the corporate market is relatively easy because corporate business comes from limited sources.

Multiple Choice

10. Key account coverage programs are useful because:

    a. they increase the efficiency of the sales staff.
    b. they help to identify and to correct any inadequate coverage of exiting markets.
    c. they provide a method for establishing better quotas and for tracking the performance of the field sales team.
    d. all of the above.

11.   Any marketing plan for a hotel should be reviewed by the owners and senior management staff because:

   a. previously approved priorities will make it easier for the marketing program to later obtain necessary funds from management.
   b. such a review can help create a team spirit throughout the hotel staff.
   c. such support ensures that affected staff members will be held accountable for carrying out the marketing plan.
   d. all of the above.

Chapter Outline

Before Construction Begins
Construction Commences—Countdown:
    24 Months to Opening
Construction Continues—Countdown:
    18 to 6 Months Prior to Opening
Construction Almost Completed—
    Countdown: 6 Months to Opening
The Soft Opening—You Are Open (but
    Quietly)
Official Opening
The Hotel's Marketing Future

Learning Objectives

1. Identify the crucial features in the
   pre-construction phase of a new hotel.

2. Identify the crucial features in the
   construction phase of a new hotel.

3. Explain the activities of the hotel staff
   during the "soft opening."

4. Identify the crucial features in the
   official opening of a new hotel.

Pre-Opening Hotel Marketing

T̶HE BEST WAY to see how the careful application of marketing principles can assist a hotel is to examine the pre-opening marketing of an emerging property. This chapter traces the development of a hypothetical hotel's marketing program from the initial feasibility study to the actual opening and beyond. Unfolding the step-by-step process of pre-opening hotel marketing will serve as an overview of many marketing applications.

> ❝Opryland is a fabulously successful convention hotel today, but the key to its success was the tremendously well-planned and well-executed pre-opening marketing period. Under Jack Vaughn's direction, we were able to put together a sound strategic plan and an effective team and [with these we] took a previously unknown convention destination and turned it into one of America's favorites.❞
>
> **—Mike Dimond**
> Vice President of Marketing
> Opryland Hotel

Opening a hotel is never easy, and marketing a hotel during its pre-opening phase is nearly always critical to the hotel's early success.

> ❝The most important element in the pre-opening marketing planning process is the development of a critical path. Simply stated, a critical path is a road map identifying what actions must be taken, by whom, and on what specific dates for the pre-opening marketing activities of a new hotel to be successful. There are hundreds of action steps that make up this critical path. They can be broken down into two general areas ... administration and marketing activities.... The administrative area includes activities such as:

- identifying and leasing office space
- hiring staff
- [getting] telephones installed
- acquiring office equipment (typewriters, computers, postal meters, etc.)
- [developing] room control books
- [setting up] function books
- [ordering] forms

The major action steps included in [the marketing] area are:

- developing the pre-opening plan
- developing the first year's revenues

- interviewing and appointing advertising and public relations agencies
- developing and assigning group room booking quotas and responsibilities

The development of the critical path is a tedious and arduous process but one that is absolutely necessary. It sets the direction and establishes the responsibility for the development of a successful marketing plan for a pre-opening hotel. **"**

—**William Hanley**
Vice President—Marketing
Radisson Hotels

The manager opening a new hotel faces enormous pressure due, in large part, to the tremendous (and sometimes conflicting) demands placed on his or her time. Nevertheless, opening a hotel can be extremely exciting, and when done successfully it may greatly benefit a manager's career.

"When we opened the Mauna Kea Beach Hotel in 1965, I said I would never open another hotel again. [Later] when I [saw] how important the marketing and execution of that first opening was and the instant fame and success [which resulted], I knew it was one of the most important contributions to the success of that hotel and would reap dividends for at least a decade to come. I am now on my fifth opening. It is a complete science unto itself and so often neglected. **"**

—**Richard Erb**
Chief Operating Officer
Grand Traverse Resort Village

Before Construction Begins

The involvement of a hotel company in the opening of a new construction project usually begins when a developer decides that a hotel might be an appropriate part of the initial conception of a particular construction project. The developer normally presents the project proposal to a financial institution in order to obtain a loan. At the same time, the developer contacts one or more hotel companies and describes the type of hotel being considered and its proposed location. If one of the hotel companies is interested in operating a hotel of this type in the proposed location, then a preliminary agreement is made to work together on the project, assuming it can be funded. Normally, to get a loan, a feasibility study must be done by one of the major accounting firms. Even though this work is an independent appraisal of the future prospects of the project, if a hotel operator has been designated when the field work begins, then the hotel operator participates in this preliminary investigative stage.

However, once the feasibility study has been completed, the operating company's involvement increases dramatically. After reviewing the feasibility study, the developer, the lending institution, and the hotel operator confer. At this point they must redefine their separate objectives and find a way to synthesize their revised goals into a single plan which satisfies all concerned. After this negotiation process, the resulting project plans may be significantly different from what the developer had originally conceived.

For example, the developer decides to build a luxury hotel at a particular site and contacts an interested hotel company. Together, they envision a property with average rates significantly above those normally achieved by other hotels in areas surrounding the proposed site. However, the feasibility study indicates that a luxury hotel in that location has little likelihood of being economically successful. This, of course, makes it highly unlikely that the financial institution will agree to lend the developer the funds necessary to build a luxury hotel. Therefore, the remaining options are to abandon the project altogether (this frequently happens), or to continue with the project but in a form vastly different from that originally considered. In the latter case, the new project would most likely be a far more modestly designed hotel with a larger number of guestrooms. This revised plan would keep the per-room cost of construction down, so the per-room rate required to make a profit would also be lower.

For the purposes of this chapter, let us consider a hypothetical case in which the developer, the hotel operator, the feasibility company, and the lender all agree that the project should be a 600-room hotel in the center of a new multi-building development. As approved by the four parties of the project, the hotel will include retail shops and apartments, plus a significant amount of function space. Because the hotel is in the capital city of a small state, it is likely to attract conventions at state and regional levels, and there is some potential at the national level also.

Let us further assume that you have been appointed general manager by the hotel operating company. While the hotel will begin operating in approximately 24 months, your job as general manager starts immediately. Your company would like your pre-opening marketing and the construction schedule to coincide.[1]

To help you in your new role, you are given the results of all of the preliminary work done by the four planning parties. You receive a pro forma financial statement, which makes rate and occupancy assumptions for the first ten years of operations. You also receive a pre-opening budget, some blueprints, and a written description of the character and features your hotel will have. Now it is up to you to apply everything you have learned about the elements of marketing as you carefully select your market mix, and then develop your marketing mix.

Construction Commences—Countdown: 24 Months to Opening

Your administration and marketing activities commence as construction of the hotel begins. You must carry out two administrative tasks early on. The first is finding office space that is not only adequate for your immediate space requirements, but also large enough to accommodate a growing staff as the project progresses. The second task is selecting the first members of your staff. These would include not only secretaries, but also sales managers—particularly those managers whose market segments will require the longest lead time (e.g., trade associations). With these tasks out of the way, you can now concentrate on creative marketing.

First of all, a marketing budget will have to be prepared. Most likely, the pro forma financial statement you were given earlier contains preliminary indications of the total marketing budget for the pre-opening period. By now you should have received preliminary figures of the anticipated marketing overheads for each of the first several years of operation. Your first challenge is to fine-tune the pre-opening budget by properly allocating the available funds for specific marketing tasks. At this point it is essential to remember that the target date of opening is approximate and, like many other hotels, it may take you longer to open than you initially anticipate. Therefore, it is crucial that you allocate monies for marketing expenses in such a way that sufficient funds are left for those many steps you will surely need to take when the hotel is just about to open. Bear in mind that the timely (or untimely) expenditure of pre-opening marketing budgets often largely determines the success (or failure) of hotels in their early years.

Once the specifics of the budget are determined, the actual marketing activities begin. Your first step must be to determine what the hotel will be and which publics it will serve. This is an absolute prerequisite for all the activities which follow, and it must represent the views of all parties involved in the hotel's marketing decisions. If there is any disagreement during this phase, a consensus must somehow be reached before any of the other marketing actions begin.

After determining your publics, several steps follow at once. First, your hotel's mission statement should be written. Second, an appropriate taste level for all of your promotions, press releases, and publicity-seeking activities should be selected. Because the mission statement and taste level determine the market segments toward which the hotel will direct its sales activity, it is imperative that these statements be broadly supported by all key people involved with the project.

Next comes the painstaking process of determining your market mix. Each segment with potential for your hotel must be described, reviewed, and either accepted or rejected. For example, you must consider which transient markets the hotel will serve. Will the hotel be primarily for the individual business traveler? Or will it serve the individual business traveler Monday through Thursday, and then switch to serving the family market on weekends? Your positioning statement and your product largely determine the answers to these questions. Your market research of each segment is crucial to the steps you will take later, so it must be done carefully. For example, if your hotel will serve the individual business traveler, you must find out what source markets this segment of your business will come from. Knowing where your marketing activity should be focused will make you a more effective marketer. You must seek source/origin data wherever it can be found. Resources such as chamber of commerce statistics, mix-of-business reports from other hotels, and arrival and departure patterns at local airports are usually available to most new hotels.

Now consider the group side of your market mix. Carefully consider all of the subsegments of group business that might be attracted to your hotel. Since the hotel has been designed with meeting facilities that would be adequate for conferences, you should look up source/origin data for groups that would be likely to hold meetings in your area. Are you in an area that would primarily attract professional associations (doctors, lawyers, teachers) and organizations from the scientific and medical communities? Or, are you more likely to do business with fraternal and service groups, ethnic associations, religious groups, and labor unions? Even though all of these groups are categorized as associations, each of them requires a separate marketing approach and, therefore, a separate allocation of your marketing dollars.

You can also differentiate among subsegments of the corporate market. Will you be doing business with corporations that come to your destination for meetings, or will business organizations be attracted to your city primarily as an incentive destination? If it is the former, then you are more likely to be booking board meetings, stockholder meetings, executive conferences, and regional or district sales meetings. All of these meetings require smaller function spaces.

If, however, you are primarily dealing with the incentive-oriented market, then the quality of your small meeting space is probably not as important as the creativity with which you assist the company or the incentive movement operator with "fan out" programs. Incentive-oriented groups generally require only one or two gatherings during their stay, and these usually take place in a large function space in the hotel. The incentive-oriented market requires that a hotel serve not so much as the center which contains the trip's attraction, but more as a hub that "fans out" to the many attractions offered throughout the entire destination site.

It is not necessary for our hypothetical case to go through each of the market segments, but in actual practice you most certainly should. You must examine the government market, universities and/or colleges, possible tie-ins with local attractions such as sports teams, symphonies, and so forth. Unless the groundwork is laid now with careful early planning, your programs will not be ready when the hotel construction is completed.

During the initial phase of pre-opening hotel marketing, you are, quite naturally, extremely busy. Therefore, you will find it helpful to delegate some marketing tasks. For example, you should select an advertising agency and a public relations firm for your hotel. Some hotels hire a full-time public relations executive as an alternative to a public relations firm; other hotels use both. With their help your hotel can begin to be recognized as a part of the community.

It is extremely important to the success of a new hotel that during its pre-opening period it be identified as a good community member. Toward this end, each executive hired for the pre-opening team should be asked to join particular organizations which take advantage of his or her personal skills and interest areas. These memberships should include but not be limited to groups of hotel professionals, such as HSMAI, AH&MA, and the International Association of Hospitality Accountants (IAHA). Participation in local service organizations contributes to the hotel's public image. Membership in your city or state hotel association, chamber of commerce, convention and visitor's bureau, and service clubs should be arranged at this time.

As your pre-opening staff grows, your administrative responsibilities increase. Now you need to select a phone system and install word processing equipment which will be compatible with the conventional hotel-based computer system. The newly established sales department must set up its sales office procedures and file system. Then the sales staff can begin an orderly solicitation of group and transient business. At this point, their calls are intended to spread the word that the hotel is coming into existence. Additionally, as general manager, you should see that an administrative reporting system, which includes weekly activity reports, a lost business log, a call report form, and a method of recording tentative and indefinite business, is developed by or with the sales department.

Also, it is not too early to begin preparing and placing advertising aimed at market segments that require the most lead time. For example, if you are going to try to reach trade associations, they generally select host cities many years in advance of their conventions.

Construction Continues—Countdown: 18 to 6 Months Prior to Opening

During the second phase of your pre-opening marketing—a period of about one year—the pace of marketing activities at your hotel accelerates. Now a more detailed schedule of specific marketing steps must be prepared. Job descriptions, quotas, and sales action plans must be put in writing for each new salesperson added to the pre-opening team.

This is a good time to take another look at the market mix you have been attempting to reach. Has your selection of segments proved to be successful? With your first six months of activities now ended, do you have as much long-term business on the books as you anticipated? If not, then you will obviously need to shift emphasis and work harder to reach your short-term markets. That is, you will now have to focus on segments that book from 18 months to 6 months in advance rather than on those segments that book further ahead. On the other hand, if you have as much long-term business as you anticipated, you can stay with your original market mix.

As construction continues and more accurate projections are possible, your advertising begins to include more date-specific information. Now your sales staff's travel schedule noticeably increases. Their sales trips are aimed at booking tentative, indefinite business.

During this second phase, you and your key subordinates ought to plan and implement promotions geared to the various publics which the hotel will serve. For example, you can schedule parties for the executives of major firms located in your area. This should help you develop business from the corporate market. Similarly, parties for local executives of major trade associations may help these officials influence their out-of-town colleagues to perceive your new hotel in a positive light.

You should begin the planning of the local corporate program as soon as possible. You need attractive and informative collateral material for distribution to executives and secretaries of the firms in your community. At the same time, you want to develop a list of the out-of-town firms with which each local firm does business in order to direct copies of your collateral material to them also.

Now you should establish a critical path countdown to opening for all marketing activities. Also the booking quotas (see Exhibit 1) established for each salesperson should be fine-tuned so that you can match them up with your backlog objectives. The backlog itself (see Exhibit 2) needs to include date-specific information so that you and the others responsible for budget planning can get a better picture of your hotel's financial future.

Having fine-tuned your probable market segments for transient and group business, you should also examine the file loads and key account lists for each

Exhibit 1   Sample Booking Quota Sheets

QUOTAS												

Individual Room Night Quotas

SALESPERSON	JAN	FEB	MAR	APR	MAY	JUN	JUL	AUG	SEPT	OCT	NOV	DEC	TOTAL

Weekly Call Quotas

SALESPERSON	PERSONAL	TELEPHONE	ENTERTAIN.
TOTAL TEAM			
TOTAL TEAM			

TOTAL TEAM

salesperson to make sure there is a good match. For example, if you anticipate a significant amount of business from the motor coach market, you ought to encourage one of your marketing executives to get actively involved with the American Bus Association (ABA) and the National Tour Association (NTA). This person should build an active prospect list of coach operators right now because they normally book business 18 to 6 months in advance. This would exactly coincide with your hotel's opening.

At this time it is also a good idea to review your internal administrative system. Make sure that your reporting procedures and tracking systems are appropriate to your needs.

A major task to accomplish during this second phase is a review of the hotel's signs and internal merchandising program. How will the guests in the building know how to get from where they are to where you would like them to be? What enticements will you use to bring them to the food and beverage outlets that will be so important to your profitability? Communicating what your hotel has to offer is necessary for productive sales results. If you postpone your review of signs and internal merchandising until the hotel is open for business, you will be missing out on sales opportunities.

Exhibit 2   Sample Backlog

ROOM NIGHTS	JAN	FEB	MAR	APR	MAY	JUN	JUL	AUG	SEPT	OCT	NOV	DEC	TOTAL
HOTEL NAME _____ DATE _____				**GROUP ROOM BACKLOG**									
1. Backlog—begin month													
2. Add: definite bookings													
3. SUBTOTAL: add lines 1 + 2													
4. Revaluations/cancellations													
5. TOTAL: used or scheduled to be used													
6. CORPORATE & INDUSTRIAL:													
a. b.													
7. Travel Industry													
8. Government													
9. Union													
10. Association													
a. b.													
11. University													
12. Athletic													
13. Other													
a. b.													
14. TOTAL													
15. OVERALL AVERAGE RATE													
16. % OCCUPANCY													

Construction Almost Completed—Countdown: 6 Months to Opening

During the last several months of pre-opening marketing, your task is to reinforce your staff's total commitment to the marketing of your hotel. As additional department heads are brought on board, you must emphasize that you expect them to manage their departments from a marketing perspective. Also, each department should have a sales action training program. For example, from day one the front office staff should know how to "sell up" (if there is a front office incentive program, they are more likely to do so). Front desk personnel should be alerted to any important guests who are expected and should be aware of any special rate arrangements made for these guests. Because you only get one chance to make a good first impression, it is essential that these sales action training programs be operative **prior to opening**, not six months after opening!

During the last days of this phase, a sales blitz, or sales attack, on the local marketplace must be undertaken. This multiple call activity is most effective when it involves more than just the sales department. A blitz is an excellent way to get all of your department heads involved in promoting and previewing the property. Participants in the pre-opening sales blitz can also gather names of prospects for the hotel's secretaries' club and names of people you may want to invite to your preview parties before the hotel officially opens.

At this critical phase of the operation, you should plan an individual sales program for each outlet of the hotel. Special emphasis should be placed on how the public will know what public the outlet intends to serve. For example, arrangements could be made for the food and beverage manager to do an interview with a local newspaper's food editor. The question of how a new restaurant is developed could be discussed using the hotel's outlet as an actual case in point. This would get the restaurant's name and identity out into the community. Plans should also be made at this time for any advertising or public relations to be done specifically for the outlets.

Your overall marketing of rooms to targeted group and transient segments also becomes much more specific now. Far more attention must be paid to representatives of the local media. Selling to the travel trade and shorter-term markets must be undertaken at this time. If university personnel, government officials, and sports teams are to be included in your market mix, now is the time to market your hotel to them. In fact, they are generally flattered to be invited for a pre-opening tour or other special "insiders" events because these are usually unique experiences for them.

By now your hotel should have amassed a very considerable number of names and addresses of people to whom your specific opening date will be important. Your mailing list should include: (1) people responsible for major social events coming up in the next year; (2) people who have held off booking space for corporate meetings (to be held soon after your grand opening) because your opening date was not yet firm; and (3) people whose responsibilities include arranging accommodations for incoming transient guests. Sequential mailings to these prospects should be undertaken at this time. Your lists of names and addresses may include some that you have purchased, but most should be the product of your hotel's solid program of sales activities during the previous 18 months. In this era of automated information storage and retrieval, computerized mailing lists are much easier to maintain than manual lists as long as the computer program for manipulating them is based from the beginning on a well-conceived plan.

You must plan ahead for an orderly transition of your administrative and sales personnel from their pre-opening location to the hotel offices. Once the transition to the main building is over, it is critical that you establish a reasonable, sensible paper flow between departments, especially between the sales department, the front office, and the food and beverage department. The more automated this paper flow is, the better. However, regardless of what form it takes, the plan for paper flow must be understood, agreed upon, and written down as an operating policy. Unless all parties involved with the plan support it, the plan will fail. Similarly, a program for function book control must be put on paper and followed.

By now you should have an operational convention coordinating department. For extra support, be sure to submit your rates and availabilities to any outside sales agencies involved in selling the property. Also begin attracting the local community's interest by announcing any introductory rate program, coupon promotion, or special club activities that you expect to launch upon opening.

As each month of this final countdown goes by, you should be getting closer to the backlog budget. A review of the backlog budget for group rooms may tell you from which source/origin markets your transient rooms business is to come. Then marketing efforts directed toward each of these source/origin markets can be reviewed. Again, the sales results versus the action plans of each individual salesperson should be scrutinized.

The Soft Opening—You Are Open (but Quietly)

The "soft opening" is when your hotel first begins to receive visitors, but before you announce that it is open to the general public. This is a trial run which allows the hotel to smooth out its operating procedures and measure the premises against the plan with which the property was conceived. Now, despite the other demands on their time, you must accelerate the personal call activity of your sales personnel in the local marketplace. Experience suggests that, although this is probably the most important time for the sales staff to be actively selling in the local community, most sales departments are so distracted by other duties at this time that they do not get on the street at all! For this reason, you may want to consider hiring some temporary employees who can conduct tours of the property and help visitors find their way through the hotel.

Promotions to travel agents, decision-makers for groups, and members of your corporate club are appropriate at this time. Also, during this period any sales representatives or corporate salespeople who represent the property in remote locations should be brought in to inspect the hotel. Because they are "part of the family," they ought to be invited to see the hotel before it is completely ready. Your food and beverage outlets, and your catering operation in particular, should be fine-tuning the sales efforts during this soft opening period.

Official Opening

Immediately following the soft opening, you need to plan the official opening of the hotel. Your marketing efforts must now become even more intense. As the general manager, you have the honor of hosting the grand opening party for people who are (or could be) important to the hotel. Of course, this means the party must be planned, the guest list compiled, and a follow-up program developed to determine which of the people you have invited to the party are actually going to come. The grand opening is a major event—a happening—which should receive media coverage in your area. It is your opportunity to show off what you've worked so hard to present to the public, so make the most of this historic day!

Now that the hotel is officially open, your advertising should shift from a countdown to a focus on specific features and benefits. Examples of some of the Sheraton Kensington's opening and post-opening ads and collateral material

Exhibit 3   Opening and Post-Opening Ads and Collateral Material for the Sheraton Kensington

Courtesy of the Sheraton Kensington Hotel, Tulsa, Oklahoma

appear in Exhibit 3. Your local advertising should also draw attention to your food and beverage outlets. Of course, from a promotional standpoint, you want to bring in newspaper and magazine food editors to shape a positive image of your project in the public mind.

You must also find time in the first 90 days of official operation for a post-opening marketing audit. This is a frank review in writing of what you thought

Exhibit 3 *(continued)*

would happen, what did and didn't happen, and what further needs to be done to address any gaps that remain in your marketing plan. One extremely important part of the marketing audit is an honest appraisal of your staff's attitude toward guests—from the guests' standpoint. Since the purpose of marketing is to meet customer needs, is your entire hotel really as marketing-oriented as it can possibly be? If in some respects it is not, what can you do about it? Your involvement as general manager is absolutely essential to ensure that the hotel maintains its marketing momentum.

Naturally you now need to redo your marketing plan to fit a newly opened hotel. Your sales staff must establish an in-house entertainment schedule. Sales personnel must continue traveling to your external markets in order to continue a strong solicitation effort. Your convention coordinating department must establish pre-convention and post-convention audit procedures. Face-to-face, customer-oriented audit procedures will give a more accurate picture than written questionnaires of how well your hotel is performing with groups.

From the very first day of operation it is important to maintain a guest history on every overnight visitor. In light of today's advanced technology, a computerized guest history system is both logical and necessary. Unfortunately, most hotels that put advance bookings on their calendars have found that the storage capacity of their systems is soon inadequate. In these cases, it is best for the hotel to arrange for time-sharing with an outside computer service company's mainframe computer. An outside service company can take over the task of maintaining some of your marketing management records. By linking your (smaller) hotel computer to an outside computer service company's mainframe computer, it will be possible to both store and retrieve all guest history information.

Because the opening of a hotel is so labor-intensive, it is especially easy at this time for your staff to lose sight of the importance of their continued community involvement. Although the management staff is required to spend many hours together when the hotel first opens, this is precisely the time when a schedule of VIP luncheons for corporation officers, association executives, local travel agencies, local airlines representatives, and your fellow hoteliers in the area is absolutely crucial. These groups are made up of individuals who are very much involved in the future success of your hotel. If your management staff excludes or ignores them at this time, you will pay the price for this lack of attention later.

Although your relations with your various publics are very important, no relationship is any more important than your relationship to the travel industry. Your actions will do more than your words in keeping the flow of business coming from this all-important source. Make sure that your commission payments are timely from the day you open.

The Hotel's Marketing Future

Now that your well-marketed hotel is open and running, you will want to develop a five-year marketing plan for the property. If you are to achieve your projected long-term rate occupancy, it is critical to have a written plan for the next five years. Of course, this should not be a rigid plan, but rather a changing and evolving document. Each year it must be fully updated, and each month it should be altered as necessary to reflect current market conditions.

This chapter has touched on virtually every principle of marketing. Reviewing your own role as the general manager of our hypothetical hotel, you should now see that you have based your planning on good market research and competition research. You have examined the marketplace in which you will compete, selected the various publics you will serve, and determined the positioning statement according to which you will serve them. You have set sales action plans, advertising campaigns, and promotional programs in motion. From two years before opening through 90 days after opening, your steps have been integrated, logical, and well-directed. You have sent sales personnel with proper collateral material about your hotel to external marketplaces, and you have advertised in those external marketplaces. You have reached out to the local community through promotions, advertising, and personal sales calls. You have brought influential local citizens into the property to experience it in a direct and personal way. Finally, your hotel has established a communications flow through direct response to your likely audiences before opening and, through your guest history system, to your previous guests after opening.

Endnotes

1. This is by no means an absolute time frame. Some major convention hotels require a significantly longer pre-opening marketing period as well as a longer construction period; other hotels can be "fast tracked." The process described in this chapter must take place, step by step, but the time allotted for each step can be greatly expanded or contracted, and some can be simultaneous activities. The hypothetical hotel described in this chapter was chosen because the normal pre-opening time frame for such a hotel would allow for a logical flow from one event to the next.

Supplemental Reading ⎯⎯⎯⎯⎯⎯⎯⎯⎯⎯⎯⎯⎯⎯⎯⎯⎯⎯⎯⎯⎯⎯⎯⎯

Pre-Opening Marketing Analysis for Hotels

by Clarence H. Peters

Clarence H. ("Pete") Peters is a manager in the San Francisco office of La-venthol and Horwath. He earned a bachelor's degree from the University of Pittsburgh before taking an M.B.A. in hotel administration at Michigan State's School of Hotel, Restaurant and Institutional Management. Following work in the management of food service operations, Peters joined L&H, where his present areas of specialization include economic feasibility, valuation, and service as a liaison between developers and lending information.

To the uninitiated, identifying and quantifying the market for a proposed lodging facility might appear to be a reasonably straightforward task. Exhibit 1 shows eight major identifiable market segments. Four of those segments appear to be concerned only with seeking shelter en route to a destination, and will probably accept the most convenient product that meets capacity and price requirements. The terminal visitors, who also represent four segments, need shelter, but as an adjunct to the real purpose of the visit that keeps them overnight in the community. Except, perhaps, for the price variable, the market analyst expects these two categories of consumers to consider all products as quite similar, so that it is not necessary to make fine discriminations between the determining factors required for the products' selection. The local resident segment, which is not represented in the diagram, is the only one that actively seeks out the product. Since those customers are primarily interested in food service and entertainment, they are more easily identifiable and quantifiable.

Unfortunately, the above categorizations of the market for lodging facilities are much too simplistic. For instance, only the current transient visitors to the area have been considered. There is another group that must be identified: the potential visitor who may come because of growth, changes in the transportation network, new commercial, industrial, or recreational developments, or even new lodging facilities. Surprising as it may seem, a new hotel in a community regularly visited by commercial travelers can change the travel pattern for a great many people. Add to these complexities another perpetual concern: a hotel is a single-purpose structure requiring a significant capital investment. Unless its design enables it to serve the major available markets, the property's economic performance will suffer. In view of all these interrelated factors, hotelmen and investors realize that pre-opening marketing analysis can be a critical ingredient in determining the ultimate success of a lodging facility.

⎯⎯⎯⎯⎯⎯⎯⎯⎯⎯

Exhibit 1   Factors Influencing Travelers' Selection of Lodging Facilities

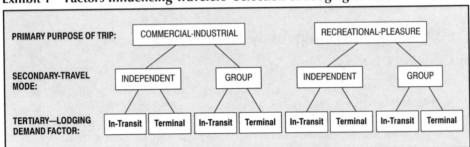

Developed by John D. Lesure, director of research, Laventhol and Horwath, and Peter Yesawich, vice president for marketing research, Robinsons, Inc.

The Community Profile

The first step in quantifying the market for overnight lodging in an area is to identify the essential reason for existence of the community or communities that make up the area. There are two major reasons to perform this step. First, it is necessary to determine the extent to which the location of the community is convenient as a stopover for persons traveling to another destination, and, second, one must identify the attractions that exist or may be developed which make the area a destination. It is important to remember that very few travelers visit a community for the purpose of staying in a hotel. Even when they are on a pleasure trip, the primary product being purchased is recreation: shelter, food, drink, and other commodities may be required, but they are secondary to the purpose of the visit. The analyst must therefore isolate and evaluate the characteristics of the community that help to create the need for overnight accommodations.

Some obvious and standard research techniques are used to obtain preliminary information. Before visiting the community, for example, a good atlas, an almanac, an encyclopedia, and various trade journals—particularly those relating to real estate—should be consulted. Once in the community, the researcher will use observation and personal-interview techniques to obtain the information necessary. Checklists can be very helpful at this stage, and some examples are presented in Exhibits 2 and 3.

The checklist shown in Exhibit 2 is intended primarily as a reminder of likely information sources; it is not necessarily an all-inclusive list of the alternatives available in every urban center. The community profile (Exhibit 3) is used to identify the essential reasons for the existence of the population center. For example, the purpose may be industrial—that is, an urban center that has developed around one or more basic industries reliant on some essential resource. On the other hand, it could be a commercial center that has developed because it is a natural transportation hub for both products and people; or it could be an educational center, containing one or more institutions of higher learning, possibly surrounded by research and scientific organizations or health-care distribution facilities. Some communities owe their existence to recreational attractions, natural or man-made, but most communities are supported by a combination of two or more of the different attribute sets identified above.

Exhibit 2   Checklist of Information Sources

GENERAL INFORMATION
Airport, highway, and port authorities
Building owners and managers' association
Chamber of Commerce
Department of Transportation—city, county, state
Municipal officials
Newspaper publishers

NUMBER OF VISITORS
Convention and visitors bureau
Customs and immigration
Industrial board
Officers of major industrial and commercial companies
Prominent bankers, realtors, attorneys
Transportation companies
Deans of universities and colleges
Administrators of health-care distribution centers
Managers of amusement, recreational, and sports centers

COMPETITIVE SERVICES AND FACILITIES
Local hotel and restaurant associations
Operators of competitive lodging and food service facilities

Exhibit 3   Guidelines for Preparing a Community Profile

DEMOGRAPHICS
1.   Prepare a complete analysis of the trends in population in the area for the past five years.
2.   For the past two years, show how the population breaks down in terms of age, sex, professions or occupations, education, income.

HOUSING
1.   List the type, number of units, and capacity of single-family and multi-family dwellings.
2.   Obtain representative price ranges and occupancy percentages for each type and note trends.
3.   Pinpoint new housing developments and growth areas.

TRANSPORTATION
1.   List types available to the area.
2.   For each type, determine capacity and volume of passengers and freight.
3.   Obtain data on proposed expansion, if any, from reliable sources.

INDUSTRIAL AND COMMERCIAL ACTIVITY
1.   Prepare a list of major employers by type of activity, employment, and value of activity.
2.   Determine plans for expansion of existing facilities and potential for new developments.
3.   List the source and volume of visitors.

HEALTH AND EDUCATION
1.   List the major health and educational institutions by type, capacity, and volume of activity.
2.   Obtain information on expansion plans from authoritative sources.

RECREATIONAL
1.   List the amusement, recreational, and sports facilities that attract visitors from outside the community.
2.   Obtain information on source, volume, and seasonality of use.
3.   Obtain information on expansion plans, if any.

UNUSUAL AREA ACTIVITIES
1.   List all special events of a recurring nature that attract visitors.
2.   Obtain data on volume.

Exhibit 4   Number of Rooms per 1,000 Population*

COMMERCIAL-INDUSTRIAL		RECREATIONAL-PLEASURE	
Chicago	8	Atlantic City	69
Cleveland	6	Daytona Beach	71
Los Angeles	7	Honolulu	35
New York	6	Las Vegas	75
Philadelphia	5	Miami	40
Pittsburgh	6	Orlando	36

*Hotel, motor-hotel, and tourist-court rooms in selected standard metropolitan statistical areas in 1972.

Source: 1972 Census of Business; 1970 Census of Population.

Physical Size and Scope

The size and scope of the market seeking accommodations in a community may range from local to national. Las Vegas, for example, is generally recognized as one of the primary recreation destinations in the United States, and attracts people from all over the world. In 1975, however, more than 47 percent of the people accommodated in Las Vegas by the reservation office of the Las Vegas Convention and Visitors Authority came from California, and a majority of these probably came from the Los Angeles metropolitan area, a reasonable driving time from Las Vegas. The developer of a property in Las Vegas could not afford to ignore the local market.

The analyst must attempt to answer the question, "where does the community draw from?" A definition of the geographic area of influence of the community is an essential step in identifying the market—and that for a suburb of San Francisco will differ substantially from that for a city in Hawaii or a community in Alaska. It is also important that the population of the area be considered, especially growth trends and demographic characteristics. There are approximately 10 guest rooms per 1,000 population in the United States, but the ratio varies substantially from one community to the next. Exhibit 4 provides a comparison of the number of rooms to population for selected commercial-industrial centers and major resort areas. Although population does not create a need for hotel rooms, the size of a community and its growth patterns, in combination with other economic indicators, bear a relationship to the market for lodging facilities.

Accessibility of the Area

The accessibility of the area must be evaluated when identifying the market. Analysis of the capacity of the transportation network is the starting point for this evaluation. Since a majority of travelers use the automobile as their major means of transport, the adequacy of the highway system should be assessed first. The local office of the state Department of Transportation should be able to provide the information necessary to answer the following questions:

- How many federal and state highways serve the area?
- What is the condition of the highways? Are there plans for improvement, relocation, or expansion?

- What is the present highway usage, including both toll and non-toll roads?

A similar study should be made of airline service to the area, if any. The local airport authority is generally a good source of information concerning: the passenger capacity of the airport; the major airlines providing service; the frequency of domestic and international flights; and records of arriving and departing passengers. If possible, the analyst should arrange personal interviews with representatives of the major airlines serving the area to obtain information about present load factors on their flights, the number of direct and stopover flights to the area, and the carrier's plans for the future. In addition, the extent to which the community is a stopover point for airline crews should be determined, because this activity can be a good source of rooms demand.

Other available modes of transportation should be evaluated, including rail, bus, ferry systems, and ocean or inland waterway transport. When the capacity of the various systems has been determined, the information should be evaluated in relation to the proximity of the community to other major metropolitan areas, and the access times to each should be computed. From these data, the analyst can construct a matrix showing the essential information on preferred travel modes of the various market segments from the major metropolitan areas, travel time, and potential demand for overnight lodging.

Evaluation of Attractions

The features of a community that give rise to visits by non-residents can be classified into the two major groups discussed in Exhibit 1, recreational-personal and commercial-industrial. Each major group can in turn be divided into two subsets— man-made or natural attractions in the personal-recreational group, and basic or sustaining developments in the commercial-industrial group. The major purpose for this disaggregation is to help the analyst identify the market. For example, a *basic* industry such as automobile assembly not only employs local residents; it also creates products for export so that funds are brought into the community and traffic is generated. A sustaining development, like a retail store, provides employment but only recirculates funds already in the community, and it generates very little traffic and attendant lodging demand. When the sustaining development is the central office of a major national chain, or when a retail outlet is part of a large, regional shopping complex, its status is upgraded because of the traffic generated by those features.

Evaluation of the attractions should be based on data obtained by observation, personal interview, and mail survey (if the number of attractions requiring analysis warrants the expenditure).

The information needed includes:

- Present physical condition and capacity.
- Planned expansion or retraction.
- New or proposed developments.
- Number of visitors by month (or other appropriate period) for the past five years.

Exhibit 5   Major Purchasers of Lodging

RANK	INDUSTRY	TYPICAL REPRESENTATIVES
1.	Wholesale trade	Salesmen for industrial products
2.	Finance and insurance	Agents; brokers; bank examiners
3.	Miscellaneous professional services	Lawyers; accountants; engineers
4.	New construction	Contractors; buyers; workers
5.	Retail trade	Buyers; salesmen
6.	Health-care services	Doctors; patients; salesmen of medical equipment and pharmaceuticals
7.	Food processors	Buyers; salesmen to the trade
8.	Motion picture production, amusement, recreation services, and commercial sports	Production companies; artists and entertainers; professional teams
9.	Nonprofit organizations	Members of business and professional associations
10.	Miscellaneous business services	Agents and employees of advertising companies; credit and computer services; news syndicates

- Number of visitors (or an estimate) requiring lodging.

The information obtained may be verified by discussing the attractions of the community with those citizens and representatives of municipal government who are most interested in the progress of the area. For example, the Chamber of Commerce and the industrial Development Board or its equivalent (if one exists) should be contacted, as should the heads of the major commercial banks and savings and loan associations. Many local business-support organizations are also good sources of published information concerning the economic and demographic characteristics of the community.

In the evaluation of the commercial-industrial base of the community, some indication of the influence that the companies may have on the market for lodging facilities can be obtained from the list in Exhibit 5. Using Input-Output tables prepared by the U.S. Department of Commerce, one can identify those industries that are the major purchasers of overnight accommodations nationally. In any community the analyst can expect that representatives of those industries will require lodging facilities if they have adequate reason to contact the companies in the local commercial-industrial base.

Factors That May Change the Market

When obtaining information on existing attractions and historical data concerning the traffic they have generated, it is imperative that the researcher be alert for evidence of plans that may alter the size and scope of the market. All avenues of growth and expansion or contraction of the commercial, industrial, or recreational development of the community should be explored as fully as possible, including the following:

- Urban renewal.
- New industrial development.

- Proposed government projects.
- Expansion of transportation modes.
- Construction of commercial office space and shopping centers.
- Proposed convention and civic centers.
- Regionalization of health-care delivery systems.
- New institutions of higher learning, or additions to existing institutions.
- Proposed amusement parks, stadium development or expansion, or planned recreational services.
- Elimination or contraction of any of the activities listed above.

Information obtained should be verified whenever possible by consulting with municipal and other officials, and all available data pertaining to expected completion dates and capacities should be recorded.

Market Characteristics

The information obtained for the evaluation of the existing attractions must next be analyzed to determine the following characteristics of the market:

- The primary, secondary, and tertiary (if applicable) purpose of visits to the community.
- The duration of visits (overnight or in-transit; if terminal, number of days at destination).
- The seasonality of visits (percentage of annual visits that occur in each month.)
- The demographic characteristics of the visitors.

When these characteristics have been determined, the analyst should prepare, on a monthly basis if possible, a projected schedule of the visitors to the community during a typical year, broken down by the market segments delineated in Exhibit 1.

Analysis of Existing Lodging Facilities

The ability of existing facilities to meet the need for overnight accommodations, as estimated by the analysis above, is calculated next. To perform this calculation, it is necessary to obtain, through observation and personal interview, the following information for each existing lodging facility:

1. Number of rooms
2. Occupancy levels (monthly)
3. Double occupancy levels (monthly)
4. Guest market segmentation
5. Rate structure
6. Average length of stay
7. Age and condition of property

8. Food and beverage facilities

    a) number of seats

    b) menu prices

    c) decor

    d) service standards

    e) type of food served

    f) ratio of food and beverage sales to total departmental sales

9. Additional amenities and facilities

    a) reservation system, if any

    b) recreational facilities

    c) store rentals; other guest services

The data should be confirmed, to the extent possible, by discussion with competing operators and representatives of convention and tourist bureaus with possible knowledge of occupancy trends. The analyst should then prepare a schedule of the number of rooms occupied monthly, based upon the data obtained.

The schedule of number of monthly visitors should be compared with the number of rooms occupied and number of guest nights developed from the accumulated data concerning existing lodging accommodations. There are four ways in which this can be accomplished:

-   By visual verification. There should be a clearly visible relationship between the number of visitors and the number of occupied rooms or number of guest nights.

-   By preparing a chart in which number of visitors is the variable or x axis and number of rooms occupied (or guest nights) is the y axis. It should be possible to draw a trend line connecting the points.

-   By linear regression. Many of the more sophisticated pocket calculators are pre-programmed for computing the trend line.

-   By computing and comparing the seasonality indices for the number of visitors and the occupancy or number of guest nights.

An Example

An illustration of the schedules that might be prepared for a feasibility study of a proposed lodging facility is presented in Exhibit 6. We have assumed that the site is in the central business district of a metropolitan area with a population of 300,000. Although mostly commercial-industrial, the fictitious city also contains a major regional health-care facility and a small college. It is a transportation hub and, because of location and facilities (a relatively new civic center), receives a good share of regional conventions. Let us also assume that it is a logical stopover point on the route to several well-known recreational resort areas.

Exhibit 6   Comparison of Number of Visitors and Number of Guest Nights

	PERCENTAGE:		NUMBER	NUMBER	NUMBER	SEASONALITY INDEX:	
MONTH	ROOM OCCUPANCY	DOUBLE OCCUPANCY	OF ROOMS OCCUPIED	OF GUEST NIGHTS	OF VISITORS	GUEST NIGHTS*	VISITORS**
JANUARY	62%	31%	35,749	46,831	37,500	78.10	76.99
FEBRUARY	67	33	34,894	46,408	40,000	77.39	82.12
MARCH	73	48	42,092	62,296	31,000	103.89	63.64
APRIL	72	52	40,176	61,068	38,000	101.84	78.02
MAY	72	38	41,515	57,291	43,000	95.54	88.28
JUNE	79	45	44,082	63,919	70,000	106.60	143.71
JULY	80	67	46,128	77,034	82,000	128.47	168.35
AUGUST	85	75	49,011	85,769	80,000	143.04	164.24
SEPTEMBER	74	45	41,292	59,873	51,000	99.85	104.70
OCTOBER	77	55	44,398	68,817	49,000	114.76	100.60
NOVEMBER	67	32	37,386	49,350	35,000	82.30	71.86
DECEMBER	55	29	31,713	40,910	28,000	68.22	57.49
TOTAL			488,436	719,566	584,500	1,200.00	1,200.00
MEAN VALUES	72%	47%	40,703	59,964	48,708	100.00	100.00

*Calculated: $\dfrac{\text{NUMBER OF GUEST NIGHTS FOR MONTH}}{\text{MEAN NUMBER OF GUEST NIGHTS EACH MONTH}}$ = GUEST NIGHTS SEASONALITY INDEX   e.g., $\dfrac{46,831}{59,964}$ = .78099

**Calculated: $\dfrac{\text{NUMBER OF VISITORS FOR MONTH}}{\text{MEAN NUMBER OF VISITORS EACH MONTH}}$ = VISITORS SEASONALITY INDEX   e.g., $\dfrac{37,500}{48,708}$ = .76989

Source: Competitive operations; Convention and Visitors Bureau; Airport Authority; Laventhol and Horwath estimates.

At the time of the study, there are 12 lodging facilities in the area with a total of 1,860 rooms considered competitive by the analyst. Using occupancy statistics obtained as a result of personal interviews and verified by observation and discussion with community officials, the number of rooms occupied and number of guest nights for the most recent 12-month period are computed.

The estimated number of visitors has been compiled from the data obtained by evaluating the various attractions in the area. From personal interviews, some telephone contacts, a mail questionnaire, and observations, the number of visitors to the commercial-industrial complex, the health-care center, and the college is computed. A discussion with the convention bureau provides data on conventions. The number of visitors who were en route to the resort area has been estimated on the basis of discussions with the Department of Transportation, analysis of traffic counts provided by that department, and observation. The aggregate of those sources is shown in Exhibit 6. Scanning the data shows some correlation, but if we assume that the analyst elects to prepare a linear regression for verification, the result of the computation, based on the formula **y** (guest nights) = **a** + **bx** (number of visitors) is: *The number of guest nights monthly equals 31,570 plus 58 percent of the number of monthly visitors.*

The correlation coefficient (r) is a fairly high .83 and shows that variations in the number of visitors accounts for about 70 percent (r = .6889) of the variation in guest nights. The large value of the **a**, or y-intercept, constant (31,570) would seem to indicate that a significant percentage of the visitors to the community stay more than one night—and, in fact, the average duration of stay for the community is 1.7 days, a figure typical of a commercial-industrial base with a high volume of in-transit visitors.

The arithmetic means of the number of guest nights and number of visitors monthly were computed and used as a basis for computing the seasonality factors (see calculations, Exhibit 6). The major variations in these indices might be interpreted as follows:

1. Extended stays by convention guests in March, April, and October provide more guest nights from fewer visitors. Those months were seasonal lows for in-transit visits.

2. Heavy travel to the recreational areas increased overnight stops in the summer months. Other lodging facilities not analyzed attracted more of the market, probably because of price.

The general conclusion would probably be that the number of guest nights and related occupancy figures are realistic estimates, and form a reasonable basis for future market projections.

Future Demand

When the data have been verified to the extent possible, the analyst has a basis for projecting future demand. The size and composition of the present transient market have been established. It now remains to determine the probable growth factors and to project the demand into the appropriate future period. By also projecting the extent to which existing lodging facilities and known additions to the capacity will satisfy that market, it will be possible to show the gap—if any—that would be filled by the proposed operation. An illustration of this calculation, prepared using a computer, is shown in Exhibit 7.

It is the final projection that will influence the design and scope of the food and beverage facilities recommended as part of the proposed property. The basic seating capacity required for transient guests can be computed based upon standard, well-established relationships, but the additional capacity for local residents is more difficult to quantify. An evaluation of that market is made primarily by observation and by polling those interviewed during the course of the study to determine their personal dining-out preferences. The analyst can also obtain some insight by visiting competing restaurants and estimating their activity during meal periods on different days during the week. If the capacity of the food service facilities is an essential element in the property's planning and design, a more elaborate study and analysis may be required.

Relating Market Demand to Design

Once the market for the proposed facility has been identified, the analyst's findings should be related to the site of the proposed facility and to the design of the building and interior space. Assuming that the economics of the project justify the development, and the decision is made to proceed, the architects and engineers will need general specifications concerning the following:

Exhibit 7 Projected Average Occupancy—Future Market Composition

PROJECTED AVERAGE OCCUPANCY—FUTURE MARKET COMPOSITION							
YEAR	COMMERCIAL	CONVENTION	TOURIST	ROOM NIGHTS DEMAND	ROOM NIGHTS AVAILABLE	AVERAGE GROWTH (PERCENT)	AVERAGE OCCUPANCY
1978	163,300	82,100	72,500	317,900	441,700	–	.72
1979	168,199	84,563	74,675	327,437	441,700	3	.74
1980	173,245	87,100	76,915	337,260	474,900	3	.71
1981	178,442	89,713	79,223	347,378	508,100	3	.68
1982	183,796	92,404	81,599	357,799	617,600	3	.58
1983	189,309	95,176	84,047	368,532	617,600	3	.60
1984	194,989	98,032	86,569	379,590	617,600	3	.61
1985	200,838	100,973	89,166	390,977	617,600	3	.63
1986	206,864	104,002	91,841	402,707	617,600	3	.65
1987	213,069	107,122	94,596	414,787	617,600	3	.67

PROJECTED OCCUPANCY OF PROPOSED HOTEL						
YEAR	COMMERCIAL	CONVENTION	TOURIST	ROOM NIGHTS DEMAND	ROOM NIGHTS AVAILABLE	AVERAGE OCCUPANCY
1978	–	–	–	–	66,430	–
1979	–	–	–	–	66,430	–
1980	19,084	10,877	9,614	39,585	66,430	.60
1981	19,656	1,214	9,903	40,773	66,430	.61
1982	18,404	9,240	8,568	36,212	66,430	.55
1983	18,955	9,518	8,825	37,298	66,430	.56
1984	20,500	10,783	9,523	40,806	66,430	.61
1985	21,115	11,107	9.808	42,030	66,430	.63
1986	21,749	11,440	10,102	43,291	66,430	.65
1987	22,401	11,783	10,406	44,590	66,430	.67

Source: Analysis of competitive properties; Laventhol and Horwath estimates of growth rates.

- The number, size, and type of guest rooms and food and beverage facilities, including function space.
- The space to be allocated for administrative, control, and general support purposes.
- The size, type, and scope of recreational facilities.
- The type of vehicle housing required and the necessary space.
- The space allocated for shops and other guest services.
- The suggested visibility of the proposed project.

The characteristics and requirements of the various market segments are the basis for judgment in developing design specifications and space allocations. Guests will fit into three standard categories: those who use the facility largely because it is convenient; those who select it after comparing the price and quality of competing facilities; and those who select it because of particular aspects of structural design, interior decor, and quality of product and services. Exhibit 8 presents a development and design criteria matrix, relating the requirements of potential

340 Chapter 12

Exhibit 8 Development and Design Criteria Matrix

| GUEST REQUIREMENTS | COMMERCIAL-INDUSTRIAL | | | | RECREATIONAL-PLEASURE | | | | LOCAL | |
| | INDEPENDENT | | GROUP | | INDEPENDENT | | GROUP | | | |
	In-Transit	Terminal	In-Transit	Terminal	In-Transit	Terminal	In-Transit	Terminal	Independent	Group
LOCATION										
Accessibility	X		X		X		X			
Parking	X	X	X	X	X	X	X	X	X	X
Proximity	X	X	X	X	X	X	X	X	X	X
Visibility	X		X		X		X			
APPEARANCE										
Decor		X		X		X		X		
Design		X		X		X		X		
Landscaping						X		X		
Structure		X		X		X		X		
LODGING										
Capacity			X	X			X	X		
Equipment		X		X		X		X		
Rates	X	X	X	X	X	X	X	X		
Room Size		X		X		X		X		
RESTAURANTS										
Capacity	X		X	X			X	X		X
Diversity		X		X		X		X	X	X
Function Space				X				X		X
Hours of Operation	X	X	X	X	X	X	X	X	X	X
OTHER GUEST SERVICES										
Laundry		X		X		X		X	X	
Shops		X		X		X		X		
Valet		X		X		X		X		
ENTERTAINMENT AND RECREATION FACILITIES										
Active		X		X		X		X	X	X
Sedentary		X		X		X		X		

customers by groups to the factors that will influence the final structural design, interior design, and space allocations.

Summary

Except for the local resident who generally selects the services of a lodging facility for some special attribute, guests are most often guided in their selection by convenience (which includes proximity) or else accept lodging services as part of a travel package. For example, the primary motivation for the member of a group is attendance at a function, not the purchase of the lodging services. Since the demand is derived from the real purpose, most customers feel that all lodging facilities are similar and will differentiate only on the basis of a bad past experience—seldom on a good one. For those reasons, the marketing thrust of the lodging industry has been based primarily upon location, brand identification, price, architectural design, or status. Little effort has been made to identify the market and to determine how the needs of the customer can best be met. Even less effort has been expended to promote the use of lodging facilities by the millions who travel, but who stay with friends and relatives or in their own vacation shelters.

My firm's analysts do not foresee that the traveler will change his habits drastically in the future, although demographic data point to a significant increase in the segment of the population that provides the best market for lodging facilities. We do believe, however, that the lodging industry can capture a greater share of the market for overnight accommodations. An important part of striving toward this goal is the recognition of the need for a more thorough market analysis early in the development of a lodging facility.

REVIEW QUIZ

When you feel you have covered all of the material in this chapter, answer these questions. Choose the *best* answer. Check your answers with the correct ones found on the Review Quiz Answer Key at the end of this book.

True (T) or False (F)

T   F   1. From the first day of operations it is important to maintain a guest history on randomly selected overnight guests.

T   F   2. The "soft opening" of a newly built hotel should be the object of concentrated promotional publicity efforts.

T   F   3. A sales blitz is most effective when just the sales department is involved.

T   F   4. "Fan out" programs are most effective in attracting the subsegment of the corporate meeting market that is attracted to a hotel as an incentive destination.

T   F   5. Attracting and developing the incentive-oriented market requires the most lead time and so should be done early in the pre-opening stages of a new hotel's marketing efforts.

T   F   6. Several days after opening, each department of a new hotel should begin a sales action training program.

Multiple Choice

7. Which of the following is *not* an administrative activity involved in the critical path of a hotel's pre-opening marketing planning process?

   a. identifying and leasing office space
   b. developing the first year's revenues
   c. hiring staff
   d. setting up function books

8. Good resources for data concerning the source/origin markets of a hotel's targeted market segments are:

   a. Chamber of Commerce statistics.
   b. mix-of-business reports from other hotels.
   c. arrival and departure patterns at airports.
   d. all of the above.

9. What form of public relations succeeds when a publicity coordinator for a newly opened hotel convinces a local newspaper's food editor to feature a story on how a new restaurant is developed?

   a. promotional publicity
   b. advancement of the industry
   c. community relations
   d. all of the above

Chapter Outline

Manager's Reception
Complimentary Coffee in the Lobby
Hosted Single Tables
Health and Fitness Programs
Bed and Breakfast
International Visitor Programs
Discount Coupons
Community Involvement Programs
Newsletters
Local Advisory Board
Trade Show Marketing
Familiarization Tours
Guest History Systems
Corporate Clubs
Speedy Check-in and Check-out
Recognition of Special Market Segments
Transportation
"Beads As Money" Programs
Weekend Packages
Combination Programs for Frequent Users
Executive Floors
In-House Marketing with Videos
Quality Guarantees

Learning Objectives

1. State the difference between sales-mindedness and marketing-mindedness, and define what is meant by a market-driven form of marketing.

2. List a number of market-driven marketing techniques, and state how each could be used to solve different kinds of marketing problems for a specific hotel.

3. List a number of internal changes that hotels have undergone as a result of a growing market-driven marketing-mindedness, and state how each could be used to solve different kinds of marketing problems.

4. List a number of cost-intensive marketing strategies, and state how each could be used to solve different kinds of marketing problems.

Marketing-Mindedness at the Property Level

I N THE PAST, many hotels combined various parts of the marketing mix according to what they felt needed to be sold. The essence of today's marketing philosophy, however, centers upon what the customer wants to buy rather than upon what business wants to sell. This is a significant change in the industry's marketing philosophy.

> 66When business is tough to get, the companies that will succeed are those that have listened to their customers. Whether those customers are the actual consumers or the intermediaries (such as travel agents), knowing what they want and enjoy and then delivering it to them is the key to success. 99

—**Gary Dischell**
President
Knightsbridge Hotel Company

An old marketing proverb captures the customer's attitude: "Don't tell me what it does good; tell me what good it does me." The hotel industry, in fact, is moving into a market-driven form of marketing. The benefits of a property for a specific audience are being featured after the target audience identifies what these benefits are.

This chapter compiles many current concepts that indicate recent and significant changes from sales-mindedness to marketing-mindedness at property levels. Many of these ideas take marketing techniques that have proven successful in one category of hotels and adapt them to other categories. The following examples intend to represent the mainstream of customer-oriented property marketing.

Manager's Reception

A mainstay feature of resort hotels, particularly at offshore sites, has long been the general manager's reception, or "rum swizzle night," or "ice breaker party" for new arrivals. Today, the same concept is being applied at commercial hotels. On a particular night (usually the slowest night in the midweek cycle) guests belonging to a particular market segment (usually corporate guests) are invited to the general manager's reception. Management encourages guests to mingle with staff and with other guests in hopes that this special treatment will motivate them to extend their stays on this visit, and will bring them back on subsequent visits. This technique is most effective in cases when people who regularly visit a city actually alter their travel patterns so they can stay in the hotel on reception night, rather than on nights which may normally be sold out.

Some all-suite hotels have further refined the manager's reception concept. These hotels frequently offer a one-hour cocktail reception in the evening for *all* room guests. This arrangement eliminates the need for the hotel to operate a full-service lounge or dinner facility during the cocktail hour while still maintaining a friendly, social atmosphere which maximizes the hotel's hospitality to its guests.

Complimentary Coffee in the Lobby

Many hotel coffee shops are strained by the cost of staying open in the morning when little revenue is contributed to the outlet because a large percentage of their customers only want a cup of coffee. Some chains, such as Days Inns, La Quinta, and EconoLodges, and individual hotels in the no-frills accommodations business have found it cost-effective to build smaller-than-normal food facilities because they serve relatively few full-service breakfasts or dinners. To compensate for this, they provide an area in the lobby for guests to help themselves to complimentary coffee. Guests who arise before the food facility is open, and guests who do not want to take the time to sit in a restaurant, can avail themselves of this feature. This amenity allows solitary travelers, who would otherwise sit alone in a coffee shop or other food facility, to mingle with each other. Many larger, more luxurious hotels are now picking up the complimentary coffee idea and promoting it to their business guests.

Hosted Single Tables

For years, hotel people talked about establishing in their dining rooms "drummers' clubs" or business traveler tables. Unescorted guests would be invited to mingle there and enjoy each other's company over dinner. While it might have sounded great on paper, for a long time this idea was not implemented very successfully in many hotels, probably due to the absence of a catalyst.

In recent years, however, as the manager-on-duty concept has become more prevalent in hotels, some properties have instituted a hosted table at which the manager on duty may buy wine or desserts for all of the single guests. Usually an invitation for a specific time is extended in one of three ways: (1) at check-in, (2) by an operator calling the guests' rooms, or (3) with an actual written invitation delivered to the guests' rooms. Hosted tables not only provide the missing catalyst which encourages single guests to feel more comfortable in the hotel dining room, they also stimulate brand loyalty and repeat business.

Health and Fitness Programs

Many hotels have had recreational facilities available for years. Resort hotels in particular have structured these activities as a part of the guest experience in a very positive way. It is only in the relatively recent past, however, that some properties have used their health and fitness programs as the main focus of their approach to various publics. In Exhibit 1, we see that the Bonaventure Inter-Continental Hotel

Exhibit 1   The Bonaventure Inter-Continental's Health and Fitness Ad

Courtesy of the Bonaventure Inter-Continental Hotel & Spa, Fort Lauderdale, Florida

and Spa uses a celebrity to communicate fitness as its main advertising theme. More and more city center hotels stress not only fitness, but also their own sensitivity to their guests' desire for fitness. Advertising features running tracks, racquetball courts, health club accessibility, and the like. Also, many properties are creating special-purpose brochures that indicate jogging routes or par course facilities located in their area.

Marketing geared to a national trend such as fitness is intelligent and effective. It allows a hotel to be perceived as both sensitive to change and willing to take the extra step and make it easy for those who are a part of that change to be comfortable in the hotel's environment.

Exhibit 2   Holiday Inn Breakfast Coupon

Compliments of the House

EXPRESS BREAKFAST
Served Monday–Friday
6:00–10:00AM

Dining Room Only
(No Cash Value)

Nº 41457

Courtesy of the Holiday Inn—Arena, Binghamton,
New York

Bed and Breakfast

In this case, we are not speaking specifically of the quaint little home-as-hotel facility commonly associated with Europe. Although this type of bed and breakfast facility is becoming more and more a part of the American hospitality scene, it is not a dominant nor even a significant part of the industry, at least not in the United States.

However, what is very noticeable is the number of hotels and inns that offer a breakfast and guestroom combination at a single price. As mentioned before, this may be a commitment in the all-suite hotels to include a single meal in the price of the room; or, in the case of some hotels with tower concepts, it may be a breakfast in the tower's lounge; or it can even be something as simple as a breakfast coupon given out upon checking in at a typical Holiday Inn (see Exhibit 2).

Hotels such as these are taking advantage of an increasingly popular bed and breakfast concept and applying it to people in mainstream market segments who may not be inclined to stay in a private home or converted private residence. For instance, the Holiday Inn coupon assures guests (whether or not they choose to use it) that their breakfast will not add to their expenses. Someone on a fixed budget may be attracted to a hotel that offers a room and breakfast combination, even though its rate per night might be slightly higher than that of hotels that do not offer such a combination.

International Visitor Programs

Today hotels not only do a much better job of reaching out to international guests, but they also provide much better services for these guests when they arrive at the hotel. More and more properties that advertise and sell to international markets are providing services that international guests find extremely important. Here are some of these services:

1. Voltage converters that allow foreign guests to use personal electrical appliances.

2. Multilingual signs and multilingual menus that allow guests who are traveling unescorted and are not fluent in English to use the hotel's food and beverage outlets comfortably.

3. A list of translation services in the community.

4. International telex equipment that is in the hotel and available for convenient use.

5. Bilingual or multilingual staff members who may be available should emergencies arise. (It helps to keep at the front desk a log of all staff members who speak foreign languages, and to have uniformed multilingual staff members wear little lapel pins with the flags of countries whose languages they can speak.)

The American Hotel & Motel Association has produced an excellent publication on this subject: *"The Care and Feeding of Guests from Abroad."*[1] The tips in this booklet were compiled primarily for hotels in the United States and Canada, but they can be adapted for use by hotels in other countries.

Discount Coupons

As a part of a specific promotional plan, some hotels provide discount coupons to be redeemed at shops contained within the hotel, or at nearby malls, or even (in some cases) at shops scattered throughout a destination. A discount coupon affords the hotel an excellent opportunity to demonstrate its community awareness and involvement. The hotel management gains additional exposure by gathering the local merchants together at the hotel to plan the discount program. What's more, the coupon program provides a tangible benefit to guests, especially to those who are shopping-minded, or to those who wish to bring gifts back from their vacation stays. Consider, for example, what a magnet it is to have an ocean-front resort hotel across from a high quality shopping mall in which merchants offer discounts, particularly in shoulder seasons, to attract hotel guests into the mall. (Shoulder seasons are the periods between peak seasons and off-seasons.) This type of program is good for everybody.

Community Involvement Programs

Managers of well-marketed hotels realize that the community's attitudes toward the hotel often greatly affect the hotel's success. For this reason, hoteliers that expect to get a significant share of their volume from local markets must also be willing to give something back. Contributions to the community can be in the form of participation in charity fund-raising drives, leadership in community events or festivals, or assistance to local service organizations, churches, or charities that put on special programs. These community activities are considered market-driven because the hotels that participate in them are responding to their local market's needs. The participation of hotel people shows their neighbors that the hotel recognizes and accepts its obligation as a corporate citizen to do something good for the community in which it functions. Such participation in these community activities creates positive attitudes toward the hotel within the local marketplace.

Newsletters

It comes as a surprise to some hoteliers to learn that their customers like to be kept abreast of developments and activities in and around the hotel. This is particularly true for hotels in destinations with repeat potential that relies on selected markets. Sending past guests an attractive newsletter listing upcoming events which might be of interest to them is a very effective way to maintain contact and encourage future visits. Shangri-La, a resort hotel in Afton, Oklahoma, regularly runs celebrity entertainment weekends and advertises these to previous guests through direct mail (see Exhibit 3) or a newsletter (see Exhibit 4).

Once a newsletter is developed, it makes sense to also send it to travel agents who would like to know what is going on at your destination. Maintaining a regular flow of information to travel agents in primary feeder markets—always with the message that commissions are paid promptly—assists some hotels in meeting their needs for volume.

Local Advisory Board

New hotels, and hotels affiliated with organizations that are new to a community, have found it useful to invite influential and active members of the local travel, banking, and corporate communities to act as a council of advisors to the hotel management. This can also be a very effective way of improving any hotel's image in the community, even if it is not a newcomer. For example, if the hotel is testing a new weekend package concept or considering a major revision of its restaurant menu, then this advisory group can function as a miniature focus group. To avoid problems, management should emphasize right from the beginning that the board serves in a strictly advisory capacity. With this in mind, the general manager, who uses the advisory board concept well, will be able to see positive results. First, the advisory board members may begin to think of the property as their own property. Also, they may use their influence in the business community to direct business to the hotel. Finally, they are likely to come up with many suggestions and ideas for promoting the hotel, some of which may be extremely practical.

Trade Show Marketing

In recent years the number of trade shows to which hotels have been invited has absolutely exploded. Now hotels have another vehicle to use in getting their message across. Many trade shows have been developed over the last few years to serve markets that heretofore had not had such opportunities. Conventions such as those of Meeting Planners International (MPI) and Insurance Conference Planners (ICP) reach out to the corporate meeting planner. The Henry Davis Shows are attended by mainline retail travel agents. Representatives of specific properties may want to consider participating in these conventions, or in any of the many other trade shows which have developed relatively recently. Most conventions and

Exhibit 3   Direct Mail Flyer Advertising Celebrity Weekends

Flyer and newsletter courtesy of Shangri-La, Afton, Oklahoma

trade shows offer an exchange of ideas as well as an exhibit area. Also, more and more sponsoring organizations are beginning to provide an education program for hotel representatives as well as for the regular attendee to fill what would otherwise be wasted time. Other organizations, whose members represent a variety of

Exhibit 4   Shangri-La's Newsletter

businesses and industries, open their educational sessions to exhibitors because the topics are generally of interest to all business people.

Familiarization Tours

Many hoteliers used to regard a familiarization tour as no more than an opportunity for people loosely affiliated with travel agencies to pay a leisurely visit to an appealing destination. However, now that professionals are organizing these tours and scheduling heavy agendas, hoteliers are capitalizing upon the familiarization tour as an excellent opportunity to reach out to those who can bring them more business. Furthermore, tours are no longer limited to the travel agency community. Today, airlines join with hotels and provide familiarization tours of particular destinations for associations' buyers, corporate meeting planners, or other groups of potential users of both air travel and hotel space.

An increasing number of hotel marketing professionals are now taking control of familiarization programs. They are designating the program participants, the program contents, and the specific travel partners eventually to be associated in the promotion. Also, the more that the professional buyers who are reached through these programs recognize an obligation to fully participate in the tour, the greater the likelihood that they will become better-informed consumers.

Many of the trends already mentioned in this chapter indicate a sensitivity to changes in the marketplace. At the hotel level, many internal changes have occurred because hotel people are listening to their markets, and are exhibiting a greater awareness of the channels of distribution which prevail today. The following sections present other major, internal changes that reflect the growing market-driven marketing-mindedness of hotels.

Guest History Systems

More and more properties, particularly the finer hotels, are using guest history systems to improve the guest experience and to solicit repeat business. This is one instance in which computers facilitate more cordial and more personalized customer service. As hotels build up information in their computerized guest histories, they can begin to customize their services to clients. For instance, rather than allowing the vagaries of chance to govern the assignment of rooms at check-in time, a good hotel with a good guest history system knows guests' preferences and assigns rooms accordingly.

Guest histories also allow front desk staff to personalize service to frequent guests. By flagging reservations to indicate "repeat guests," the front desk person can alert rooms personnel to greet the guests by name as they check in, even though they may have never met before. Guest history systems also make it easier for hotels to solicit repeat business. For example, names of guests who have visited a luxury hotel for theater programs in the past can be retrieved from the hotel's guest history systems, and the guests can be invited to attend similar or improved programs in the future.

Corporate Clubs

Today hotels are providing benefits to corporate customers that exceed those offered to infrequent guests. Usually the corporate guest must sign up in advance as a member of the corporate club (or be signed up by his or her company). Specific amenities offered to corporate club members may include: speedy check-in and check-out, turndown service each night with a mint and brandy next to the bed, and a complimentary morning newspaper at the door. These and other niceties are provided to corporate guests on the assumption that they will speak favorably of the hotel to the local office that made the reservations and that they will request that hotel on any return visits.

Speedy Check-in and Check-out

While some hotels consider rapid check-ins and check-outs as special benefits for corporate club members only, more and more guests today are requesting these same benefits. Speedy check-in basically means preregistration and preassignment of guestrooms. If the reservation has been taken properly and rooms are available, the guests should be able to sign in immediately and be quickly on their way to their rooms.

Speedy check-outs are not quite as simple. By its handling of check-outs, the hotel reveals some of its attitudes toward guests. Good hotels with real sensitivity to their customers' needs have recognized that speedy check-outs will eventually be the rule rather than the exception and they are already moving toward this future by trying to meet these demands today. However, some hotels are still reluctant to let the guest leave without having that one final opportunity to verify that the bill will be paid. Unfortunately, this policy can lead to customer dissatisfaction, especially if the guest is forced to waste a great deal of time waiting to check out at the front desk. As a waggish hotelier once said, "I don't think the guy who has been stuck in your check-out line for 45 minutes is there because he wants to skip!"

Recognition of Special Market Segments

Because of today's increased emphasis on market segmentation, special programs are being developed for specific categories of travelers. This chapter has described a number of programs for the corporate traveler, but some hotels are breaking down the category of corporate traveler even further. These hotels are reaching out for special segments within the segment.

For example, a number of hotels identify businesswomen travelers as a target market subsegment, and provide them with a package of special benefits. Similarly, at certain times of the week as a part of their marketing program, other hotels provide "extras" for government travelers, members of the clergy, or students and faculty. If overdone, these programs can become patronizing and offensive to the targeted subsegment; but if they are done properly, they can become a business magnet. Before you institute such programs in your hotel, your marketing decision-making should carefully weigh their advantages and disadvantages in your marketplace.

The beauty of a marketing plan is that it gives you the "big picture." If you are marketing-minded, you consider the demands of all your market segments before you make major changes in service. Suppose, for example, an airline crew is always booked into your hotel because you offer 24-hour coffee shop service. Before you decide to discontinue around-the-clock service, you certainly ought to carefully analyze its effect on this market segment. Similarly, if you have "golden ager" motor coach tours in your marketing mix, these early risers would be quite pleased to know that your breakfast room just changed its opening time to accommodate them. Remember, your goal is to respond to major trends in your target markets without being pressured to react to short-term or temporary conditions.

The final section of this chapter focuses on more cost-intensive marketing strategies. Certain hotels have made these major adaptations, and other hoteliers may want to consider them in the future. Although these programs require an even greater financial commitment than the policy changes previously cited, certain markets have indicated (1) that these programs will become trends in the industry, and (2) that they will be successful if properly implemented.

Transportation

Many hotels suffer from the disadvantage of being too distant from certain attractions. For instance, a new hotel, built to capitalize on future growth when the city develops a new central business district, may be too far away from the current central business district to attract business travelers, particularly if taxi service is difficult to obtain. In this case, the only way to attract business travelers who need to be in the current central business district may be to provide them with transportation to and from their business appointments.

Similarly, a resort hotel may lack certain recreational opportunities in its immediate area, such as white-water rafting or horseback riding. If the only opportunities for certain recreational activities are located several miles from the resort, and if the guests who fly into the resort destination do not rent cars, then a hotel may want to consider absorbing the expense of operating a transportation system in order to please those guests who wish to explore the destination more completely.

Other hotels decide to offer their own transportation because public transportation to and from the airport is either limited or of inferior quality. Unfortunately, hotel transportation systems are sometimes viewed negatively by local public transportation companies because they represent added competition. Therefore, this type of reaction needs to be considered in making any marketing commitment to transportation.

"Beads As Money" Programs

The positioning suggested by the slogan, "Do more in a week than most people do in a lifetime," fits the guest experience provided by Club Med and other hotels and resorts participating in full-destination promotions. These hotels, which are reaching out to the young (or the "I wish I were young") audience that is affluent, hardworking, and looking for an escape (notice how the ad for Club Med shown in Exhibit 5 combines all of these elements), have had remarkable success with the "beads as money" programs. These properties have found a way to help guests enjoy buying drinks, food, and services without having to carry cash. They use beads joined into necklaces as a medium of exchange.

Weekend Packages

In this chapter on market-driven changes in the marketing mix of hotels, it is sufficient to simply mention the weekend package. The Club Med example just cited

Exhibit 5   Ad for Club Med

Courtesy of Club Med, New York City

can be seen as an extension of the "within 75 miles" concept. That is, most successful special interest or "escape" weekend packages are marketed within a two-hour drive (or one-hour flight) from the hotel site.

Combination Programs for Frequent Users

Some hotels in certain markets have the opportunity to combine with the very successful frequent user programs sponsored in their area by airline and car rental companies. These programs, which offer a free trip to the frequent user's family, are worth the consideration of hoteliers who want to expand their share of the frequent traveler market.

On the negative side, combination programs can carry a very heavy price tag and often are available only to chain-affiliated hotels. Another disadvantage is that some companies are opposed to these programs. Thus, they are reluctant to allow their personnel to be involved in sweepstakes or in other incentive promotions. However, the majority of companies have not taken this position, and they do allow their employees to participate.

Executive Floors

While some of the older, more elegant hotels have had "tower" sections for many, many years, most of these have been facilities for long-term residents. Only in recent years has the concept of "a hotel-within-a-hotel" been extended to service new markets. Frequent business travelers, in particular, want the convenience of a major hotel location, but want to avoid the frenzied activity found in many large, mixed-usage hotels. For this reason, executive floors or special tower sections have become very popular. Nice, private amenities such as honor bars, complimentary breakfast in the lounge area, turndown service, and 24-hour room service are perceived by many travelers as well worth the room price differential.

Executive floors seem to be most successful when carried out as a full program rather than as a partial effort. Usually a check-in/registration area separate from the main hotel front desk is necessary.

In-House Marketing with Videos

Many hotels are taking advantage of technology to satisfy the guest's desire to know what is available in the hotel by advertising their facilities on one channel of the guestroom television. Videotapes can be ingeniously programmed in-house so that only the facilities that need additional volume on a given day are mentioned. On the days when demand from customers outside the hotel is expected to be exceedingly high for a certain outlet, that outlet is not advertised in-house.

For example, if a property wishes to generate more dining room traffic from its guestrooms on weeknights (say from Sunday to Thursday), then on those five nights of the week its in-house video program could feature the dining room. If, however, the same hotel dining room does extremely well with the local market on weekends, increasing the demand from in-house guests might cause long lines, delays, and frustration for both markets. In this case, therefore, the dining room message would be extracted on Friday and Saturday nights from the continuously running video. Hotels—and destination resorts in particular—using an in-house video marketing system can speak directly to guests and can tell a more complete story of what their facilities offer. Theoretically, this marketing technique should produce more profit-making opportunities for the hotel's outlets.

Quality Guarantees

Some hotels are finding it important to tell guests in advance that they will enjoy their stay—or they won't have to pay for it. Holiday Inn's "No Excuse Guarantee" and Dunfey's "Good Night Guarantee" are examples of this apparently gutsy marketing approach. In actuality, most of these programs do allow for a period of time after a complaint is registered during which management can either resolve the complaint or offer another room before the first room becomes complimentary. Therefore, the actual risk in a well-run hotel is relatively small. Nevertheless, guarantees are psychologically advantageous because (1) they comfort guests, most of whom have probably had a bad hotel experience at one time or another; (2) they indicate a commitment to excellence in the operation; and (3) they are consistent with a hotel's objectives to satisfy guests and to encourage them to return. Again, each hotel must decide whether or not to incorporate this market-driven concept.

This chapter has presented many examples of marketing-mindedness manifested at the property level in various hotels. It is doubtful that a single property anywhere uses all of these concepts. However, there is such diversity within the worldwide spectrum of hotels that most hotels should be able to use some of these ideas.

Endnotes

1. *The Care and Feeding of Guests from Abroad* (East Lansing, Mich.: The American Hotel & Motel Association, American Express Company, and the Educational Institute of AH&MA, 1980).

REVIEW QUIZ

When you feel you have covered all of the material in this chapter, answer these questions. Choose the *best* answer. Check your answers with the correct ones found on the Review Quiz Answer Key at the end of this book.

True (T) or False (F)

T F 1. A manager's reception is most effective when the invited guests belong to a wide range of market segments.

T F 2. The major goal of market-driven hotel marketing is to react to short-term, temporary conditions.

T F 3. Today's marketing philosophy centers on what the business wants to sell and not on what the customer wants to buy.

T F 4. In a market-driven form of marketing, a property features benefits for a specific audience after the target audience identifies what these benefits are.

Multiple Choice

5. Which of the following market-driven forms of marketing is directed toward very specific market segments?

   a. complimentary coffee in the lobby
   b. corporate clubs
   c. speedy check-in and check-out
   d. newsletters

6. In-house video marketing can be a most effective:

   a. pricing technique.
   b. advertising technique.
   c. promotional publicity technique.
   d. sales technique.

7. Which of the following is not evidence of a market-driven form of marketing?

   a. selling up at all points-of-purchase
   b. hosted singles tables
   c. health and fitness programs
   d. manager's reception

8. Which of the following market-driven forms of marketing benefit an entire destination?

   a. newsletters
   b. discount coupons
   c. familiarization tours
   d. all of the above

Chapter Outline

Opryland Hotel
The Sheraton at St. Johns Place
The Americana Congress Hotel
The Sheraton at Steamboat

Learning Objectives

1. Identify the problem of each of the four hotels examined and briefly summarize the strategic planning that solved each hotel's particular problem.

2. Recognize the continuity behind a hotel's targeted market mix and the hotel's particular marketing mix.

Strategic Marketing in Action: Case Histories

> ❝A strategic plan in itself will not ensure success. However, I doubt seriously that you achieve success without a formal plan. The plan should provide a direction, structure, and strategies necessary to be successful.❞

—**Gary Morgenstern**
Managing Director
Americana Congress Hotel
Chicago, Illinois

THIS CHAPTER PRESENTS CASE STUDIES of four very different hotels and discusses how each hotel implemented a strategic plan to solve its particular marketing problems. The first case concerns Opryland Hotel: a destination resort that was created from scratch and which turned into one of the finest convention sites in the country soon after it opened.

The Sheraton at St. Johns Place is the subject of the second case study. This hotel did not open successfully because (among other reasons) the community was not made ready for it. However, by vigorously pursuing a strategic plan, within a year it became one of the hotel industry's great turnaround stories.

The next case involves an old, very large hotel in Chicago—the Americana Congress Hotel. The area surrounding the hotel was purported to be decaying, but the Congress refused to give in. By changing its marketing strategy, the Congress has re-established itself as a viable force in the Chicago marketplace.

Finally, the Sheraton at Steamboat is examined. This case illustrates the marvelous results that can be achieved when the marketing efforts of a fine hotel are backed by strong corporate involvement and support.

As you study each of these success stories, notice how well they demonstrate key marketing principles. Also, pay special attention to the careful planning and implementation of the plan adopted in each of these cases.

Opryland Hotel

Prior to the opening of Opryland Hotel in Nashville, the state of Tennessee was not widely recognized as a convention destination. In early 1975, Jack Vaughn, Vice President and General Manager, and Mike Dimond, Vice President of Marketing, arrived in Nashville with some ideas on how to change that fact. Mike Dimond graciously agreed to tell the Opryland Hotel story. The story begins well before the

Opryland Hotel's Conservatory—a Victorian garden beneath more than two acres of skylights with 200 private balconies.

hotel's November 1977 opening, and closes years later with the hotel's first major expansion.

    ❝To be competitive in the Southeast, and to impact the marketplace, the design of the hotel was very crucial to our success. Our 'mission statement' was simply to introduce a new product in the Southeast that could be competitive with Atlanta, New Orleans, and Miami in terms of convention business. This ran contrary to the conventional wisdom at that time. The market for a Nashville hotel was thought to be restricted to tourists, individual corporate travelers, and small local, state, and regional groups. However, we were convinced that the multi-billion-dollar convention, association, and meeting market could indeed be penetrated. Based on our study and analysis of indicated market demand, we estimated potential room demand for the new project (Opryland Hotel) to be

161,512 room-nights for our first full year of operation (1978) or an annual occupancy of 75%.

We estimated that rooms demand for the Opryland Hotel would be derived from the following sources:

Demand Source Total	Estimated Annual Room Demand	Percentage of Total
100-day park season	57,820	36%
82-day tourist and Opry-goers	47,412	29%
183-day conventions and group meetings	56,280	35%
TOTALS	161,512	100%

Keep in mind that these estimated figures did not include any projections for individual, corporate, and industrial (that is, walk-in business). Fifty transient rooms a night would have increased our estimated occupancy by 8.3%.

The hotel's physical features were as follows:

Features	Capacity
• Guestrooms (including 56 suites)	601
• Sitting rooms (deluxe parlors)	15
• Coffee shop	225 seats
• Theme restaurant	210 seats
• Cocktail lounge	90 seats
• Show lounge	382 seats
• Sub-rentals (shops)	6,100 sq. ft.
• Surface parking lot for cars	1,313 spaces
• Indoor lot for valet parking of cars	125 spaces
• Olympic-sized swimming pool	
• All-weather, lighted tennis courts	
• Four special features:	

    Three-story vaulted skylight
    Roof galleria, treated with earth
      stone and natural greenery
    A mid-rise structure of three to five stories
    90,000 sq. ft. total meeting and exhibit space

While this design by no means gave us the largest hotel in the Southeast, it gave us more meeting and exhibit space than most 1,000-room properties. The 90,000 square feet of space initially consisted of 15,000 square feet of prefunction area, a 20,000-square-foot ballroom with a permanent stage, a 30,000-square-foot exhibit hall, and 18 break-out session rooms, all on one floor. With this type of product, we were able to quickly identify appropriate market segments, and with our experience, we knew how to reach them.

Our main focus would be on group business, and we set our priorities accordingly. The people at *Successful Meetings* magazine were very helpful in defining the target market for us. From *Successful Meetings'* data bank, we were able to determine that the single largest market would be national associations, followed by corporations, and then regional and state associations.

Our research also told us that to be competitive in the three major markets—Washington, Chicago, and New York—we would need representation, since every major chain was represented in each of these cities. We entered into a working relationship with the Krisam Group because we could not afford the luxury of having our own individual offices. That relationship proved to be most satisfactory; in fact, we are still with them nine years later.

Opryland Hotel, by design, positioned itself in the marketplace as a convention hotel with over 80% of its business coming from meetings and conventions. Our advertising strategy was simply to convince potential clients that, because of its physical size, its favorable geographical location (50% of the population of the continental United States is within a 600-mile radius), the management team, and the value received for their dollar, Nashville's Opryland Hotel would be a viable alternative for their group meeting needs. Since we were positioning ourselves as a group hotel, the tone of the advertising was straightforward to fit this target market.

The media objective was simply to focus on the group meeting planner rather than the transient; very few dollars were spent on consumer advertising. Careful consideration was given to the placement of ads in meeting-related publications such as *Meeting News, Meetings and Conventions, Successful Meetings, Insurance Conference Planner, Association Management, Hotel & Travel Index, Hotel & Motel Red Book,* and *Official Meetings and Facilities Guide.*

Realizing that national associations, corporate conventions, and meetings offered the greatest potential for sales, our sales strategy was simply to have the sales team concentrate their efforts on making personal contacts with national trade shows and industry-related shows such as JCMC Sales Blitz, LIMRA, NAEM, ASAE, NSTD, Dialog, Meeting World, and MPI.[1]

In November 1977 Opryland Hotel opened its 600 rooms, ancillary facilities, and supportive amenities. Our strategy of targeting the meeting and convention market segments was soon justified. Our hotel's offerings were recognized immediately, and now Opryland is respected as one of the premier hotels for major conventions in the nation. Because the hotel's primary target market was selected at the conceptual stage, we were able to design the hotel specifically for this market. The hotel's immediate and continuing success is largely due to its acceptance by the meetings market. The following figures show Opryland's actual performance against our annual occupancy projections and industry averages for the first five full years of operation.

Year	Budget Projection	Actual	Variance	Industry Average	Variance
1978	75%	79.5%	+4.5	72.8%	+6.7
1979	80%	82.1%	+2.1	72.6%	+9.5
1980	80%	84.1%	+4.1	69.9%	+14.2
1981	80%	84.2%	+4.2	67.3%	+16.9
1982	80%	84.4%	+4.4	65.0%	+19.4

As the actual occupancy percentages continually outstripped our stated goals, we did some specific tracking and then decided that an addition was in the offing. In contemplating an addition, we knew that with 90,000 square feet of meeting and exhibit space, we could easily justify expanding to 1,000 rooms. But we planned carefully in order to have the same advantages with a 1,000-room hotel that we had with the original 600-room hotel. From opening, we had kept lost business reports on groups that we turned away because their dates were sold out, local catering groups were unavailable, or whatever. We also tracked the groups that had indicated they would meet at our hotel if we had 1,000 rooms or more. Now extensive research was done on all groups of 1,000 to 3,000 people that had met in the Southeast previously.

We also learned that an airport expansion was definitely planned, in light of the airport's passenger projections for inbound and outbound traffic for the next five years. We felt that a convention center would inevitably be built in Nashville so we had to prepare ourselves accordingly. We decided it would be advantageous to offer the largest in-house hotel exhibit facilities in the country—large enough to accommodate 90% of all the trade shows held in the United States annually.

After researching various properties of 1,000 rooms or more throughout the United States, we felt that we could strengthen our overall position in the marketplace by adding 400+ rooms and bringing our total meeting and exhibit space to 225,000 square feet. We carried out our expansion as planned. At this point in time, our convention facilities are the largest in the country and we now have 1,067 rooms. The annualized occupancy projections for our first full operating year after expanding are an unbelievable 80%. Now phase three, the building of an additional 500 to 700 rooms, is already on the drawing board. **"**

—**Mike Dimond**
Vice President of Marketing
Opryland Hotel

The Sheraton at St. Johns Place

In late 1980, the Sheraton at St. Johns Place opened in an urban redevelopment area of Jacksonville, Florida. Located across the river from downtown, the hotel is quite close to the Hilton Hotel, but not near the central business district. From the start, the occupancy of the Sheraton at St. Johns Place was significantly below budget. For this reason, local, divisional, and corporate executives of The Sheraton Corporation were brought together to find ways to meet the needs of the hotel. The major problem identified by the problem-solving team concerned the local market. The property was not being used by the Jacksonville community. Local businesses needed to be wooed. The committee recommended that the hotel's general manager and director of marketing immediately begin hosting a series of luncheons with key business leaders in the community. The owners of the hotel and their local representatives were asked to participate since they had contacts in the community at a very senior level. Specific offices within specific companies were targeted, and a miniature action plan was executed.

The Sheraton at St. Johns Place was, physically speaking, a very attractive but also a somewhat unusual property. The team of trouble-shooters decided that a special incentive would be needed to stimulate first time trials. A bonus coupon was extended to the public offering a ten dollar discount for every night's stay at the hotel. This special offer was communicated through advertising in newspapers and in-flight magazines. All guests who checked in during the promotion were also informed of the discount by front desk personnel. This program, which was originally intended to last for only a limited period of time, was later extended due to its success.

Borrowing on corporate strength, the Sheraton at St. Johns Place gained exposure by taking advantage of corporate programs. For example, a sales blitz was arranged involving personnel from the hotel and from other franchise properties in the state. Those who were brought in to help with the blitz were allowed to distribute their own material as well as material from the Sheraton at St. Johns Place. The hotel repaid the efforts of the other corporate properties by providing complimentary rooms and a VIP gift to the members of the blitz team.

Other actions were taken to solve the occupancy problem. Internal merchandising was reviewed. Point-of-purchase distribution of hotel material in the form of pocketed dioramas for brochures and coupons was worked out at the Jacksonville Airport. The hotel secured a large billboard at the airport exit. Pickup service was provided for downtown businesses to bring people to and from the hotel during the day. Overnight guests were transported to the central business district in the morning and back to the hotel in the evening. On nights when the rooms were not sold out, guests were upgraded to the best accommodations available.

Special sales efforts were directed toward the state association convention market. Through these efforts, a 1981 meeting of the Florida Society of Association Executives was booked into the hotel. The property continued to benefit from this great exposure long after the meeting was over.

Additionally, every effort was made to involve the hotel in local promotions and charity benefits. The staff was active in a personal way with these charities and promotions, so that the hotel would be considered as the preferred site for any events connected with these programs.

Eventually, an energetic new general manager was added to the team. Under his strong direction, many of the programs already under way took on a new impetus. The Sunday brunch program was expanded and advertised locally to increase awareness of the hotel as much as to increase the cover count. The general manager became very active in local clubs and selected local leaders to serve on a public relations council to help increase the community's awareness of the hotel. In addition, he became very active in hosting a weekly general manager's party. New emphasis was also placed on the hotel's secretaries' club.

At this point, the Sheraton at St. Johns Place took the initiative and contacted the air carriers, particularly People Express which was new to the area. The hotel management hoped that its dialogue with the air carriers would persuade them to give more attention to Jacksonville as a destination with this fine new hotel as a magnet. The dialogue worked; all of the airlines pitched in and volume started to grow!

Next, another sales blitz was scheduled to follow up on the leads uncovered during the first blitz. Very close ties were forged to Jacksonville's Convention and Visitors Bureau which, in itself, was becoming a more active force. Whenever and wherever an opportunity was presented to participate with the bureau in sales blitz activities or in outside calls, the opportunity was seized.

Eventually, by using local guest history and the Sheraton reservation system, the hotel was able to detect patterns of business from feeder markets. Hotel sales personnel along with regional sales personnel made sales calls and sales trips into those feeder markets. Research was also done on the sources of travel-agent-based business. Whenever these markets matched up with markets where corporate

The Americana Congress.

accounts were being sought, calls were made on travel agencies as well as on corporations. Other special markets such as the relocation market, the government market, and the retiree motor coach market were examined and attacked.

This marketing program was reinforced, of course, by a very strong selling effort. The results were impressive: an almost instantaneous improvement in the occupancy, a tremendous lifting of employee morale, a better working relationship between the ownership group and the operating company, and a healthier hotel for all concerned. Indeed, this was a case of strategic marketing in action.

The Americana Congress Hotel

Located in one of the less desirable sections of downtown Chicago, the Congress Hotel was deteriorating as a product. The Congress found it difficult to compete in the corporate meeting and convention markets because it was perceived as an old, very large hotel in an area purported to be decaying.

Realizing that it was rated as a second or third choice by the planners scheduling conventions and meetings in Chicago, management decided to attract alternative markets by slightly repositioning the hotel. The Congress Hotel wanted to capture long-term contract or "permanent guest" business without sacrificing its present business. The goal was 500 contracted rooms. The management wanted to project an image of the hotel as a very acceptable product at an attractive price.

In its strategic plan the Congress Hotel used aggressive pricing tactics to attack major sources of contract room business, such as airline crews, railroad crews, and people in training. The hotel researched the question of whether its rates should include food and beverage, transportation, valet service, money exchange, check cashing, or even discounts in local restaurants. Mail-grams, describing the benefits of long-term contract rooms at the Congress, were sent out to the chief financial officers of airlines and railroad companies in the Midwest. Price and availability of tailored packages were strongly featured as selling points. Follow-up sales calls were made to these financial officers. Again, the affordability of the product was emphasized. These calls resulted in a large number of site inspections. Once the decision-makers visited the hotel, the Congress succeeded in closing sales a large percentage of the time.

The hotel developed a new philosophy about maintaining its contract business: it would keep this business by taking care of the permanent guest. The Congress Hotel wanted to make sure that the needs and wants of the permanent guest were met. Therefore, 80% of its rooms were refurbished, and a new concierge service was added to take care of these groups.

The Congress Hotel found that late-night restaurant hours and a diverse menu selection were important to their long-term contract guests. So the hotel began serving eggs 24 hours a day and expanded its restaurant menus. These examples show how the hotel's food and beverage support was structured around its marketing philosophy.

Another major segment that the Congress pursued was the tour and travel market. In particular, bus tour operators were attracted by "best buys" and special packages. The Congress directed its marketing efforts toward major tour operators. Many of these operators arranged tours of the United States for visitors from Asia and Europe. To reach this specialized market segment, the Congress visited national and local trade shows. The hotel's action plan again featured aggressive pricing tactics and special services such as foreign currency exchange and late-night food options. This approach created a strong demand from the motor coach tour operators.

With the hotel now positioned as an acceptable product at an attractive price, the Congress decided to pursue the entertainment market segment. In this case the potential guests were out-of-town residents attending theater and ballet performances at a nearby major auditorium. The Congress Hotel put together specially priced packages tied in with the shows to attract these transient guests. The business it succeeded in capturing from this new market helped to increase the hotel's occupancy during slack periods.

The hotel also created and sold other promotional packages for transient guests. For example, the Congress offered "Shopper's Delight" in December, "Baseball Weekend" during the spring and summer months, and "Family Fling" for which families paid a special rate and children were allowed to stay free. Each package involved its own unique features related to a special event in the hotel.

By properly executing a good strategic marketing plan, the Congress Hotel developed long-term demand in new segments and increased its occupancy from 52% to 80% in a three-year turnaround.

The Sheraton at Steamboat

The case of the Sheraton at Steamboat, Steamboat Springs, Colorado, is a classic example of what marketing can do for a hotel that has inadequate business volume. Although Steamboat was a very successful ski resort with ample business volume in winter, it had become extremely worrisome to top management at The Sheraton Corporation. This was because Sheraton had invested heavily in its Steamboat property, greatly expanding the hotel and significantly improving the product quality; yet, except for the winter season, the hotel was doing relatively little business.

As of August 1981 the resort's future bookings were not encouraging. The summer of 1981 had been very slow, and by 1982 there would be even more competing products on the market. Something had to be done.

Once again, Sheraton's solution was to bring in a team of corporate marketing executives to work with the hotel staff. This team spent several days examining what could be done. Soon the group focused on the question "What is there to do during the off-season at Steamboat?" Answers were solicited, primarily from the local residents. The trouble-shooters learned that the summer months at Steamboat were wonderful and that there were many things to do, but that the public just didn't know this. They decided that the property would have to make commitments of staff, transportation, and money to launch a major promotional campaign. The goal was to communicate how much there was to do at Steamboat and how easy it could be for guests of the resort to utilize the facilities of this destination.

With the property's advertising agency heavily involved, a campaign called "The Way It Wuz Days" was created. Although Sheraton could have run this promotion on its own at the property level, the decision was made to offer the program to the entire destination. The umbrella theme, the logo, and graphics were offered to local businesses. Merchants were encouraged to put together a book of discount coupons for visitors. This would mean more store traffic for them because tourists would have to visit the shops in order to use the coupons. The opportunity to participate fully was even extended to the hotel's competition. This calculated risk was taken on the basis that regardless of who spread the word about Steamboat being a great destination at this time of year, it could only have a positive effect on the Sheraton hotel's business. (This assumption proved to be quite correct!)

Arrangements with hot air balloon companies, Indian tribes, a local theater camp, and other groups were worked out for specific weekends during the target period. One weekend Steamboat took on the air of nineteenth century life when it hosted "The Mountain Men"—a group of executives who led normal lives five days a week, but camped primitively in the wilderness on weekends. The Mountain Men added authenticity to "The Way It Wuz Days."

Transportation was provided at an activities desk, where information on activities in the area was available to guests. This transportation network represented a substantial investment, but it was a key factor in helping guests participate in the programs offered around Steamboat. Horseback-riding establishments, white-water rafting companies, and nearby recreational facilities cooperated by accepting vouchers for payment by the hotel. In this deferred payment system, guests who used a participating facility merely signed a payment voucher. These would be turned over to the hotel and added to the guests' bills. Of course, this made it much easier for guests to enjoy the attractions around Steamboat.

Furthermore, trade-out promotions were coordinated with Denver-based television stations. They would promote the various weekend events at Steamboat in return for rooms credits to be used in station promotions, or station staff meetings, or employee incentives. Because much of the group business for the property was expected to come from Denver, a remote sales office was established there to handle the solicitation of short-term group business. Again, partners in travel were sought to broaden the impact of the marketing effort.

Finally, a very complicated but very effective arrangement was worked with United Airlines, which is the major carrier from the hotel's distant target markets to Denver, and with Rocky Mountain Airways, which is the primary commuter service from Denver to Steamboat.

It is significant that the management of the hotel welcomed the assistance they received. In fact, instead of resenting outside involvement, they kept the Sheraton team constantly involved with the progress of the project. The completion or elimination of suggested action steps was communicated very effectively. In light of this cooperation, it is not surprising that the results were outstanding. The hotel's summer occupancy improved by more than 40 points comparing August 1982 to August 1981. This was in spite of the fact that during that 12-month period, over 200 additional rooms were opened by the competition in Steamboat. The effectiveness of the Sheraton at Steamboat's program continued to grow in subsequent years.

An enormous investment in time and dollars was made to support the Steamboat program, but the Sheraton's problems were serious and without such a program they would have continued. All in all, the Steamboat story illustrates an important point: no matter how severe a problem—no matter how remote a turnaround may appear—great minds using great resources can turn a challenge into an opportunity and progressively improve the situation.

The case studies cited in this chapter furnish a cross-section of marketing-mindedness. Other examples of marketing-mindedness in action at other types of hotels could have been selected. No doubt, the successes of your own marketing program deserve to be told. However, these cases were chosen for a variety of reasons.

The main reason is that they all involved the application of combinations of marketing resources. The marketing problems you may encounter are likely to be similarly complex. In these case studies a one-dimensional approach to marketing would have been inadequate. For example, better selling alone would not have solved the Steamboat problem, but better selling was certainly a necessary part of its solution. Combination promotions with the airlines did not make Jacksonville an overnight success, but they certainly helped it become a long-term success story.

Moreover, none of the solutions presented in this chapter were permanent, nor could they be, since conditions are always changing. All of these programs required constant attention to keep them working. If the marketing efforts had not been maintained in every one of these cases, a drop in occupancy would have been almost immediate. That these hotels have continued to be success stories is a tribute to the marketers involved and to the organizations which they represent.

Endnotes

1. The acronyms stand for: Joint Conference Medical Convention, Life Insurance Marketing Research Association, National Association of Exhibit Managers, American Society of Association Executives, National Society of Training Directors, and Meeting Planners International.

Supplemental Reading ─────────────────────────────

Evaluating Hotel Marketing Effectiveness: The Audit

by Peter Goffe, Associate Professor
School of Hospitality Management
Florida International University

Hotel management is increasingly looking for ways to evaluate marketing effectiveness. A system is needed to assess objectives, strategies, and performance. The Marketing Audit provides a workable, worthwhile tool for managers to assess current performances and long-range goals.

Hotel marketing today has achieved a high degree of sophistication and skill compared to a few years ago. It has made major strides in taking advantage of contemporary general marketing theory, especially with regard to consumer goods. Today's marketing textbooks use hotel examples to illustrate established principles where they would not have done so a few years ago. Hotel marketing is gradually receiving authoritative recognition as having come of age.

As the level of sophistication has risen, however, so has the pressure for performance. A number of factors are responsible for this. One is the increasing complexity of the decisions and choices to be made. Greater knowledge among hotel marketing management about the intricacies and potential of advanced market segmentation techniques, computer-assisted marketing information systems, highly-specialized market research, advertising media alternatives, and other variables in making decisions is changing hotel marketing into a much more demanding function than ever before.

Another factor placing even greater demands on hotel marketing management is intense competition. Not only has the number of competitors risen significantly everywhere, but competitive marketing tactics have grown increasingly aggressive and proficient. No market position or area of marketing activity is sacred, and even the most well-established properties can no longer eschew active competition. Effective hotel marketing management must compete competently.

A third factor in the pressure on hotel marketing management today is rapid and radical increases in costs and expenditures. This sector of management is increasingly being held accountable for greater return on marketing investment, cost-effectiveness, and profitability as expenditures continue to rise inexorably. The size of the marketing budget is increasingly being questioned, especially the way in which it is derived, and management is more than ever expected to demonstrate a direct, measurable, predictable correlation between expenditure, sales volume, and profits. Hotel marketing management must respond to this pressure as well.

All these factors have combined to increase the pressure on management to perform and to find ways to evaluate strategic marketing performance and

From Florida International University Hospitality Review, Vol. 1, No. 2 (Fall 1983): pp. 51-65. Reprinted by permission of *Florida International University Hospitality Review.*

effectiveness. Some hotels, of course, are not yet as aware of the pressure as others, while those that are may respond differently to it.

Many hotels seem content to do without any systematic, comprehensive attempt to evaluate their marketing effectiveness. This attitude is the result of a failure by top management to understand or accept the total marketing concept and the persistent belief that marketing is synonymous with sales. Top management may be more concerned with short-term results than with long-range growth, stability, and profitability. In such a situation, marketing effectiveness is evaluated in terms of short-term sales performance, as indicated by such measures as occupancy and average rate. But occupancy and average rate results in the short term may be due more to factors outside the hotel's control than to effective or ineffective marketing.

Even hotel managers who question strategic marketing performance and desire to evaluate marketing effectiveness systematically and comprehensively can find little guidance on how to proceed. Hotel marketing literature has conspicuously failed to address this area, and there seems to be no practical precedent for such a procedure in the industry. Other types of marketing review do exist, such as that which surrounds the preparation and monitoring of the execution of the annual marketing plan. But they are not designed to make a thorough, dispassionate examination of long-term marketing objectives, strategies, organization, policies, and procedures. Lacking the needed tools, marketing managers at these hotels continue from year to year without any real attempt to evaluate whether they are doing the best they can with what they have to ensure long-run profitability.

What is needed is a system to analyze and evaluate how the marketing function is being performed in order to improve the hotel's overall continuing marketing effectiveness, a tool to assess and appraise long-range performance. The questions to be answered include the following: Is our marketing as effective as it should be? How can we know? What factors determine marketing effectiveness? How can we improve?

One tool which can make a valuable contribution is the marketing audit. It offers a useful mechanism for evaluating hotel marketing effectiveness.

The Marketing Audit: What is It?

The marketing audit is not a new idea. Leading management consulting firms have been doing such audits since the early 1950s. However, the marketing audit is not yet as widespread and accepted a business practice, nor is its methodology as well-developed and sophisticated as the accounting audit. Unlike the latter, which seeks to determine quantitative accuracy and adherence to established procedures, the marketing audit is intended to expose inappropriate or uncoordinated objectives, strategies, policies, and procedures and guide the hotel toward the practice of the marketing concept as a strategic orientation. The methodology of the audit is also primarily one of judgmental analysis, without the quantitative precision of the accounting audit methodology.

A full-scale marketing audit is comprehensive. It covers not just specific marketing activities such as advertising and personal selling, but also objectives and strategies, and analysis, planning and control systems. Like the accounting audit, it should be done according to an established sequence of systematic steps, going from the general to the specific, without jumping any step. And, again like the accounting audit, it should be scheduled as part of the regular calendar of recurrent management events. It should not be reserved to diagnose problems as they arise or seen as a source of quick solutions to produce fast results. It is these characteristics that distinguish the marketing audit from other, less sophisticated types of review and evaluation.

The marketing audit, like the accounting audit, evaluates people's work. As a result, its conclusions and recommendations can have strong political repercussions within the hotel organization. With regard to who should do the marketing audit, the best choice would be to use an external, independent auditor with hotel marketing auditing experience. However, while a self audit is not likely to be equally objective, it may yet provide a useful stimulus for significant improvement and a further, external audit. In the case of hotel chains, corporate, divisional, or regional offices might provide relatively objective internal marketing audit services to member hotels either on request or as a matter of policy. Whoever does it, pains should be taken to have it perceived as non-threatening and supportive, although some people will be defensive nonetheless.

The Marketing Audit Procedure

The first step in doing a marketing audit is establishing its objectives, scope, data sources, and expected duration in consultation with the responsible hotel executive prior to beginning any data collection. This is essential to ensure unrealistic expectations are avoided and a positive, cooperative attitude is established throughout the audit between the auditor and the executive. Once this is done, a detailed determination of the documentation required should be made and a request made to the appropriate sources for organizational charts, marketing plans, advertising and sales promotion material, advertising media schedules, publicity clippings, sales call reports, other sales force reports, and all other forms and reports which can reveal the internal marketing information system.

The next step is to draw up an interview plan. This identifies who is to be interviewed, where and when the interview is to take place, and the questions to be asked. When a team of auditors is used, this step would also specify who is to be interviewed by whom. Careful preparation and implementation will significantly reduce auditing time and cost, and improve how the audit and the auditor are perceived by those whose cooperation is needed.

A decision has to be made whether to require individual interviews or group discussion. For individual instances, it is important to rehearse precisely which questions will be asked of whom in advance, and to prepare separate questionnaires for each person to be interviewed. This will better concentrate the focus of each interview. A decision must also be made whether to supply interviewees with advance copies of their respective questions. Submitting questions in advance is helpful for the more quantitative questions, but eliminates spontaneity, which may be especially valuable for qualitative, judgmental questions. Some questions are best asked of a team of those directly responsible and involved.

Interview reports, whether individual or group, should be prepared daily to reveal any areas requiring further clarification or exploration while the audit is still in the data collection stage.

The marketing audit should never rely too heavily on those being audited or on any one person, even if senior or experienced. Information obtained in interviews should be cross-checked and adjusted for bias where justified.

The marketing audit should also include interviews of hotel guests, major client accounts, travel agents and tour wholesalers who do business with the hotel or its competition, sales agents and hotel representatives, advertising and public relations agencies, and physical transportation middlemen such as airlines, car rental firms, and other ground transport operators. Often these outside information sources are more important than those within the hotel. Information should also be collected by simple observation.

During this data collection stage, the marketing auditor should meet at least once with the responsible executive to review progress against the original plan, identify and resolve any problems, and modify the scope, as may be necessary. However, no preliminary recommendations or decisions should be made or opinions formed at this time until the audit is completed.

At the end of the data collection stage, after all interviews have been conducted, preliminary conclusions, suggestions, and general recommendations should be verbally presented to the responsible executive prior to preparing the final, written report. Discretion may also justify making only a verbal report of any material especially disparaging about anyone audited. The final report should restate the original objectives and scope, report the findings in detail, and make specific recommendations for action. Recommendations should be prioritized according to urgency, probable cost, and ease of implementation, and each should be assigned to a person who becomes responsible for implementation and is allotted a prescribed time for completion.

While these procedures may seem at first to be disagreeably time-consuming and difficult to put into practice, in fact they are no more so than the standard accounting audit already long in use. Initial, start-up problems can be expected, of course. But with recurrent use, the marketing audit can quickly become as routine as the accounting audit. Moreover, for hotels committed to maximizing marketing performance, its benefits outweigh its limitations.

The above procedure is only meant to illustrate the marketing audit technique in general terms. Before doing an actual audit, a more detailed procedure would need to be designed and tested on a small scale. Some audits might be more complex than others, involving other stages and information sources.

Corporate Marketing Audits

While attention here is focused exclusively on the individual hotel, marketing audits find equal application as a technique for analyzing and evaluating corporate strategic marketing effectiveness of a hotel chain. A corporate marketing audit of a chain would examine marketing objectives, policies, and procedures at the corporate level in terms of the marketing performances of the company as a whole. It would need to assess the corporate marketing information system, planning and competitive strategy, and communications, organization and control in terms of the company as a single business unit, rather than its constituent hotels. Although the specifics of the marketing audit procedure would need to be modified to accommodate the different focus involved, the general direction would remain the same.

A Marketing Audit Framework

One obstacle in the development of hotel marketing audits has been the need to produce a framework of logical, detailed points of inquiry, custom-fitted to hotel operations and marketing activities. These points should evolve from the recognition of what constitutes marketing effectiveness for a hotel and what factors determine it. The checklists that follow suggest basic guidelines and starting points for such a framework. They show the direction to follow and are meant to stimulate and precipitate more detailed questions. The checklist approach is useful because it provides an orderly, methodical procedure and avoids the danger of forgetting important topics. Checklists also save time in data collection and allow comparison of results obtained over time. However, they should not be used restrictively, but should be subject to modification for improvement at the discretion of the marketing auditor.

Hotel marketing is today under ever-increasing pressures to perform because of such factors as the increased variety of variables involved in making marketing decisions, the intense competition, and the runaway marketing costs. Hotel marketing managers should make a deliberate, determined effort to respond constructively to such pressure for their own best interests. A new tool must be developed and perfected to aid in the assessment and appraisal of hotel marketing effectiveness. The hotel marketing audit offers a workable, worthwhile mechanism to accomplish this goal. The purpose here has been to suggest a feasible approach in this direction.

Marketing audit methodology is not yet so sophisticated as to be immediately implementable in every hotel. Each would need to invest the time and other resources necessary to develop its own marketing audit procedures before doing one, but the benefits to be derived in terms of revealing opportunities for improving marketing performance and productivity seem eminently timely and worthwhile.

The Audit Checklist

Part I: Marketing Information Checklist

The marketing audit should begin with a look at the hotel's overall marketing information system to determine the extent and effectiveness of its role and contribution in making marketing decisions. An advanced, planning-directed, marketing information system is purpose-built exactly to provide maximum input into marketing strategy decision making, and is distinguished from a rudimentary system made up of assorted procedures and reports with low impact on marketing decisions. Generally, the more committed management is to a planning-directed marketing information system, the more advanced the system is likely to be, and the more each of its component parts—market intelligence, market research, and internal reports—is likely to be carefully structured and managed. Key points to look for are:

- **Market Intelligence:** Is management very knowledgeable about its competition and their marketing efforts, both current and future? Does management appear to be in touch with current trends in the marketplace? Is the sales force encouraged and expected to spot and report new market development? Has management specified the kinds of market information it wants regularly collected and by whom? Are the front office and food and beverage units also involved in collecting market information? Is the system formally organized or treated casually? How are sales force reports used? Are they studied and discussed?

- **Market Research:** Does management do any research into the hotel's markets and sources of business? What market research projects have previously been done? Has management made any effort to measure the cost-effectiveness of varying marketing expenditures to see what happens when they spend more or less in any area?

- **Internal Reports:** Are accounting reports in a form that permits easy, regular use by marketing? Are accounting and front office reports respected and valued by the marketing department for their accuracy, timeliness, and relevance in making marketing decisions? How does marketing use the reports? What changes in recordkeeping and report formats could be made to improve the usefulness of internal reports in making decisions? What information does marketing want that it is not now getting?

Part II: Marketing Planning

The objective in examining the hotel's marketing planning activities and methods is to evaluate management's approach to and use of planning in its competitive strategy. The audit should look at the hotel's planning philosophy through its policies and procedures, forecasting, objectives and strategies, and actual marketing plan document. The auditor must be careful, however, to avoid undue emphasis on the hotel's marketing plan, and go beyond token symbols of planning to the real planning process as it is in practice. Some of the main criteria to use are:

- **Policies and Procedures:** Does management do any formal marketing planning? Is there a documented planning cycle policy? Is the planning cycle enforced? Does the cycle include stages for review while plans are in the process of being prepared? Is there both long and short-range marketing planning? Does planning appear to be done mainly to satisfy a corporate policy rather than being valued in its own right? Do managers tend more to plan what they think their superiors want to see than what they themselves genuinely believe?

- **Forecasting:** What forecasting methods are used? How accurate have forecasts been in the past two years? What time periods do they cover? Are there immediate, short-term, medium-term, and long-term forecasts? Are there optimistic, most-likely, and pessimistic forecasts? Are forecasts made by market segment? Is market share measurement used? Is market share measured for each target market? How are the hotel's market shares explained? How are competitors' market shares explained? What trends in market share are projected?

Is any attempt made to measure the current and future sales potential and profitability of different market segments? Have growth markets been identified? Which departments use which forecasts, for what purpose and how? Are forecasts generally respected by all departments for their accuracy and reliability? How can forecasting accuracy be improved? Would the benefit be worth the cost?

- **Objectives and Strategies:** Have target markets been clearly identified, prioritized, and profiled? Are there separate marketing objectives and strategies for each? Are the objectives clearly stated, logically related to, and appropriate for the hotel's competitive position, resources, and identified target opportunities? Are the strategies clear, logically derived from and compatible with the objectives? Are there strategies that are not documented but are being implemented in practice? Is there any confusion among marketing staff about the hotel's marketing objectives and general strategies?

- **The Marketing Plan:** Does the hotel have a formal, written marketing plan? Is there an annual as well as a five-year plan? How detailed is it? Does it cover all the key areas? Does it contain detailed analyses of the hotel's markets, competition, product, rates, marketing communications, sales channels, marketing information system, and marketing organization? Does it contain clear statements of objectives and strategy for each target market? Have strategies been translated into specific, measurable action plans? Is there provision for periodic progress review and control?

Does it contain detailed forecasts and marketing expenditure budgets? Is it fully circulated to all those with an active responsibility for implementation, including non-marketing personnel? Is there evidence that the plan is used throughout the year for reference, guidance, and control? Are the marketing resources adequate to achieve the goals set? How large is the gap? What resources are needed to close the gap? Will they be made available?

Part III: Product

Here begins the examination of each marketing-mix element. It may be useful to clarify the product concept on which this section is based. The product of a hotel is the total experience offered to and expected by the target market in the form of benefits. The purpose of the marketing audit is to identify and appraise the hotel's product objective and strategy in relation to its target markets and competition. Often, the hotel's product objective is implicit in its product strategy rather than clearly articulated or understood, or there may be no discernible, coherent product objective or strategy at all. The highly intangible nature of the hotel's product makes a clear, specific product objective especially valuable for the strategic marketing focus and reference point it provides. Some of the factors to look for are:

- **Objectives:** What kind of hotel experience is management aiming to offer its guests? Has this been clearly stated and effectively communicated to all levels throughout the hotel? Is there consensus about it? Has the intended experience been determined and based upon the hotel's best capabilities and management's understanding of guests' desired benefits? What benefits does the experience aim to offer guests? Have different versions of the experience been designed to satisfy different kinds of guests? What is the hotel's positioning objective? In what way is the experience being offered favorably differentiated from the competition? Is there an official image objective?

- **Strategy:** What are the hotel's features? How effectively do they provide the intended benefits for each target market? How do current guests evaluate the hotel's strengths and weaknesses, appeals and drawbacks? How do they evaluate competing hotels? How does management think guests rate the hotel and its competition? Which features and benefits desired by guests are not being provided by the hotel? What factors prevent the hotel from providing these features and benefits? How can the hotel's drawbacks be overcome? Do the guests get a trade-off for the drawbacks?

  Is there an active, continuous practice of generating, screening, and implementing new ideas to offer guests more satisfaction and value for their money? Are these ideas generally original or copied from the competition? Does the stimulus for innovative change come more often from operations or finance considerations rather than a guest satisfaction orientation? What are the projections for innovation in the features and benefits provided by competing hotels, both existing and planned?

Part IV: Rates

The marketing audit is not concerned with establishing or recommending rates, but rather it seeks to analyze and evaluate how the hotel uses rates in relation to its general marketing objectives, competitive marketing strategy, and other market-mix elements in each target market. Key areas the audit should cover are:

- **Objectives:** Is there a clear purpose regarding how rates are to be used to achieve overall marketing objectives in each target market? Has management defined the role of rates in achieving profitability and market share objectives? How do competitors use rates?

- **Strategy:** How are rates determined and structured? Do they support the positioning objective? How do rates compare with competitors' rates? What discounts are offered by the hotel and by the competition? How closely are rates administered and controlled? To what extent are rates used competitively and exploited for competitive advantage? To what extent are rates used as a promotional tool?

  Is there any widespread rate resistance from any market segment? How well are rates received? To what extent are rates in or out of line with each target market's perceived value of the experience offered by the hotel? How does this compare with their perceived value of competing offers? How are rates changed? Have recent rate increases been justified to the market by real improvements in guest satisfaction and value for money?

Part V: Trade Middlemen

Because the hotel is unlikely to carry out all its marketing activities entirely on its own, it is important to identify those marketing tasks it expects others to perform or assist in performing, and assess their suitability, effectiveness, and working relationship with the hotel in terms of the hotel's target markets, competition, resources, and trade motivational efforts. In general, trade middlemen would assist the hotel in making its product more efficiently available, accessible and known to its target markets, and would include wholesale and retail travel agents, general sales agents, hotel representatives, customer transportation firms, and marketing research and communications specialists. Examples of criteria to use are:

- **Objectives:** What tasks does management assign to independent trade middlemen to assist in achieving marketing objectives in each target market? To what extent is management dependent on wholesale, retail, or other selling agents and outside marketing specialists to achieve these objectives? How does this compare with the competition?

- **Strategy:** What trade middlemen does management use? What criteria are used in the selection of which wholesalers, sales agents, or hotel representatives to work with? How effectively are they kept informed, motivated, and evaluated on a regular basis? What support services does the hotel offer its wholesale, retail, or other selling agents? How does this compare with the support services offered by competing hotels? What services and assistance would these agents value that are not now being offered by the hotel? What are the hotel's policies regarding special rates and booking and payment terms for these agents? How do they compare with those of the competition?

    What effort is made to stimulate agency cooperation and performance? Does management appear to understand agency operations and problems? Is there any special program to improve agency relations by helping them achieve their goals? Is management generally indifferent or distrustful toward agents? Are there joint, agency-hotel marketing efforts?

    Is there a strong, cooperative relationship with transportation intermediaries such as airlines and car rental firms? Are there joint marketing efforts between the hotel and these transportation firms? What outside marketing specialists are used? How are they selected, motivated, and evaluated? How closely do they cooperate with each other and work as a team on the hotel's behalf? Is there any conflict or competition between them? How do selling agents, transportation firms, and outside marketing specialists evaluate the hotel, its marketing strategies, and its competition?

Part VI: Marketing Communications

The goal here is not to measure the return-on-investment productivity of advertising, sales promotion, or public relations expenditures, but rather to identify and evaluate objectives and strategies for each from an integrated, targeted, marketing communications perspective. All three elements should be mutually supportive and planned together for optimum, combined impact, and results in relation to the hotel's target markets, competitive strategy, and marketing communications resources. Important factors to cover are:

- **Objectives:** Are there clear objectives for advertising, sales promotion, and publicity? Are these objectives practical and measurable? Are they mutually supportive and interconnected? Are those responsible for implementing advertising, sales promotion, and publicity efforts aware of them?

- **Strategy:** Is there an established creative strategy, indicating the desired appeal to be used for each target market? Does the appeal effectively promote benefits rather than hotel features? Is each target audience clearly defined and profiled? On what basis was the target audience and desired theme chosen? How is the advertising budget determined? Is it prepared by market segment? Does the advertising being done conform to the creative strategy in design and copy? Are the advertising media used well-chosen? What methods are used to evaluate advertising effectiveness? What do the sales force and agents think of the advertisements? Is there a direct mail program and do campaigns conform to the established creative strategy? Do they have quantitative goals?

  How are sales promotion expenditures established? What consumer and trade promotion tools are used? Do they conform to the established creative strategy? Is trade show participation well-chosen and effective? Is there a sales promotion plan for each target market? How do sales promotion activities compare with competitors' efforts? How is their success evaluated? How is publicity used? What methods are used to obtain publicity for the hotel? How is the effectiveness of publicity efforts evaluated? Is there a detailed publicity plan? How does the publicity generated by the hotel compare with its competitors' efforts?

Part VII: Marketing Communications: Personal Selling

The hotel's sales force should be examined to determine its principal marketing role and how efficiently and effectively it performs it. The marketing audit should look at its structure and resources, and its day-to-day operations, including actual sales calls. Some key points to look for are:

- **Objectives:** What tasks is the sales force expected to perform to help the hotel achieve its marketing objectives in its target markets? How are these tasks ranked in importance? How does this compare with what the competition expects from its sales force? Is the sales force expected only to produce the budgeted sales volume, with little involvement in producing guest satisfaction and profitability?

- **Strategy:** How well is the sales force fulfilling its expected role? What is the size of the sales force and how is it determined? Is the sales force large enough for the task it has been assigned? Is it organized along territorial or market segment specialization lines or both? Is the type of sales force organization appropriate for the assigned task? How does the hotel's method and level of sales force compensation compare with competitors? How is the sales force recruited? What training do they receive? What is the level of turnover? What is the major cause? Does the sales force in general display high morale, ability, and effort?

How does the sales force feel about the job? Do they seem very knowledgeable? How many days per month are actually spent selling? What can be done to reduce the amount of non-selling time? What is the average number of calls per day? How many calls are made to solicit new business? What percentage of new business comes from sales force solicitation? To what extent is telephone selling used? How does the sales force perform on calls? Does top management often accompany the sales force on calls, make telephone sales calls, or meet clients on site inspection? Does the sales force feel their activities are effectively supervised and controlled by management? Do they use time efficiently and effectively? Is the general working atmosphere highly pressured or calmly efficient?

How is the hotel's sales force perceived by clients in comparison to the competition? How do other departments evaluate the efficiency and effectiveness of the sales force? Are there any major interdepartmental problems and conflicts? Do the salespeople work well with operations people to resolve issues in the interest of guest satisfaction? Are interdepartmental relations genuinely close and team-spirited or merely cool?

Part VIII: Marketing Organization and Control

Any evaluation of the efficiency and effectiveness of the hotel's marketing organization must first consider the hotel's commitment to the marketing concept as a strategic philosophy. This will heavily influence its attitude toward sales versus marketing and how it assigns sales and marketing authority and responsibility. The marketing auditor must be careful, however, not to take titles at face value. Often, a title with "marketing" in it has more form than substance in terms of genuine authority and responsibility. The audit should also examine those formal techniques and procedures used to track and control the performance of each marketing-mix element. Examples of areas to cover are:

- **Philosophy:** Is management largely operations- or market-oriented? Is more attention paid to operational efficiency and productivity than to identifying and satisfying guests' desires? When there is a conflict between the two, which is more likely to prevail? Is efficient operation taken as an end in itself or as a means toward guest satisfaction? Are guests' complaints generally considered more a routine nuisance to be endured than an opportunity for improvement?

- **Structure:** How is marketing authority and responsibility assigned? Is overall marketing authority and responsibility fully brought together in a specific position at the highest executive level? Is the assignment of personal selling responsibility clearly distinguished from the assignment of responsibility for other marketing activity?

- **Marketing-Mix Controls:** Are periodic techniques in use which are designed to measure performance against projected results? Do they reveal any variance? When identified, are such variances analyzed to determine their cause, and alternative courses of possible action evaluated for their suitability to remedy the variance? Is there evidence of corrective action being taken after such an analysis? What policies and procedures exist to control and ensure the quality of the guests' experience at the hotel? How effectively is guest dissatisfaction identified and resolved? Is there any recurring pattern of guest dissatisfaction? Is there an observable commitment to reduce and minimize guest dissatisfaction?

How are the setting and quoting of rates controlled? Is rate control considered too rigid or too lax by the sales force of the front office? Are variances from rack rates adequately monitored? Is there formal, on-going measurement of agency productivity? How is the productivity data used? How is advertising and public relations agency performance evaluated? What quantitative marketing control instruments are used? Are advertising-to-sales and sales-staff-to-sales ratios monitored? Are there sales force productivity standards? How are they used? How is the sales force evaluated? Do sales force evaluations appear to be frank and improvement-oriented?

References

Aubrey Wilson's Marketing Audit Check Lists. Maidenhead, England: McGraw-Hill Book Co., 1982.

John Naylor and Alan Wood, *Practical Marketing Audits*. New York: Wiley, 1978.

Philip Kotler, "The Marketing Audit Comes of Age," *Sloan Management Review,* Winter 1977, pp. 25–43.

From *Florida International University Hospitality Review,* Vol. 1, No. 2 (Fall 1983): pp. 51–65. Reprinted by permission of *Florida International University Hospitality Review.*

REVIEW QUIZ

When you feel you have covered all of the material in this chapter, answer these questions. Choose the *best* answer. Check your answers with the correct ones found on the Review Quiz Answer Key at the end of this book.

True (T) or False (F)

T F 1. The marketing strategy used at The Sheraton at Steamboat is an example of market expansion.

T F 2. The Americana Congress Hotel gave up on its permanent guests and concentrated on the tour and travel market, especially on bus tour operators.

T F 3. The Sheraton at Steamboat engaged heavily in full destination promotions.

T F 4. The case studies in the chapter indicate that a one-dimensional approach to marketing is most effective.

T F 5. The Opryland Hotel made effective use of its lost business reports.

T F 6. The Sheraton at St. Johns Place effectively used the concept of a local advisory board.

T F 7. The Americana Congress Hotel decided to strongly feature price and availability as selling points to its targeted markets.

T F 8. The Opryland Hotel repositioned itself away from meeting planners and concentrated its marketing efforts on local public relations programs.

T F 9. The Sheraton at Steamboat and the Opryland Hotel faced almost identical marketing problems.

T F 10. The late-night restaurant hours and diverse menu selection devised by the Americana Congress Hotel reveal a strong emphasis on sales-mindedness.

T F 11. The Sheraton at St. Johns Place had to address the problem of occupancy during the off-season summer months.

Multiple Choice

12. The Opryland Hotel examined and approached which of the following markets?

   a. relocation markets
   b. government market
   c. retiree motor coach market
   d. group business

Part V

Strategic Planning: Managing for Growth

This section focuses on strategic planning as a growth philosophy. Chapter 15 addresses the reasons companies may adopt strategic planning as a growth philosophy and illustrates how the concepts of "common thread" and "synergy" provide directions for growth. The chapter also presents a variety of growth strategies open to many hospitality properties. Chapter 16 concludes this text with a discussion of how properties that manage for growth may gain and sustain a competitive advantage by attending to current trends and future possibilities that affect the hospitality industry.

Chapter Outline

Business Definitions and the Common
    Thread
Synergy
Intensive Growth Strategies
    Market Penetration
    Market Development Strategy
    New Product Development
Integrative Growth Strategies
Concentric Diversification
    Atlantic City
    Las Vegas

Learning Objectives

1. State general reasons companies may have for pursuing growth opportunities.

2. Explain what is meant by economies of scale.

3. Explain what is meant by experience-curve effects.

4. State the purpose of a business definition in the context of strategically planning for growth.

5. Explain what is meant by a common thread.

6. Explain what is meant by synergy.

7. Describe intensive growth strategies.

8. Describe integrative growth strategies.

9. Describe concentric diversification growth strategies.

15

Growth Strategies

ORGANIZATIONS CAN GROW in many dimensions. Three of the most important are: sales, profits, and people. Most companies would like to grow in all three of these dimensions. Companies differ, however, in the degree to which they actively pursue growth opportunities. Firms that actively pursue growth reinvest a considerable amount of available funds in the expansion of their operations. Some of the reasons that companies may have for pursuing growth opportunities include: developing personnel within their organizations by providing professional growth opportunities, capitalizing on cost benefits through economies of scale and experience-curve effects, and diversifying through the development of strategic business units (SBUs).

Company growth provides psychological and financial rewards as well as promotion opportunities for managers and employees. Salary increases, profit-sharing plans, and bonuses are some of the potential financial rewards derived from working in a growing, healthy organization. Opportunities for promotion often attract and keep managers who possess the kind of entrepreneurial spirit that can keep an expanding company on a growth direction.

A second reason for actively pursuing growth is that it can lead to economies of scale and experience-curve efficiencies that improve a company's cost structure. An economy of scale can be thought of as a cost advantage that is simply the result of a company's size. An example of an economy of scale in the hotel industry is the ability of a large firm to gain a cost advantage over its competitors by spreading advertising costs over a larger number of properties. Experience-curve efficiencies, on the other hand, are cost advantages gained over time as a company's knowledge accumulates and the number of its business units increases as well. The cost benefits usually come about simply because a company gets better and more efficient at what it does.

Most companies start out by serving one customer group with one specific product or service. However, this situation may leave a company vulnerable if the product or service goes out of style, if a substitute product comes along, or if a competitor enters the market with a better product or service. To offset this vulnerability, some companies actively pursue growth as a means of developing a set of semi-autonomous businesses, called strategic business units (SBUs). The Marriott Corporation is an example of a lodging company that has implemented the SBU concept. In addition to its core business of hotels, Marriott has a restaurant SBU that includes the Roy Rogers and Big Boy food service chains, and also a contract food service SBU. In a centralized organization, SBUs can support one another because resources can be funneled from units that generate cash to those units which require cash to realize their full growth potential. Another advantage of the SBU concept is that it spreads risk, much in the same way that sophisticated investors spread their risk by developing diversified investment portfolios that consist of stocks, bonds, real estate investments, and precious metals. According to this analogy, the more diverse a company's businesses, the better may be its chances of withstanding changes in the economic environment.

Some firms have found out the hard way that diversity does not guarantee strong financial performance. Diversity requires the ability to successfully operate separate businesses that may vary greatly in terms of necessary production processes, technological abilities, managerial talents, and marketing skills. Also, diversification is not the only growth strategy open to companies in the lodging industry. Later sections of this chapter will discuss other growth strategies such as market penetration, new product development, and international and domestic expansion.

The kind of strategic planning which normally precedes a successful growth venture is very similar to the early phases of strategic marketing planning. Strategic marketing planning begins with a concise mission statement which clearly defines what the business is and what the business is not. Strategic planning as a growth philosophy also begins with a basic definition of the company's business activity. This business definition guides the company's search for a "common thread" which could link its present business concerns to future growth possibilities.

Business Definitions and the Common Thread

In his classic article, "Marketing Myopia," Theodore Levitt suggests that a business should look to a broad range of growth options by defining itself in relation to the generic need being fulfilled. Thus, railways would view themselves as in the transportation business, petroleum companies in the energy business, and lodging companies in the leisure time business. Defining a business in terms of generic need can be extremely useful in fostering a creative search for strategic growth opportunities. In particular, the generic need concept helps managers avoid an internal, product-oriented focus and frees the business to seek new growth directions.

However, defining a business in terms of generic need leaves some unanswered questions: Does it follow, for example, that railroad companies should be in the long-haul trucking business? What about taxicabs or the rental-car business? These are all transportation industries, but they may have little in common with the skills, facilities, and experience necessary for the effective and efficient operation of a railway system. Also, are petroleum companies really in the energy business? Should they diversify into synthetic uranium fuels for atomic power plants? The managerial, technical, production, and marketing skills necessary for each operation may be entirely different.

Some years ago, Holiday Inns, Inc. broadened its business definition to include the travel industry and acquired Trailways, Inc., the nation's second largest bus company, and Delta Steamship Lines, Inc. In 1978, however, the company redefined its business as a hospitality industry and decided to limit the scope of its operations to food service, lodging, and entertainment, and so divested itself of Trailways and sought a buyer for the steamship line.[1]

Frederic V. Malek, Executive Vice President of the Marriott Corporation in the mid-1970s, recalls that:

> ❝In the early seventies, a serious effort was made to define what we were.... The broadly defined answer was: leisure time. From there it was an easy jump from restaurants, contract feeding, and hotels to cruise ships and theme parks. We said, 'Aren't theme parks just restaurants with entertainment? Aren't cruise ships floating hotels?'❞[2]

Marriott has since moved to a more internal focus and has de-emphasized theme parks and cruise ships, focusing instead on opening more hotels and serving a wider range of customers with its institutional food service.

Defining a business by the generic need it seeks to fulfill may reveal many growth options, but it may be insufficient in terms of providing actual direction for growth. A more adequate guide to practical growth opportunities may arise as companies first define their businesses in relation to their current product/market positions, and then search for a common thread which could link their present business concerns to immediate possibilities for expansion or diversification.

Traditional business definitions in manufacturing industries focus on the "product line"—what the business offers for sale. However, in terms of lodging and food service operations, a product line definition focusing on rooms or food would miss the necessary service element of these hospitality industries. Other business definitions in manufacturing industries concentrate on the technology employed to satisfy consumer needs. However, in a service industry, the technology dimension is only a part of the necessary service delivery system. People, not equipment, are at the center of the hospitality industry.

Many businesses erroneously define their operations in terms of specific customer needs their companies attempt to satisfy. This procedure could result in an unwieldy and confusing definition because any given customer will frequently have an indefinite number of unrelated needs such as: needs for food and shelter, entertainment needs, vacation needs, psychological needs, and so on. Needs are best defined as states of felt deprivation of some basic satisfaction. They are not created by marketers; rather, they are implicit in the human condition. Wants, on the other hand, are desires for specific satisfiers of deeper needs. For example, a person needs food and wants a hamburger, needs clothing and wants an L. L. Bean jacket, needs esteem and wants a Cadillac. In each society and culture, wants are shaped by social forces and institutions such as churches, schools, families, and businesses.

Customer groups, not customer needs, should be the basis for defining a business's immediate activity. Customer groups are groups of consumers with related needs. A customer group is an economic unit (such as an individual, family, or even another business firm) that possesses a need for specific products or services, and the means by which to satisfy that need.

A practical business definition that provides a concise statement of a company's current product/market position addresses product characteristics of the lodging firm, technological and human resource dimensions of the firm, and the customer groups which the firm attempts to serve. The link between the present and the future is the "common thread"—a natural extension of the firm's current product/market position through some core characteristic or capability of its current business operations. The common thread points the direction for future growth and provides clear guidelines on where the organization's resources can be applied most effectively.

Synergy

The starting point for defining the common thread is synergy. Synergy refers to the interaction that takes place between two or more businesses, product lines, or functional areas which share a common resource or capability. Areas that can experience synergistic effects include:

- Sales and advertising—through shared image or sales force
- Use of facilities—through shared meeting, banquet, or public space
- Research and development—through shared knowledge and expertise

An example of synergy is the acquisition of major hotel companies by airlines: Intercontinental by Pan Am (acquired in 1981, but sold in 1982), Hilton International by TWA (1967), Westin Hotels by United Airlines (1970), and Meridien Hotels by Air France. Another example of synergy is a mixed-use project in which a hotel is located close to primary demand generators such as commercial and residential developments. Royce Hotels' West Palm Beach property, for example, integrates office, hotel, lounge, and limited retail operations with atrium costs shared by offices and the hotel. Office tenants get to use the hotel's health club facilities as well as meeting and banquet facilities.[3]

The key to capitalizing on potentially synergistic relationships is identifying a firm's distinctive competencies or business strengths. A distinctive competence is something the organization is particularly good at, such as marketing or human resource development. Capitalizing on synergistic relationships is really a two-step process. It begins by asking, "What are we good at? What can we do better than our competitors?" It concludes by asking, "How can we build on our strengths (or overcome our weaknesses)?" An inventory of a firm's assets and distinctive competencies will often reveal both strengths and weaknesses. Assets may include financial resources, facilities, managerial talents, efficient operating systems, a successful image, a loyal customer base, and more.

The identification of strengths and weaknesses can be strongly influenced by characteristics of managers such as the level of their positions in the organization, their backgrounds, and their lengths of service with the company. For example, managers tend to be more optimistic about the analysis of a company's strengths and weaknesses. Therefore, in order to get a complete picture of the firm, it is necessary to get input from a variety of perspectives. Differences among various managers within the same company may suggest that frank and open discussions are needed to ensure that the resulting list of strengths and weaknesses is not superficial.

Growth opportunities must be evaluated in terms of how synergistic they are with a company's primary business area and basic distinctive competencies. Synergy is the key criterion used to evaluate growth options and guide investment and new-product development decisions. It is especially critical in regard to considerations involving diversification because decisions in this area often involve taking on businesses that may be new and unfamiliar to current management officials. Financial troubles may result from overextended resources when a company fails to evaluate growth opportunities in terms of basic synergies.

Synergy is not the only criterion used in making growth decisions. Businesses with a marketing orientation that are considering some form of expansion or diversification will generally address such concerns as: potential customer benefits, potential cost efficiencies, potential differences between the company's current marketing, research, service, and distribution systems and those that may be needed to operate successfully in the area of expansion or diversification. The corporate culture of an organization must also be considered. Simply put, corporate culture refers to everything behind the common phrase: "This is the way things are done around here." Every organization has a history of aims, policies, and accomplishments. These formal aspects of an organization's corporate culture, and informal aspects such as the current preferences of owners and top-level managers, are important factors which affect not only growth decisions, but also the initial decision to even consider growth opportunities.

The business definition of a firm and the identification of a common thread for guiding growth decisions represent starting points for a company's growth strategy. There still remains the task of defining the precise direction for growth. Growth moves by companies can be characterized as either aggressive or defensive. Aggressive growth moves generally offer new products or services that make use of an outstanding competence or asset possessed by the company. Defensive growth moves generally seek new business ventures that will themselves supply some key competence or asset which the company currently lacks. There are three broad growth strategies:

- Intensive growth
- Integrative growth
- Concentric diversification

While these strategies are *not* mutually exclusive, any combination of them will obviously entail more involved kinds of resource allocation decisions.

Intensive Growth Strategies

Intensive growth strategies seek to develop new products or new markets. Strategies for capitalizing upon intensive growth opportunities include market penetration, market development, and product development.

Market Penetration

This strategy involves growth in relation to markets which the company already serves. Growth in this area can occur by increasing product usage, gaining market share, or encouraging non-users to use the product. The advantage of pursuing a market penetration strategy is that the company already knows the key success factors required to compete in the market.

Increasing Product Usage by Current Customers. This can take place either by increasing the frequency of use or by developing new applications for current product users. As previously explained, the demand for lodging accommodations is generally a derived demand; consequently, it is unlikely that people will increase their frequency of use without stimulating primary sources of demand in the community (such as the construction of new tourist attractions in the community and near existing hotels), or stimulating favorable economic factors (such as increasing the leisure time or disposable income of individuals). Obviously, it is in the interest of lodging companies to take active roles in promoting tourism in their areas by lobbying in state and federal legislatures for increased tourist-related expenditures. Finding new applications for current product users could also involve promoting the facility as an ideal vacation getaway for a businessperson's family while, at the same time, promoting the property as an ideal place for business meetings. However, this strategy may blur the property's image in the marketplace.

Gaining Market Share. Gains in the share of a particular market are usually less expensive to achieve during the rapid growth phase in a product's life cycle. This is usually the case because the market is growing fast enough so that share gains do not come solely at the expense of competitors' sales. Instead, they come from capturing a disproportionate share of incremental sales and through sales to new users of the product. New users entering the market are relatively easy targets since they have no established loyalties and habits. Increasing market share at the expense of existing competitors can be difficult and is usually achieved through short-term tactical decisions in regard to advertising, promotions, or pricing considerations.

Converting Non-Users. Finally, a lodging operation could try to convince non-users of hotel accommodations to start staying at hotels. Special incentives, similar to those used to increase usage or gain market share (such as special discounts to senior citizens), could also encourage non-users to try the lodging market.

Market Development Strategy

This growth strategy looks for new markets whose needs might be met by current products and services offered by a lodging operation. This can take place either by bringing new users to the property, or by expanding the distribution network. Expanding the distribution network can be directed either toward international expansion or domestic expansion.

Bringing New Users to the Property. This was the strategy followed by the Sheraton at Steamboat, a destination resort in Steamboat Springs, Colorado, which generated demand by publicizing and promoting the area's attractions.

Expanding the Distribution Network. Geographic expansion can involve expanding to another country, from one region to another, or even from a regional operation to a national operation. Before adopting international or domestic expansion strategies, lodging companies need to address several concerns. First, operations within the current market must be sound. Second, if expansion means developing a new market, special attention needs to be given to differences in consumer habits, attitudes, and preferences. Third, plans must be developed to adjust to new conditions of expansion.

International expansion entails both risks and potential benefits. One risk is in site selection. For example, it is difficult for an executive from a lodging firm in the United States to discern the best location for a new hotel in New Delhi, India. Moreover, opening and operating offices overseas to deal with problems like site selection entails its own set of risks and administrative hassles:

- Financing can be more difficult to secure and, in many international markets, real estate is difficult to obtain and far costlier than in the United States.

- Hotels, like any other international business, have problems with currency fluctuations and restrictions on repatriating profits.

- Many food items and various supplies can be extremely expensive in foreign markets. For example, a hamburger-dominated menu is far costlier to provide in those countries where all beef is imported.

- Franchising standards can be difficult to enforce.

- Construction techniques or customs can be radically different. For example, the construction of the Mecca Intercontinental was supervised entirely by closed circuit cameras because the company's Western engineers were not permitted into the Islamic Holy City.

Operating foreign hotels often requires different standards and involves different customs. For example, virtually every American hotel company is involved in some kind of promotion whereby the customer receives a prize or discount for staying in the hotel. By contrast, Europeans often perceive American marketing programs as gimmicky, if not gauche. Some promotions and incentives are not only unpopular in Europe—in some countries, they are illegal.[4]

Finally, there is considerable competition from foreign chains, particularly in the more attractive operating environments. Britain's Trusthouse Forte, for example, is one of the world's largest hotel companies. Grand Metropolitan Hotels (also British) was large even before it acquired Intercontinental Hotels. Canada has its CP Hotels, CN Hotels, Auberge Des Gouverneurs, and Four Seasons Hotels Limited (the latter company now operates several luxury hotels in the United States). France has several worldwide chains, including Meridien, Club Mediteranee, Novotel, PLM-ETAP-Frantel International Hotels, and the Relais et Chateau Association. In fact, virtually every major country or region of the world has its own home-based chains and many of them have grown into international organizations, rivaling the international presence of American companies.

Holiday Corporation, Sheraton Corporation, and Ramada Inns, Inc., are currently the three largest hotel chains in the world, and all are looking to expand internationally even more in the future. Sheraton expects to increase its number of overseas operations by 250 properties, which would give them 700 hotels, inns, and resorts in 70 countries by the end of the decade.[5] One factor inhibiting the overseas growth of these companies is that much of the world is only now developing the transportation infrastructure that led to the hotel boom in the United States in the 1950s and 1960s.

To take advantage of the opportunities of global expansion, and to avoid some of the problems of overseas expansion, marketers in the lodging industry increasingly need to recognize the international nature of their business and develop a better understanding of other countries and cultures, particularly their languages.

Opportunities for domestic expansion with current products may exist even for large chains whose traditional markets are saturated. Opportunities arise in the form of improved site selection techniques. Access to and visibility from interstate highways and major traffic arteries are important site criteria, as well as proximity to office centers, central business districts, commercial and industrial concentrations, medical and educational complexes, regional shopping malls, and airports.

Opportunities for domestic expansion also arise in those parts of the country that are experiencing economic prosperity. For example, despite assertions by industry analysts that Holiday Corporation has saturated its middle-market base, the nation's largest hotel chain sees opportunities for domestic expansion in the western states and in the East.[6]

Like international expansion, domestic expansion is seldom haphazard. Many expansion strategies are guided by the concepts of adjacency, clustering, and filling-in. Adjacency refers to locating new motor inns within approximately 300 miles of existing properties. This improves service to franchisees as well as enabling closer contact with area developers. Clustering refers to building multiple inns in a major statistical metropolitan area. Filling-in refers to moving into secondary cities (populations under 100,000) within existing market areas.

New Product Development

Companies that fail to meet their growth objectives in existing (or new) markets with their current products may turn to a strategy of new product development. The maturity of the lodging industry and the wide variety of potential markets have induced many, but not all, hotel companies to turn to new product development for existing markets. Most of the companies that are developing new products are currently competing in the large, but crowded, mid-price market segment. Most operators on the high end of the scale, and almost all operators of budget hotels, have remained one-product companies.

The following sections discuss some of the challenges of new product development that arise in relation to resource allocation, fragmentation of functional activities, and image-related issues.

Resource Allocation Problems. Deploying limited financial resources across products in a multi-product, multi-market firm can create resource allocation problems. Some of the company's products and services may be in strong positions relative to competitors while other products or services may be in weaker positions. Some products may need cash to finance growth or fight competitive battles, while others may be generating more cash than they need. Even deciding whether or not to invest in new product development may be costly in terms of using valuable management time.

Fragmentation of Functional Activities. Hotel companies have created their new brands by purchasing existing hotel chains or properties, or by developing a new brand internally. The management of new brands may be structured in one of two ways: existing management may oversee the new brands, or a new division may be created within the company. Industry experts disagree on the appropriate organizational structure for a new, qualitatively different brand.

Daniel Lee argues that different kinds of hotels require different management skills:

> **❝**Most hotelmen operating luxury hotels would chaff at the economies necessary to make a budget motel successful. Similarly, most budget motel operators would have difficulty convincing themselves to spend money on the extravagances necessary in a luxury hotel. **❞**[7]

On the other hand, Gerald Petitt, Chief Operating Officer of Quality Inns, doesn't think the management skills are all that different:

> **❝**The difference is mostly in facilities and amenities. There shouldn't be a difference in the idea of providing service, and the basics, like smooth operation of the front desk and good housekeeping, are the same across all levels. **❞**[8]

Radisson Hotels and Quality Inns are among the hotel companies that have extended their product lines using existing management. Holiday Corporation is an example of a company that has created a separate division to manage its new product. Only its Crowne Plaza brand is run directly by Holiday Inns management; Holiday's other brands are entirely separate divisions, and to accentuate the differentiation from the Holiday Inn brand, two of the new division headquarters are located far from Holiday's Memphis headquarters. Residence Inns is located in Wichita, Kansas, and Embassy Suites is located near Dallas, Texas. In addition to using separate management teams, at least two of Holiday's chains (Hampton Inns and Embassy Suites) operate separate reservation systems while sharing equipment, communication circuits, and satellite communication systems.

Image-Related Issues. Creating a broad product line may tend to confuse customers and may be disadvantageous to an already predominant and well-known name. Different products often require separate national advertising since each brand may cater to very different markets. Reservationists may require a great deal more time to explain the differences to confused clients.

Another potential problem that may arise as lodging companies expand through developing new product lines is that differences within segments of the industry may begin to disappear. This places new demands and challenges for lodging industry marketers. According to Daniel Boorstein, Harvard sociologist:

> **❝**There is clearly a conflict between the homogenizing of all experience, the attenuation of space and time, the expectation of the same facility by the customer in every place, and, on the other hand, the expansive need to discover new wants, the need to provide new novelties for customers.... It seems to me that nowadays in a society where all places are becoming more alike, one of the responsibilities of the hotel business … is to think of more creative and appealing occasions for drawing people together. **❞**[9]

Integrative Growth Strategies ———————————————————————

Integration represents a second major potential growth strategy. Integrative growth attempts to operate in two or more areas of the marketing-channel stream through vertical integration. Vertical integration is the combination of technologically distinct production, distribution, selling, and/or other economic and business functions within a single firm. As such, it represents a decision by the firm to develop certain capabilities in-house, rather than going outside to have them performed. Daniel R. Lee identifies several ways by which vertical integration is accomplished in the lodging industry:

- Development: Locating the site, arranging financing, and coordinating the design

- Construction: Designing and actually building the property, usually as a general contractor

- Rooms Operations: Renting guestrooms

- Ancillary Services: Operating restaurants, bars, telephones, dry cleaning, shops, casinos, health clubs, etc.

- Referral Services: Reservations networking

Not all hotel companies wish to vertically integrate. International hotel chains, for example, often avoid becoming developers, contractors, or even investors, since site selection, the potential for real estate appreciation, and political risk are difficult to assess in an unfamiliar country. Large chains in the United States have been selling or franchising their hotels to private investors and then contracting to operate them. Sheraton, for example, a leader in selling and franchising, now owns only 14 of its 482 hotels. Ramada Inns owns only 12,000 of its 80,000 rooms. Of the 145 Marriott hotels and resorts, Marriott now owns only 20.[10]

Operating as a management company is a shrewd strategy and amounts to taking a capital intensive business (hotels) and making it noncapital intensive. A hotel chain puts up money to build a hotel, then sells it to a group of investors, either an insurance company, limited partnership, or real estate investment trust. The attractions for investors include a possible tax shelter, the prospect of growing cash flow, and possible capital gains in the future. Meanwhile, the management company makes money whether the hotel does so or not. With little cash in a project, the hotel company has money to build more hotels and sell them—allowing for rapid expansion. The trade-off is that while the hotel company avoids losses, potential profits are limited because it can't claim 100% of the profits. Furthermore, if it wants to make improvements in the hotel, it must often negotiate with the owners.

Concentric Diversification ———————————————————————

The third growth option available to lodging firms is concentric diversification. This strategy seeks to develop new businesses that have synergies with current businesses. Concentric diversification is an attractive growth option because it allows a chain to preserve its core business, while at the same time capitalizing on its business strengths and spreading the risks.

For many lodging companies, diversification means casinos. Marriott is one of the few large hotel companies to avoid the gaming business while diversifying in the areas of theme parks, timesharing, airline food service, cruise ships, and contract food service. Because gaming is so important to lodging companies, the following sections discuss the topic from the point of view of the two major casino areas in this country: Atlantic City and Las Vegas.

Atlantic City

As of August 1985, Atlantic City had ten casinos.[11] Now a year-round resort, Atlantic City boasts an overall occupancy of 85–90%. All the original casino hotels have expanded their capacities. Resorts International, for example, is adding 1,200 rooms to its current capacity of 686 rooms. Resort International's slot machine area boasts a total of 1,750 machines—this is more than are allowed in some countries!

Atlantic City's strength has always been its location. It is on the beach with a boardwalk and near the intersection of two major highways. More important, Atlantic City is the only major gaming facility in the East and is within 300 miles of some 54 million people. By comparison, there are approximately 17 million people within 300 miles of Las Vegas. However, transportation systems have posed some problems for the casino hotels in Atlantic City. While there is a major airport just a few miles from the city, there is yet no scheduled airline service. Major airlines seek a guarantee of room availability before scheduling regular flights, but the high occupancy rates of the casino hotels makes this impossible. The hotels have relied heavily on other modes of transportation such as private automobiles, small aircraft, and special bus services. Recently, Resorts International initiated its own helicopter service from Manhattan directly to its heliport.

Las Vegas

Total gaming revenues for Clark County, which encompasses Las Vegas, have grown astronomically. During the 1970s, the industry became accustomed to growth rates of 15% per year and the myth developed that gaming was recession-proof. However, growth rates tumbled sharply from 1981 through 1984.

Hotel rooms are important to Las Vegas. The city receives some 12 million visitors per year and the average stay is approximately 4.2 nights. Las Vegas hotels are currently targeting a new market—the middle and working classes. Some casinos have added recreation vehicle parks, low-stake slot machines, and fast-food restaurants. Circus-Circus Enterprises operates more casino space in Nevada than any other company and has attracted waves of "low-rollers" by offering moderate room rates and opening a 41-acre recreational vehicle park.

Endnotes

1. *Hotel & Resort Industry,* January 1985, p. 19.
2. "Holiday Inns: Refining Its Focus to Food, Lodging—and More Casinos," *Business Week,* July 21, 1980, pp. 100–104.

3. "Out of the Clouds; Back into the Kitchen," *Forbes*, May 15, 1978, p. 182.

4. "Four Differences Between U.S. and Foreign Hotel Operations," *Lodging*, January 1985, pp. 65–66.

5. "Kapioltas Leads Sheraton through Changes and Expansion Program," *Hotel & Restaurant Industry*, March 1985, p. 18.

6. Sally Clark, "Holiday Inns Forges Ahead with Ambitious Segmentation Plans," *Hotel & Restaurant Industry*, August 1984, p. 52.

7. Daniel R. Lee, in a marketing study by Drexel Burnham Lambert, January 1984.

8. Glenn Withiam, "Hotel Companies Aim for Multiple Markets," *The Cornell Hotel & Restaurant Administration Quarterly*, November 1985, p. 46.

9. Daniel Boorstein, "The Service Society," *The Future of Service*, Chicago: Renaissance, Inc., 1966, p. 3.

10. Howard Ruditsky, "What Do the Sellers Know that the Buyers Don't?" *Forbes*, October 7, 1985, p. 119.

11. Stuart I. Feiler, "Casinos: Is the Take Worth the Trouble?" *Hotels & Restaurants International*, July/August 1985, p. 116.

REVIEW QUIZ

When you feel you have covered all of the material in this chapter, answer these questions. Choose the *best* answer. Check your answers with the correct ones found on the Review Quiz Answer Key at the end of this book.

True (T) or False (F)

T   F   1.   Diversification guarantees strong financial performance.

T   F   2.   Economies of scale benefit smaller operations more than they do larger operations.

T   F   3.   The function of a business definition is the same as that of a company's mission statement.

T   F   4.   A need is best defined as a state of felt deprivation of some basic satisfaction.

T   F   5.   A common thread links a company's current product/market position to future possibilities for expansion or diversification.

T   F   6.   Synergy is the starting point for defining the common thread.

T   F   7.   Distinctive competencies represent the weaknesses of a company.

T   F   8.   Synergy is the key criterion used to evaluate growth options.

T   F   9.   Intensive growth strategies capitalize on existing product opportunities.

T   F   10.   Integrative growth strategies are primarily designed to develop new products or new markets.

T   F   11.   Concentric diversification seeks to develop new businesses that have synergies with current business functions.

Multiple Choice

12.   Which of the following is not a reason for a company to pursue growth opportunities?

   a.   personnel development
   b.   cost benefits
   c.   diversification
   d.   market saturation

13.   Defining a business in terms of the generic need it fulfills:

   a.   is sufficient in terms of providing practical growth options.
   b.   can be extremely useful in fostering a creative search for strategic growth opportunities.
   c.   provides managers with an internal, product-oriented focus.
   d.   all of the above.

14. Intensive growth strategies:

    a. include market penetration, market development, and product development.
    b. work through vertical integration.
    c. are based solely on the concept of synergy.
    d. none of the above.

15. Which of the following growth strategies focuses on vertical integration?

    a. intensive growth strategies
    b. integrative growth strategies
    c. concentric growth strategies
    d. none of the above

Chapter Outline

Trends in the U.S. Lodging Industry
    Consolidation
    Market Saturation
    Brand Proliferation
Well-Marketed Hotels of the Future
The Managers of the Future
Evolving Hospitality Technology

Learning Objectives

1. List what lodging marketers must do to gain and sustain a competitive advantage in the market.

2. Identify current trends affecting the lodging industry.

16

Current Trends and Future Possibilities

Economists often dream of a "perfectly competitive" industry in which many small sellers offer undifferentiated products to many small buyers. Here, no single firm can earn an above-average rate of return, charge exorbitant prices, or unduly influence industry events. The dream suggests that firms which habitually earn less than a minimal rate of return quickly draw the attention of competitive investors. Subsequently, a new wave of competition enters the marketplace and drives down the high returns previously enjoyed by a handful of firms. Once again, competition is balanced until some firms go out of business and others achieve high rates of return. In other words, perfect competition creates a perfect cycle which endlessly repeats itself. Obviously, the economists' dream of "perfect competition" applies to very few industries.

For firms to consistently achieve high rates of return, they need to gain and sustain a competitive advantage over similar firms in the market. The implication for lodging marketers is clear: they must differentiate their products by establishing strong brand images and cultivating consumer loyalty. Marketers must also constantly strive for a strong product-market fit. This task increasingly requires formal market research to gain an in-depth understanding of what existing and potential customers need and want.

To help increase their competitive advantage, hoteliers should capitalize on current trends and continually anticipate future possibilities for the industry. This chapter explores some of the present issues which are shaping the way hotels are organized and marketed as well as some of the factors which may affect hotel marketing in the future.

Trends in the U.S. Lodging Industry

Service industries, and especially the lodging industry, must be sensitive to changing market conditions and customer preferences. Successful marketers must be able to adapt the strategic plans of their properties to current trends in the business environment and be able to respond quickly to the changing needs and wants of consumers. This section examines three trends which challenge today's lodging industry: (1) consolidation, (2) market saturation, and (3) brand proliferation.

Consolidation

Consolidation can best be explained by way of a brief illustration. Few people can remember when the U.S. automobile industry comprised over 100 companies including such manufacturers as Hupmobile, Pierce Arrow, and Stutz Bear Cat. Today, the automobile manufacturing business has tapered to three major corporations—Ford, General Motors, and Chrysler Corporation—each of which offers a variety of product lines and brand names.

Is the hotel industry following a similar path toward consolidation? In 1948, only 4.7% of all hotels belonged to a chain organization.[1] Today, over 33% of hotel properties and 70% of all industry rooms carry some type of chain affiliation.[2]

Given the rapid rise of hotel/motel chains, it's important to look beyond the figures and examine factors which may be contributing to an industry trend toward consolidation. At present, five significant reasons may be cited for the increase in chain affiliation: accessibility of financing, growth of management companies, cost advantages, higher occupancy rates, and cost barriers to new firms.

Accessibility of Financing. The availability of money for real estate ventures through such sources as real estate investment trusts, limited partnerships, and syndications created vast opportunities for growth in the hotel/motel industry. This direction for growth encouraged chain affiliation because most lenders prefer to deal with hotel companies under some form of professional management.

Growth of Management Companies. As the industry continued to develop, management companies gained experience and cultivated reputations for operational expertise. In essence, the growing supply of strong management companies created its own demand.

Cost Advantages of Chains. Economies of scale and experience-curve efficiencies provide large hotel multi-unit chains with major cost advantages over single-unit or small firms.

Higher Occupancy Rates. Due to sophisticated, centralized reservations systems and other marketing resources at the disposal of large hotel/motel chains, chain affiliated properties typically enjoy higher occupancies than many independent hotel/motel properties.

Cost Barriers to New Firms. New firms seeking to enter the marketplace may experience such barriers as high capital costs for state-of-the-art equipment or extensive marketing expenditures. Such barriers may accelerate consolidation since the economies of scale inherent in chain affiliation help to surmount such cost hurdles.

Market Saturation

Market factors of supply and demand may affect the trend toward consolidation. The total domestic lodging demand is estimated to be increasing at only 1.8%.[3] Should the growth of chains and outlets far exceed the demand for rooms, certain areas of the country would soon be overbuilt and market saturation would result.

Market saturation is a critical concern for hoteliers because the hospitality industry is characterized by substantially high fixed costs and depends on high occupancy percentages. It appears that more and more cities are becoming overbuilt, thereby increasing the inventory of available rooms faster than it can be absorbed. The net effect is reduced occupancy for large and small properties alike. Factors that may contribute to overbuilding and market saturation include construction cycles, approaches of investors, tax legislation, industry exit barriers, and the different cycles of supply and demand that affect the lodging industry.

Construction Cycles. The construction cycle, which begins with the initial decision to build and ends with the actual opening of a property, is typically two to four years. To project the environmental conditions of a specific area that far into the future is often difficult, if not impossible.

Approaches of Investors. Investors often invest in capacity expansion at the peak of the business cycle and expect continued high occupancy rates, room rates, and profitability. Additionally, many investors are "product-oriented." They feel that their product has an edge in the marketplace and can defy supply and demand.

Tax Legislation. The tax legislation enacted in 1981 provided large and rapid depreciation write-offs for new corporate assets and consequent tax savings. As a result, investors found new hotels offered more desirable investment ventures than older ones. However, industry experts forecast that the revisions in tax legislation considered in early 1986 would temper such development trends.

Industry Exit Barriers. Relatively high exit barriers exist in the hotel industry since it is ordinarily difficult to phase out an older hotel from the marketplace. Unlike product industries, rooms cannot be sold in a clearance sale, be stored in a warehouse, or be easily adapted to other uses.

Cycles of Supply and Demand. Lodging supply and demand tend to follow different cycles. In recessionary periods, supply growth normally exceeds that of demand and results in excess capacity and slow industry recovery. During healthier economic times, demand growth exceeds that of supply and absorbs the supply backlogs built up during recessions. Also, the lodging industry normally lags behind conditions of the domestic economy by four to eight months. This is due in part to the fact that vacation reservations are often made several months in advance and that businesses usually reduce travel budgets when profits decline and increase them once profits improve.

Brand Proliferation

If E. M. Statler were asked today what three factors contribute to a successful hotel, he might modify his response "location, location, location" to mirror the formula proposed by Stephen Selka, President of Royce Hotels: "location, product, and identity."[4] Today's consumers have become increasingly sophisticated and value conscious. Consumers have a specific image of the services they want and the price they want to pay. In other words, consumers are less likely to accept a hotel that just falls short of their needs and more likely to seek a hotel that meets their needs exactly. Many hotel operators have had to face the possibility that their lodging product is boring since guests today are better educated, more well-traveled, and less inclined to accept standardized products.[5] In response to this diversity of demand, hotel companies have segmented the market extensively and developed a wider range of products to meet specific consumer needs.

Hotels today are shifting more and more from the typical market segments which dominated the pre-1980s. To meet the changing needs of consumers, new lodging concepts have emerged which appeal to narrowly defined market segments. Rather than offer one line or service level, many hospitality companies offer several different types under the umbrella of their brand name. This trend is known as brand proliferation.

Some companies such as Super 8 Motels tend to stick to their typical product and service line while other companies comprise a diverse group of operations but resist the term "proliferation." Hyatt, for example, maintains that it has only one brand and that its properties differ only in terms of "scale."[6] Still other lodging companies such as Royce Hotels try to preserve a unified identity by offering minor service level variations under a single brand name. "Hybrid" concepts have also been created which capitalize on a company's name while projecting a different image to consumers than that of the company's core offering. Typical examples of this concept include Marriott's Courtyard properties and the Holiday Corporation's Crowne Plazas. A few chains are establishing new product lines under entirely new names such as AIRCOA's Clarion Collection and Wynfield Inns, and Doubletree Hotels' Compri Hotel Systems.

Whatever the phenomena is called—brand proliferation, segmentation, or multiple-market strategy—it has produced an astonishing array of lodging offerings. Other factors contributing to this trend include market saturation, and competitive and cost pressures.

Market Saturation. A number of hotel chains are nearing saturation in their traditional markets. In order to continue growing, these companies have opted to target other market segments and produce products which match the particular constraints of the site. This appears to be the case with Marriott's Courtyard concepts which are typically located on small lots in suburban areas.

Competitive and Cost Pressures. Some companies are simply reacting to a combination of competitive pressures and higher construction and site-acquisition costs in particular markets. For example, when established mid-range properties moved into downtown or airport markets, they found themselves competing head-on with world-class hotels. Faced with such a situation, these companies were forced to develop comparable brands that would appeal to the typical market mix of the area.

Well-Marketed Hotels of the Future

In order to compete in a changing environment, lodging marketers will have to be familiar with the tools used to maximize product differentiation. Hoteliers should develop a solid understanding of the traditional marketing tools and be able to promote ideas for research and development, new product planning, packaging, and design. In the consumer package goods industry, each of these areas has evolved into a sophisticated and distinct discipline. Indications are that a similar evolution will take place in the lodging industry as tomorrow's marketers look for ways to carve out unique positions for their individual properties or groups of properties.

❝The greatest challenge of the eighties and nineties will fall within the sales function and specifically with the need for a commitment by management to train salespeople in market awareness. College graduates are entering the field with adequate business management knowledge but, too often, with no understanding of the difference between association meetings and corporate meetings; the evolving role of the travel agent; the decision-making processes of various client groups; the importance of the small meetings market in approaching large meetings; client attitudes; and more. Also, all too often the individual is granted the title of Sales Manager or Director of Sales and is simply told to 'go sell,' with emphasis on cold calls, blitzes, and telephone solicitation [but,] again, with inadequate preparation regarding customer identification and needs.

Long-term success in hospitality marketing in the next two decades will [require] that the marketing executive: (1) be given the investment of continuous training, (2) be provided salary and benefit levels commensurate with the responsibility in order to minimize industry transience and develop loyalty, and (3) be included in the mainstream operational decisions which greatly influence the marketing executive's ability to work effectively.❞

—**Buck Hoyle**
Executive Vice President
HSMAI

Buck Hoyle sees the need to change the way the lodging industry develops and challenges its people. Bill Newman foresees the challenge of teaching marketing people to use the emerging techniques and technology of marketing.

❝One thing is the degree to which automation and computerization will be used in marketing. There will be more and more opportunities for retrieval of hard data and for processing that data in a way that allows for sound marketing and management decisions. We [will be] able to tell at the punch of a button or two whether a prospective piece of business will be profitable or not or whether a booking a salesperson has made meets the financial needs of the hotel and, if not, why not. [This] will eliminate the guesswork and allow for fine-tuning of room rates, food prices, and the other variables offered to the customer.

[Our industry is] almost complete in the evolution from an operational orientation to a point of view which makes marketing an equal partner. Younger managers, who have been exposed to sophisticated marketing techniques as part of their educational process, come to properties ready to work with directors of marketing in a climate of mutual respect and understanding.

I think you'll also see more and more directors of marketing moving into general managers' slots.... And the day is really not too far down the road when, at some hotels, you'll [have] a manager for operations who runs the physical plant and a manager from marketing who makes all the other decisions—not just guestroom marketing but meal pricing, valet and laundry prices, virtually anything that has to do with generation of revenue.

That [prediction] comes out of the sad truth that you can be the best general manager and have the best hotel in the world operationally, but if you don't have any guests, who cares?❞

—**Bill Newman**
Senior Vice President—Marketing
Westin Hotels

From an operations standpoint, the hotels of the 1980s became much more complicated than the hotels of the past. The traditional hotel types overlapped tremendously in the scramble to meet a significantly more fickle and sophisticated market. In downtown areas, there may be small hotels for the senior executive, hotels-within-hotels, massive convention facilities, and hotels with no facilities other than guestrooms. Destination resorts, which used to live or die on the quality of their in-season business, are now adding facilities to make themselves attractive to meeting planners during the off season. Such resorts are doing an imaginative job of marketing the shoulder seasons as well. Today's airport hotel includes everything from a no-nonsense economy (e.g., Thrifty Scot, Super 8) to massive convention properties such as those located around Los Angeles International Airport. Even the highway intersection motel has been replaced by a convention-oriented hotel that may also offer a weekend escape package complete with an indoor pool and health club.

This evolution is still continuing. Whereas, in the past, hotels were built in a particular location because of what was already there (e.g., a railroad terminal, an airport, a convention center), hotels today are built into development projects to increase the value of the locations. As more American cities recognize the need for growth and resurgence in their downtown areas, virtually every proposed city center project contains one or more hotels. Even proposals for shopping centers include hotel facilities as part of the development package. Why? Because hospitality marketing makes these new hotel facilities magnets that add to the value of the developments. When the creative practice of hospitality marketing is combined with the imaginative marketing concepts of other business entities, projects are much more likely to succeed financially in the long run. Because even greater business challenges will be imposed upon the hotels of the future, new types of managers will be needed to run them successfully.

The Managers of the Future

There is no question that the individuals who are emerging as leaders in the hotel industry today are increasingly marketing-minded. Some started out in management but recognized that marketing skills were fast becoming essential within the industry. Others started out as marketing people and grew into executive positions. In the future, managers will need an even greater sensitivity to and familiarity with marketing if they are to succeed in the hotel business.

The hotel manager of tomorrow will still have to be able to deal with the needs and problems of guests. But, additional challenges will be presented by having to deal with another very important aspect of the hotel business: the owner. In general, today's hotels are not owned by the hospitality company that operates them. Instead, they are owned by insurance companies or business enterprises for which hotel ownership is only a sideline, or they are owned by groups of individuals who have invested in hospitality real estate for purposes of their own. Sensitivity to the business needs of owners is becoming as fundamental to success in the hospitality field as the ability to properly check in a guest. As owners increasingly come to the hotel business from other successful enterprises, they will demand more and more interface and dialogue with the people who are managing their valuable real estate.

Today's owners are increasingly basing their evaluations of operating companies on the effectiveness of the marketing program. Therefore, it is extremely important that the hotel schools that train the managers of tomorrow take into account the realities of ownership today and prepare students for the challenges that lie ahead. Generally, hotel schools do a better job today than ever before of teaching principles of marketing to the managers of tomorrow. More hospitality-oriented schools have substantial marketing faculties now than those of a few years ago. However, in their curricula, careful attention should be given to preparing future managers to deal with owners. If this need is not met on campus today, it will have to be met sooner or later by the hotel companies themselves. Already it is clear that companies which make the effort to prepare their managers tend to be more successful in obtaining management contracts.

To be successful, hospitality managers of tomorrow will certainly need to know about guests' needs; evolving markets; and the mechanics of operating a hotel, running food and beverage facilities, and controlling costs. However, there will be an increasing dependence on technical equipment and technology in the management of future hotel operations.

Evolving Hospitality Technology

The successful hotel manager of tomorrow will be accustomed to and even comfortable with the use of computers and computer-based data in running a property. Naturally, future data management techniques will include all that is now becoming standard information-handling in the hotel industry. Automated night audits; computer-based daily, weekly, and monthly reporting; and energy control will all be handled through computerized property management systems. Tomorrow's managers will also use automated data processing to become more adept at handling the internal and external marketing data for their hotels.

This prediction prompts a question. What method will be used in the coming years to gather leads on new sources of business? The literature of sales and marketing and of other related fields suggests that there will be more reliance on external data-gathering sources than on internal ones. This by no means suggests that individuals who earn livings by marketing hospitality facilities will be out of their jobs. Rather, it points to the possibility that the conventional techniques of hotel selling may eventually become obsolete. Already the selling tools used by salespersons are changing form; in many cases they are electronic instead of paper-based. More and more salespeople today are carrying sales information in the form of videocassettes rather than relying exclusively on brochures and folders. Trade show displays are becoming more elaborate, too. Providing realistic videotapes of the property in action is more convincing than presenting cold statistics in an old-fashioned manner.

The characteristics (such as personality and empathy) that traditionally made the hotel salesperson successful may become less important. A more technically minded, logical, and profit-oriented individual may emerge as the new "typical salesperson." Nevertheless, it is unlikely that the trait of a strong ego drive will ever disappear from the profile of the marketing professional.

The marketing professional of the future will be fully prepared to use all of the data available, both internal and external, in writing a marketing plan. The sales travel plan will be based on internal facts about source/origins for the existing hotel if the data is statistically significant. External data about traffic to the destination may be used if that is the best information available. This information will be combined with statistics on the spending patterns of guests from the various source/origin markets. Then all of this will be intertwined with internal projections of what will constitute profitable business for the hotel in the future.

The successful marketing professionals of the coming decade will be better prepared, more broadly educated, and more market-sensitive than any people who have ever been involved in business departments of the hotel industry. Because the education of these future marketers will increasingly focus on how profits are made rather than on how revenues are generated, they will be prepared to generate satisfactory returns to the hotel owners. As they succeed in benefiting their companies they will build outstanding careers for themselves.

The hospitality industry is a tremendously exciting one in which to work because of its challenges and rewards. Hotels are very much a part of the mainstream of today's business world, and the hotel industry will always remain a unique field in which you can combine personal satisfaction and career enrichment while, at the same time, providing for the needs of those whom the hospitality industry has always and will always recognize as its guests.

Endnotes

1. "Chain Gangs are Your Link to Big Bucks," *Hotel & Motel Management*, April 1985, p. 51.

2. Laventhol & Horwath, *A Special Analysis*, The Sixth Annual National Hospitality Industry Investment Conference, New York City, June 1984, p. 4. Cited by Gregory Casserly in *A Strategic Analysis of the U.S. Lodging Industry and The Quality International Franchise Development Survey*. Washington, D.C.: Quality International, 1984, p. 22.

3. Daniel R. Lee, in a marketing study by Drexel Burnham Lambert, 1984.

4. Stephen Selka, "Your Keys for the 80s: Location, Product, and Identity," *Hotel & Motel Management*, December 1984, p. 31.

5. Glenn Withiam, "Hotel Companies Aim for Multiple Markets," *The Cornell Hotel and Restaurant Administration Quarterly*, November 1985, p. 42.

6. Joan Livingston, "A Burst of Tiers," *The Cornell Hotel and Restaurant Administration Quarterly*, November 1985, p. 34.

REVIEW QUIZ

When you feel you have covered all of the material in this chapter, answer these questions. Choose the *best* answer. Check your answers with the correct ones found on the Review Quiz Answer Key at the end of this book.

True (T) or False (F)

T   F   1. Consolidation is a trend which has resulted in increased chain affiliation among hotels.

T   F   2. The overbuilding of hotels in more and more cities has not contributed to market saturation in the hotel industry.

T   F   3. Hotels of the future will become less dependent on marketing techniques to sell their products and services.

T   F   4. Managers of the future will have less need to communicate with owners than they have today.

Multiple Choice

5. Which of the following current trends poses the greatest threat to the lodging industry?

    a. economies of scale
    b. market saturation
    c. brand proliferation
    d. none of the above

Index

A

action plans, food and
    beverage sales, 291, 294
advertising
    agencies, 216, 218–220
    broadcast, 222–224
    budgeting, 225–226
    collateral, 220
    design, 142
    food and beverage, 294
    manager, 162
    objectives, 216–218
    outdoor, 224–225
    point-of-purchase, 259–260
    print, 221–222
    videos, in-house, 357
"Advertising That Sells
    Hotels," 238–242
Air France, 390
airlines, acquisitions of hotels,
    390
airport hotels, 126
alcoholic beverages
    guestroom service, 296
    service, 294–296
    specialty drinks, 295
    suggestive selling, 295
    traffic accidents and,
        294–295
    wine service, 295
all-suite hotels, 118–120, 266
allocentric personality, 149
amenities, luxury, 116,
    124–125
American Express, 173
American Hotel & Motel
    Association (AH&MA),
    227, 231, 349
Americana Congress Hotel,
    367–368 (case study)
Americana Great Gorge
    Resort, 82–83
Americana Hotels, 172, 287
"Analysis of the Hotel Room
    Rate Pricing Decision,
    An," 261
Anheuser-Busch, 9
Arrowwood, 180
*Association Management
    Magazine*, 283

B

Bagley, Colleen, 255
bartering, 222–223
bed and breakfasts, 116–117
Belz family, 217
Best Western, 129
Bonaventure Inter-
    Continental Hotel and
    Spa, 346–347
Boorstein, Daniel, 395
Bostonian, The, 125
"Breaking Free from Product
    Marketing," 57–68
Bush, Melinda, 177–179
business orientations
    marketing, 6–8
    product, 5
    selling, 6
    societal marketing, 8

C

Canas, Jon, 12
Canyon Hotel Racquet and
    Golf Resort, 172
*Care and Feeding of Guests from
    Abroad, The*, 349
casinos/hotels
    Atlantic City, 12–13, 397
    Great Britain, 51
    Las Vegas, 11–12, 13, 397
chain hotels, 129–131
Cigahotels, 121
Circus-Circus Enterprises, 397
city-center hotels, 126
Claritas Corporation, 173
Club Med, 152, 355–356
Coffman, C. DeWitt, 10–11
Coffman Process, 166
"Comparing Marketing
    Management in Package
    Goods and Service
    Organizations," 68–74
competition, 3, 86–89, 139,
    154, 262, 296
conference centers, 118
consumer/guest relations,
    236
consumer loyalty, 145–147

hard-core, 145
shifting, 146
soft-core, 145
switchers, 146
consumers
    expectations of, 45, 46
    market segmentation of, 89
    needs of, 6–7, 8, 121–122,
        389
    participation in production
        by, 55
    perceived risks and, 47, 49
    at point of service, 48
convention hotels, Canadian
    vs. U.S., 110
convention services manager,
    161–162
corporate culture, 391
corporate market, selling to,
    196–200
Crystler, Julia, 164

D

data bases, 173
Days Inns of America, 79, 120,
    123, 292
Days Lodges, 120
Del Webb, 11
Delta Landing Project, 8
derived demand, 53
destination (resort) hotels,
    127–128
"Developing a Balanced
    Market Mix," 297–305
differential pricing, 52–53
Dimond, Mike, 315, 361, 365
Dischell, Gary, 345
Disneyland Hotel, 127
distinctive competencies, 390
Drucker, Peter F., 4, 7, 15, 80
Dumazedier, Joffre, 151
Dunfey's, 357–358

E

Econo Lodges, 123
Econo-Travel Motor Hotels,
    123

STRATEGIC HOTEL/MOTEL MARKETING

REVIEW QUIZ ANSWER KEY

The numbers in parentheses refer to the page(s) where the answer may be found.

Chapter 1	Chapter 2	Chapter 3	Chapter 4
1. T (4)	1. F (43)	1. T (80)	1. T (105)
2. T (4)	2. F (43)	2. F (80)	2. F (108)
3. F (5)	3. T (43)	3. F (80)	3. T (108)
4. T (5)	4. T (44)	4. T (81)	4. F (111)
5. F (7–8)	5. T (45)	5. T (83)	5. d (105–106)
6. F (5)	6. F (45–46)	6. T (82)	6. c (108)
7. T (4)	7. T (46)	7. F (83–84)	
8. F (5)	8. T (47)	8. T (84)	
9. F (6)	9. T (47)	9. T (84)	
10. T (7)	10. T (48)	10. F (84)	
11. F (8)	11. F (48)	11. F (86)	
12. T (9)	12. T (49)	12. c (81)	
13. T (10)	13. F (49)	13. d (82)	
14. F (12)	14. F (51)	14. b (83)	
15. F (11)	15. F (53)		
16. a (4)	16. b (54)		
17. d (3)	17. b (52)		
18. c (8–9)	18. c (55)		
19. b (6)	19. b (47)		
20. d (8)	20. b (53)		

Chapter 5	Chapter 6	Chapter 7	Chapter 8
1. T (115)	1. T (138)	1. T (161)	1. T (195)
2. F (116)	2. T (138)	2. F (162–163)	2. T (196)
3. F (116–117)	3. F (139)	3. F (163)	3. T (196)
4. F (118)	4. T (139)	4. F (164)	4. T (196)
5. T (119)	5. F (142)	5. F (165)	5. F (196)
6. T (120)	6. F (142)	6. T (165)	6. T (196)
7. F (123)	7. T (142)	7. F (165–166)	7. F (197)
8. T (123)	8. T (142)	8. T (167)	8. F (198)
9. T (123–124)	9. F (143)	9. T (167)	9. F (198)
10. F (126)	10. T (144)	10. F (168)	10. F (200-202)
11. T (127)	11. F (145)	11. F (173)	11. F (202)
12. F (129)	12. F (148)	12. T (175)	12. F (202)
13. F (129)	13. F (149)	13. F (177, 179)	13. T (204)
14. T (131)	14. T (151)	14. T (182)	14. F (206)
15. F (130)	15. T (153)	15. T (182)	15. F (207)
16. c (118)	16. d (138)	16. d (161–163)	16. d (196–199)
17. d (118–120)	17. c (140)	17. d (167)	17. a (196–197)
18. b (122)	18. a (142)	18. a (168)	18. d (197)
19. d (129)	19. b (151)	19. b (175)	19. b (203)
20. a (130)	20. c (153)	20. d (179)	20. d (204)

Chapter 9			

1. T (218)
2. T (222)
3. F (226–227)
4. F (227)
5. F (221)
6. T (227)
7. F (216)
8. F (218)
9. T (231)
10. F (231)
11. T (218)
12. F (217)
13. F (234)
14. F (216)
15. F (236)
16. b (236)
17. a (216)
18. c (236–237)
19. d (225)
20. d (227, 231, 237)

1.
2.
3.
4.
5.
6. 1
7. T (265)
8. F (252)
9. F (257)
10. F (261)
11. F (261, 268)
12. T (258)
13. T (263)
14. d (255)
15. a (257–258)
16. d (262)
17. d (258–259)
18. d (261, 262, 266–268)

ა. ┌ (280)
7. F (278)
8. F (291)
9. F (280)
10. d (288)
11. d (285–286)

Chapter 12	

1. F (327)
2. F (324)
3. F (323)
4. T (319)
5. F (320)
6. F (322)
7. b (315–316)
8. d (318)
9. d (323)

Chapter 13	Chapter 14	Chapter 15	Chapter 16
1. F (345)	1. T (369)	1. F (388)	1. T (404)
2. F (345)	2. F (367–368)	2. F (387)	2. F (404)
3. F (345)	3. T (369)	3. F (388)	3. F (406–407)
4. T (345)	4. F (370)	4. T (389)	4. F (408–409)
5. b (353–354)	5. T (364–365)	5. T (389)	5. b (404–405)
6. b (357)	6. T (365)	6. T (390)	
7. a (345)	7. T (367–368)	7. F (390)	
8. d (349, 350, 352)	8. F (361–365)	8. T (390–391)	
	9. F (361, 369)	9. F (391)	
	10. F (368)	10. F (396)	
	11. F (365)	11. T (396–397)	
	12. d (363)	12. d (387)	
		13. b (388)	
		14. a (391)	
		15. b (396)	

The
Educational Institute Board of Trustees

The Educational Institute of the American Hotel & Motel Association is fortunate to have both industry and academic leaders, as well as allied members, on its Board of Trustees. Individually and collectively, the following persons play leading roles in supporting the Institute and determining the directions of its programs.

Steven J. Belmonte, CHA
President & COO
Ramada Franchise
    Systems, Inc.
Parsippany, New Jersey

John Q. Hammons
Chairman & CEO
John Q. Hammons
    Hotels, Inc.
Springfield, Missouri

David J. Christianson, Ph.D.
Dean
William F. Harrah College of
    Hotel Administration
University of Nevada,
    Las Vegas
Las Vegas, Nevada

Arnold J. Hewes, CAE
Executive Vice President
Minnesota Hotel & Lodging
    Association
St. Paul, Minnesota

Caroline A. Cooper, CHA
Dean
The Hospitality College
Johnson & Wales University
Providence, Rhode Island

S. Kirk Kinsell
President—Franchise
ITT Sheraton World
    Headquarters
Atlanta, Georgia

Edouard P.O. Dandrieux, CHA
Director
H.I.M., Hotel Institute,
    Montreux
Montreux, Switzerland

Donald J. Landry, CHA
President
Choice Hotels International
Silver Spring, Maryland

Valerie C. Ferguson
General Manager
Ritz-Carlton Atlanta
Atlanta, Georgia

Georges LeMener
President & CEO
Motel 6, L.P.
Dallas, Texas

Douglas G. Geoga
President
Hyatt Hotels Corporation
Chicago, Illinois

Jerry R. Manion, CHA
President
Manion Investments
Paradise Valley, Arizona

Joseph A. McInerney, CHA
President & CEO
Forte Hotels, Inc.
El Cajon, California

William R. Tiefel
President
Marriott Lodging
Washington, D.C.

John L. Sharpe, CHA
President & COO
Four Seasons-Regent Hotels
   and Resorts
Toronto, Ontario, Canada

Jonathan M. Tisch
President & CEO
Loews Hotels
New York, New York

Paul J. Sistare, CHA
President & CEO
Richfield Hospitality Services
Englewood, Colorado

Paul E. Wise, CHA
Professor & Director
Hotel, Restaurant &
   Institutional Management
University of Delaware
Newark, Delaware

Thomas W. Staed, CHA
President
Oceans Eleven Resorts, Inc.
Daytona Beach Shores, Florida

Ted Wright, CHA
Vice President/Managing
   Director
The Cloister Hotel
Sea Island, Georgia

Thomas G. Stauffer, CHA
President & CFO
Americas Region
Renaissance Hotels
   International, Inc.
Cleveland, Ohio